Treason in the Northern Quarter

# Treason in the Northern Quarter

WAR, TERROR, AND THE RULE OF LAW
IN THE DUTCH REVOLT

*Henk van Nierop*
*Translated by J. C. Grayson*

PRINCETON UNIVERSITY PRESS
PRINCETON AND OXFORD

First published in the Netherlands by Uitgeverij Bert Bakker under the title
*Het verraad van het Noorderkwartier* in 1999
English edition copyright © 2009 by Princeton University Press
Published by Princeton University Press, 41 William Street,
Princeton, New Jersey 08540
In the United Kingdom: Princeton University Press, 6 Oxford Street,
Woodstock, Oxfordshire OX20 1TR

Cover: Torturing of Jan Jeroenszoon. Etching in Richard Verstegan,
Theatre de Scruautez de Sheretiques de Nostretemps, 1587
(photo library of the University of Amsterdam)
Cover design by Jason Alejandro

All Rights Reserved

First paperback printing, 2018
Paperback ISBN 978-0-691-17804-2
The Library of Congress has cataloged the cloth edition as follows:

Nierop, Henk F. K. van.
 [Verraad van het Noorderkwartier. English]
 Treason in the Northern Quarter : war, terror, and the rule of law
in the Dutch revolt / Henk van Nierop ; translated by J.C. Grayson.
   p.   cm.
 Includes bibliographical references and index.
 ISBN 978-0-691-13564-9 (hardback : acid-free paper)
 1. Netherlands—History—Wars of Independence, 1556-1648. 2. Catholic
Church—Netherlands—History—16th century. 3. Netherlands—Church
history—17th century. 4. Friesland (Netherlands)—History. I. Title.
 DH186.N5413 2009
 949.2′03—dc22      2009006696

British Library Cataloging-in-Publication Data is available

This book has been translated with the generous support of The Netherlands
Organization for Scientific Research (NWO)

This book has been composed in Sabon

Printed on acid-free paper. ∞

press.princeton.edu

Printed in the United States of America

Mark well reader everything that is written here, and marvel at this troubled, tormented and wild, desolate time in which we have lived.

—*Wouter Jacobszoon*, 6 February 1573

# Contents

*Preface* ix

CHAPTER ONE
Introduction 1

CHAPTER TWO
The Northland 12

CHAPTER THREE
Believers 28

CHAPTER FOUR
Revolt 51

CHAPTER FIVE
War 72

CHAPTER SIX
Treason 93

CHAPTER SEVEN
Vagabonds 121

CHAPTER EIGHT
Peasants 136

CHAPTER NINE
Citizens 165

CHAPTER TEN
Law against Terror 186

CHAPTER ELEVEN
Jan Jeroenszoon Again 222

CHAPTER TWELVE
Historiography and Propaganda 239

CHAPTER THIRTEEN
Conclusion 259

*Abbreviations* 265
*Bibliography* 267
*Index of Persons* 285
*Index of Places* 293

# Preface

THIS BOOK GREW OUT of an article written in 1995, in which I attempted to give a brief explanation of what the Revolt of the Netherlands was actually about. I wrote that the Revolt was a conflict about two issues: liberty and religion. The struggle was so complex and ultimately insoluble because contemporaries attached different meanings to these concepts, and because they were inextricably intertwined. That conclusion was far from original. From the very beginning the rebels had been unable to agree if they were fighting for liberty or for religion, and the debate continued among historians until well into the twentieth century.

That article appeared in two versions,[1] the earlier of which concluded: "But these motives must not make us forget that for most contemporaries the Revolt was probably not about anything at all. For them the war was simply a disaster, a nightmare from which they hoped to awake as soon as they could." In the later version these sentences were omitted. On reflection I felt that it was not very helpful to close an article that tried to explain what the Revolt was about, by suggesting that in fact it was not really about anything.

Yet the idea continued to preoccupy me. It was fed by press reports of the civil wars of the last decade of the twentieth century that tore apart the former Yugoslavia, the former Soviet Union, and several African countries, with their mass slaughter and unmanageable floods of refugees. The impression was confirmed when I read Wouter Jacobszoon's journal, a blood-curdling eyewitness account of everyday life during the Revolt written by one who was himself a fugitive from war.

And so I came to the idea of writing a book on the Revolt that would not see the struggle as the heroic birth of the Dutch nation, but as the miserable ordeal it must have been for most of those who lived through it. My research very soon showed me that for some the Revolt was a far more horrible nightmare than I could initially have imagined. But it also became clear to me that I would have to qualify my original idea: that the Revolt was not about anything for most of its contemporaries. The poor vagrants and peasants whom Sonoy's commission of inquiry sentenced to death probably had hardly any notion of what the conflict was about, but

---

[1] Van Nierop, "Om de vrijheid" and "Troon van Alva," the latter translated into English as "Alva's Throne."

the more educated townsfolk, both Protestant and Catholic, were imbued with a strong civic republican ethos. Many of them firmly believed that the authorities, both the lawful government of Philip II and Alba and the rebel regime of William of Orange, ought in the last analysis to be subject to the law, even in wartime. Hence the subtitle of this book: *War, Terror, and the Rule of Law in the Dutch Revolt*.

Many people helped me in writing this book. The enthusiasm of the students who took part in a class that I devoted to the subject confirmed my belief that I was on the track of something special. I made very profitable use of the master's theses of Henk Looijesteijn and Loet Schledorn. Jan de Bruin drew my attention to some important archive sources in Hoorn. Rob Huijbrecht was my guide through the labyrinthine archive of the Court of Holland. Guido and An Marnef offered hospitality and friendship during my research in the Belgian State Archives. Geoffrey Parker showed me the way in the Spanish archives. Clé Lesger and Christel Verhas answered my requests for information helpfully. Florike Egmond generously permitted me to make use of the results of her unpublished research. Alastair Duke allowed me to profit from his vast knowledge of the Reformation in the Northern Quarter. He and Jonathan Israel, Phil Benedict, Jim Tracy, and Ben Schmidt enabled me to present my ideas to critical audiences in England and the United States. Gabrielle Dorren, Paul Knevel, and Judith Pollmann read all the chapters separately, and Juliaan Woltjer read the whole manuscript. My Dutch publisher Mai Spijkers at Uitgeverij Bert Bakker believed in the project from the beginning and kept me at it. The book owes a great deal to their criticism and readiness to share their thoughts. The faults that remain are my own.

The translation of this book was possible thanks to the generous support of The Netherlands Organization for Scientific Research (NWO). Chris Grayson was as punctual and creative a translator as ever, and a friend. I am also grateful to Ian Malcolm and the Princeton University Press editorial team for their support in bringing this book about. My wife Tine and my children Leonie, Samuel, and Gulian were understanding whenever I yet again hung out my "I'm not in" sign.

Treason in the Northern Quarter

The Northern Quarter of Holland in 1575, after Joost Janszoon Beeldsnijder alias Bilhamer.

The Netherlands in the sixteenth century.

CHAPTER ONE

# Introduction

IN THE SPRING OF 1575 the Northern Quarter of Holland, the region north of the River IJ, was a fortress under siege. The Beggar rebels who held it were cut off from their fellow insurgents in South Holland and Zeeland. The government army had dug itself into a heavily fortified but not easily defensible bridgehead, which extended from Naarden and Muiden in the east through Amsterdam to Haarlem, thus driving a wedge between the two areas in rebel hands. For the central government in Brussels it was vitally important to reconquer North Holland from the rebels, and so break through the virtual encirclement of Amsterdam, which had remained loyal to Church and King. The Amsterdammers were suffering great hardship, above all because the rebels in North Holland had cut their trade and shipping routes. On 26 April Wouter Jacobszoon, a monk who had taken refuge in Amsterdam, noted in his diary a rumor that the Spanish army was getting ready for a new campaign. "A gruesome apparatus of war" was being prepared to "attack or overpower" the rebels by force.[1]

Not long before, Brother Wouter had been leading a peaceful and orderly life as prior of the Augustinian monastery at Stein near Gouda. But when his fellow townsmen opened their gates to a Beggar band in June 1572, he and many others had fled. Although he found a temporary refuge in Amsterdam he did not feel safe there. The city was swarming with asylum seekers, who posed serious problems for the magistrates. As long as the rebels kept up their blockade, it was hard enough for the beleaguered city to feed its own population. Moreover, even in Catholic Amsterdam the inhabitants were anything but kindly disposed toward monks and other clerical refugees.

While the ex-prior waited for better times—which would never come—he recorded his daily observations in his journal. We do not know exactly what he had in mind in keeping such a record, but it was certainly not a mere private diary. Probably Wouter Jacobszoon wanted to bear witness to his readers—perhaps his fellow monks now scattered in exile?—of the extraordinary times in which he found himself, when in a way not seen in living memory the Lord showed how he would punish sinners and put

[1] *DWJ*, 492.

his faithful to the test. "Mark well reader," he wrote in February 1573, "everything that is written here, and marvel at this troubled, tormented and wild, desolate time in which we have lived."[2]

It is to Wouter Jacobszoon's eagerness to keep a record that we owe one of the most fascinating works of the age of the Revolt. His recurrent accounts of hunger and misery, petty humiliations and savage massacres, his hopes of a speedy end to the war, and his fears that it would only grow worse, remind us that the Dutch Revolt was a true revolt for only a very few. For the great majority of the people of the Netherlands the Revolt was not a course they had chosen but a calamity that overwhelmed them. The catastrophe displayed the familiar features of a war. Yet it was not the heroic struggle for national liberation that nineteenth-century historians wanted to see in it, but an ordinary "dirty" war. For most contemporaries the most urgent question was not how to win it, but how to survive it. Many joined Wouter Jacobszoon on the road to exile, contributing to an enormous refugee problem.

As always, the poor, and above all the rural poor, were the first and hardest hit of the war's victims, as every page of Brother Wouter's journal testifies. But what makes it such a special document is its wealth of vivid detail, which evokes a concrete and sometimes almost apocalyptic picture of a society torn apart by war. In November 1572, for example, Wouter reported that many poor folk from Amsterdam had gone to the Diemermeer to take the carcasses of dead cattle floating on the water. The animals, at least a hundred of them, had been stolen from the farms by the Beggars and driven over the ice, but had fallen through it and drowned. The poor people were willing to eat the meat of the carcasses. This, as Brother Wouter pointed out, "well showed . . . what suffering of hunger and misery has befallen this age."

In January 1575 Wouter heard from a soldier who had found a woman with a child at her breast sitting by the dike near Ter Hart, a country house between Amsterdam and Haarlem. When he took a closer look he saw that she was dead and frozen stiff, but must have had some milk left in her breast, at which the child was suckling. The baby was brought to the Spanish camp, as a "sign to be wondered at."

Children were the first and most defenseless victims of the war. A woman carrying a seven- or eight-week-old infant on her shoulder was shot by the Beggars "so that its intestines burst out of its body and it died." In November 1573 some children whose father had died were brought from Beverwijk to the Lily convent in Haarlem. Some of them were so malnourished they would have been taken for dead if they had

---

[2] Ibid., 179; on Wouter Jacobszoon, ibid., i–xvi. The passages cited below are from *DWJ*, 179, 76, 121, 81, 337, 343, 280, 494, 492, 499–502.

not stirred from time to time. Two of them died within two weeks and were buried together in a single coffin, a used one that the gravedigger dug up and emptied for a small fee. In the same month Wouter Jacobszoon heard that people were lying dead on the dike between Haarlem and Amsterdam, with no one to remove or bury them. Birds and dogs had gnawed at their bodies.

Soon after Haarlem fell to the Spanish army, Wouter took the opportunity to visit his old friend and colleague, the prior of the monastic house at Zijl in Haarlem. On 23 July 1573 he walked along the dike beside the River IJ to Haarlem. After months of siege the countryside presented a forlorn and eerie sight:

> And as I journeyed there, I saw on the way the frightful desolation to which the land has come through the troubles in this present year. I found very few houses between Haarlem and Amsterdam that had not been burned. All the churches along this road that we saw were either burned down or at least miraculously damaged and broken. In many places the land was altogether waste without any cattle.
>
> I also saw on the way, among many animals that lay here and there, a naked body lying in the middle of the road in the cart tracks, and it was dried out by the sun, and almost crushed, so that a decent person must shudder to look at it. And it was especially amazing that no one was found who saw fit to remove the body from the road, or cover it with earth, but it remained lying there like the carcass of a beast.

Yet even in the darkest years of the war there were glimmerings of hope. For a short time in the spring of 1575 it was not the miseries of war that kept Wouter's pen busy but the hope of peace. Negotiations were under way in Breda between representatives of the Spanish governor of the Netherlands, Luis de Requesens, and the rebel leader William of Orange in the hope of ending the war, which had now lasted three years and which seemed to be unwinnable by either side. Brother Wouter eagerly followed the reports of the peace conference. On 6 May he wrote that the man in the street in Amsterdam was convinced that peace was already a fact.

Wouter's optimism was short-lived. The very same day he spoke to a traveler from Brabant, who told him that no one any longer believed in peace. Discouraging reports had been circulating as early as 28 April, and Wouter wrote that many now doubted that peace would be made because so many soldiers were afoot, and there was an impression that this time the Spaniards would strike at the Northland. It was also rumored that Hierges, the king's Stadholder of Holland, had come to Utrecht to be briefed on communications with the Northern Quarter. For Wouter this was a clear sign that some dreadful event was imminent.

On 22 May, Wouter had more certain news about the resumption of hostilities: the smiths in Amsterdam had been ordered to work day and night making shovels, spades, and other digging tools for the war effort. Next day the Stadholder Hierges himself arrived in Amsterdam. Wouter realized the campaign would be "for the Northland, for the same to be destroyed by fire and sword." A day later he watched a large fleet of transport and escort ships sail out of the harbor of Amsterdam to Muiden, to pick up the infantry assembled there. On the 25th Spanish cavalry passed the city on the way to Beverwijk, where the expedition to invade North Holland was gathering. On the same day it was proclaimed to the sound of trumpets in Amsterdam that the citizens had leave to go to the camp as sutlers (victuallers). More troops passed through the city the next day, and there was now a rumor that Alkmaar would be besieged and that the rebels in the North had cut the dikes again.

On 27 May, Brother Wouter learned that the army had left its camp at Beverwijk and was marching north. The rumor mill was now working overtime: the Prince of Orange was said to have advised Alkmaar to surrender to the king and admit the royal army. But the very next day refugees from Alkmaar arrived, who claimed that the truth was exactly the opposite. "The Northlanders," they insisted, "were ready to wade up to their knees in their own blood rather than return to the Catholic faith and their obedience to the King." Others claimed to know for a fact that South Holland was willing to yield, but that the north of the province would stand firm. Letters from Utrecht and Gouda reported that peace was now beyond doubt, especially with the towns of South Holland. But only two days later the prospect of peace seemed to have vanished once more.

On 29 May, Wouter heard that the army had returned to Beverwijk. The invasion plan had come to nothing. The troops had been in great danger and had barely escaped with their lives. If Requesens really wanted to subdue the North, people felt, he would first have to send reinforcements.

About a week later all hope of the recapture of the North was gone. On 7 June the army left its camp in Beverwijk and began to lay siege to the small town of Buren in the Betuwe. No one understood the implications of this; some were still hoping for peace, while others dreaded even worse to come. "One saw the people walking about wholly defenseless and desperate, like men who had no hope at all but dreaded further sorrow and misery."

Why had Hierges abandoned his campaign in North Holland so suddenly? The wildest rumors were in the air. Many suspected that the expedition had been no more than a diversionary maneuver, intended to lure William of Orange's army out of South Holland. But others hinted at treachery.

As early as 31 May it was being said in Amsterdam that certain Beggar captains had been willing to betray the city of Alkmaar and some of the forts to Hierges. The scheme had been discovered and the traitors put to death, "so it was said," Wouter added cautiously. On 4 June he had more certain information. The plotters—seven cartloads of Beggar soldiers—were supposed to have been brought captive into Alkmaar, "for they were accused as traitors, as having an alliance with the Spaniards, cunningly to deliver up to them the forts that stood in the way of their coming into the Northland." The plan had been exposed, and the traitors had been arrested and executed. The Spanish army had no choice but to withdraw without achieving its objective.

This book is about Hierges's failed invasion of the Northern Quarter, the frustrated plot, and the chain of dramatic events that it set in motion. On the first rumors of treason Diederik Sonoy, the Prince of Orange's governor in the Northern Quarter, had ordered the arrest of all suspect strangers. About twenty vagrants were seized, tortured, and executed after a summary trial. The vagrants named as the men who had incited them some North Holland peasants, who in turn were arrested and interrogated. One of them died under torture, two others obdurately continued to deny the charge in spite of exceptionally long and cruel tortures. Finally their resistance was broken, and they accused several Catholic townsmen, among them Jan Jeroenszoon, an advocate from Hoorn. The hysterical campaign against the alleged traitors began to assume the dimensions of a witch hunt, which threatened to engulf the burgomasters of Hoorn as well. The town sprang to the defense of its accused citizens, William of Orange concerned himself with the question, and the investigation became bogged down in a succession of laborious proceedings. The Pacification of Ghent—the peace treaty of 1576 between rebel-held Holland and Zeeland and the other provinces of the Netherlands—ought to have put an end to the affair, but the prisoners demanded a fair trial in which they could prove their innocence. After the Court of Holland acquitted them, they in turn brought actions against Sonoy and the commissioners who had investigated the plot.

The treason affair in the Northern Quarter and all its repercussions remained a cause célèbre in the historiography of the seventeenth to the nineteenth centuries. For Protestant historians who took the official pro-States view it was a well-known black page in their otherwise glorious national history. Catholic authors, in contrast, saw it as yet another proof of the scandalous outrages perpetrated by the Beggars on the Catholic majority of the population. In the twentieth century the treason of the Northern Quarter has been all but forgotten.

Why then devote a whole book to this old story? I had three aims in view in writing this book. My first is the simplest: the betrayal of the

Northern Quarter is a story that is still worth telling again to a new generation of readers. The way in which Nanning Coppenszoon and Pieter Nanningszoon withstood long and inhuman torture, to avoid accusing innocent people, still arouses our astonished admiration. We can still sympathize with the ingenuity and tenacity of Jan Jeroenszoon, while his unshaken confidence in the law as the protector of the powerless against unbridled authority has lost none of its relevance. The cynicism of the commissioners who carried out the investigation, and who were more concerned to close their file than to respect the individual rights of the accused, is another aspect that is still as timely as ever. In short the history of the betrayal of the Northern Quarter is a story with many of the qualities of an epic, a gripping tale with every appearance of authentic villains and untarnished heroes. It is also a case that raises a number of currently topical questions in the most striking and concrete form: questions that concern the nature of the Revolt and its significance, the role of law in society, civil rights, and the limits imposed on them in time of war and time of peace.

The first historian to relate the plot in detail was Pieter Christiaenszoon Bor in the third impression of his monumental work on the "Origin, Beginning, and Continuation of the Wars of the Netherlands" of 1621.[3] Bor combed the archives so thoroughly that not a single historian since his time has bothered to investigate them anew. My second aim has therefore been to reconstruct the events from the original documents, both the sources that underlay Bor's work and others. Only where they have been lost does Bor remain an indispensable and not necessarily unreliable guide. Still, new archive research has revealed some new details.

Finally, in this account I have tried to reconstruct the historical context as broadly as possible. The background to the events, which was still self-evident for readers in the seventeenth and eighteenth centuries, can no longer be taken for granted. That background posed no problem for historians such as Bor, Pieter Corneliszoon Hooft, and Jan Wagenaar, whose readers in the Dutch Republic lived in an age when the Revolt in many respects was still a past imperfect. Much of the context in which the events had to be understood was still as alive in the seventeenth and eighteenth centuries as it had been in the Revolt. Such questions as the autonomy of the towns from the central government, the importance of urban privileges and the different social positions of townsmen, country folk, and foreigners were still vitally relevant and familiar to everyone. The Revolt had begun precisely to protect these and other privileges against the centralizing policy of the government. Because the Revolt achieved these

---

[3] Bor, book VIII. On the historiography of the treason of the Northern Quarter, see also chapter 12 of this book.

goals in the seven northern provinces of the Netherlands, the same constitution and the same institutions survived there until the time of the French Revolution. Anyone who brought a case before the Court of Holland at the end of the eighteenth century followed exactly the same procedure as Jan Jeroenszoon and his fellow prisoners two centuries earlier.

That situation changed in the nineteenth century. The coming into being of a unitary state (the Kingdom of the Netherlands), the principle of the equality of all citizens before the law, the introduction of the Napoleonic Codes, and the separation of Church and State all drew a line under the republican past and made the sixteenth century appear suddenly much more remote. Yet nineteenth-century historians were scarcely aware of this greater gulf, and carried on as if the historical context that had still been self-evident in the time of the Republic were as obvious as ever.

This lack of historical distance was partly explained by the role that historical writing played in the nineteenth century in legitimizing the national state. That state was undeniably the heir of the old Republic, which in its turn had been founded in the Revolt; and because the Dutch national state was regarded as a good thing, the Revolt must therefore have been a good thing as well. From this teleological and determinist perspective nineteenth-century liberal historians saw the Revolt as a struggle for national liberation, the overthrow of a foreign oppressor who had failed to respect the peculiarities of the (North) Netherlands nation. In this way the writers of nineteenth-century nationalist history reclaimed a past that was now definitively over, and remodeled it to suit their own needs.[4]

Much the same can be said of nineteenth-century Catholic historians. Once Catholics had won political equality in the constitution of 1798, confirmed by the liberal constitution of 1848, they sought to achieve complete social emancipation. The writing of history was one of their chief means to this end. Naturally, Catholic historians traced a direct line of descent from the humiliations inflicted on the victims of the Beggars to the social inferiority that they themselves chafed under. The sixteenth-century martyrs could only serve as inspiring examples if they were presented as fellow-sufferers who had fought the same cosmic battle as their nineteenth-century descendants. These historians did not always see quite so clearly that there had been great changes between the sixteenth and the nineteenth centuries.[5]

Around the middle of the twentieth century the Revolt of the Netherlands moved definitively from past imperfect to past perfect. Those who want to invoke history to support "national" values or national unity

---

[4] Blaas, "Nederlandse geschiedschrijving"; on the historiography of the Revolt see Smit, "The present position"; Woltjer, "Beeld vergruisd"; Groenveld, "Beeldvorming en realiteit."
[5] Vermaseren, *Katholieke Nederlandse geschiedschrijving*.

appeal instead to a more recent past, the Second World War. Of course the unity of the Dutch people in the Second World War is, up to a point, no less a myth than their unity in the struggle against "Spain," but the new myth lends itself more easily to such manipulation than the old. After all, the Revolt of the sixteenth century was not just a struggle for freedom, but also for religion. Although contemporaries were very well able to distinguish between them, the two issues were nevertheless linked in a complex symbiosis. The Reformed Church claimed a privileged place in the state and society that emerged from the Revolt, while Catholics had to accept relegation to the rank of second-class citizens. In the conditions of sixteenth- and seventeenth-century Europe such a result was probably inevitable, but it certainly prevented the Revolt from serving as a symbol of national unity in the independent state to which it gave birth.

The Revolt was a civil war of Catholics against Protestants, loyalists against rebels (to say nothing of the large middle groups who were unwilling to choose either party and who were dragged along against their will by events).[6] The efforts of such nineteenth-century national liberal historians as Robert Fruin and Petrus Johannes Blok to force the Revolt into the mold of a general struggle for national liberation were so at odds with the facts that they were ultimately doomed to failure.

There are several reasons to retell an old tale from the original sources and place it in the widest possible historical context. In the first place attention is paid to the period that was once known, with magnificent partiality, as the "heroic phase of the Revolt." Until the middle of the twentieth century the history of the Revolt of 1572 and the subsequent four years of war in Holland and Zeeland took center stage in Dutch historiography (the spotlights being focused on the heroic defense of Haarlem, Alkmaar, and Leiden), but in recent decades historians have shown relatively little interest in these events.[7]

Also new is the geographical focus of this study, the Northern Quarter of Holland. Except for the siege of Alkmaar the history of the war of 1572–76 has been written almost entirely as the affair of South Holland and Zeeland.[8] No one at the time could have suspected that, as the Dutch

---

[6] The first author who explicitly described the Revolt as a civil war was Van Gelder, "Historiese vergelijking." On the importance of the middle groups see Woltjer, *Tussen vrijheidsstrijd en burgeroorlog*.

[7] Important revisionist contributions were made by Woltjer, *Tussen vrijheidsstrijd en burgeroorlog*; Hibben, *Gouda in Revolt*; Janssens, *Brabant in het verweer*; Swart, *William of Orange*, chapter 1. As perspective shifted from a national liberation struggle to a revolt, interest grew in the motives of that revolt. In what circumstances were subjects permitted to revolt against their lawful ruler? On this see especially Van Gelderen, *Political Thought*, and Mout, "Van arm vaderland."

[8] Cordfunke, *Alkmaar ontzet*.

saying goes, victory began at Alkmaar. Forced to withdraw when the rebels cut the dikes and allowed the sea to flood the land, the Spanish army abandoned the reconquest of North Holland for the time being and marched south to lay siege to Leiden. Historians, glorified war correspondents as always, followed in its tracks: via the intermezzo of the battle of Mook Heath, through the relief of Leiden, the sack of Oudewater, and the capture of Zierikzee to the Pacification of Ghent, which ended the war on the soil of Holland and Zeeland for good.

No contemporary, rebel or loyalist, could have foreseen that the relief of Alkmaar would herald the final victory of the Revolt. In the following years the Spanish army made repeated bids to reconquer the rebel Northern Quarter. Hierges's frustrated invasion in May 1575 was only the last of those attempts. History written from the viewpoint of the victors has said almost nothing about the final fruitless efforts of the Spanish army after Alkmaar. Yet in August 1573 the royal army recaptured the Waterland villages of Landsmeer, Zuiderwoude, Zunderdorp, and Broek. In February 1574 it launched assaults on Wormer, Wormerveer, Jisp, and Krommenie. On Whit Sunday 1574 it suffered a catastrophic defeat at Wormer; after the battle the rebels slaughtered 150 German prisoners of war in cold blood.[9] It will become evident that the character and course of the war in the Northern Quarter were largely determined by the geography of the region, its isolation and exceptional abundance of water. Moreover, this study will be more concerned with the war in the countryside than older works, which concentrated almost exclusively on the towns.

A final novelty in this book is that it describes the war from the viewpoint of its victims: the vagabonds and vagrants, of whom we often know no more than their name and place of origin, and the Catholic exiles who, like Wouter Jacobszoon, tried to survive in extremely difficult conditions in Amsterdam. That does not mean, however, that they must be regarded purely as passive victims of the Revolt. War and revolt often forced them to make dramatic choices. Some of them strained every sinew to free the country from the Spanish army, while others fled and lived as refugees in Amsterdam, where they had to accept the loss of their possessions, friends, and families.[10]

The story of the treason affair in the Northern Quarter is the history of scandalous excess. One may wonder how far it is representative, and what it tells us about the Revolt in general. It is by no means my intention to suggest that all sixteenth-century court officials were unscrupulous

---

[9] The best account of military events in the Northern Quarter is still found in Velius. For the conflicts mentioned here see Velius, 216, 235, 239–42.

[10] On the effects of the war on the civilian population, see Van Deursen, *Mensen van klein vermogen*, 229–59, and Gutmann, *War and Rural Life*.

power seekers, or that all the leaders of the Revolt saw a traitor behind every tree. The history of loyalty, treason, and alleged treason in the Revolt of the Netherlands is a rich topic that deserves further research,[11] but one must not expect it to bring to light numerous comparable cases. I am convinced, however, that the study of exceptional events and persons, as long as it is embedded in a social, political, economic, and cultural context reconstructed in as much depth as possible, can often yield a more penetrating insight into social reality than the study of "normal" practice and patterns of behavior. By looking at the abnormal, the exceptional, and the bizarre, the historian can form a clearer picture of the normal and everyday. The confused ideas of the cosmos of a sixteenth-century miller from Friuli can shed light on religious thought in the age of the Reformation; the minute examination of a single village in the Pyrenees in the thirteenth century tells us more about social and cultural relationships than a massive statistical investigation could reveal.[12]

The events described in this book took place chiefly in the part of Holland that lies north of the River IJ. In the sources this region goes under various names: the Northern Quarter, North Holland, West Friesland, the Northland, Waterland. All these names are more or less ambiguous, and they do not designate a clearly defined area. It will therefore be useful to explain them briefly.[13]

The name the *Northern Quarter* was in common use in the sixteenth century and still is today. In normal usage it designates the whole of the mainland of Holland north of the River IJ, but in the war years 1572–76 the southwestern corner of this area was still held by the Spanish army, and after 1576 it continued to be administered as part of the Southern Quarter of Holland. In his book on the Northern Quarter, A. M. van der Woude therefore confined the use of the name, for practical reasons, to the region between the IJ and an imaginary line drawn from Hoorn through Alkmaar to the North Sea. He referred to the area north of this line as West Friesland and to the whole peninsula north of the IJ and the *banne* of Velsen as North Holland.[14]

The name *North Holland*, often used to refer to the Northern Quarter, must be distinguished from its use as the name of the present-day province, which also extends south of the IJ.[15]

The name *West Friesland* applied in the strict sense to the bailiwick within the West Friesian enclosure dike, that is northeast of Kennemer-

---

[11] There is a good analysis of the problems in Duke, *Reformation*, chapter 8.
[12] Ginzburg, *Cheese*; Le Roy Ladurie, *Montaillou*.
[13] Wagenaar, *Tegenwoordige staat*, V, 361–74.
[14] Van der Woude, *Noorderkwartier*, 19–30. A *banne* was a jurisdictional district.
[15] Bor, 502.

land and north of Waterland, but it was also used in a more general sense for the whole Northern Quarter outside Kennemerland, as in the phrase "The States of Holland and West Friesland." Similarly, contemporary authors sometimes used the name *North Holland* to mean only the northern part of the peninsula, and sometimes the whole Northern Quarter or North Holland.

*Waterland* was properly the name of the bailiwick within the Waterland sea dike, but was also used as a synonym for the whole region, undoubtedly because of its exceptionally waterlogged landscape. The use of Waterland in this wider sense was particularly common on the government side. "The whole quarter of Holland that is called West Friesland, which is the Waterland, has long been full of Anabaptists," Provost Morillon wrote to Cardinal Granvelle.[16]

In this book the names *Northern Quarter*, *North Holland*, *West Friesland*, *Northland*, and *Waterland* will be used to refer to the whole peninsula north of the IJ and the *banne* of Velsen. Whenever a geographical name designates a more restricted area, for example the bailiwick of Waterland, that fact will be made clear.

A second point of terminology that needs to be clarified is the expression the *Spanish army*, already used several times. In this *Spanish* army Spaniards were in the minority. In January 1575, for example, the army numbered 56,850 infantry, of whom 25,240 were Netherlanders, 23,600 Germans, and only 7,830 Spaniards (13.8 percent).[17] To be sure, the Spanish companies formed the best-trained and most-experienced units of the army, which explains why contemporaries, both rebels and loyalists, spoke of the *Spanish* army when they meant the government forces. I shall follow this custom, but do not wish to imply that the Revolt must be seen as a conflict between Netherlanders and Spaniards. On the contrary, the size of the contingent recruited in the Netherlands shows how far the Revolt was in the first place a civil war.

[16] *CCG*, IV, 174, Morillon to Granvelle, 13 April 1572.
[17] Parker, *Army*, 271 (appendix A) and 25–35.

CHAPTER TWO

## The Northland

IN THE SUMMER OF 1575 the Amsterdam sculptor, engineer, and cartographer Joost Janszoon Beeldsnijder, also named Bilhamer, put the finishing touches to a new map of the Northern Quarter (plate 8).[1] The depiction on the map of a seaman or surveyor equipped with plumb line, compasses, and Jacob's staff suggests that Bilhamer used the most modern surveying techniques. Compared with other maps of the time (plates 9 and 10) Bilhamer's work is remarkably detailed, especially in showing the position of roads, dikes, canals, and streams. Bilhamer's attention to North Holland's system of land routes and waterways was no accident, for he was commissioned to produce the map by the Duke of Alba himself. Alba hoped to be able to use it in the reconquest of the Northern Quarter, a rebel stronghold since the summer of 1572.[2] As on a modern ordnance map Joost Janszoon had precisely delineated all the roads, dikes, and dams that were supposed to unlock the Northern Quarter to the king's army. But he also meticulously marked the countless lakes, channels, and ditches that would obstruct the army's path. His map extended as far south as Leiden and Utrecht, where much of the Spanish army was encamped. Of course the region south of the River IJ does not belong in a map of North Holland, but it was of the greatest importance for planning the route and the supply lines of the government forces.

Careful examination of the map reveals signs of war everywhere. In the harbor of Amsterdam Bilhamer drew the wrecked ships the rebels had sunk in 1573 to prevent the government fleet from leaving port. Around Leiden he drew the sconces or fortifications dug for the siege of the city but hurriedly abandoned by the Spanish army in October 1574, with their exotic names: Forte Lalame, Forte Lacruijse, Forte Gran Victoen, Forte Casse Vasse, Forte Satane.

Bilhamer did not complete the definitive version of his map until 31 July 1575, two months after Hierges's campaign in the Northern Quarter, yet Hierges must have used the Amsterdam cartographer's work, presum-

[1] Kölker, *Kaart van Noordholland*; Lambooij, *Getekend land*, 17; Ter Gouw, *Geschiedenis van Amsterdam*, V, 461; VI, 394–96.

[2] Although Pontanus, *Beschrijvinghe*, 287, states that Alba ordered the map around 1571, when he "thought of again reducing the Northern Quarter to obedience and duty," he must mean 1572.

ably in a hand-drawn version. Brother Wouter Jacobszoon knew as early as 28 April that Hierges had gone to Utrecht, where he "had been shown through what places or roads one must pass to reach the Northland."[3] The rebels north of the IJ had also scented danger. On 27 May, the day that Hierges's army marched northward, Sonoy's second in command, Lieutenant Hendrik van Broekhuijsen, wrote from Wormer that he had heard that "two men from the Northland" had gone to Amsterdam to show Hierges "a new map," in which the region was depicted "from stream to stream and from channel to channel." They had received a hundred guilders each for this. These men must have been Bilhamer and his assistant.[4] Broekhuijsen's letter confirmed Sonoy's conviction that treason and all its calamitous consequences were lurking around every corner.

The sight of the natural obstacles that faced him in the North, as they appeared on Bilhamer's map, must have horrified Hierges. It seemed as if the larger part of the region consisted of water rather than land. The extraordinary ubiquity of water must have made him even more pessimistic about his chances of success. In themselves the mercenary forces of the rebels and the hastily mobilized North Holland peasants were no match for the experienced Spanish *tercios*, but the rebels' control of the inland waterways and the sea enabled them to cause immense difficulties for the government army. Twice already, at Alkmaar and Leiden, the rebels had literally washed the Spanish troops away by opening the dikes.

What did Hierges see in Bilhamer's map? The decisive factor in the geography of the Northern Quarter was the River IJ, a broad estuary that ran westward almost as far as the line of sand dunes, and thus separated the Northern Quarter from the rest of Holland. The IJ, which a medieval charter had called "the wild sea," was a formidable barrier to communication between north and south. In 1489 the Holy Roman Emperor Maximilian had almost been shipwrecked in a storm while crossing from Amsterdam to Spaarndam.[5] The river made the Northern Quarter a true peninsula, linked to the rest of the province only by a narrow strip of land. On four sides it was washed by the waves of the North Sea, the Zuiderzee and the IJ itself.

The northern coastline of the peninsula lay much farther south than it does now. It began at Petten and meandered via Kolhorn and Medemblik to Enkhuizen. The strip of dunes between Petten and Huisduinen, which had once formed the island of 't Oge, had been joined to the mainland of

---

[3] *DWJ*, 492.
[4] Bor, 620–21; Kölker, *Kaart van Noordholland* (unpaginated); Soeteboom, *Nederlandsche beroerten*, fol. A3v and pp. 53–54.
[5] Ter Gouw, *Geschiedenis van Amsterdam*, I, 39; Wiesflecker, 348; *Kaiser Maximilian*, I, 222.

Kennemerland by the Hondsbosse Zeewering since the end of the fifteenth century.[6] The closing of this gap had made it possible to drain and build dikes around the Zijpe in 1553, but all the land just won was lost again in the catastrophic All Saints' Day flood of 1570. Not until 1597 was the Zijpe to be definitively reclaimed from the sea. The neat straight lines parceling out the Zijpe polder, drawn in the upper left corner of Bilhamer's map, must have been added to the new edition of 1608.

Seawater was not the only obstacle that confronted an invader of the Northern Quarter, for within the dikes there was a complex of extensive lakes, or meres, that made military campaigns an awkward business. The two largest were the Waard and the Schermer in the north, separated from each other only by the Huigendijk. Only slightly smaller were the Beemster, Purmer, and Wormer meres around the town of Purmerend. In addition to these there were countless smaller lakes and meres, many of them the lasting result of earlier dike breaches. Most of these bodies of water were connected by a system of waterways, on which dams had been built at many places to regulate the flow. Thanks to locks and portages they did not form a significant hindrance to the rebels' shipping. Besides these main channels the North Hollanders had also developed a very fine-meshed network of streams and ditches to drain the low-lying meadows (plate 1). In such a waterlogged landscape it was impossible for the main body of the Spanish army to operate away from the main roads, which ran along the tops of the dikes. For cavalry the attempt to traverse the marshy country, crisscrossed by streams, was a nightmare.

Excessive water was not a problem for the government forces alone. The inhabitants of the peninsula of North Holland had a hard time keeping themselves dry. To protect themselves against the waters they had built many dikes and dams. As a result the landscape east of the Kennemerland dunes was in fact made up of several islands, each of these larger units being enclosed within a communal dike. In the north lay the bailiwick of West Friesland, surrounded by the old West Friesian enclosure dike; in the south lay the bailiwick of Waterland, which shared an enclosure dike with the eastern and western Zaan districts. In between were the smaller Zeevang and Schermer islands. The links between the inland waterways and the sea—the Korsloot, the Purmer Ee, the Zaan, and the Krommenie—had long been dammed, thereby combining Kennemerland in a single geographical unit with West Friesland, Zeevang, Waterland, and the Zaan district, centered on Schermer Island. Outside the dikes lay vast salt marshes and reed beds, which were unattractive terrain for the operations of a modern army. For the guerrilla tactics of the rebels, though, they were ideal.

[6] Schoorl, *'t Oge*.

The people of North Holland had to be constantly on their guard against the inundation of their low-lying and waterlogged land. In the middle ages several causes had combined in a vicious circle to make it increasingly difficult for them to keep the upper hand in the struggle against the waters. Improved drainage techniques allowed the farmers to lower the water table, but the lower groundwater in turn caused the upper layers of the peat fen to oxidize and shrink, so that the land surface was lowered again. This made even deeper drainage necessary, which once more caused the ground level to sink.[7]

The situation was all the more dangerous because the fall in the land surface caused by human intervention coincided with a gradual rise in sea level. This twofold disturbance of the natural equilibrium had led to several great breaches of the dikes, the origin of the meres of North Holland, which again reduced the area of land available. The prevailing westerly winds whipped up violent waves, which undermined the banks of the meres. In 1544, for example, the inhabitants of Schermer Island explained that in the last eighty or ninety years, by their estimate, they had seen three hundred *morgen* of their land washed away. In the same year the *schout* (sheriff) of Oudkarspel declared that he could well remember a time when there had been so much land on either side of the Huigendijk that a man standing on top of it could not see the water. But now the dike was washed on both sides by the Waard and the Schermer.[8]

Around the middle of the sixteenth century the war against the water took a turn for the better. This was thanks in part to natural changes in the environment, as the so-called Late Medieval Transgression gave way to the Little Ice Age, a cold period characterized by harsh winters, a fall in sea level, and a decline in the frequency of storm surges.[9] Between 1502 and 1575 North Holland had had to cope with twelve dike breaches. These natural disasters were, however, concentrated in the early part of the century, six of them between 1502 and 1518. After the great All Saints' Day flood of 1570 there were two more storm surges in 1573 and 1575, coincidentally the very years in which Sonoy flooded the Northland to defend it against the enemy.[10]

The improvement in the control of the waters was also a result of better techniques and organization. The fifteenth century had seen the invention of the smock mill, a type of water mill that could be turned to face and be driven by a wind from any direction. This new technology allowed the

---

[7] De Vries and van der Woude, *First Modern Economy*, 17–18.

[8] Van der Woude, *Noorderkwartier*, 43. The Graftse *morgen* was about 1.85 acres. Verhoeff, *Oude Nederlandse maten*, 20.

[9] Lambert, *Making of the Dutch Landscape*, 212.

[10] Van der Woude, *Noorderkwartier*, 55; Gottschalk, *Stormvloeden*, 723, 738–40.

inhabitants to pump water out of the sinking polders and into the higher outlet pools.[11] The struggle to master the waters took a great step forward in 1544, when Charles V granted a charter for the incorporation of a *waterschap*, a body to centralize the various local efforts.[12] This also put an end to the system under which each landowner liable for the duty of maintenance was responsible for the upkeep of a section of dike. Landowners whose property was subject to this obligation could either maintain the portion of dike themselves or contract it out. It is obvious that such a system entailed great risks, even though the dike authorities could impose fines on negligent owners after an inspection. By then in most cases it was already too late.[13]

The most spectacular proof that the balance between man and nature had at last tipped in favor of the former was supplied by the great drainage projects of the seventeenth century, which were to change the face of the landscape forever; North Holland would cease to be a land of water and become a land of meadows and pastures. That transformation had already made a modest start in the middle of the sixteenth century, when three small meres were drained in the 1540s, followed by seven more between 1561 and 1567. Two of these were larger meres to the west of Alkmaar, the Egmondermeer and the Bergermeer, a joint project of the Count of Egmond and the Lord of Brederode.[14]

By sixteenth-century standards North Holland's system of water control was impressive, but its effectiveness must not be exaggerated. The means available to drain the waterlogged land were so primitive they could not prevent the meadows flooding in winter. Around the middle of the seventeenth century a French traveler, Jean-Nicolas de Parival, could still write that the meadows in October were under water "because of the wind, storms and continual rains . . . when the water is stirred up by the wind, in many places only the dikes, houses and church towers are visible as if they were rising from the sea."[15] In 1591 the Utrecht man of letters Arnoldus Buchelius described the country north of the IJ as "a wet district, everywhere overflowing with water, so that in many places the only way to leave one's house is by boat." The Waterlanders, Buchelius punned, sailed not just on the sea but on the soil as well (*salum non modo sed et solum navigant*). The flat country was intersected by numerous ditches, and Buchelius claimed with astonishment that not a single tree

---

[11] De Vries and Van der Woude, *First Modern Economy*, 18, 28.
[12] Belonje, *Hoogheemraadschap*.
[13] Van der Woude, *Noorderkwartier*, 41, 44.
[14] Ibid., 616; appendix I; see also Lambert, *Making of the Dutch Landscape*, 214.
[15] De Parival, *Délices*, 9.

was to be found in the whole region.[16] The Catholic hagiographer Petrus Opmeer also recorded that there were so few trees the country dwellers had to make do with dried cattle dung for fuel and the townsfolk with "turves of peat the color of pitch."[17] Trees could not be grown on the dikes for safety reasons, while in other places their growth was hindered by the sinking land surface and high water table, which must have been brackish because of the seepage of sea water.

Lodovico Guicciardini, a Florentine resident of Antwerp, whose *Descrittione di tutti i Paesi Bassi* ("Description of All the Low Countries," 1567) became a bestseller, was also impressed by the watery landscape. He devoted a learned discussion to the meaning of the name Holland, and offered two possible etymologies. The first was that the name derived from "*holt* or *hout* land," because it was assumed that the region had once been covered in woodland (Dutch *hout*). But Guicciardini preferred the second explanation: this derived the name from "hollow" land, "for when one rides in a carriage or on horseback here, one sees the earth trembling in many places, as if it were floating on the water."[18]

Guicciardini found the evidence for the second theory in an amazing event that had occurred near Haarlem around 1565. A cow had fallen into a deep water-filled pit and had drowned. Three days later its body was found floating in open water, some distance east of the site of the accident. It was obvious that the cow must have been carried *under the land* by the water.[19]

> And although it may appear strange or almost impossible that such a great tract of land should float on water, yet one sees clearly that if not all the land, at least part of it has no other foundation than the water, and is borne by the water; as is the case in the district called Waterland [cioè Paese dall'acqua].[20]

In a country so wet that not a tree would grow, agriculture was bound to be a troublesome business. The inhabitants were compelled to live by raising cattle. This meant that they had to import the necessary bread grains and pay for them by exporting butter and cheese and providing shipping services. In this way the Northern Quarter became part of the modern commercial economy.

---

[16] Van Buchell, *Diarium*, 310: "*arborem regio non alit.*" See also Guicciardini, *Beschrijvinghe*, 192.

[17] Opmeer, *Martelaarsboek*, 19.

[18] Guicciardini, *Descrittione*, 369. Cited from the Dutch translation of 1612, *Beschrijvinghe*, 191.

[19] "onde si compresa che ella, sprofondata di terra nell'acqua et dall'acqua traportata, venne a far tal reuscita."

[20] Guicciardini, *Descrittione*, 369.

In the sixteenth century agrarian prices rose faster than the general price level. Rising rents for leases of farmland and pasture indicate that agriculture was becoming more profitable; the drainage schemes begun in the 1540s are another sign of this. The peasants of Waterland supplied the Amsterdam market with dairy products. Large quantities of butter and cheese were shipped from such market and port towns as Hoorn, chiefly to Antwerp for sale in its hinterland in Brabant and Flanders, and also to Germany, England, and Spain. According to Guicciardini four thousand head of cattle were kept in the village of Assendelft alone, which gave at least eight hundred *stoop* (about four hundred gallons) of milk year round. In Holland it was said that more milk was produced in Assendelft, Oostzaan, Westzaan, Krommenie, and Krommeniedijk than Rhenish wine was imported through the staple at Dordrecht.[21]

In spite of the relative importance of dairy farming in North Holland, most peasants made a fairly modest living. The poorly drained meadows could support only a few cattle. The fifty-four households that made up the West Friesian village of Westwoud kept no more than two hundred cattle on eight hundred *morgen* of pasture. A single cow needed four *morgen* or almost 8.4 acres. Average herds were small; a few wealthy farmers might keep ten to twelve cattle, the average four to six, the poorest peasants no more than two or three animals. By modern standards the cattle were small and their milk yield low.[22]

The small scale of most dairy farms meant that the average farm household could not support itself from farming alone. Farmers were forced to supplement their incomes from all kinds of outside work. Many country folk went to work for hire in the merchant fleets of North Holland and Amsterdam ship owners. The *Informacie*, an inquiry into the potential tax yield of the towns and villages of Holland in 1514, gives a characteristic description of Ransdorp in Waterland. The men went to sea while "their wives might keep a cow or two."[23] The North Hollanders eked out their income from farming with a variety of other activities, including the herring fishery, freshwater fishing, bird catching, cutting reeds, digging peat, transport by barge or wagon, building and maintaining dikes and ditches, or working on reclamation projects.

In 1514, the year for which we have the fullest information, North Holland had about eighty-two thousand inhabitants, roughly 30 percent of the total for the province of Holland. Lack of employment in the agrar-

---

[21] Guicciardini, *Beschrijvinghe*, 193.

[22] De Vries, "De boer," 288; De Vries, *Dutch Rural Economy*, 70–71; De Vries and Van der Woude, *Nederland 1500–1815*, 237. But cf. Van Buchell, *Diarium*, 310, who asserts that the ordinary farmers (*mediocres villici*) kept twenty-four cows.

[23] *Informacie*, 213.

ian sector had led around twenty-two thousand inhabitants, or 27 percent of the population, to live in one of the six walled towns of the Quarter.[24] The population rose rapidly in the sixteenth century. In the half century from 1514 to 1561 the number of households, and therefore the number of people, grew by nearly 70 percent.[25] In 1622 there would be almost 192,000 people living in the Northern Quarter, a third of them in the towns. Large open villages also grew in the second half of the sixteenth century in the Zaan area and on Schermer Island, where the population was entirely engaged in nonagrarian pursuits, such as shipping, sea fishing, shipbuilding, and baking ship's biscuits.

Alkmaar, Hoorn, and Enkhuizen were the three largest and most important towns. Alkmaar, which had about nine thousand inhabitants on the eve of the Revolt, was the oldest.[26] Before the draining of the Schermer and the Beemster the harbor had been accessible to seagoing ships, but Alkmaar's chief function was as a regional market and service center. Farmers from the surrounding villages brought their cheese and other dairy produce to market and used the specialized services that could only be found in the town. Alkmaar notaries, for example, drew up deeds for these villagers. Hoorn, well situated on a natural bay on the Zuiderzee, combined the functions of regional market and service center with that of international port. In 1560 its population numbered about eight thousand.[27] Its chief imports were timber from Norway and salt from Portugal. Enkhuizen, which had about seven thousand inhabitants at this time and occupied a strategic position at the entrance to the Zuiderzee, developed into the most important port for the herring fishery and imported salt to preserve its catch.[28]

[24] Based on De Vries, *Dutch Rural Economy*, 86, and Naber, *Terugblik*, 36–37. The population figure includes 7,770 inhabitants of the islands of Wieringen, Texel, and Vlieland. Purmerend was not yet a walled town in 1514. See also Lesger, *Hoorn*, 222; around 1560, 32.4 percent of the West Friesian population lived in the towns of Hoorn, Enkhuizen, and Medemblik.

[25] Van der Woude, *Noorderkwartier*, 153; Van der Woude's calculation refers to the district between the IJ and West Friesland, but there is no reason to assume that the demographic development of the rest of the region followed a different course.

[26] In 1561 there were 1,778 houses in Alkmaar. Van der Woude applied a coefficient of 4.7 persons per household in the towns in the year 1514. I have assumed an average of 5.0 persons per household in 1561, taking into account the strong growth of population since 1514 and the residents of the urban monastic houses and convents, which are not included in the number of houses. Van der Woude, *Noorderkwartier*, 85–89, 622; see also Lesger, *Hoorn*, 219–20.

[27] Lesger, *Hoorn*, 22, gives a total population for Hoorn, Enkhuizen, and Medemblik. I am grateful to Clé Lesger for making available the underlying numbers of houses, based on the assessment registers for the tenth penny tax of 1561–62: Hoorn 1,628, Enkhuizen 1,407, and Medemblik 489 households.

[28] Willemsen, *Enkhuizen*.

The three remaining towns, Medemblik, Edam, and Monnickendam, were much smaller. Medemblik, with about twenty-five hundred people, gained a strategic importance from its castle, and imported timber through its harbor. In 1517 the Gelderlanders reduced the town to ashes, and in 1555 it burned down again.[29] Edam ("where they make the good cheeses of Holland") had about four thousand inhabitants in 1561.[30] It too imported timber for shipbuilding, its most important occupation. In 1561 the little town had forty-five shipyards, which must have employed several hundred inhabitants. In Monnickendam the cloth industry and shipbuilding were the most important activities of the three thousand inhabitants, but there were also salt refineries and shipyards. Like Medemblik, Monnickendam suffered two disastrous fires in the sixteenth century, which spared only the church and a handful of houses.[31]

The predominance of timber and salt in the region's imports reveals its heavy economic dependence on Amsterdam. The ship owners, who came mainly from the smaller towns and villages of Waterland and East Friesland, sailed largely for shippers in Amsterdam. The majority of the Dutch ships that passed through the toll on the Sound had their home ports in the towns and villages of North Holland. Waterlanders and West Frieslanders owned a larger share of the total merchant fleet than the Amsterdammers, but this obscures the fact that their ships did not usually load and unload their cargoes in their home ports, but at Amsterdam. Except for bulky timber and salt, the Northern Quarter drew practically all its imported goods from the port of Amsterdam.[32] The most vital import for a region that had specialized entirely in cattle rearing was rye and other bread grains from the Baltic countries. The other goods the Northern Quarter imported through Amsterdam included wine and copper from Germany, wool and cloth from England, wool, oil, and spices from Spain and Portugal, wine from France, and silk and alum from Italy.[33]

When Amsterdam became almost the only place in the rebel-held area to remain loyal to the government between 1572 and 1578, the ports of North Holland saw an extraordinary opportunity to profit from the city's temporary eclipse. But when Amsterdam regained its place as the economic hub of the region in 1578, this did not lead to the immediate stagnation of North Holland's economic development. The resurgence of Am-

---

[29] Sigmond, *Nederlandse zeehavens*, 53.

[30] Cited in CCG, IV, 180, Morillon to Granvelle, 15 April 1572. In 1561 Edam had 806 houses, a number that had grown to 898 by 1569. Van der Woude, *Noorderkwartier*, 156, 286, 458, 622.

[31] In 1561 Monnickendam had 616 households. Van der Woude, *Noorderkwartier*, 155, 286, 330–31, 622.

[32] De Vries and Van der Woude, *First Modern Economy*, 353–54; Posthumus, *Uitvoer van Amsterdam*, 211–22.

[33] De Vries and Van der Woude, *First Modern Economy*, 360.

sterdam's economy after the Alteration of 1578 generated plenty of work and prosperity to spare for the city's hinterland in North Holland.

Nature had made the Northland an isolated region, cut off from the rest of Holland by the IJ, and almost inaccessible to travelers on foot or on horseback because of the ubiquitous water. But that did not mean the Northern Quarter was a backward or inward-looking area. From the favorably placed harbors on the Zuiderzee travelers and merchants' goods could reach Amsterdam and other Dutch ports quickly, safely, and in comfort. There were good shipping connections with more distant ports in Norway, northern Germany, and Portugal. The water could both divide and unite.

The Northern Quarter has never been a hotbed of culture and learning, yet the international craze for humanism did not pass it by. The painters Jan van Scorel (Schoorl) and Maerten van Heemskerck worked in the new Italian style, though not in their native land but in Utrecht and Haarlem. In Alkmaar the Latin School flourished under one learned rector, Johannes Murmellius, while another, Petrus Nannius, was a famous scholar who became a professor at the Collegium Trilingue in Leuven.[34] Hoorn was the birthplace of the erudite physician, philologist, poet, and historian Hadrianus Junius, who settled in Haarlem after spending some time in Italy, Paris, and London.[35] Even so, the Northland was too small for really eminent artists and scholars.

According to the current Galenic theory of the humors, the damp climate of North Holland was bound to influence the outward appearance and inner character of the population. Petrus Opmeer, the author of a Catholic martyrology, assumed a clear connection between the nature of the soil, the climate and diet, and the character of the people.

> Marshy West Friesland, dismal in appearance and raw in climate . . . has a flat landscape, abounding in grass to support beasts, which supplies us with a wealth of milk and leafy vegetables . . . just as the people in that country are coarse and large of body, so they are also dull and slow-witted, living for the most part on milk and black rye bread.[36]

There were hardly any noblemen, but all the more plebeians. "Everyone's worth is valued by his power and wealth," Opmeer wrote disparagingly, "so that men who excel in virtue are little esteemed there."[37] By sixteenth-

---

[34] Van Gelder, *Geschiedenis der Latijnsche school*.
[35] Veldman, "Enkele aanvullende gegevens."
[36] Cited from the Dutch translation of 1700: Opmeer, *Martelaarsboek*, 19, and Opmeer, *Historia martyrum*, 11.
[37] Opmeer, *Martelaarsboek*, 20 and Opmeer, *Historia martyrum*, 12: "Nobilitas ei praecipue invisa, censu et divitiis cuiusque dignitatem metiuntur, virtuteque excellentes viros aegre ferunt. Plebeii fere omnes."

century standards, therefore, the Northern Quarter was a rather egalitarian society, and the baneful consequences were obvious to everyone. The country had been "dishonored by so many insurrections and the murder of William the Holy Roman Emperor and several other princes."[38]

Indeed, nature and history had joined forces to give the Northland a character all its own. There was hardly a nobleman to be found outside the Kennemerland dunes. In large parts of the countryside feudalism was unknown. Many villages (called *bannen* in North Holland) had never been granted in feudal tenure.[39] Although they had no walls, many of the villages possessed town rights. The peasants of the Northern Quarter were free proprietors, conscious of their status as citizens of self-governing communities.

In the towns, too, except for Alkmaar, the citizenry enjoyed a greater degree of participation in political life than was customary elsewhere in Holland. In a roundabout, two-stage but relatively democratic electoral procedure, known as "going to the bean," a large proportion of the male population was directly involved in the annual renewal of the magistracy. Each year, using bags of white and black beans, they cast lots for a list of nominees chosen from among themselves, from which the sheriff made the final choice of magistrates.[40] Every town of the Northern Quarter, like all the others in Holland, also had its *vroedschap*, or council, on which the most eminent citizens had seats for life. The sheriff represented the authority of the ruler, but had to be a citizen of three years standing in the town in question.

This deviant political structure had its roots in the history of the Northland. The region had originally been independent and was not united with the County of Holland until quite a late date. After first incorporating Kennemerland, the counts of Holland in the twelfth and thirteenth centuries waged a long series of wars to bring West Friesland and Waterland under their rule. They faced the same geographic and strategic obstacles that would be the despair of Alba and his successors centuries later. The West Frieslanders dug themselves in behind a water line that ran from the Zijpe to Alkmaar and on past the Schermer to the IJ. Alkmaar was the only place where the armies of the counts of Holland could force an entry

---

[38] Opmeer, *Martelaarsboek*, 20.

[39] An *ambachtsheerlijkheid* was the right of jurisdiction over a defined area, mostly a village. This jurisdiction was granted by the ruler. The lord, who was usually a noble, had the right to appoint the sheriff and to collect the incomes that were derived from the administration of justice. Other more or less lucrative rights were also attached to the *ambachtsheerlijkheid* proper: Van Nierop, *The Nobility*, 104–8, 141–47.

[40] De Lange, "Ontwikkeling van een oligarchische regeringsvorm"; Van Hasselt, "Hoorn's stadsbestuur"; Kooijmans, *Onder regenten*, 38; Bossaers, *Van kintsbeen*, 39, 42–43.

into West Friesland, but heavily armed cavalry were of little use on the quaking fenland. Winter was the best season for campaigning, when the water was under a thick layer of ice and the ground had frozen hard. In 1256, during one of these winter expeditions, William II, Count of Holland and King of the Romans, fell through the ice near Hoogwoud with his horse and was slain by the West Friesland peasants. Under normal circumstances the peasants were no match for the knightly armies of the counts of Holland, but on this occasion they turned the natural features of the country to their advantage. Exploiting their superior knowledge of the terrain and the support of the local population they waged a guerrilla war, avoiding pitched battles and luring the Hollanders into traps.[41]

After Count Floris V of Holland finally subdued the region in 1289, he allowed it to remain a separate administrative unit. From this date, besides that of count of Holland and Zeeland he also took the lesser title of "lord" of West Friesland, tacitly including Waterland and the Zeevang. Unlike Kennemerland, which had been conquered earlier, he did not introduce feudal tenures here, but left the old Friesian administrative and legal institutions largely in existence.

That administration can be described as local self-government by free peasant proprietors.[42] The basis of the legal and administrative organization was the *banne*, in which the count was represented by a *schout*, or sheriff. Each year the sheriff chose a college of *schepenen* (justices) from a list of names put forward by the villagers themselves. While in Kennemerland and the rest of Holland the feudal nobility formed a connecting link between the count and the villagers, in West Friesland the latter were directly under the count.

In the early fourteenth century the counts of Holland took the administrative and legal organization of the West Friesland countryside to its logical conclusion by granting town rights to all the West Friesland *bannen* and most of those in Waterland. These places were quite different from what one would imagine as a normal medieval town. They were not walled, and they had not lost their agricultural character. Town rights simply meant that their jurisdiction was detached from the surrounding countryside; the neighbors composed the administrative and judicial bodies, and the peasants became *poorters*, or citizens who enjoyed the protection of their own laws. Sometimes two or more *bannen* were combined in a single grant of town rights; or *bannen* were incorporated under the rights of an existing town. In 1406, for example, Zwaag was brought under the law of Hoorn, followed two years later by the villages of the

---

[41] De Graaf, *Oorlog om Holland*, 210–49.
[42] Pols, *Westfriesche stadsrechten*; De Goede, *Swannotsrecht*; De Goede, "Bestuurspolitiek"; De Goede, *Waterland*.

area known as the Veenhoop. In 1413 Warder, Middelie, and Kwadijk came under the law of Edam.[43] The villages were not simply brought within the sphere of influence of the town, but the villagers gained the same privileges as the citizens of the towns. Sometimes the inhabitants of the incorporated *bannen* sent one or more delegates to the college of aldermen and the council of the chief town, as Lutjebroek and Hoogkarspel did when they were added to Grootebroek. In other cases the *bannen* under a single law were governed by their own administration, made up of "peacemakers."[44]

In the conflict between Jacqueline of Bavaria and Philip the Good of Burgundy the country towns of North Holland opted massively for the Bavarian countess. Alkmaar, Kennemerland, and West Friesland rose in revolt in 1425 and laid siege to Haarlem. Only the three larger West Friesland towns of Hoorn, Enkhuizen, and Medemblik, and the smaller towns of Schellinkhout, Westwoud, and Hem, sided with the Burgundians. After his victory over Jacqueline, Philip punished the insurgent towns with heavy fines and the loss of their town rights.

The new ruler seized the opportunity to curb the independence of the West Friesland communes. He introduced feudal tenures in the area for the first time, granting them to the commanders who had put down the rebellion and to some of the bastards of the house of Bavaria.[45] The villages of Geestmerambacht, which had only recently been brought under the law of Alkmaar, lost their town rights for good. Philip rewarded the towns that had supported him by extending their authority over surrounding villages. In 1426, for example, he ruled that the inhabitants of Wognum, which had earlier been united with Hoorn on a footing of equality but had supported Jacqueline, must in future stand trial in Hoorn. Henceforth the burgomasters of Hoorn would appoint the peacemakers in Wognum.[46]

This retribution did not put an end to the spirit of independence in North Holland. In 1491 and 1492 the bloody rising of the Cheese and Bread Folk broke out in the Quarter, an antitax revolt of peasants and urban day laborers, behind which lay resistance to the growing power of the Burgundian state.[47] In the Northern Quarter there was widespread opposition to the raising of the *ruitergeld*, a tax levied by the ruler Maximilian of Austria to pay for the suppression of a rebellion in Flanders. In April 1491 the North Hollanders, their discontent aggravated by an

[43] Pols, *Westfriesche stadsrechten*, xx, xx–xxiii; De Goede, *Swannotsrecht*, 109, 119–20.
[44] De Goede, *Swannotsrecht*, 117.
[45] Pols, *Westfriesche stadsrechten*, xxvii.
[46] De Goede, *Swannotsrecht*, 150.
[47] Van Gent, "Pertijelijke saken," 389–92; Scheurkogel, "Kaas- and broodspel"; Jansen, *Hoekse en Kabeljauwse twisten*, 98–106; Hugenholtz, "Kaas- en Broodvolk."

economic recession, refused to pay it. Rebellious nobles, members of the Hoek faction, fled to the islands of Texel and Wieringen, from where they mounted raids on the countryside of North Holland. When Stadholder Jan van Egmond raised bands of armed men to collect the hated tax, he provoked a violent reaction. On Easter Day in 1491 a furious mob plundered the house of the chief tax collector of North Holland in Alkmaar.

The collection of the *ruitergeld* was suspended after this, but the malcontents were not appeased. The opposition organized a general diet, or assembly, of the Northern Quarter in Oude Niedorp, attended by delegates from all the towns except Enkhuizen. They raised a peasant army, which followed banners bearing images of loaves and cheeses, a symbol of their economic grievances. In May 1492 the peasant rebels captured Haarlem with the support of sympathizers in the city. They lynched the sheriff of Haarlem, a former chief tax collector in North Holland, and set fire to title deeds and tax records.

An attack on Leiden, however, was repelled, and this turned the tide. Maximilian's commander Albert of Saxony crushed the insurgents at Heemskerk. The town of Beverwijk, which still offered resistance, was sacked and razed to the ground. The leaders of the revolt were executed. The rebellious villages and towns, including Alkmaar, were condemned to pay heavy fines and to forfeit their privileges. Alkmaar was forced to pull down its walls, gates, and towers. This left it a defenseless prey to the Gelderlanders, who plundered the city during their incursion into North Holland in 1517.

How far did the peculiar administrative institutions of the North and its people's attachment to their autonomy help to develop a sense of regional identity? The sources give no hint that the North Hollanders felt they shared a common fate. Apart from the single assembly at Oude Niedorp they never attempted to create supralocal organs to promote the interests of the region as a whole. On the contrary, their jealously guarded local autonomy embroiled the towns and villages of North Holland in numerous quarrels with one another.[48]

In the administrative center of Holland, The Hague, the North Hollanders rarely put in an appearance. The provincial States, the States of Holland and West Friesland to give them their official name, grew over the half-century before the revolt into a self-conscious body politic,[49] but the towns of the Northern Quarter took no part in that process. Until 1572 only the six great towns, all of them south of the River IJ, participated in the deliberations of the States. Only in special cases that directly concerned them were the smaller towns occasionally summoned to The

---

[48] Aten, *Als het geweld komt*.
[49] Tracy, *Holland under Habsburg Rule*.

Hague. In 1540 the seaports of the Northern Quarter were called to take part in the discussion of the anchorage money tax, in 1547 of the herring fishery, and in 1559 of the salt tax.[50] Such attendance was too intermittent to secure North Holland a permanent voice in The Hague.

It was the second estate, the knights and nobles, that was supposed to speak for the interests of the countryside and the smaller towns in the States assembly. But in the Northern Quarter noblemen were very thin on the ground outside Kennemerland. In that area the nobles with the largest estates were the count of Egmond, followed at a distance by the lords of Brederode and Assendelft.[51] All three were powerful lords, who could wield influence and patronage in The Hague and at the court in Brussels, where the central government of the Netherlands was based. They meant little to the Northern Quarter. Lamorael van Egmond resided mainly in Flanders, where he was Stadholder of the province and owned important estates as Prince of Gavere. Hendrik van Brederode was out of favor with the government and spent most of his time in his free town of Vianen. Gerrit van Assendelft, who held an extremely important post as presiding counselor of the Court of Holland, was the chief informant on Holland affairs of the Regent in Brussels, but was more often in The Hague than at his castle of Assumburg near Heemskerk. He does not appear to have cast himself in the role of spokesman for the interests of the Northern Quarter.[52] Only three lesser nobles with estates in North Holland were regularly summoned to attend the States, and only one of them appeared regularly, but he held posts in South Holland as well.[53]

In the sixteenth century a powerful caste of high administrative officials grew up around the institutions of government in The Hague. These officials wielded great power in the various organs of the administration, such as the Chamber of Accounts and the Court, and kept up good contacts with the central government in Brussels, but there was not a North

---

[50] Fruin, *Geschiedenis der staatsinstellingen*, 80.

[51] The Count of Egmond held the lordships of Egmond binnen and Egmond aan Zee, Huisduinen, Petten, Warmenhuizen, Harenkarspel, and Bakkum, and in Waterland Purmerend, Ilpendam, Purmerland, and Nek. Brederode held the lordships of Bergen, 't Oge (Callantsoog), Velsen, Schoorl, and Camp. The Lord of Assendelft possessed Heemskerk, Castricum, and Assendelft. Van Nierop, *Van ridders tot regenten*, 255–63, appendix I.

[52] On Egmond and Assendelft see Tracy, *Holland under Habsburg Rule*, 188–91. On the position of Hendrik van Brederode in Holland see Van Nierop, *The Nobility*, 39–40, 146, 160, 182, 186–89.

[53] Van Nierop, *Van ridders*, appendix I, and 180, 184. The lords of Egmond van Kenenburg (with Sint Maartensrecht), the lords of Beieren van Schagen (with Barsingerhorn, Harenhuizen, and Burghorn), and the lords of Duvenvoirde (with Obdam and Hensbroek). Otto van Egmond van Kenenburg served in The Hague as a counselor in the feudal court and master of the registers of Holland. He was also a *hoogheemraad* (water official) of Delfland.

Hollander among them.[54] With no representative among the towns or the nobles in the States, and no powerful noblemen or top officials who could protect its interests, the Northern Quarter thus played hardly any part in the process of state formation that gathered pace in the Netherlands during the reign of Charles V. This does not seem to have troubled it. Remote, inhospitable, and politically isolated, the Northern Quarter wanted only to be left in peace.

[54] Koopmans, *Staten van Holland*, 273–80, appendix 2.

CHAPTER THREE

# Believers

INACCESSIBLE AND REMOVED from the centers of Habsburg power in the Netherlands, the Northern Quarter had an unenviable reputation as a nest of heretics. In 1565 the counselors of the Court of Holland reported that "the Northland of Holland and also Waterland will be worst affected by heresy, since the inhabitants there border closely on [East] Friesland, Emden and other eastern cities, which are of a different and indeed a contrary religion."[1] Immediately after the fall of Brill in April 1572, Provost Morillon, the well-informed Brussels correspondent of Cardinal Granvelle, was worried about the loyalty of the Northern Quarter, which was "full of Anabaptists."[2]

They had good reason to be concerned. The urbanization of the Quarter, the need for a great part of its people, including the rural population, to earn a living by going to sea, and the orientation of North Holland's shipping above all to the eastern ports of Emden, Hamburg, Lübeck, and Gdansk, combined to expose many of the inhabitants of the Northland to a variety of evangelically inspired ideas from an early date.[3] The Court singled out the pernicious influence of "foreigners who sail to and fro."[4] No less dangerous was the nearness of Amsterdam, which in the 1530s became the focal point of Anabaptism, and thirty years later in the Wonder Year 1566 was the center of the Reformation movement in Holland.

Other causes helped to spread the influence of Reformation ideas. As early as 1526 the Court of Holland saw a need to launch an inquiry into a Lutheran play that had been staged by the "rhetoricians" of Monnickendam.[5] Many of the towns of North Holland had these "chambers of rhetoric," active literary and debating societies, that also produced plays. They were not the hotbeds of heresy that conservative clerics feared, but in the semi-intellectual milieu of their craftsmen membership the new evangelical ideas must have been frequently and sympathetically discussed.

---

[1] "Verslag," 54. The counselors of the Court of Holland tried to give the impression in this report that the Catholic faith was not faring too badly. See also Van Beuningen, *Lindanus*, 187–91.
[2] CCG, IV, 170, 174, 292.
[3] Voets, "Hervorming," I, 220.
[4] "Verslag," 55.
[5] CD, V, 171.

Many of the plays performed by the rhetoricians in these years showed a marked biblical influence, though this did not necessarily make them "Protestant."

Alkmaar and Hoorn each had its Latin School, where the teachers were enthusiastic devotees of the new humanistic learning. The study of the *bonae litterae* was no more automatically likely to lead to the adoption of unorthodox beliefs than membership of a chamber of rhetoric, though many conservatives feared that it did. But the presence of the schools and their corps of humanistically educated teachers provided an intellectual climate in which new books and new ideas were keenly debated. The rector of the Latin School in Alkmaar, the priest Laurens Jacobszoon Zas (d. 1557), had studied at the Collegium Trilingue in Leuven and was well known as a student of Greek, Latin, Hebrew, the arts, philosophy, and the writings of the Church Fathers. Around him he gathered a circle of evangelically minded friends, among them Cornelis Cooltuyn, who has been called the father of the Dutch Reformation.[6]

While the intellectual climate of North Holland favored the dissemination of evangelical ideas, it was far from favorable to their suppression. Antiheretical measures were more effective the closer one came to the centers of the ruler's power. The authorities in the towns and villages were fiercely attached to their autonomy, and had no appetite for helping outsiders who came among them to hunt heretics. Moreover, the Northern Quarter was hard to reach from The Hague, and the numerous meres, creeks, and reed beds offered fugitives from persecution abundant opportunities to hide from the prying eyes of the Inquisition.

In the Court of Holland's report of 1565, mentioned above, the counselors complained of a lack of cooperation from the judicial authorities of Medemblik in tracking down and punishing violators of the edicts against heresy. They wrote that the Court would be glad to assist the sheriff of Medemblik if only the distance between the two towns were not so great. It can be taken for granted that the miscreants had gone into hiding long before the authorities from The Hague arrived on the scene.

The Court had already been snubbed when it tried to arrest several heretics on the islands of Texel and Vlieland. The need to change carriages and boats so often en route made it impossible for the prosecutor-general's substitute and his men to conceal their movements. When the judicial officers from The Hague finally arrived on Texel the birds had flown, "since the aforesaid island lies surrounded by water [!] and on the coast of the sea, open to the navigation to the East."[7]

---

[6] Vis, *Cooltuijn*, 17.
[7] "Verslag," 77–78, 90.

Evangelical pamphlets and tracts must have been hidden in many a bale of rye and load of timber that the Holland shippers carried home. Yet it was not the seamen who first imported evangelical ideas into North Holland in the 1520s, but the professionals, that is, the parish clergy. Cornelis Pieterszoon, parish priest of Krommeniedijk since 1520, preached daily

> diverse errors, especially touching the order of the Holy Church and the invocation of the saints, just as Luther and his disciples [had] written and taught. [He is] reputed among those who know him to be enlightened by Luther's darkness, which fame and reputation has its origin in conversation with suspect persons.[8]

One of those suspect persons was Dirck Allaertszoon, a blind dissenter who had been banished from Leiden in 1525 and who had gone into hiding in the house of Heer Cornelis Pieterszoon (*Heer*, or Sir, was the title by which a priest was addressed). He organized conventicles throughout the Zaan area, illegal meetings of critical believers, where forbidden writings were read and discussed, and at which the priest of Krommeniedijk often took the lead. In his own parish church Heer Cornelis forbade the lighting of candles before the sacrament and the saints. He refused to say the *Ave Maria*, and when one of his parishioners asked him what he thought of the sacrament of the altar, he gave an evasive but all the more eloquent answer: "You ask me too much, I cannot advise you on this, the doctors have enough to do with it."[9] Finally his ideas brought him into conflict with the ecclesiastical authorities, who dismissed him from his parish. Yet he remained at his post, even after the bailiff had threatened his flock with punishment if they did not remove him. The dissident priest knew that he had the support of his parish, because "by far the most honorable people and the most capable part of the inhabitants there were very well content with him or desired to keep him."[10]

Most adherents of the "Lutheran sect" were to be found in Hoorn and Monnickendam. At a meeting of the States of Holland, Hoorn was even named in the same breath with Amsterdam and Delft as one of the three towns most infected with Lutheranism. The authorities of Monnickendam (popularly known as Luiterschendam) were summoned to The Hague several times to answer for what the Court of Holland regarded as their leniency toward those who adopted the new doctrines. In April 1527 a fugitive monk had preached in public for an hour or more, clothed in a tabard he had borrowed from the town clerk.[11]

---

[8] De Hoop Scheffer, *Geschiedenis*, 563.
[9] Ibid., 564–66.
[10] Ibid., 564.
[11] *CD*, V, 180, 193–97; De Hoop Scheffer, *Geschiedenis*, 578.

Even more worrying than the laxity of the magistrates was the presence of clerics who proclaimed the new ideas. Monnickendam was the home of three priests who held "bad views" on the sacrament of the altar and were unwilling to say mass.[12] In Hoorn the priest Gerard Peelt preached a variety of unorthodox opinions in the town churches, and ended up in prison in 1525.[13] His colleague Jan Hetersen joined "a professed nun and a servant" in marriage, and was generally considered a Lutheran, reason enough for the town magistrates to forbid him to accept the chaplaincy for which he had just paid six Flemish pounds.[14]

Willem Ottenszoon, another influential preacher, had been imprisoned in Utrecht for his ideas but escaped, was imprisoned again in Amsterdam, and after his release settled in Hoorn as pastor of the Beguines.[15] Ultimately he could no longer reconcile himself to the priesthood, and laid down his office to live as a layman, calling the tonsure the *signum bestiae* (mark of the beast). Leaving the priesthood, which was strictly forbidden by law at the time, did not mean the end of his spiritual leadership, for he now acted as a preacher at conventicles. A pamphlet he wrote against the parish priest of one of the Hoorn churches earned him another arrest and trial, followed by imprisonment in The Hague and the castle at Medemblik. When called back to The Hague, Willem recanted his errors, although he made difficulties because he said that God had forbidden the swearing of oaths. Once again released, he surfaced in Monnickendam, where with the sheriff's cooperation he "took a young maiden as his wedded wife." When even Monnickendam became too hot to hold him, after the Court launched a new investigation, he and his young bride fled to Emden, where a ship was said to be waiting to carry him on to the "Eastland" (the Baltic). A year later he was reported in Delfshaven near Rotterdam, where he earned a living in the herring fishery ("sailing east and west for herring").

Jan Corneliszoon Winter, the vice-priest of the parish church of Hoorn, was less fortunate.[16] Winter proclaimed from the pulpit that the institutions of the Church were of no value, being merely human opinions, and that the legends of the saints were lies; he also taught unorthodox views of penance, satisfaction, and purgatory, and distributed among the children in the parish school tracts in the vernacular containing biblical sayings, the Lord's Prayer, and the Apostolic Confession of Faith. The Court of Holland ordered him to recant his errors, but when this failed he was

---

[12] *CD*, V, 156–58, 160–61.
[13] *CD*, IV, 394–95.
[14] *CD*, IV, 311–12; De Hoop Scheffer, *Geschiedenis*, 571; Voets, "Hervorming," II, 2.
[15] *CD*, IV, 337–38; V, 10, 21, 73, 74, 77, 89, 109–16, 170, 270–71; De Hoop Scheffer, *Geschiedenis*, 572–78; Voets, "Hervorming," II, 3–5.
[16] Velius, 137; De Hoop Scheffer, *Geschiedenis*, 75–76; Voets, "Hervorming," II, 11–12.

arrested and tried before the episcopal court in Utrecht, which unfrocked him, declared that he had forfeited all his clerical privileges, and handed him over to the secular arm. After eleven months in jail, Winter was executed as a heretic at Utrecht in July 1533. According to the Hoorn chronicler Dirck Velius, on the scaffold he sang the "wonderful song of Augustine and Ambrose, *Te Deum Laudamus,* and when he reached the verse *Laudant te omnes martyres* (all martyrs praise thee) the sword cut through his neck."

Where clergy led the way in adopting new opinions, laymen would follow. Criticism voiced by dissident clerics merged seamlessly into a widespread anticlericalism, expressions of which can be found in North Holland as elsewhere. In 1526 three men from Monnickendam were arrested for committing acts of vandalism in the Cistercian monastery of Galilee outside Monnickendam. In 1529 three religious houses outside Hoorn were attacked. In Hoorn one Simon Gerbrantszoon de Glaesmaker accused the Dean of West Friesland of "selling God for a farthing."[17] The dean can hardly have been surprised by this charge, for he himself had written that the peasants of West Friesland said "the people favor Luther because the priests sell one another churches and ecclesiastical property."[18] In any case he hardly dared to show his face on the street, and in December 1524 he handed in his resignation.[19] This may have been a sensible move, for in 1530 in Monnickendam a parish priest died of his wounds after being attacked by a "Lutheran cut-throat."[20]

Some of those who welcomed Reformation ideas gathered in conventicles, at first probably as well as attending mass, later instead of it. In 1526 the sheriff of Hoorn broke up one such heretical network.[21] Reylof Jacobszoon, Claes van Midwoud, Jannytge Schoenmackers and her son Neel Jan van Melles, and Cornelis Allert "with the crippled hand" from Zwaag had met at Reylof's house and violated the edicts by "holding secret meetings . . . to preach and do other things." They were sentenced to do public penance by walking bareheaded and barefoot in procession before the holy sacrament, each holding a burning half-pound candle in the hand. In the same year another group in Hoorn was given the same sentence (but this time they were to wear a "figure of the chalice and host" on the front and back of their clothing) for blasphemy and

[17] *CD,* IV, 172; Duke, *Reformation,* 35.

[18] *Bronnen voor de geschiedenis van de kerkelijke rechtspraak,* VII, 386; see also Post, 518.

[19] Duke, *Reformation,* 61, 77; *Bronnen voor de geschiedenis van de kerkelijke rechtspraak,* VII, 385–87.

[20] Duke, *Reformation,* 61.

[21] *CD,* V, 126; De Hoop Scheffer, *Geschiedenis,* 573; Voets, "Hervorming," II, 6.

"speaking ill of almighty God and the Holy Sacrament of the altar."[22] One Claes Henricxzoon of Hoorn was fined and banished for six years because he had spoken publicly about the Gospels and the Epistles of Paul, and—worse—had sung in public and in his own home from a "scandalous" booklet.[23]

Not everyone was happy about all the new ideas that were circulating, both from the pulpit and in taverns, on ferries, and in the markets and streets. They threatened to split the civic community. In 1527, following the arrest of a woman in Hoorn for uttering bad sentiments about confession and the sacrament of the altar, her husband and son assaulted the sheriff.[24] In September 1527 the magistrates of Hoorn complained that great disunity had been caused among the common people, and that the townsfolk were insulting one another in taverns and on the street, saying: "You are a Lutheran of the new light," or: "You are of the old light and the Devil."[25] It is doubtful that the by-law they issued to suppress this controversy brought any improvement.

Although the authorities always spoke of "Luther" and "Lutheranizing," the Wittenberg reformer really had little influence on the evangelical movement in the Northern Quarter. At first sight those who followed the new ideas appear to have held mainly negative opinions.[26] They were against the cult of Mary and the saints, against the burning of candles in church, against pilgrimages, the veneration of relics, processions, and confession. They denied the existence of purgatory, the sense of monastic life and the value of celibacy, and they objected to the administration of the sacraments. Their fiercest condemnation was reserved for the sacrament of the altar; they scorned the consecrated host as "Bread God" and "Jan Flour." The dissidents thus denied the central Roman Catholic dogma of the real presence, the doctrine that Christ is really present in the bread and wine that the priest consecrates on the altar. The name of *Sacramentarians* given to these early evangelicals does not, however, imply that they already formed an organized sect or movement, still less an alternative church.[27] They wanted to remain inside the existing Church and reform it from within.

What then did these critical Catholics believe in? Although it is difficult to generalize about the ideas of the Sacramentarians, who remained wholly unconfessional, their criticisms of existing institutions and cus-

---

[22] *CD*, V, 176.
[23] *CD*, V, 148; Voets, "Hervorming," II, 6–7.
[24] *CD*, V, 196, 204, 231, 247–48.
[25] Duke, *Reformation*, 36.
[26] For the early Reformation movement see Duke, *Reformation*, 29–70.
[27] E.g., Knappert, *Ontstaan*, 111–61.

toms can also be interpreted in a more positive sense.[28] For all their disagreements, they had one thing in common: they rejected everything material in the life of the Church and its liturgy. For how could material things form a bridge between the believer, who is by definition a creature of matter, and God, who is pure spirit? The only positive element in which the evangelicals placed their trust was the Bible, in which God had revealed His intentions to everyone who wished to read it, and which therefore ought to be available in the vernacular. Stripped of all externals, the core of their belief remained the sacrifice of Christ, by which He had redeemed the sins of mankind. Those who put their trust in Him could count on sharing in eternal grace.

The crass materialism of the Sacramentarians—bread is bread and God is God—is clear from the recorded opinions of one Master Jelys Vrientszoon, or Vincentszoon, who was arrested at an inn at Hoorn in 1528.[29] He scandalized his judges by declaring that he had no more reverence for the Mother of God than for "a piss-pot or a chimney." At first sight the comparison appears purely blasphemous (and it is certainly not Lutheran), but on closer analysis it relates to the views of other early Dutch dissenters, who compared the Virgin Mary to a sack of cinnamon, "of which only the sweet smell lingered," an empty bag of flour, or a lantern without a candle.[30] It was the content that mattered and not the container. Master Jelys also believed that the Devil had written the Apostolic Confession of Faith, and that St. Laurence, the third-century martyr, had rightly been roasted on a slow fire, because he had absconded with the money of the local poor fund. Perhaps because Jelys had obviously been drunk when he made these remarks, the judges treated him leniently, letting him off with a public penance and a fine of twenty-five guilders.

Much more consistent in her opinions and certainly not drunk was Wendelmoet Claesdochter of Monnickendam, the first female Protestant martyr.[31] She was arrested in May 1527 and tried before the Court of Holland in The Hague, where she was

> found to hold evil opinions of the worthy Holy Sacrament, of all human institutions and generally of all that is done and performed outwardly in the Holy Church, the which she despises, alleging many authorities from the Holy Scriptures, and she claims that she is willing to die for

---

[28] Augustijn, "Anabaptisme," 23–25.

[29] Duke, *Reformation*, 26, 70; Voets, "Hervorming," II, 8–10; Conclusie genomen tegen mr. Jelis Vincentsz [deposition taken against Master Jelis Vincentszoon], 1528, WFA, OA Hoorn, inv. no. 81.

[30] Duke, *Reformation*, 25, 42.

[31] De Hoop Scheffer, *Geschiedenis*, 81–87; all the documents in *CD*, V, 225, 229–30, 232, 236–37, 272–85, 312, 315, 370–71, 381, 385–86, 388.

her errors, so that we [the Court] have very little hope of being able to bring the said woman back [to the true faith]."[32]

The core of the charges against Wendelmoet was that she despised all the outward forms of the Holy Church. Asked her opinion of the Eucharist she declared: "I regard your sacrament as bread and flour, and where you believe it to be a God, I say that it is your Devil." She refused a confessor, for "I have Christ, and to him I confess." Questioned on her view of holy unction, she replied: "Oil is good on a salad, or to clean your shoes with."[33] Her fate was inevitable. On 20 November 1527, steadfast to the last, she was burned at the stake.

The religious situation in the Northern Quarter began to change with the rise of the Anabaptist movement around 1530.[34] While the early evangelicals had hoped to reform the Church from within, the Anabaptists were the first to break openly with the existing Church. Adult baptism was the outward sign that they had left behind the old Adam and entered on a new spiritual life. Most Anabaptists were simple folk, craftsmen, day laborers, fishermen, and seamen. They believed that the end of the world was at hand, and they were preparing for the imminent second coming of Christ. Whereas the evangelical movement of the 1520s had had its centers in Hoorn and Monnickendam, the Anabaptists recruited chiefly in the countryside of Waterland, the Zaan, and West Friesland.

The local magistrates had very little sympathy for the exalted chiliasm of the Anabaptists, but they judged that these simple souls did little harm. The Anabaptists were certainly misled, but they did not deserve to be put to death. Moreover, the magistrates realized that the very size of the movement would pose great problems for them. To hunt down so many people and bring them to trial, as the edicts required, would be impossible. In April 1534 the Court wrote to the Regent Mary of Hungary that two out of three inhabitants of Monnickendam were infected by Anabaptism, certainly an exaggeration. "We find the matter very perplexing," the counselors wrote, "for if we proceed as the law prescribes, then all these persons have forfeited their lives, but the multitude is so great and so many."[35] The Court tried to escape from this dilemma by persecuting the leaders of the movement, even offering a reward of twelve guilders per head, while treating their followers with leniency. Two counselors wrote to the Stadholder and the regent that many of the Anabaptists were remorseful and felt deceived:

[32] CD, V, 225.
[33] Ibid., V, 281.
[34] Krahn, *Dutch Anabaptism*.
[35] De Hoop Scheffer, *Geschiedenis*, 587.

so that they shriek and howl, some of them roaming about the country like raving madmen, abandoning their wives and children, and to execute all of them by the sword seems to be hard, and would cause great unrest in the country, since they have many friends and relatives, of simple estate and married to one another.³⁶

The situation became even more explosive after the Anabaptists occupied the episcopal city of Münster in Westphalia to wait for the end of the world there, while practicing polygamy and communism of property. On the one hand the religious revolutionaries ruthlessly banished from the city everyone who refused to be baptized again. On the other hand they invited everyone who wished to escape God's imminent judgment of the world to make haste for the city where the saints would be preserved.³⁷ Thousands of Hollanders heeded this call in March 1534, sold their scanty possessions, and set off for the Westphalian Jerusalem. The great majority of this Anabaptist migration came from or through North Holland. More than thirty ships of Anabaptists sailed from Monnickendam, but there were only six from Amsterdam and five from Haarlem.³⁸ They got no farther than Hasselt in Overijssel, where the authorities arrested the leaders and sent back the rest, about three thousand men, women, and children. That was not the end of the danger, for there was still a strong chance the Anabaptists would seize a town and repeat the Münster experiment. The prosecutor-general of the Court of Holland feared that they would occupy Monnickendam or Edam, "where they are in great favor"; and Anabaptists from Waterland and Kennemerland were supposed to have played a large part in a foiled attack on Amsterdam on 18 March 1534.³⁹

That was reason enough for the Court to intervene decisively, all the more so since the local authorities were still reluctant to take action against the Anabaptists. With a force of a few hundred soldiers, Prosecutor-General Reijnier Brunt set out on a hunt for Anabaptists in Purmerend, Wormer, Jisp, Knollendam, and the surrounding hamlets in March 1535. The terrain worked in favor of the Anabaptists, allowing fifty of the eighty who were being hunted to escape in boats.

> They mostly fled in their boats through the waterways, a great many of which they have behind their houses. We could not occupy these

---

³⁶ Mellink, *Wederdopers*, 157; *Documenta Anabaptistica*, V, 21 (17 February 1534).
³⁷ Mellink, *Wederdopers*, 31.
³⁸ Ibid., 158. On the migration to Münster, ibid., 30–39.
³⁹ Ibid., 158. In reality the share of the Waterland Anabaptists in the assault on Amsterdam on 10 May 1535 was a small one. Ibid., 163.

waterways because the villages are a mile long and the channels debouch into the meres, where we lay in wait for them.[40]

Those Anabaptists who did not escape recanted. The houses where baptism had been given were burned down or demolished. From Waterland, Brunt and his band of soldiers moved on to West Friesland, "where we spent three or four days with a troop of men seeking out and pursuing the Anabaptists from one village to another, who all ran away and fled before we came."[41] Only three Anabaptists, who had been injured while offering resistance, fell into the hands of the law and were put to death without any form of trial in Nieuwe Niedorp. In Kolhorn and Barsingerhorn the Anabaptists turned on the soldiers and attacked them, forcing Brunt to take refuge in a church.

The debacle in Münster, where the city was recaptured by the bishop's soldiers and the population put to the sword, had a sobering effect on the Anabaptists. A period of harsh reprisals began in the Netherlands as well, which compelled many Anabaptists to reconsider their position. Under the leadership of the Friesian ex-pastor Menno Simonszoon (or Menno Simons) the Anabaptists shed their radicalism and transformed themselves into a sect that was pacifist on principle. Nevertheless they continued to face severe persecution. Indeed, the great majority of all the victims of persecution before 1566 were adherents of the Mennonite movement, yet even in this repressive period they managed to win many new members, and once again the sect flourished above all in North Holland.

In 1543 Menno was traveling through West Friesland, where he is reported to have converted a priest in Eenigenburg to his views during a debate in Latin.[42] The great champion of Mennonism in the region, however, was not Menno himself but the Zeelander Lenaert Bouwenszoon. He spent much of his time in East Friesland, from where he paid numerous visits to the Netherlands.[43] Lenaert was active between 1551 and 1582, and in those years he is said to have baptized at least 10,252 persons in the Netherlands and East Friesland, most of his successes being in Friesland. He performed the greatest number of baptisms (4,499) in the years 1563–65, on the eve of the troubles of the Wonder Year 1566. The same period also accounted for the lion's share of baptisms in the Northern Quarter, namely 801, to which we can add 91 baptisms on the northern Wadden Islands, which belonged to Holland. In Holland south of the River IJ, Lenaert only baptized 549 converts in the same period, of whom 168 were in Amsterdam and 79 in Haarlem. His list of baptisms has sur-

[40] Ibid., 161.
[41] Ibid., 167.
[42] Voets, "Hervorming," II, 20.
[43] Vos, "Dooplijst"; cf. the less reliable version in Blaupot ten Cate, *Geschiedenis*, I, 24.

vived and gives a remarkable picture of the attraction exerted by the Mennonite movement in the Northern Quarter.

The Anabaptist congregations in Hoorn and Alkmaar were notably large. In Hoorn, Lenaert Bouwenszoon baptized 186 persons between 1563 and 1565, more than in Amsterdam, the capital of Dutch Anabaptism. The size of the Mennonite congregation in Hoorn is put in perspective when one recalls that Hoorn had no more than eight thousand inhabitants in 1560, against nearly thirty thousand in Amsterdam. Alkmaar was in third place with 120 baptisms. Even more spectacular were the large numbers of converts in some of the villages of North Holland, most of which numbered no more than one hundred households. One person in every four households in such Waterland villages as Ransdorp and Landsmeer had himself baptized.[44] In Kennemerland, on the contrary, the Anabaptists gained hardly any converts, perhaps because the higher and dryer land was more accessible to the forces of order in The Hague.

| | |
|---|---|
| Hoorn | 186 |
| Alkmaar | 120 |
| Ransdorp | 82 |
| Medemblik | 63 |
| Monnickendam | 62 |
| Zaandam | 40 |
| Hoogkarspel | 35 |
| Kolhorn | 32 |
| Barsingerhorn | 32 |
| Landsmeer | 27 |
| Middelie | 25 |
| Grootebroek | 24 |
| Beets | 19 |
| Edam | 15 |
| Enkhuizen | 14 |
| Watergang | 14 |
| Durgerdam | 11 |
| Northern Quarter | 801 |
| Vlieland | 45 |
| Wieringen | 25 |
| Terschelling | 12 |
| Texel | 9 |
| Wadden Islands | 91 |

[44] In 1561 there were 332 houses in Ransdorp, 109 in Landsmeer; Van der Woude, *Noorderkwartier*, 622–23.

The growth of the congregation in Hoorn was stimulated by the extraordinary leniency of the town's magistrates. In the Anabaptist year of disaster, 1535, the Court of Holland had urged the magistrates to take tough action against the Anabaptists. The result was the public execution of three men and two women, but the harsh sentences only aroused revulsion among the population and the regents.[45] Since then the magistrates had practically ignored the religious edicts, which prescribed death at the stake for stubborn heretics and death by the sword for those who recanted. It is true that Charles V's antiheresy laws were widely sabotaged all over the Netherlands in these years, but one has the impression that the magistrates of Hoorn carried religious tolerance much further than most.[46] Indeed, the Anabaptist congregation in Hoorn had been led since 1550 by the son of a burgomaster, Joost Ewoutszoon.[47] The magistrates were believed to turn a blind eye to "public hostels," a sort of Anabaptist maternity home, where women could give birth without the midwife reporting their children to the parish church for baptism, as the law required.[48]

The moderate religious and political climate in the town was very attractive to co-religionists who were being hunted down in Amsterdam, South Holland, Zeeland, and Utrecht. The result was that Hoorn's commerce and industry prospered as never before.[49] The Anabaptists could profess their faith in peace, as long as they did not do so too openly. When the city was in a state of alarm in May 1567, after some of Brederode's Beggar troops appeared before its gates, the citizens took to arms, but the pacifist Mennonites were officially allowed to equip themselves with baskets and shovels and report for trench-digging duties.[50] The incident reveals the semilegal status that the Anabaptists had managed to win in the civic community of Hoorn.

The situation in Medemblik was much the same. There, too, women from Texel and elsewhere were said to flock to the town to give birth in secret.[51] At the end of December 1564, Regent Margaret of Parma wrote to the Court of Holland that she was alarmed by the spread of Anabaptism in the town.[52] The counselors warned the magistrates, who replied that there was no reason whatever for concern. The Court passed on this reassurance to the regent, but acknowledged that it had nevertheless or-

---

[45] Velius, 136–37; Mellink, *Wederdopers*, 168–69.
[46] Woltjer, *Friesland*, 123–43; Duke, *Reformation*, 152–74; Tracy, *Holland*, 147–75.
[47] Voets, "Hervorming," II, 21.
[48] "Verslag," 75.
[49] Velius, 158.
[50] Sol, "Reformatie," 139.
[51] "Verslag," 79.
[52] Van Beuningen, *Lindanus*, 152–53; "Verslag," 76–79.

dered the sheriff of Medemblik to keep a close eye on things, "so that the aforesaid damned sect should be put down and rooted out." Margaret remained mistrustful and pressed the Court to make a new investigation. In 1565 it appeared that the bench of justices in Medemblik had acquitted parents who could not prove that they had had their children baptized. The justices had inverted the burden of proof by demanding that the sheriff should prove that the children were not baptized.[53]

Disturbing rumors also came from Alkmaar, Edam, and Hoorn.[54] Parents were said to have forcibly prevented the baptism of their children, sometimes seizing them from the arms of the midwife in the church. The father of newborn twins from Egmond had already hidden one child in the dunes and came home to fetch the other, but found it had already been taken to church. In all these cases the magistrates had "proceeded very laxly and badly."

There is no doubt that the Anabaptists were the largest group among dissenters in the Northern Quarter. They had visibly removed themselves from the Church on principle. But there were still priests and others with highly objectionable opinions, who nevertheless wanted to remain within the Catholic Church. Leonardus, the parish priest of Sijbekarspel, owned works by the German reformer Antonius Corvinus, on which he drew for his sermons.[55] The vice-pastor of Oosterland on Wieringen Island, Nicolaes Hendrickszoon, became parish priest of Twisk in 1540. He preached against the veneration of saints ("They have no power. God is alone"), denied the doctrine of transubstantiation ("That the sacrament of the altar is no more than a figure"), and rejected celibacy ("That priests ought to take wives"), setting an example of the last himself. Yet he did not find this a reason to break with the Church, nor did his parishioners see anything unusual in their pastor's views. The orthodox priest in neighboring Opperdoes, meanwhile, had said that one who was unwilling to believe in the real presence of Christ in the sacrament must be condemned. The result was that two brothers, Jan and Laurens Pieterszoon, complained to him that his preaching disagreed with that of his colleague in Twisk; in future they would prefer to go to church there.

There must have been several more such "Protestantizing priests,"[56] but it is difficult to identify them or say how many there were, for we only hear of those who came into conflict with the ecclesiastical authorities. If their parishioners were satisfied with them, and no one denounced them,

---

[53] "Verslag," 79.

[54] Van Beuningen, *Lindanus*, 154–55; "Verslag," 71–72.

[55] Voets, "Hervorming," II, 222–23, wrongly calls him Andreas Corvinus. *Bronnen voor de geschiedenis van de kerkelijke rechtspraak*, 406, 422, 424, 428.

[56] Woltjer, *Friesland*, 90–104.

such clergymen could go on spreading their unorthodox ideas for years without leaving a trace in the archives. The alacrity with which many parish priests in North Holland hung up their vestments, married their mistresses, and proclaimed the new doctrine from their pulpits when Protestant preaching was briefly allowed in the summer of 1566, suggests that orthodoxy was not too firmly rooted before that year.[57]

The vicar of the Great Church in Hoorn, Maerten Pieterszoon, had died in 1564.[58] The burgomasters were happy with the nomination of an equally peaceable and tolerant man as his successor, and they and their candidate, Clement Maertenszoon, traveled to Brussels and Leuven to have his appointment confirmed by the secular and ecclesiastical authorities. A few years previously this Clement Maertenszoon had not objected to conducting the secret burial at night of a man who had refused the sacrament for the dying and therefore could not be buried in the parish church. The authorities apparently found him too unreliable, for they passed him over in favor of the more orthodox Dirck Corneliszoon. Their suspicions would later prove justified, for Clement was to break with Rome in the summer of 1566, marry, and lead the field preaching outside the walls of Hoorn.[59]

The most important figure in the development of Protestantism in North Holland was Cornelis Cooltuyn.[60] He began his career as a priest in Alkmaar, where he combined the performance of Catholic ritual with the preaching of evangelically inspired sermons. In the middle 1550s he became chaplain or pastor of the St. Pancras, or South, Church. His sermons earned him the love of his flock but brought him into bad odor with the Court of Holland in The Hague. Thanks to the protection of the inquisitor Ruard Tapper, himself a native of Enkhuizen, the matter was hushed up. On Tapper's advice Cooltuyn devoted himself in future to caring for the poor and the sick, and refrained from saying mass. Cooltuyn was so popular among his flock that some civic militiamen forcibly broke into the house of his orthodox colleague Balthazar Platander, the pastor of the church of St. Gommarus, because they suspected him of denouncing Cooltuyn to the Inquisition.[61] When Cooltuyn was summoned to The Hague for the second time in 1557, he left Enkhuizen and settled in his birthplace Alkmaar, where he succeeded Laurens Jacobszoon as rector of the Latin School. His duties in that capacity included preaching, but after two weeks and two sermons he was no longer willing to

---

[57] Voets, "Hervorming," II, 42–43; Van Vloten, "Noordholland," 147.
[58] Velius, 159; Voets, "Hervorming," II, 31; Sol, "Reformatie," 130.
[59] Velius, 162; Voets, "Hervorming," II, 41; Sol, "Reformatie," 134.
[60] Vis, *Cooltuyn*; Kaplan, "Cooltuyn."
[61] Duke, "Onbekende en mislukte aanslag"; Vis, *Cooltuyn*, 24; "Verslag," 72.

have anything to do with "the gruesome idolatrous services." He left for Emden, where in 1559 he was called to become minister of the Reformed city church.[62] Cooltuyn was the author of the influential tract *Dat Evangeli der armen* ("The Poor Folk's Gospel"), a dialog between a reformer and a sick Catholic woman, which was intended to console and instruct Protestants living under persecution.

The sermons of Cooltuyn's successor in Enkhuizen, Andries Dirckszoon of Castricum (Andreas Castricomius), were also evangelical in tone.[63] In July 1561 the dean of West Friesland summoned him to Hoorn and imprisoned him. Some of his Enkhuizen parishioners broke into the prison in secret at night to free their pastor, who then found it advisable to move to Friesland. In 1566 the infant Reformed congregation of Enkhuizen recalled him to become their leader. Heer Lieuwe, who had been chaplain of the West Church until 1566, also preached to the Enkhuizen congregation in the Beggar times.

Before the long, hot summer of 1566 there was no trace in the Northern Quarter of a strictly organized Calvinist communal life, or "churches under the cross," like those that came into existence at this time in Antwerp and other southern cities.[64] There were some rather informal Protestant congregations of a more flexible sort, which made do for the time being without a consistory or regular administration of the sacraments.[65]

Many critical Catholics felt less and less at ease in the existing Church, which since the introduction of the plan to create new dioceses (1559) and the close of the Council of Trent (1563) had been defining the frontiers between orthodoxy and heresy ever more strictly. They felt alienated from the existing Church, but for the moment they had nowhere else to turn. In two letters dated from Amsterdam on 20 March and 1 September 1565, a pair of anonymous writers complained to Théodore de Bèze (Beza), Calvin's successor in Geneva, of the freethinking doctrines that were being proclaimed by the spiritualist Dirck Volkertszoon Coornhert, and urged him to take up his pen against them. The authors of the letters refer to themselves as *fideles* or *fratres per Hollandiam sparsi* ("believers or brothers scattered through Holland").[66] Presumably these *fideles* were already so far outside the Church that they could no longer reconcile it with their consciences to receive the sacraments.

But even if they did not set up alternative church congregations, these stray Christians were in need of instruction, admonition, and consolation.

---

[62] Vis, *Cooltuyn*, 27.
[63] Voets, "Hervorming," II, 30, 41.
[64] Marnef, *Antwerpen*, 95–107.
[65] Vis and Woltjer, "Predikanten."
[66] Vis, *Cooltuyn*, 54; Pettegree, *Emden*, 125.

In 1558 some anonymous "brothers of Amsterdam" wrote to Emden asking to be sent a preacher. The consistory in Emden sent them Nicolaes Carinaeus, a native of Edam; but he was so ineffective against the Anabaptists that there were soon calls for his replacement. Cooltuyn, by now preacher of the congregation in Emden, wrote to the Alkmaar basket maker Jan Arentszoon, asking him to come and serve the congregations in Holland.[67] Jan Arentszoon accepted, and Cooltuyn himself may also have made a few journeys to Holland, where he is said to have preached God's word to groups in Edam, Monnickendam, Purmerend, Medemblik, and Schagen.

We know little detail of Jan Arentszoon's activities, but he must have preached in secret to small, informal groups of evangelically minded people, conventicles rather than congregations. He probably also administered baptism, for in their inquiry into the state of religion in Holland in 1565 the Brussels authorities asked if any children in Alkmaar had been baptized "in the manner of Calvin."[68] The same inquiry investigated a conventicle held in Medemblik, where two to three hundred people were said to have been present, and a Calvinist doctor had disputed on the sacrament of the altar with the pastor for three or four hours. The Court claimed to know nothing about it, but admitted that in 1563 a foreigner (Jan Arentszoon or Cooltuyn?) had spoken on the Gospel in a private house in nearby Wervershoof. The parish priest had been invited and had held a long debate with him, though according to the Court they had not gathered "conventicle-wise," but in order to bring the heretical teacher to better opinions. The doors had remained open, "so that many people went in and out, some drunk and others sober."[69]

The turbulent events of the Wonder Year 1566 shook the Church to its foundations north of the River IJ as they did to the south. In April 1566 a few hundred nobles, who had banded together in a sworn association, or Compromise, submitted a petition to Margaret of Parma, in which they pleaded with her to put an end to the persecution of heretics. Fearing violence, the regent suspended the existing antiheretical laws. The clandestine Calvinist congregations, at first in Flanders and Brabant but later also elsewhere, exploited this de facto religious freedom to organize public preaching in the open air.

The first "hedge preaching" in Holland took place north of the IJ. Once again the remoteness of the Quarter allowed the Reformers to experiment more or less undisturbed. The initiative came from Amsterdam, where some adherents of the new doctrines decided that the time was now ripe

---

[67] Pettegree, *Emden*, 78–80; Vis, *Cooltuyn*, 35, 52–53, 63; Vis, *Jan Arentsz*, 42–43.
[68] "Verslag," 61.
[69] Ibid., 79.

to organize open-air sermons in Holland too. Because these were banned, and the organizers expected the city magistrates to enforce the ban, the first sermons would be preached near Hoorn, on Sunday 14 July in a meadow next to the monastery of Westerblokker, just to the north and outside the jurisdiction of Hoorn. The ex–basket maker Jan Arentszoon preached before a crowd of more than a thousand from Hoorn, Berkhout, and the villages of the district.[70] The following Sunday he preached again in a cornfield owned by Brederode. A week later he led a meeting at Den Ilp in Waterland. Jan Arentszoon was in hiding in Waterland through late July and early August, being picked up in a boat to preach in the neighborhood of Monnickendam and Edam. Only on 31 July did the Calvinists venture to hold an open-air sermon before the gates of Amsterdam itself. It was 18 August, five weeks after the first sermon near Hoorn, before they dared to risk preaching farther south.

On 10 August groups of itinerant Calvinists in West Flanders began to destroy images and altars in their parish churches and monasteries. On 20 August the iconoclastic fury reached Antwerp; on 23 August it spread to Amsterdam, and then it was the turn of the other towns of Holland: Delft, Leiden, The Hague, Brill, Asperen, and Vianen. In the towns of the Northern Quarter the damage was confined to the Franciscan church in Alkmaar. In some villages owned by Hendrik van Brederode the churches were purged by the local authorities.[71]

While traveling around Holland in July to drum up support for the Compromise of the Nobility, Brederode visited his lordship of Bergen, where he inspected new polder works. Inspired by the landscape of dunes and beaches he wrote enthusiastically to Orange's brother Louis of Nassau that "the Beggars are sown as thickly here as the sands of the sea."[72] Soon after the iconoclastic riots in Amsterdam, Brederode was back in the Northern Quarter. He sent his steward Willem van Sonnenberg, who will play an important part later in this book, to his North Holland estates to remove the church ornaments in an orderly manner.[73] Brederode claimed that his main concern was to place the valuables in safekeeping for the moment, and not to equip the churches for the benefit of Reformed worship. But for the time being mass was no longer said here.

Brederode and his lengthy retinue moved on from his lordship of Callantsoog to Medemblik, Hoorn, and Alkmaar, where on 2 September he visited the Franciscan church. The Reformed leaders in Alkmaar had previously tried in vain to persuade the town authorities to let them use the

---

[70] *Correspondance française*, II, 307–8; Vis, *Jan Arentsz*, 49.
[71] Scheerder, *Beeldenstorm*.
[72] *Archives*, II, 130.
[73] Brederode's commission to Sonnenberg in Van Vloten, "Noordholland," 333, n. 1.

church for their worship. Half an hour after Brederode left the town, the images were smashed, not without his knowledge and probably on his authority.[74] On 24 August, the day after the images had been destroyed in Amsterdam, there had already been an attempt to destroy the images in the church of St. Laurence in Alkmaar, but the magistrates had managed to restore calm, ordered the guilds to remove their altars, and closed the church to prevent further trouble.

Hoorn escaped an iconoclastic fury, perhaps because of the moderate attitude of both the local magistrates and the ex-pastor Clement Maertenszoon.[75] But as winter approached the Reformed in Hoorn felt the need of a roof over their heads, "since they, the Beggars, had preached long enough in the rain and the wind, and wanted to have a church."[76] On 23 November some of their followers tried to break open the doors of the Great Church, which had been locked for safety since the summer. The attempt failed, and the Hoorn Calvinists continued to hold their services in the open air. The Reformed worshipers in Enkhuizen, led by the ex-pastor Andries van Castricum, a former exile, used a salt works outside the walls.[77]

Thus, pro-reform groups had been active in North Holland since July 1566, organizing Reformed gatherings at first outdoors, later in barns, sheds, and private houses. The adherents of the new doctrine had their children baptized in the Calvinist form, while some congregations even appointed elders and deacons, and celebrated communion by the Reformed rite for the first time around Christmas 1566. Besides the old Church and the Anabaptists, there were now clearly identifiable more or less Calvinist congregations present in the towns. It is impossible to say how large they were; the hedge sermons had drawn mass audiences, but many who came must have been led by curiosity rather than a thirst for the true word of God. The townsfolk had a choice: they could join the new faith or stay with the old Church. Although the parish churches in the towns remained closed between the end of August and Christmas 1566, the faithful were allowed to attend mass in one of the monastic houses, where "God's service was continued with open doors, in the old manner."[78]

The options were less straightforward in the countryside, where the attitude of the local parish priest chiefly determined how far the villagers were exposed to the Reformation movement. Three possibilities presented

---

[74] Vis, *Jan Arentsz*, 71.
[75] Velius, 163; Sol, "Reformatie," 135.
[76] Sol, "Reformatie," 137; Velius, 163.
[77] Voets, "Hervorming," II, 42.
[78] Van Vloten, "Noordholland," 149.

themselves: the parish priest might remain loyal to the old Church, he might become a Protestant, or an evangelically minded preacher might be sent to the villagers from outside.

In the villages of Kennemerland, south of Alkmaar, in Waterland, the Zeevang and the Streek district between Hoorn and Enkhuizen, there is little evidence of any difficulties. The parish priests were good Catholics, and the congregation attended mass apparently without grumbling. During the inquiries into the events of the Wonder Year held by the commissioners of the Council of Troubles, the special court set up by Alba to punish the ringleaders of the iconoclastic riots of 1566 and 1567, the parish priest of Assendelft could truly declare that "there were no especially bad humors";[79] but sometimes the authorities painted a flattering picture of the reality. The priest of Castricum, who had only held his living for six months, undoubtedly claimed in good faith that his flock had behaved honorably, yet his colleague in neighboring Heemskerk told the commissioners that during the troubles Castricum had been served by one Jan Petri (Pieterszoon), "being a sectary and apostate."[80]

There were more such clergy who had gone over to Protestantism. The Dean of West Friesland, Jan Gruwel, told the commissioners that in his deanery (except for Clement Maertenszoon and Jan Clein of Hoorn), the parish priest and the sexton of Eenigenburg, the priest of Sint Maarten, both parish priests of Schagen, those of Barsingerhorn, Sint Pancras, Nieuwe Niedorp (with the sexton and the curate), Twisk, and Sijbekarspel had "repudiated their priesthood and betaken themselves to the married state, and continued the preaching of Calvinus' and other reprobated doctrine."[81] Other witnesses named the two pastors of Castricum, and those of Oostzaan, Petten, Warmenhuizen, Schoorl, and Camp.

Jan Jordaenszoon of Schoorl, the pastor of Petten, was one such priest who turned Protestant. In November 1566 he announced to his flock that they must pay attention, because he was about to tell them something that concerned their salvation. To the consternation of his hearers he then began to denounce the mass and struck up a psalm. After the service he laid aside his vestments and left the priesthood for good.[82] The presence of some prominent Reformers from Alkmaar in the church at Bergen, among them Guillaume Mostaert and Guillaume van Triere, whom we shall encounter again, suggests that this gesture had been carefully prepared. Jan Jordaenszoon's functions were taken over by one Heer Wigger,

---

[79] Ibid., 323–28; passage cited on 325.

[80] Ibid., 326. Cf. *Sententiën*, 185, for the banishment of "Sire Jehan Pieters apostat jadiz pasteur de Castricom."

[81] Van Vloten, "Noordholland," 145.

[82] Ibid., 329–30.

a Friesian and a "good Catholic." But after he had said mass, he resigned his place to the ex-pastor, who used the same parish church to preach to his followers in the new style. Petten thus achieved toleration in practice. The inhabitants could choose whose flock they wished to join.

The local population was not always so charmed with their pastor's behavior. When the parish priest of Sint Maarten, Claes Scheeltkens of Warmenhuizen, who would later serve the Amsterdam congregation as Nicolaes Scheltius, ventured to preach without first donning his vestments in August 1566, the majority of his congregation ostentatiously walked out.[83] Once Scheeltkens had left the village things were quiet again.

There was less chance of calm when the local lord imposed a new preacher, commonly a former priest, on the villagers. Lancelot van Brederode, a bastard brother of the Beggar leader Hendrik van Brederode, caused the ex-pastor of Nieuwe Niedorp Pieter Dirckszoon, "being of the sect of Zwinglius," to take the pulpit of the parish church at Warmenhuizen. Laurens Claeszoon, the ex-pastor of Eenigenburg, and Jan Jordaenszoon of Petten also preached here, and their conduct evidently sowed discord among the villagers. At the end of September "certain wicked people" stormed the parish church and broke the images, but another witness declared that the 1,025 communicants of the parish were good Catholics.[84]

In Schoorl and Camp, where Hendrik van Brederode was lord, the community was "very altered" after the basket maker Jan Arentszoon preached four or five times "in the cattle-market" at the request of some of the villagers.[85] Brederode's steward Sonnenberg took the church plate into his custody, and the parish priest, one Heer Reyer, who had previously "wavered somewhat," now no longer said mass, but began to preach "in the Beggar fashion." Others who preached here included the Protestant pastors of Eenigenburg, Petten, and Nieuwe Niedorp, and one Pieter Corneliszoon, formerly a fish auctioneer in Alkmaar, "a thin and pale little person," who preached before an audience of about twenty or thirty. Once the church plate was returned about two or three months later, the chaplain resumed saying mass. The parish priest himself did not celebrate mass until Whitsun 1567, after the government had restored order. In Schoorl and Camp the Reformed obviously still had some followers; how many we do not know, nor can we tell if there was a genuine congregation with elders and deacons and a regular celebration of communion.

[83] Ibid., 331–32.
[84] Ibid., 332, 340.
[85] Ibid., 335–38.

48 • Chapter Three

In Oudkarspel, the villagers wanted nothing to do with religious innovations.[86] Here in January 1567 the sexton introduced Jan Jordaenszoon. He preached his "erroneous teaching" for a while, but was finally "chased out with stones, dung and other materials by the young folk of the village, who were drinking to celebrate the New Year as usual."

Most of the parishes where the parish priest went over to the new faith lay in the far north of the Quarter, with a striking concentration around the recently reclaimed Zijpe polder. This cannot have been mere chance. Once again the distance from the centers of power must have determined the possibilities open to them. When the Reformation was introduced into the countryside in 1566, the attitude of local nobles such as Brederode and Reformed townsmen in Alkmaar also played an important part, but without the collaboration of the local clergy they could have achieved little. The priests who became Protestants must have formed a network of dissidents within the Church even before 1566. Claes Scheeltkens, Jan Jordaenszoon, Pieter Dirckszoon, Laurens Claeszoon, and Heer Reyer knew one another from the school in Schoorl, an institution with a bad reputation. Pieter Dirckszoon, Jan Jordaenszoon, and the pastor and priest of Eenigenburg had also studied with Cornelis Cooltuyn in Leuven.[87] These educated clergy must have had objections to certain aspects of Catholic doctrine for some time. Their isolation in this bleak northern outpost left them free to experiment almost undisturbed with many of the new ideas. In the Wonder Year they believed the time was ripe for a definitive break with the old Church.

The freedom the Reformed had enjoyed in the Northern Quarter came to an end in the spring of 1567. Many who had compromised themselves in the eyes of the government went into exile, in many cases to relatively nearby East Friesland. The Council of Troubles pronounced sentence of banishment on forty-three persons from Enkhuizen, thirty-four from Alkmaar, fifteen from Hoorn, eleven from Medemblik, forty-two from Edam and Monnickendam, and one from Purmerend. It condemned sixteen others from various villages in North Holland for attempting to bring the Northern Quarter over to the cause of the Prince of Orange in 1568, but hardly anyone in the countryside was sentenced for his activities in 1566.[88] In total the Council of Troubles sentenced 162 persons in the Northern Quarter, but the number of fugitives must have been much greater; 350 inhabitants are said to have fled from Enkhuizen

---

[86] Ibid., 346.

[87] For the school in Schoorl see ibid., 335–36.

[88] *Sententiën*, 35, 38, 118, 142, 171, 185, 202. Some of those sentenced in Enkhuizen actually came from villages in the Streek.

alone.[89] At Emden in East Friesland and elsewhere they joined the local Reformed churches, and while in exile many of them moved toward a stricter and more dogmatic Calvinism than they had known in Holland in the Wonder Year.[90]

In spite of harsh repression, order was not completely restored in the Northern Quarter. Was it once again the isolation of the region that ruled out more effective measures? In any case, in November 1567 the bailiff of Kennemerland was foiled in his attempt to arrest some of the priests who had gone over to Protestantism and who were in hiding in Schoorl and Callantsoog. The priest of Ilpendam gave evidence before the commissioners of the Council of Troubles that his apostate predecessor was still continuing his clandestine Protestant activities. In Enkhuizen the place of the fugitive Andreas Castricomius was taken by a local lay preacher.[91]

The great absentee in this chapter is the majority of the population of the Northern Quarter. Outside the handful of Reformers who came to the fore in 1566, and the relatively extensive Anabaptist congregations, who stayed quiet, the majority of the population undoubtedly remained Catholic. But what are we to understand by this? The sources contain much information, some of it spectacular, on heretics and other unorthodox people of many hues and shades of opinion, some of them inside the Church, others outside it. But anyone who went to confession at least once a year, took communion, had his children baptized in the parish church, and for the rest refrained from expressing contentious views, never came under the notice of the judicial system. We know as good as nothing about the spirituality of the silent majority.[92]

The official government policy of implacable suppression of religious dissent probably had very few supporters in the Northern Quarter. Some Catholics were exposed for a longer or shorter time to a variety of heretical opinions, proclaimed from the pulpit by their own pastors. This exposure may have made some of them feel sufficiently at ease with evangelical doctrine to have little difficulty in accepting the new preacher in 1572. In some cases, after all, that new preacher was none other than their old priest.[93] But there were also Catholics for whom all these changes just went too far. They wanted to have their children baptized in the same way that they themselves, their parents, and grandparents had been

---

[89] Brandt, *Historie Enkhuisen*, 100.
[90] Woltjer, *Tussen vrijheidsstrijd*, 89–120.
[91] Duke, *Reformation*, 201–2.
[92] For the problem of the attitude of the Catholics to the Reformation movement see Woltjer, *Geweld*.
[93] *Acta*, I, 8, 240–45; Voets, "Hervorming," II, 65.

baptized. They felt it important to be present when mass was said, whatever their opinions about the precise significance of the Eucharist. After the Beggars seized power in 1572 these traditional Catholics were left in a vacuum.

The Catholics in 1572 elude the grasp of the historian; but in a sense they were beyond the grasp of the new men in power as well. They were in the majority, but they dropped out of sight when every organized form of Catholic worship and spiritual care was suppressed. It may be assumed that they had serious grievances against the new regime. Would none of them become potential traitors?

CHAPTER FOUR

# Revolt

THE WAR IN THE NORTHERN QUARTER began in the town of Enkhuizen, and it began as a revolt, a true revolution. In May 1572, after a few weeks of unrest, armed citizens deposed their town authorities, opened their gates to an occupation force of Sea Beggars and acknowledged the leader of the rebellion, the Prince of Orange, as Stadholder of Holland. From their base in Enkhuizen the rebels then brought the other towns and the countryside of the Northern Quarter over to the side of the Revolt. In Hoorn, too, it was the inhabitants, under pressure from Enkhuizen, who took their town into the rebel camp. The other towns of North Holland were conquered by the rebels, although they offered very little resistance, and in all of them there were supporters of the Revolt.

In all the towns the population was divided. Committed adherents of the Revolt were in a minority at first, but thanks to the dynamic of events they made the running and brought the moderate majority in some towns over to their side. Likewise, in all the towns there were opponents of the rebellion, who foresaw that it would be the beginning of a period of violence and privation with no end in sight. Many of them abandoned their homes, the first of a swelling stream of refugees. The Revolt became more than just a war, it became a civil war.

Not one of the North Holland towns that went over to the rebels in the summer of 1572 was ever to be brought back under the lawful rule of Philip II. The period of the Revolt merged seamlessly into the age of the Republic. Looking back, historians therefore assumed that the goal of the rebels must have been to free "the Netherlands" from "Spanish domination," in other words to depose Philip II and to establish a free and independent republic. In the nineteenth and early twentieth centuries above all the Revolt was seen as a national liberation struggle waged by the whole people. "The revolution effected here [in Enkhuizen] was purely the work of the people, of the mariners and burghers of the city," wrote the American historian John Lothrop Motley around the middle of the nineteenth century. Motley's greatest Dutch contemporary, Robert Fruin, also believed that William of Orange had "only protected and promoted what the people wanted and intended."[1]

---

[1] Motley, *Rise*, II, 395; Fruin, "Prins Willem I in 1570," 165.

This nationalist interpretation of the Revolt was hard to reconcile with the facts, and it did not escape criticism. Between the world wars Pieter Geyl and H. A. Enno van Gelder began to argue, firstly that the Revolt had been essentially a civil war comparable to the conflicts that raged in France at the same time; and secondly that most of the towns of Holland and Zeeland had not risen in revolt, but had simply been conquered by force of arms.[2] The Beggars, most of them exiles of 1567 led by noblemen, and convinced Calvinists or at least fiercely anti-Catholic, formed the active element in the Revolt, the rest of the population "merely the sounding board."[3]

Since then J. J. Woltjer has made clear the complexity of the relationships within urban society. Woltjer underlined the importance of the moderate middle groups, the political center. Only a minority of radicals wanted to join the Revolt, but Alba's regime had provoked revulsion even among the moderate parts of the population. The result was that, faced with the choice between a Spanish garrison or admitting the Beggars, they accepted the latter as the lesser of two evils. It was precisely where it had been relatively quiet in the Wonder Year 1566–67, for example in the towns of the Northern Quarter, that hatred of Alba's rule was most intense. The towns of Holland could have defended themselves against the Beggars if they had wanted to; but that will was lacking.[4]

The capture of Brill on 1 April 1572, which historians have identified as the beginning of the Revolt of 1572, can hardly be regarded as an example of a spontaneous revolutionary uprising.[5] The Beggar captains Lumey and Treslong seized the small town at the mouth of the Maas with the help of a fleet of twenty-six well-armed ships and about eleven hundred men, among them two hundred Walloon mercenaries. The crews used a ship's mast as a battering ram to break open the seaward gate and plundered ecclesiastical property, but they distributed among the poor the grain they found in the monastic houses. Most of the townsfolk had already fled the town in disorder through the gate on the landward side. They were the first refugees of the conflict.

A few days later a genuine insurrection broke out in Flushing.[6] Billeting officers who came to requisition quarters for a Spanish garrison were thrown out of the town by a crowd of angry citizens. The townspeople would accept a garrison of Netherlanders if they had to, but not Span-

---

[2] Van Gelder, "Nederlandse adel," 161; Van Gelder, "Historiese vergelijking," 36; Geyl, *Nederlandse stam*, I, 277.

[3] Boogman, "Overgang," 112.

[4] Woltjer, *Tussen vrijheidsstrijd*, 48–63 and 137.

[5] De Meij, *Watergeuzen*, 90–99; Bor, 365–66; CCG, IV, 173 (Morillon to Granvelle, 13 April 1572).

[6] Parker, *Dutch Revolt*, 133–34; Bor, 369; Van Gelder, "Nederlandse adel," 159.

iards. Two days later, when a Spanish architect arrived in Flushing with plans for the construction of a new citadel and the collection of the hated new tax, the Tenth Penny, he was attacked by a furious mob and lynched. A few days later still the people of Flushing expelled the Walloon garrison. On 22 April they let a fleet of fourteen Beggar ships into their harbor and declared for the Prince of Orange. From Flushing the rebels brought most of the other towns of Zeeland under their control. Only Middelburg remained stubbornly loyal to the lawful ruler until February 1573, when it had to surrender to the rebels after months of siege.

One month after Flushing welcomed the Beggars the Zeeland pattern was repeated in the Northern Quarter. On 21 May armed citizens of Enkhuizen took their town over to William of Orange's cause, against the will of the magistrates; a month later, on 18 June, the citizens of Hoorn voted more or less democratically to admit the Beggars. The rebels took the other towns by force: Medemblik (8 June), Alkmaar (20 June), Edam and Monnickendam (both 27 June). Toward the end of the month practically the whole of the Northern Quarter was in rebel hands. Alba's stadholder in Holland, Maximilien de Hennin, Count of Boussu, was in despair: "It seems as if the stones in Holland rise up against me," he wrote to his chief on 17 June.[7]

William of Orange had already made two attempts to ignite a revolt in the Northern Quarter in 1568 and 1570, but they were badly organized damp squibs.[8] Why did the population support a revolt in 1572, when it had shown no enthusiasm for one in earlier years?

The fundamental cause of the success of the Revolt of 1572 was in the first place the popular revulsion from Alba's tactless behavior. That revulsion was the other side of the popular attachment to urban autonomy, the right to be master in one's own house, and if necessary to defend that house against outsiders. To that was added a grave economic crisis, which had reduced many Hollanders to penury since 1570. The depredations of the Beggars exacerbated the results of the recession, but the population blamed the government and not the Beggars. In these circumstances unemployed seamen and fishermen were willing to gamble on the rebels. The third cause of the success of 1572 was the presence and organized intervention of returned exiles. They managed to win support among the discontented population for the rising that the Prince of Orange had unleashed. That rising could never have succeeded if the government had

---

[7] "Il semble que les pierres se levent contre moi (en ce pays de Hollande)." Van Vloten, *Nederlands opstand*, II, lxxiv.

[8] "Rooftocht"; Bor, 330; Fruin, "Prins Willem I in 1570," 149–54; De Meij, *Watergeuzen*, 48–53.

had troops at its disposal in Holland. The fourth cause of the success of the Revolt was therefore the absence of garrisons in the towns of Holland.

The immediate trigger of rebellion in Flushing, Enkhuizen, and Hoorn was the citizens' fear that the government would quarter soldiers in their towns after Brill fell to the rebels. Except for a handful of returned Calvinist fugitives, who were in the vanguard of the disturbances everywhere, the question of religion played no part in the revolution of 1572.

The choice for William of Orange, for the Beggars, and thus for the Revolt can only be explained if one realizes how deeply rooted hatred of Alba's rule had become.[9] Many considered his actions downright illegal, because they violated the treaties, special charters, and customs (the privileges) that Philip II had sworn to uphold when he became Count of Holland. Until 1567 the Habsburg rulers had always appointed members of the princely family to govern the Netherlands. Alba, in contrast, was a general, and what was more, a Spaniard who surrounded himself with Spanish advisers and did not listen to the native counselors and nobles. He and his army did not treat the Netherlands as the lawful hereditary lands of their common ruler, but as a conquered territory.

Moderate public opinion in the Netherlands had always been repelled by the fanatical persecution of religious dissidents,[10] in favor of tolerance and inclined to give the Protestants a chance in 1566. The iconoclastic fury and the maltreatment of priests, monks, and nuns, however, were repugnant to them, and held them back from supporting Brederode and the radical Calvinists, who had been eager to rise in armed revolt as early as the end of 1566. This attitude made it relatively easy for the government of Margaret of Parma to subdue the rebel towns in the spring of 1567 and to expel the hastily recruited Beggar armies. When Alba arrived in the Netherlands at the head of a great army in August 1567 the Revolt was already beaten, and most of the Protestants and other ringleaders had fled abroad. The moderates were chastened and willing to cooperate with the government, which only needed to consolidate its victory. It would have made sense for Alba to seek the support of the political center to heal the wounds that the events of 1566 had opened up in society.

He did the very opposite. The new governor punished, not just the Protestants and iconoclasts, but everyone whom he accused of conniving at the troubles by not enforcing the letter of the law. The counts of Egmond and Hornes, loyal Catholics who had done as much as their consciences allowed them to resolve the difficulties by moderate methods, were accused of high treason, condemned, and executed. Alba's Council

---

[9] Janssens, *Brabant*, 186–203; Maltby, *Alba*, 138–58.
[10] What follows is based on Woltjer, *Tussen vrijheidsstrijd*, 39–44 and 68.

of Troubles was a flagrant violation of the legal order and customs that applied in the Netherlands. In its six years of operation this special court sentenced more than a thousand persons to death and more than eleven thousand to perpetual banishment, in both cases confiscating their property. Such rigorous punishment was unprecedented in sixteenth-century Europe. Even the Spanish Inquisition claimed fewer victims in proportion to the size of the population.

Alba made himself even more hated through his proposals for tax reform, the infamous Tenth and Twentieth Penny taxes.[11] It has been argued that the Tenth Penny was more rational than the existing tax system and would have been more favorable to the less well off, but the introduction of this sales tax would have robbed the States assemblies of the only weapon at their disposal. The custom in the Netherlands was that the provincial States only granted taxes (called *bedes* or *aides*) to the central government if the government was willing to accommodate their demands. Rational or not, virtually everyone in the Netherlands was convinced that the new tax would spell ruin for the country. Provost Morillon wrote at the end of April that the Hollanders held the Tenth Penny in such abhorrence that "they say they would rather live under the Turk than in such slavery."[12]

At the very moment when Alba wanted to begin levying the Tenth Penny, the country was in the depths of a grave economic crisis.[13] A seven years' war between Denmark and Sweden led to several blockades of the Sound, bringing Holland's shipping and above all the import of grain to a standstill. Although a peace was signed in 1570, uncertainty remained. In 1571 a harvest failure struck the whole of northwestern Europe.[14] In Poland and on the Baltic shores of Germany so little grain was harvested that Gdansk exported none in the autumn of 1571 and only a few hundred loads in the following year. In October 1571 Amsterdam forbade the export of corn for the first time since the grain crisis of 1565.[15] The collapse of the grain trade brought down with it the Baltic market for salt, which Hollanders shipped from Spain and Portugal. The malaise in the Baltic trade caused widespread unemployment and poverty in North Holland. The price of rye, which had averaged 2.44 guilders per *mud* between 1566 and 1570, rose to 2.98 guilders in 1571 and 4.50 guilders

---

[11] Grapperhaus, *Alva*.
[12] *CCG*, IV, 203 (Morillon to Granvelle, 28 April 1572). "Ce x^e est tant abhorri des Hollandois, qu'ilz aymeront mieulx, ad ce qu'ilz dient, vivre soubs le Turcq que en telle servitut."
[13] De Meij, *Watergeuzen*, 299–306.
[14] Abel, *Massenarmut*, 37–45.
[15] Parker, *Dutch Revolt*, 128; Ter Gouw, *Geschiedenis van Amsterdam*, VI, 389–92.

in 1572. The purchasing power of Haarlem bricklayers fell by 58 percent between 1570 and 1572.[16]

On 1 November 1570 a severe northwesterly storm drove the waters higher than at any time in living memory. Some of the sea dikes gave way, and the All Saints' Day flood left practically all of the Northern Quarter under water, so that the country "was a flat sea, on which the boats sailed to and fro."[17] In Edam the storm drove two ships through the breach in the dike and left them high and dry. The Zijpe polder, only recently drained and enclosed, was again submerged. The whole village of Callantsoog, all three hundred houses, was washed away except for its church. Damage to crops and herds was so enormous that tax farmers successfully petitioned the States of Holland for exemption from payment.[18] Little more than a year later in January 1572 the country was hit by another severe storm. This time the sea dikes held firm, but east of Alkmaar the Galgendijk and the Huigendijk were breached, inundating the whole of Geestmerambacht. All but one of the windmills in the Northern Quarter were blown over.[19]

Many in government circles above all were convinced that the poverty of the people was the root cause of the rebellion of 1572. "The canaille of Enkhuizen has again risen in revolt," Boussu wrote to Alba on 22 May, "and that is largely caused by poverty." A week later: "A general rebellion is to be feared here, for the poor people are beginning to feel such a lack of foodstuffs that they do not know where to turn; no grain at all is coming from the Baltic, on which the whole country depends."[20] On 26 June, Morillon blamed the fall of Medemblik and Hoorn to the rebels on "the pure poverty of the subjects. Because they no longer have the means to provide for their lives, they are in despair and rise in revolt against their magistrates, who cannot control them any longer." Because all of Holland was dependent on commerce, he feared that the other towns would soon follow.[21]

---

[16] Daily wages expressed in rye prices, Noordegraaf, *Hollands welvaren*, 202, 204; Posthumus, *Nederlandse Prijsgeschiedenis*, I, 67. Rye prices on the Utrecht market were in line with prices in Holland, see Noordegraaf, *Hollands welvaren*, 23.

[17] Velius, 175; Dirk burger van Schoorel, *Chronyk*, 294–95.

[18] De Meij, *Watergeuzen*, 300; Schoorl, *'t Oge*, 88–94.

[19] Bor, 595.

[20] "Le canaille d'Enchuyse s'est de rechief revoltée [ . . . ] et ce est causé en grand parti par la pauvreté." "Il est à craindre icy une revolte generale; car jà les pauvres commencent à resentir telle necessité de vivres, qu'ils ne sçavent où se tourner, et n'en viennent aucuns grains d'Ooste, qui est l'entière sustentation de ce pays." Van Vloten, *Nederlands opstand*, II, lxii and lxvi (Boussu to Alba, 22 and 28 May 1572).

[21] "Par pure povreté des subgectz, lesquelz n'ayantz moyen de gaigner leur vie, se desesperent et se levent contre leurs magistrats qui n'en peuvent etre les maitres," CCG, IV, 280 (Morillon to Granvelle, 26 June 1572).

The consequences of the economic crisis were exacerbated by the raids of the Sea Beggars. A complaint of the States of Holland of 1570 reveals the havoc they were inflicting on the fishermen and seamen. Many Dutch ship captains had gone abroad "because of the sick and sorry state" of commerce at home. More than two hundred Holland ships had been sold to residents of the Hanseatic cities in the last few years. At the end of the year the States concluded that in their province "there is neither commerce nor welfare, because of the spoliations and robberies that daily take place at sea," while "those of Holland cannot long subsist without the seafaring trade."[22] Everywhere the signs of decay were visible. In Edam, where forty-five shipyards had still been busy in 1561, the number had fallen to thirty-six in 1569 and these "lay empty, because of the evil times." The crane that was used to raise the ships' masts was not leased that year, "for the land is now without commerce and few ships are being built, may God better it."[23]

The Northern Quarter had to suffer more frequently from the onshore raids of the Sea Beggars, who plundered and destroyed churches and monastic houses, but often allowed the local people to buy immunity from looting. In 1569 and 1570 the Beggars had raided only in Groningen, Friesland, and the Wadden Islands, but after they were expelled by Count Edzard of East Friesland and the Stadholder of Friesland, Caspar de Robles, Lord of Billy, the freebooters transferred their activities to the west in the following year. Between January 1571 and April 1572 they made twenty-three raids on land, six of them in the Northern Quarter.[24] On 2 March 1571 the Beggars sacked Monnickendam and Schellingwoude, very near Amsterdam. On 28 and 29 March it was the turn of Huisduinen and Petten, and a few days later of thirteen villages at the tip of North Holland: Camp, Groet, Schoorl, Callantsoog, Bergen, Schagen, Oude and Nieuwe Niedorp, Winkel, Barsingerhorn, Kolhorn, Haringhuizen, and Keins. These were the same villages, far from the centers of government power, where the parish priests had gone over to the new religion in the Wonder Year. The locals offered the Beggars hardly any resistance. The men capable of bearing arms in the villages, whose job it was to defend them, were in the words of the bailiff of Schagen "almost dead with fear, as peasants usually are."[25] Petten was overrun by only eight Sea Beggars, who exacted eighty guilders as the price for not burning the village and pressed fifty men to serve in their fleet.

[22] Cited in De Meij, *Watergeuzen*, 297.
[23] Van der Woude, *Noorderkwartier*, 458–59.
[24] De Meij, *Watergeuzen*, 55–57 and appendix I.
[25] Ibid., 249.

An account of the raid on Monnickendam gives an impression of just what such a raid on a town could be like.[26] On the evening of Friday, 2 March 1571, between nine and ten o'clock, when most of the townspeople were already in bed, two men arrived at the north gate, claiming to be local citizens who had been drinking outside the town and had forgotten the time. The gatekeeper's widow (the gatekeeper himself had recently been drowned at sea), opened the gate, suspecting nothing, and was badly wounded. Three hundred Beggars then forced their way into the town, among them twelve or fourteen inhabitants of Monnickendam who had been in exile since the troubles of 1566–67. They overcame the night watch, occupied the town hall so that the tocsin could not be rung, and spread out through the streets to prevent the citizens from gathering. They took the keys from the town jailer and released five prisoners, whom they soon conveyed to safety outside the town. Obviously this was the real motive for the raid. They then looted the house of the bailiff of Waterland, who saved his life by hiding in a pigsty, where he lay low for five hours "in nothing but his nightshirt." The Beggars stole all the church ornaments from the parish church, but left the altar and images intact. In the nunnery they stole the silver and destroyed a few images, but failed in their attempt to burn down the building.

Then it was the turn of the citizens. Summoned by a trumpet call the attackers forced their way into more than seventy houses and robbed them of everything that took their fancy. Finally they forced the boomkeeper to open the boom that closed off the harbor and sailed away with their booty, six pieces of artillery and two ships that they had found in port. The chaplain of the parish church, whom they took captive with them, did not survive the ordeal.

The entire episode had lasted no more than four hours. It was carried out efficiently and without mercy. Undoubtedly thanks to the help of the Beggars who were natives of Monnickendam, the attackers were well informed on local conditions. Such raids did not make the Beggars popular among the local people, so it is all the more remarkable that they found as much support as they did, especially in the first months of the Revolt. One explanation is the universal hatred of Alba, who was held responsible for the damage the Beggars caused.

If the government had stationed a few companies of troops in the Northern Quarter it could undoubtedly have prevented much of the damage and Revolt of 1572. Why had Alba omitted to put an adequate defense force in Holland?[27] One consideration was presumably that the province was already responsible for equipping the fleet. When danger

---

[26] Van Vloten, *Nederlands opstand*, I, 317–19.
[27] De Meij, *Watergeuzen*, 226–65; Williams, *Actions*, 34–35.

threatened, the Stadholder could always quickly summon troops from neighboring Utrecht, which bore an exceptionally heavy burden of garrisons. In the spring of 1572, for example, eight Spanish companies were based in Utrecht. Holland had in fact called on these resources occasionally in 1569 and 1571, but as soon as the danger from the Beggars had passed the soldiers were sent back to Utrecht.[28]

In addition, the defense of Holland was not Alba's highest priority. To be sure, the Duke had an eye for the harm the Sea Beggars had inflicted on Holland's trade and fishery, but he did not regard them as a strategic threat. He expected—rightly, as it later proved—that the invasion would come over the frontiers from France and Germany, where he accordingly concentrated the main strength of his army in 1572. The old Duke despised the pirates. "They are not soldiers who have struck these blows at me, but seamen and vagabonds, of the same stripe as those who smashed the images in previous years," he wrote scornfully to the king on 2 July.[29] It was no accident therefore that Alba did not inform the king of the seizure of Brill until 26 April, after he had already written five letters on other matters and he himself had been informed by Boussu as early as 2 April. "No es nada" (it is nothing), he is supposed to have commented on that occasion.[30]

On 24 May, three days after Enkhuizen went over to the Revolt, Louis of Nassau captured Mons in Hainault, and on 10 June the Prince of Orange's brother-in-law, Count van den Bergh, took Zutphen. Alba marshaled all his forces to deal with this threat, which in his eyes was far more serious. Once he had dealt with the invading armies in the South and East, he expected to have little difficulty clearing Holland and Zeeland of a handful of pirates.

In the spring and summer of 1572 Boussu therefore had hardly any resources that he could use to maintain and where necessary restore his authority in Holland. The only unit he could rely on, the Lombardy *tercio*, was disposed along the Maas to contain the Beggars at Brill, and could not play any significant role in the Northern Quarter. In his letters to Alba, which were at first worried but gradually grew almost hysterical in tone, he pressed the duke time and again to send him men, but all his pleas were refused. Although Alba himself never contemplated sending troops to the Northern Quarter, it was paradoxically enough their fear of a government garrison being billeted on them that had driven the inhabitants into revolt.

---

[28] On the garrison of Utrecht see Bor, 357–61.
[29] *CP*, II, 266 (Alba to the King, 2 July 1572).
[30] Ibid., II, 245 (Alba to the King, 26 April 1572); De Meij, *Watergeuzen*, 98; Fruin, "Alva's Bril," 378–79.

In Enkhuizen the whole month of May was one of continual unrest.[31] A fleet of twenty Holland warships lay at anchor in the roadstead, being fitted out on Alba's orders to recapture Brill and Flushing. The presence of these ships made the local people extremely nervous. They suspected that their own magistrates were plotting to use them to convey soldiers into the town in secret, to defend it against the expected assault from the Sea Beggars.

In this tense atmosphere there were frequent clashes when the soldiers on board the ships provoked the townsfolk.[32] A band of soldiers who reported at the gate, ostensibly to go on board, was refused entry by the militiamen. Soldiers who were already on board and who came into town to buy goods were forcibly removed from it by armed citizens.

Fearing the town authorities would secretly admit an occupation force, the people of Enkhuizen took drastic action. They hauled artillery pieces from the harbor and from a warship moored there, and placed them on the walls, occupied the gates and walls of the town, and doubled the watch. When the ferry arrived from Amsterdam with a large quantity of guns and gunpowder intended for the fleet, the rebels seized this cargo as well. Such disobedience was serious enough in the eyes of the government, but the citizens made it worse when they dragged the admiral of the fleet, the Amsterdammer Frans van Bosschuijzen, from his bed and held him prisoner in the town hall. But the citizens had not yet chosen the side of William of Orange. Instead, by maintaining armed neutrality, they sought to keep all foreign troops, government or Beggar, outside the walls of their town.

In these extremely tense circumstances a few exiles returned from Emden and other places where they had spent the last five years. One of them was Pieter Luijtgeszoon Buijskens, whose orders from the Prince of Orange to make himself master of the town were dated 20 April, about ten days before the troubles in Enkhuizen began.[33] The returned exiles had a great deal of influence among the discontented citizens, especially unemployed fishermen and seamen.

It was clear that the town authorities were no longer in control of events. By taking the side of the government in the conflict, they forfeited the confidence of their own citizens. When the burgomasters called on the militia "to strike these Beggars, these scoundrels, these rebels dead," most of the militiamen refused to take action against their fellow townsmen,

---

[31] For the transition of Enkhuizen see *CP*, II, 254–55 (Alba to the King, May 1572); Bor, 371–77; Velius, 179–82; Van Meteren (more concise and less careful than the above), fol. 55; Brandt (chiefly based on Bor, Velius, and Van Meteren), 107–25. More recent summaries of the older literature in Swierstra, "Enkhuizen" and Willemsen, *Enkhuizen*.

[32] *CP*, II, 254 (Alba to the King, May 1572); Bor, 371.

[33] His commission in Brandt, *Historie Enkhuisen*, 111–12.

especially when they heard that ship captains and fishermen were being mobilized.³⁴ A peremptory ultimatum from Boussu, demanding that the guilty should be punished and that the citizens should swear a new oath of loyalty to Alba as governor and himself as Stadholder, was the final provocation that prodded the town into revolt. The militiamen refused to serve; rebellious citizens broke down the door of the town hall with a beam of timber, took the burgomasters into custody, flew the Prince of Orange's flag from the town walls, and proclaimed that the town had declared for his cause. Four new burgomasters, among them Orange's man Buijskens, swore an oath to remain loyal to the King of Spain, the Prince of Orange, and the town of Enkhuizen, and to resist "Alba and his following, the Tenth and Twentieth Penny and the tyrannical Inquisition."

Now that the balance had tipped in favor of William of Orange's rebellion, a clash with the lawful government was bound to follow sooner or later. Enkhuizen, the key to the Zuiderzee, defended by its recently built walls, which Morillon compared to those of Antwerp, was of great strategic importance.³⁵ "The salvation of the country depends on the recapture of Enkhuizen," wrote Boussu, rather dramatically.³⁶ It was clear that the town's own defense forces, its armed citizens, would not be enough for an armed conflict. And so a town that had risen in revolt to prevent the admission of a garrison was forced to call in military help.

Only a day after the revolution twenty-six ships sailed in from Emden with five hundred men on board. The seizure of power at Enkhuizen must have been carefully prepared, for the fleet must have left Emden before the coup of 21 May. A few days later some detachments of Beggars arrived from Brill. On 2 June, Diederik Sonoy appeared in the town bearing a letter of commission from the Prince of Orange, who gave him full powers to act as governor of Enkhuizen and the whole of the Northern Quarter, which was still to be captured. Like the instructions for Pieter Buijskens, Sonoy's commission was dated 20 April, before the disturbances in Enkhuizen had even begun.

It is clear that the citizens of Enkhuizen were divided about the course to be followed. "The citizens were up everywhere, and one brother hardly dared trust another," Bor wrote of these events.³⁷ Yet a pattern can be discerned in these civil discords. The administrative elite, the burgomasters, and the majority of the *vroedschap* sided with the lawful authorities. The population suspected them, rightly or wrongly, of wanting to quarter

³⁴ Knevel, *Burgers*, 84–85; Grayson, "Civic Militia," 91.

³⁵ Bor, 371; *CCG*, IV, 203 (Morillon to Granvelle, 28 April 1572): "fortifié de murailles nouvelles, aultant quasi que la ville d'Anvers."

³⁶ "Du recouvrement d'Enckhuysen dependoit la salvation de ce pays." Van Vloten, *Nederlands opstand*, II, lxvi (Boussu to Alba, 29 May 1572).

³⁷ Bor, 373.

soldiers in the town after the fall of Brill, to defend it against the expected attack from the Sea Beggars. It was, as we saw, highly unlikely that Alba would really have protected them. The magistrates must have had some support among the citizenry, but not much. Only a few of the militiamen, in Bor's opinion "few but the wholly pro-Spanish Catholics," were willing to protect them from the unruly citizens.[38]

The town magistrates were opposed by the lower levels of the population, the "fishermen, boatmen and the rest of the rough mob."[39] They had been hardest hit by the economic crisis and had least to lose. Although to begin with they were only concerned to prevent the billeting of a garrison in the town, they were the first who were willing to take Enkhuizen over to the Orangist cause.

In between the loyalist magistrates and the rebel seamen was the citizenry, composed of more or less affluent merchants, ship owners, entrepreneurs, craftsmen, and shopkeepers, the backbone of every Holland town.[40] This middle class, and especially its armed members, the militia, played a decisive part in the conflict. As long as there was no garrison in the town, the armed citizenry, its core being the militia companies, formed the only local military force. Without the support of the militiamen the discontented citizens could do nothing. But the magistrates were equally dependent on the militias for protection. Ultimately it was the refusal of the militiamen to use force against their fellow citizens that brought the town over to the side of the Revolt. The harshness of Boussu, who had loyally enforced Alba's hard line since 1567, drove them into the arms of the Prince of Orange, whose propaganda accused the "Spanish" government of tyranny and promised to restore the old privileges.

Things would never have gone so far without the activities of a few returned Calvinist exiles. They cannot have been many; Boussu had originally promised to pardon fourteen or fifteen of them, but this small band had strong reasons to win Enkhuizen for the rebel cause.[41] The activities of the exiles were directed from Emden. Urged on by Sonoy, Jan Arentszoon, the hedge-preaching ex–basket maker, who was now a preacher in Emden, had asked four exiles to return.[42] When the choice between obedience and revolt hung in the balance, this handful of dedicated zealots could decide the issue.

Medemblik was the rebels' next target. The strategic importance of the little town for both rebels and government lay in its castle, which stood

[38] Ibid., 373.
[39] Velius, 181.
[40] Knevel, *Burgers*, 82–91.
[41] The Council of Troubles had banished forty-three inhabitants of Enkhuizen in October 1568. *Sententiën*, 171.
[42] Bor, 372.

next to the town and dominated the countryside and the entrance to the Zuiderzee. The castle was not garrisoned, however; instead, its defense was entrusted to a guard drawn from the townsmen. In September 1569 two companies of soldiers had been based there for a short time, but once the immediate threat from the Beggars had passed they were sent back to Utrecht. In January 1571, as a late reaction to the surrender of the castle of Loevestein to the Beggars, Alba ordered the castellan of Medemblik to raise a company of citizen guards to defend the castle. The population had little enthusiasm for guard duty. The guard of three men was increased to eight, but after a month they were again dismissed.[43]

Boussu saw the importance of Medemblik, and soon after Enkhuizen had gone over to the revolt he sent two hundred arquebusiers from Stavoren. The castellan Cornelis van Rijswijk and his modest force refused to admit them to the castle, and the troops returned across the Zuiderzee to Friesland with nothing to show for their journey.[44] Boussu's unsuccessful attempt to secure Medemblik earned him a reprimand from his chief. Alba believed that the advantage of retaining Medemblik was outweighed by the risk to which Boussu had exposed Groningen by shipping soldiers to North Holland.[45] The large force based in Groningen was there to defend the northeastern frontier, Alba's priority.

The citizens of Medemblik were as unwilling to admit a garrison as their counterparts in Enkhuizen, but that did not mean they were now ready to admit the rebels. A delegation from Enkhuizen, which arrived at the gate with a proposal to come over to the Orangist cause, was refused admittance. Yet Medemblik could not stay neutral for long. A few days later, on 8 June, Sonoy sent two troops of soldiers, who broke through the east gate while two companies of militia from Enkhuizen forced the west gate. Many of the townspeople fled to the castle, from where they opened fire on the invaders, until the latter used the remaining women and children as human shields between themselves and the castle. That left the defenders of the castle with no choice but to capitulate.[46] Rijswijk, who had refused to admit the government forces, remained in his post as castellan.

While Medemblik was taken by force, Hoorn followed the pattern of Enkhuizen.[47] As in Enkhuizen the difficulties began with disagreement between the magistrates and the townsfolk on the admission of an occupying garrison. Immediately after their neighbors in Enkhuizen had joined

---

[43] De Meij, *Watergeuzen*, 233, 245.

[44] Van Vloten, *Nederlands opstand*, II, lxvi (29 May) and lxviii (3 June).

[45] Ibid., II, lxviii (Alba to Boussu, 3 June 1572).

[46] Bor, 377; Dirk burger van Schoorl, *Chronyk*, 22–23; "Kroniek van Medemblik."

[47] For Hoorn's transition to the Revolt see Velius, 182–88; Van Vloten, *Nederlands opstand*, II, lxii–lxxiv; Knevel, *Burgers*, 86.

the Revolt the burgomasters of Hoorn tried to quarter soldiers in their town to prevent its capture. In Hoorn, too, this brought hundreds of armed citizens onto the streets. As in Enkhuizen the townspeople were divided on the policy to be followed: the magistrates and their supporters wanted to bring soldiers into the town, while most of the population hoped to defend the town against both Spaniards and rebels. Immediately after Enkhuizen had gone over to the Revolt, Hoorn also saw the return of some exiles, who were able to exert great influence in the unstable situation.

To broaden the base of their authority in the town, the magistrates created a new representative body, a Broad Council in which the burgomasters and *vroedschap* consulted with the officers of the militia and the heads of the guilds, who represented the broad citizenry, or urban middle classes. The magistrates also took 450 of the humble commonalty into their service as soldiers, to help the militia defend the town against an attack from either side. This measure both reinforced the militia and gave the unemployed sailors and fishermen a temporary income, while attaching them to the town by requiring them to swear an oath of loyalty.

The burgomasters could do nothing without the consent of the town's middle classes. That does not mean the citizens of Hoorn were now ready to welcome the Beggars. When nine wagons of soldiers from Enkhuizen appeared before the gates of Hoorn, the citizens refused to admit them and threatened to drive them away by firing their cannon. Yet there were some who favored admitting the Beggars. The captains of the civic militia agreed secretly with Enkhuizen that they would open the gates to the rebels. The plan leaked out, and the military leaders of the militia managed to convince them "with good reasons and suitable presentations," to renounce the idea.[48]

While Hoorn wavered between revolt and loyalty, returned exiles and neighboring Enkhuizen gave the final little push that was needed to bring the town over to rebellion. A proposal from Sonoy and the magistrates of Enkhuizen, urging Hoorn to come over to their side and threatening economic blockade if it refused, caused serious disagreement. Attempts by the burgomasters to put off a decision failed, as did the efforts of the Broad Council to reach an agreement with Edam and Monnickendam on a joint line of action.

Threatened by Enkhuizen and with no prospect of help from Boussu, Hoorn could not maintain its neutrality. The Broad Council had to decide if the town should admit a government occupation force or a detachment of Beggars. The council could not reach a consensus and left it to a vote. The representatives of the militia and the guilds, supported by a few dissi-

---

[48] Velius, 187.

dents on the *vroedschap*, outvoted the burgomasters and the rest of the *vroedschap*; it was decided to open the gates to the Beggars. The burgomasters and a few of their adherents, "most of the most prominent men in both wealth and reputation," took responsibility and left the town.[49] One of the burgomasters was persuaded to return, and three new colleagues were chosen to serve alongside him, all of them returned exiles.

The revolution in Hoorn was as bloodless as it had been in Enkhuizen. The decision to admit the rebels was taken in an extraordinarily democratic manner by sixteenth-century standards, by a body that represented the town's middle classes. The same groups who decided the outcome in Enkhuizen were active in Hoorn: the majority of the civic elite, which wished to impose a government garrison on the town against the will of the majority of its people; the lower classes, suffering from unemployment and poverty, and politically unreliable; and a middle group organized in the militias and the guilds, which at first hoped to defend the town against both sides, but gradually came round to supporting the revolt, under pressure from the rebels in Enkhuizen and the returned exiles.

The citizens of Alkmaar were equally unwilling to have anything to do with a military occupation by government forces, of which they had very painful memories.[50] A year earlier in April 1571 Boussu had tried to quarter two regiments of Spaniards on the town to defend it and the surrounding countryside from the raids of the Sea Beggars. While the *vroedschap* met to discuss the request, armed citizens gathered to resist the foragers who had been sent ahead to prepare the way. The burgomasters had to intervene to prevent a bloodbath. The citizens had then occupied the walls and closed the gates, and Boussu himself had to come to Alkmaar to compel the town to admit the force. The troops were billeted on the citizens, who had to provide their food; the townsfolk complained that they were being eaten out of house and home, because the soldiers expected meat, fish, beer, and wine on the table twice a day. Shortly afterward Boussu recalled the troops to Utrecht.

Presumably for this reason the magistrates did not ask for a garrison after Enkhuizen went over to the Revolt, but were just as reluctant to open their gates to the rebels. Sonoy made himself master of the town by a clever ruse.[51] He ordered the peasants of North Holland to report for military service equipped with a firearm or a pike. Placing two or three peasants alongside each soldier, he then drew up the troops with about two or three stones' throws between each company. With this little army, packed to look bigger than it was, he marched along the Huigendijk from

---

[49] Ibid., 188.
[50] Boomkamp, *Alkmaer*, 171–74.
[51] Van der Woude, *Kronyck*, 64; Boomkamp, *Alkmaer*, 179.

Hoorn to Alkmaar, where the inhabitants soon concluded that they were no match for such a superior force. Since they were well aware that they could not expect help from government troops in the near future, and that the Prince of Orange's adherents in Alkmaar were just waiting to hand over the town, they opened their gates to Sonoy on 20 June.[52] Unlike their counterparts in Hoorn and Enkhuizen, the burgomasters of Alkmaar were not replaced for the time being.[53] The five Beggar detachments did not stay long, and soon moved on toward Waterland and the River Zaan.

A week later it was the turn of Edam and Monnickendam. These two small towns did not join the Revolt of their own free will either.[54] Four freebooters, encouraged by their success in Enkhuizen, had already appeared in Monnickendam on 8 June, carrying letters from Lumey, who demanded that the astonished citizens should open their churches and hand over the reliquaries to the bearers. It proved that they had completely misjudged the situation, for they were promptly arrested and sent to Boussu. After the fall of Alkmaar, however, there was little hope that Edam and Monnickendam could keep the rebels out without help from government forces. On 27 June they had to open their gates. Apparently not everyone agreed. The burgomasters of Amsterdam wrote to Alba that Edam had been taken "not without resistance of the men of good will in the same town."[55] There was evidently some opposition to the decision of the town's magistrates, but nothing more is heard of any resistance to the rebels in either town.

Once the six towns of the Northern Quarter had gone over to the Revolt or had been seized for it, the rebels were also masters of the countryside. Whether they had town rights or not, without walls and gates the villages had to accept the authority of the towns. Shortly after Enkhuizen was in rebel hands about a hundred men marched on the surrounding countryside, called the Streek, where they sacked some villages and forced the magistrates and villagers to swear an oath of loyalty to the Prince of Orange. The force that captured Medemblik followed this up by a tour of the twelve surrounding villages, where they seized all the weapons.[56] Only

---

[52] Boomkamp, *Alkmaer*, 177, gives the date as 28 June, but on 21 June Boussu wrote that "hyer sur les quatre heures apres disner les pirates sont entrez en Alcmaer," Van Vloten, *Nederlands opstand*, II, lxxv. See also Schulten, *Beleg*, 64.

[53] Jacob van Warendel, who had been appointed burgomaster before the transition, represented Alkmaar at the revolutionary assembly of the States of Holland in Dordrecht on 19 July. Boomkamp, *Alkmaer*, 180, 183–84; Bakhuizen van den Brink, "Eerste vergadering," 195.

[54] Van Vloten, *Nederlands opstand*, II, lxx, lxxvii, lxxx–lxxxvi; Vermeer, "Overgang"; Driessen, "Waterland."

[55] Van Vloten, *Nederlands opstand*, II, lxxxi.

[56] Ibid., II, lxv; Dirk burger van Schoorl, *Chronyk*, 23.

Zaandam and the adjacent area remained in government hands. Boussu had put a garrison there at the eleventh hour, after a Beggar captain disobeyed Sonoy's order to seize the locks on the River Zaan and deserted.[57]

The Beggars enjoyed an extraordinary popularity in the countryside, certainly in the first weeks of the Revolt. Immediately after Enkhuizen went over, the Beggars in Brill landed large forces on the beach between Petten and Schoorl, which then made their way via Krabbendam and Schagen to Enkhuizen. The peasants, to whom Boussu had entrusted the defense of the country against the Beggars, did not put a single obstacle in their path.[58] On the contrary, when a company of Spanish soldiers quartered on Egmond to prevent landings tried to break out to Warmenhuizen, it encountered fierce resistance everywhere. The peasants rang the tocsin, demolished bridges, and dug trenches across the roads, forcing the soldiers to withdraw hastily to the castle and abbey of Egmond. Undoubtedly the rural population preferred the Beggars to the Spaniards. Two drummers sent by Boussu on 25 May to Waterland to raise men for the fleet returned without a single recruit; but, they reported, if they had wished to raise a thousand men for the Beggars, they would have had no trouble.[59] The sailors in government service also proved unreliable. When Boussu finally managed to collect a small fleet on the Zuiderzee, after great efforts, three of the ships deserted to the rebels.[60]

The events in the Northern Quarter offer no evidence to support the theories of Motley and Fruin of a spontaneous popular uprising, or those of Geyl and Van Gelder of a brutal war of conquest. In all the towns the population was divided on the line to follow, and the moderate middle groups were radicalized as pressure from the rebels increased and support from the government failed to arrive. The towns also joined the Revolt in different ways: Enkhuizen and Hoorn went over on their own initiative; Medemblik defended itself; Alkmaar, Edam, and Monnickendam capitulated under pressure but did not offer resistance.

The attitude of the towns during the revolutionary events of 1572 was determined largely by the policy of their magistrates. Where they openly favored admitting a garrison of government troops, they lost the support of the citizens, who took to arms to resist the threat. In Enkhuizen and Hoorn that soon led to the overthrow of the burgomasters and the admission of the rebels. But where the town authorities showed no eagerness to call in outside help, civic unity remained intact. These towns also went

---

[57] Bor, 397.
[58] Van Vloten, *Nederlands opstand*, II, lxiv, lxvi, lxix, lxxi (Boussu to Alba, 26, 27, 28 May, 5 June, 12 June).
[59] Ibid., II, lxvi (Boussu to Alba, 28 May 1572).
[60] Ibid., II, lxxvi (Boussu to Alba, 24 June 1572).

over to the Revolt, but not as a result of civic discord. The sitting magistrates were able to remain in office for the time being.

A comparison with Amsterdam makes this clear. Amsterdam remained loyal to the government during the crisis of 1572, but like the other towns of Holland it refused to allow government troops within its walls, relying instead on its own armed citizens to resist the rebels.[61] The situation in Amsterdam had similarities to that in Enkhuizen: warships were also being fitted out on the IJ to sail against the rebels in Brill and Flushing. As in Enkhuizen, a few dozen soldiers arrived at the city gate in late May, claiming that they wanted to go on board; and they too were refused admittance by the Amsterdammers.[62] The citizens shared Enkhuizen's fear that the soldiers on board the fleet would seize the city, and the *vroedschap* therefore forbade them access, even to buy provisions.[63]

The difference from Enkhuizen was that in Amsterdam it was the city authorities who took measures to keep out the soldiers. Time and again the burgomasters wrote to Boussu to protest against the threatened billeting of troops. Defending the city's interests in this way allowed them to maintain civic unity. If the burgomasters of Amsterdam had followed the example of their counterparts in Enkhuizen and tried to impose a government garrison against the will of their citizens, they might have provoked an insurrection, which could have taken the city into the camp of the Revolt. Even after virtually the whole of Holland had fallen into rebel hands, the magistrates of Amsterdam still refused to accept a garrison, to the despair of Alba and Boussu. Not until the city was besieged by the rebels in August 1572 were they forced to agree to admit four or five companies of Spaniards.[64]

The events in Medemblik are further confirmation of this connection. Nothing is known of the attitude of the burgomasters, but the castellan Cornelis van Rijswijk refused to allow the troops from Stavoren to enter, and held the castle against the rebels with the aid of the citizens. In Medemblik, too, civic unity was preserved, and the castellan remained in office.

Throughout the summer of 1572 the rebels in Holland and Zeeland scored one unexpected success after another. After overrunning the Northern Quarter the Revolt spread to South Holland: Gouda, Dordrecht, and Gorinchem opened their gates to the rebels by the end of

[61] Ter Gouw, *Geschiedenis van Amsterdam*, VII, 13–31.

[62] Van Vloten, *Nederlands opstand*, II, lxv (Boussu to Alba, 27 May 1572).

[63] Resolution of 3 July 1572, SAA, Archief Vroedschap, inv. no. 5026/2, fol. 219v.

[64] Van Vloten, *Nederlands opstand*, II, lxix, lxxviii (Boussu to Alba, 7 June and 3 July 1572); *CP*, II, 266, 268, 272, 276 (Alba to the King, 2 July, 18 July, 21 August, 6 September 1572); Wagenaar, *Amsterdam*, 325; Ter Gouw, *Geschiedenis van Amsterdam*, VII, 48–58. According to Alba (*CP*, II, 276), the city took in five companies; according to Bor, 404, four.

June, and most of the other towns followed in July. On 19 July delegates from the rebel towns met on their own authority at Dordrecht to hold a revolutionary assembly of the States of Holland, which formed a provisional administration for the province.[65] While the States deliberated, Boussu recalled the few troops he still had left in Holland to defend the frontier against the expected French invasion. With that the last strongholds of the government in South Holland fell into the hands of the rebels, who now controlled all of Holland and Zeeland except for Amsterdam and Middelburg.

But that was the end of the honeymoon for the Revolt. In August it suffered its first reverses, and in October the tide appeared to be turning permanently. Many moderates realized that their original decision to admit the Beggars and to keep out a garrison of government forces had not brought the advantages for which they had hoped.

The first reversal for the rebels was their failure to take Amsterdam.[66] The citizens failed to rise as expected, and the city finally received a government garrison, which beat off a short siege by William of Orange's lieutenant in South Holland, Lumey. At almost the same moment (23–24 August 1572), far from Holland, the French government instigated a bloodbath of the Huguenots. The Massacre of St. Bartholomew was to have far-reaching consequences for the Revolt of the Netherlands,[67] for it prevented the expected French assistance from reaching the Prince of Orange, and thereby crippled his offensive in the South. For the next four years the struggle was to be waged entirely in Holland and Zeeland. On 19 September, without French support, Louis of Nassau was forced to surrender Mons in Hainault, which had been surrounded by Alba for some time. William of Orange, who had failed to relieve the city, hastened back to the North. One after another the towns of Brabant that had declared for the Revolt surrendered to Alba. At the end of October the Prince of Orange fled to Enkhuizen and Holland, expecting, in his own prophetic words, "to make my sepulcher there."[68]

Alba decided to strike hard against the rebel towns. At the beginning of October he let his soldiers loose on Mechelen for two days and two nights, even though the city had opened its gates to them voluntarily. The soldiers, who had not been paid for some time but had not been allowed to sack Mons, "did not leave a nail in the walls," as a shocked Spanish secretary reported to the king. Even clerics, counselors of the Great Council, and government officials were not spared. "But the worst were the

---

[65] Boogman, "Overgang"; Bakhuizen van den Brink, "Eerste vergadering."
[66] Bor, 404; Velius, 192; Ter Gouw, *Geschiedenis van Amsterdam*, VII, 48–58.
[67] Parker, *Dutch Revolt*, 138, especially note 14. See. also *DWJ*, 2.
[68] *Archives*, IV, 4.

tortures that they inflicted on many married women, boys and girls to find out where they had hidden the gold and silver, before they put them to death."[69] The slaughter had the intended result. In a few days all the rebellious towns of Brabant had surrendered.

On 14 November it was the turn of Zutphen, which had admitted the army of Count van den Bergh without a fight in June. Alba ordered his commander, his son Don Fadrique de Toledo, "not to leave a man alive and . . . to set fire to the town."[70] This massacre caused the collapse of resistance in the East. By the end of November the Revolt was confined to Holland and Zeeland. The government army marched westward, apparently hoping to mop up the remaining resistance in a quick campaign. The atrocities at Mechelen and Zutphen had not achieved the desired results here. Boussu wrote to Alba that he hoped the example of Mechelen and the other towns would teach them a lesson, but added that this did not look likely in Holland, where things were going from bad to worse, and he pleaded with Alba to send him the means "to repress the audacity of this canaille."[71]

Naarden became the turning point of the war. Don Fadrique repeated the formula already tried in Mechelen and Zutphen, firmly convinced that the rebel towns of Holland would fall into his lap like ripe fruit. On 1 December his army slaughtered practically the whole population and burned the little town to ashes. As Alba wrote with grim satisfaction to the king, "they cut the throats of citizens and soldiers without a living soul escaping."[72]

But the consequences were the opposite of what Alba had expected. The brutality of the Spanish soldiers, who drew no distinction between military men and civilians, supporters of the Revolt and loyalists, adherents of the Reformation and good Catholics, or between laymen and clergy, only made most Hollanders even more grimly resolved to defend themselves to the last. Many Catholics and other loyalists who until then had been skeptical about the new regime decided to fight the Spanish army. They would rather die in battle than be massacred unresisting by the Spaniards.[73]

---

[69] *CP*, II, 299 (Esteban Prats to the King, 30 November 1572); Bor, 409; Parker, *Dutch Revolt*, 141; Janssens, *Brabant*, 176–77.

[70] *CP*, II, 295 (Alba to the King, 19 November 1572); Bor, 414–15.

[71] "réprimer l'audace de ce canaille." *CCG*, IV, 507 (Boussu to Alba, 11 October 1572).

[72] *CP*, II, 300 (Alba to the King, 19 December 1572). "degollaron burgeses y soldados, sin escaparse hombre nascido." For the bloodbath in Naarden see Bor, 417–20.

[73] Bor, 420; Strada, 521. See also *CCG*, IV, 526 (Morillon to Granvelle, 9 December 1572): "Ce n'est pas pour donner grande envie aux autres villes de se rendre." Cf. also *CCG*, IV, 532 (Morillon to Granvelle, 16 December 1582): Haarlem will not put itself in Alba's mercy, to avoid the fate of Naarden.

That was soon apparent in Haarlem, the next target of the government army.[74] While its burgomasters negotiated in Amsterdam with Don Fadrique on the terms for capitulation, radical militiamen staged a coup in Haarlem and put the city into a state of defense. The siege that began on 11 December cost the Spanish army seven months, heavy losses, and damage to its prestige in the Netherlands and abroad before the city surrendered unconditionally on 13 July 1573. The greater part of the rebel force in Haarlem was put to death, 1,250 men by some estimates, as many as 1,700 by others. Some of the rebel leaders were also executed, but most of the citizens were spared, and the city was allowed to buy off the threat of plunder.

Alkmaar was supposed to follow Haarlem.[75] On 21 August the army began to surround the town. The citizens and the Beggar forces hastily brought into the town at the eleventh hour beat off some attempts to take it by storm, but it was ultimately saved by the natural features of the Northland. Sonoy ordered the sluice gates of the inundated Zijpe polder to be opened, and on 8 October the royal army began to withdraw. "Victory begins at Alkmaar," the later saying would claim, but the inhabitants of the Northern Quarter could not yet predict the future. They faced three more anxious years of war.

---

[74] For the siege of Haarlem see Bor, 421–44; Wijn, *Beleg*; Verwer, *Memoriaelbouck*.
[75] Bor, 444–55; Schulten, "Beleg"; Foreest, *Cort verhael*.

CHAPTER FIVE

# War

THE TREASON AFFAIR in the Northern Quarter began with the attempt of Gilles de Berlaymont, Lord of Hierges, to overrun North Holland. Our account must therefore also begin with his fruitless campaign, which baffled contemporaries. What were the strategic and operational objectives of the Spanish military command? Why did they want to subjugate the Northern Quarter, why at this particular moment, and what resources were at their disposal? Why did the campaign fail, or, in other words, why were the scanty bands of rebels able to withstand an army that was still regarded as the best-trained and most formidable in Europe?

The failed invasion raises questions about the conduct of the war in North Holland. Except for the well-documented siege of Alkmaar, it is little known. No one could have predicted that the end of the siege of Alkmaar would later come to be seen as the turning point of the war. There was no sign of this at the time. In 1573, 1574, and 1575 the North Hollanders were again alarmed by large-scale Spanish invasions. And even though the rebels held some important trump cards, such as the watery geography of the Northern Quarter and their control of the sea, it was far from a foregone conclusion that their stronghold in North Holland would stand firm.

A glance at the map that Joost Janszoon Bilhamer had produced for the Spanish military command is enough to show that the strategic position of the rebels in the Northern Quarter was precarious. The wide arm of the sea formed by the River IJ and the fortified cities of Amsterdam and Haarlem divided the mainland of Holland in two.

When he began the siege of Haarlem in December 1572 Don Fadrique stationed a few companies of Spaniards at Beverwijk, and placed a unit of cavalry in the castle of Egmond to patrol the beach. The role of these forces was to prevent an attack from Alkmaar or Waterland in the rear of the Spanish army.[1] In this way the Spaniards cut off communication by land between the rebels in the Northern and Southern Quarters of Holland, a situation confirmed by the fall of Haarlem in July 1573. Because the Spaniards dominated the greater part of Kennemerland from Bever-

---

[1] Mendoça, *Commentaires*, 188–89; see also Brouwer, *Kronieken*, 226–27; Wijn, *Beleg*, 48.

wijk, the rebels in the Northern Quarter were also exposed to the threat of invasion from that side. Danger also threatened them from the East, across the Zuiderzee, where Stavoren and Harlingen had good harbors that could be used as springboards for an invasion.[2]

Even so, the position of the rebels in the North was not hopeless. They managed to stay in touch with South Holland and Zeeland by the sea route from Enkhuizen through the Marsdiep and by the North Sea to the river Maas.[3] They also remained firmly in control of the northern shipping lanes to northern Germany and the Baltic, and so safeguarded their overseas trade, their troop transports, and communications with the Prince of Orange and the States of Holland. In practice, however, the geographic and strategic features of the region held by the rebels dictated the possibilities open to them. North Holland had to defend itself with its own resources.

The continued presence of the rebels in North Holland confronted the Spaniards with grave problems, not least the blockade of Amsterdam. Between 1572 and 1578, while its overseas trade routes were cut off, Amsterdam's commerce was crippled. This created serious difficulties for the import of food, especially grain, in all the loyalist areas of the Netherlands. The rebel blockade continued even after the Pacification of Ghent. It was largely this economic warfare that eventually forced Amsterdam to go over to the rebel side in 1578. Once the blockade was lifted, the city rapidly recovered its prosperity.

As early as August 1572, at a meeting of the States of Holland in Haarlem, Sonoy declared himself in favor of blockading the port of Amsterdam. At the time the States found the plan too expensive and resolved instead on a siege of the city. It was begun in the same month, by Lumey, but soon had to be abandoned.[4] In May 1573 the North Holland rebels sank a large number of old decommissioned hulks in the IJ near Nieuwendam, ballasted with sand and brick from demolished monasteries and churches.[5] The object was to prevent the government fleet, which was being fitted out in the harbor of Amsterdam, from putting to sea against the rebels. But evidently the sinking had been mismanaged, for when the Zuiderzee fleet sailed in September 1573 the sunken ships were not

---

[2] Bor, 449, on an unsuccessful plan to attack Enkhuizen from Friesland in August 1573.

[3] For example NHA, GNK, inv. no. 236, 17 and 18 August 1585; it was decided to send three companies of soldiers to South Holland as quickly as possible.

[4] Bor, 404; Wagenaar, *Amsterdam*, I, 325.

[5] Velius, 211. The sunken ships were seized from persons who had sided with the enemy. WFA, OA Hoorn, inv. no. 2519, and NHA, GNK, inv. no. 235, 3 June 1575. They included Jan Simonszoon Rol, the vice-admiral of the government fleet and a native of Hoorn. If the owners were later found to be adherents of the "common cause" they were to be compensated.

enough to stop it.⁶ In October the hulks floated to the surface again, which an excited Wouter Jacobszoon interpreted as a sign that God was obviously on the side of Amsterdam and the lawful government.⁷ But on 11 October the rebels destroyed the Amsterdam fleet on the Zuiderzee between Hoorn and Enkhuizen; and so the barriers on the IJ lost their point. To bring the city to its knees it was enough for the rebels to send a small squadron to close the outlets to the sea at the Marsdiep and the Vlie.⁸

The blockade had disastrous consequences for Amsterdam's economy. The city lost its position as the central entrepôt for grain and other Baltic products, and could barely feed its own inhabitants adequately. Furthermore, its population had been swollen by numerous refugees and, since August 1572, by several companies of Spaniards. The city's economic collapse is apparent from the figures in its accounts. The revenue from the "great excise," levied on such primary necessities of life as grain, beer, and wine, which had amounted to 9,500 pounds Flemish in 1571, fell to 6,600 pounds in 1572, 6,000 in 1573, 5,300 in 1574, and 5,200 in 1575.⁹ The collapse of the grain trade was chiefly responsible for this decline. Revenues from the corn excise fell from 844 Flemish pounds in 1571 via 329 and 169 to 113 pounds in 1574, a fall of 87 percent.¹⁰

The *vroedschap* of Amsterdam at this time was continually preoccupied with securing the food supply for its population as best it could. In early 1573 it resolved that refugees who arrived in the city from outside must deliver a *mud* of rye, wheat, or barley to the city at a fixed price.¹¹

The most vivid images, as usual, were those drawn by Brother Wouter Jacobszoon. On 10 October 1572 he described the arrival of the last fleet of grain ships, convoyed past Enkhuizen by warships. Everyone went down to the harbor to witness their arrival, "for they had been greatly yearned for."¹² Next day the government fleet was defeated by the rebels, and from that date Wouter complained incessantly of the dearth of food.¹³ On 11 January 1573 he looked on as a crowd besieged a baker's shop on the Dam square:

> And that throng gathered only to get bread for money. I heard someone say that he had stood three hours before he could get any bread. Great

---

⁶ Bor, 455.

⁷ *DWJ*, 25–26.

⁸ NHA, GNK, fol. 154, 25 February 1575: six ships in the Ems, seven in the Vlie, eight on the Zuiderzee.

⁹ Lievense-Pelser, "Alteratie," 53.

¹⁰ Ibid., 42.

¹¹ *Vroedschap* resolutions, 15 January and 20 February 1573, SAA, archief vroedschap, inv. no. 5026/2, fols. 231v, 236.

¹² *DWJ*, 25.

¹³ For example ibid., 105, 120, 171, 368, 370 (December 1572, January 1573, February 1574).

lamentation was to be heard, as one wailed while another took on terribly; and particularly because everyone said that there was no bread to be had anywhere.[14]

In January 1574 Wouter lamented that even priests and clerics must go begging before the doors of the good folk for something to still their hungry bellies. A nun who came from a wealthy convent in Hoorn had fallen into such destitution that she went out in the evening to sing "devout spiritual songs" before the doors for a piece of bread. "She went out in the evening when it was dark, for she was ashamed to do so in the daytime, being honorable in her heart."[15]

On 13 October 1574 the magistrates of Amsterdam wrote to Governor Requesens to explain exactly where the shoe pinched.[16] The blockade had made it impossible for merchants "from east or west" to enter the city; instead, merchants were compelled to unload their cargoes in the rebel-held towns, whose commerce was flourishing mightily, so that they had an ample supply of food while the Amsterdammers were falling into poverty and misery. The dearth of food had already caused an epidemic of plague. In Emden there were large stocks of food from the Baltic countries, from which the king's subjects and his army had been fed last year. The rebels had now sent so many warships to patrol the shipping lanes between Emden and Friesland that the trade between Friesland and Amsterdam had been brought to a standstill. Prices of all foodstuffs in Amsterdam had risen to extraordinary levels and would rise even further unless Requesens sent a fleet to drive the rebel warships from the River Ems. If he failed to do so, "the good subjects of the King's Majesty will perish and die of hunger this coming winter, which would be a very lamentable matter." In the circumstances it is understandable that the magistrates pressed the governor so urgently to expel the rebels from the Northern Quarter.

The Spanish military commanders had yet another reason to be interested in the subjugation of the North Holland peninsula. The presence of the rebels there represented a constant threat to the long and narrow supply lines from Utrecht via Amsterdam to Haarlem on which the Spanish army depended. Even though the rebels did not have the military strength to force Amsterdam or Haarlem to surrender to a regular siege, an attack on the dikes and the roads that ran along them between the loyal cities was by no means beyond them. With their relatively simple and limited resources they could still cause serious difficulties for the Spanish army.

---

[14] Ibid., 131.
[15] Ibid., 364.
[16] CCG, V, 504.

In March and June 1573 Sonoy had twice attacked the dike between the IJ and the Diemermeer. By thus closing the passage between Utrecht and Amsterdam, and preventing supplies from reaching the Spanish army encamped before Haarlem, he hoped to relieve the city. But on both occasions the Amsterdammers had managed to chase the Beggar forces away after violent skirmishes.[17]

The fall of Haarlem in July 1573 improved the strategic situation of the Spanish army. In the late summer and autumn of 1573 the Spaniards drove the rebels from the fortifications on the Waterland dike north of the IJ and recaptured the southern part of Waterland and the Zaan.[18] The district between the IJ and the Purmer and Wormer meres became a ghostly no man's land, the scene of regular fierce and bloody fighting, where now the rebels and now the Spaniards held the upper hand. This struggle bore little resemblance to the regular warfare described in general works on the "military revolution." There were no lengthy and orderly sieges of walled towns surrounded by modern fortifications in the Italian style. The war in Waterland was a guerrilla war of numerous unconnected fights, skirmishes, and ambushes.[19] Sconces, villages, and isolated houses and huts were defended, captured, surrendered again, and burned to the ground. Prisoners of war were sometimes killed in cold blood. In June 1574, for example, after a great Spanish defeat near Wormer, 150 German prisoners were loaded onto ships and drowned in the Zuiderzee off Hoorn.[20]

Between October 1573 and October 1574 the Spanish army did not need to be too worried about the security of its communications. North of the IJ it was protected by a buffer zone, while on the south side there was nothing to fear as long as it was still besieging Leiden. The situation changed in October 1574 when the mutinous army abandoned the siege of Leiden and evacuated the countryside of South Holland.[21] From that moment the military barrier that divided North from South Holland was reduced to a narrow and extremely precarious bridgehead, an advanced position exposed to the threat of attack from both north and south.[22]

---

[17] Velius, 205–9; Bor, 437, 439; Wagenaar, *Amsterdam*, I, 328–30; Ter Gouw, *Geschiedenis van Amsterdam*, VII, 77, 85–86, 93–95. Sonoy had made an earlier attempt on 21 December 1572, but had to abandon it after a few hours.

[18] Velius, 216, 228.

[19] For guerrilla warfare in the Dutch Revolt see Parker, *Army of Flanders*, 12–13.

[20] For the fights at Wormer and Purmerend at Whitsun 1574, see Velius, 239–42; Bor, 496–97. Velius, 242, calls the murder of the prisoners of war one of the cruelest and most outrageous deeds committed by the rebels in the war. Bor does not mention it.

[21] *CP*, III, 191 and 196 (Requesens to the King, 6 and 18 November 1574); Bor, 583.

[22] Cf. *CCG*, V, 250 (Morillon to Granvelle, 12 October 1574) with reference to the relief of Leiden: "If our people leave Holland, Haarlem will then be lost and Amsterdam will not be able to hold out for long. Once the Diemerdijk is abandoned, the enemy will get as far as Utrecht." Requesens's concern for the lines of communication is evident, inter alia, from

It was the spring of 1575 before Sonoy exploited his new opportunities. At the beginning of April 1575 he made an assault on the Barndegat, an inlet on the north bank of the IJ. He threw up an earthwork and dug through the dike to open up a passage for his galleys to the IJ from the inland waterways of North Holland.[23] At the same time he urged the Prince of Orange to launch an attack from the Southern Quarter on Ter Hart, the fortified house that dominated the locks between the IJ and the Haarlemmermeer. By seizing these two strong points, one on either side of the IJ, Sonoy hoped to make himself master of the estuary, drive the Spaniards out of Waterland, and isolate their garrison in Haarlem. But the aid from the South never arrived, partly because the States were at that moment negotiating peace terms with the Spaniards in Breda. In the meantime the towns of the Northern Quarter vacillated about sending Sonoy sufficient reinforcements. To his great rage and frustration he had to abandon his positions on the bank of the IJ for the third time.[24]

Although all Sonoy's plans had ended in failure, there was still every reason for the Spanish commanders to take the threat to their positions seriously. In previous years the army command had already devised several means to expel the rebels from the Northern Quarter. Alkmaar was the most obvious point of entry to the region. If the government army once captured the town, it could either advance eastward from it along the Huigendijk, which separated the Waarder mere from the Schermer mere, or northward across the higher ground of the Vroonlanden before turning east by Schagen and the villages of Oude- and Nieuwe Niedorp. But the Spanish siege of Alkmaar in October 1573 collapsed after Sonoy opened the sluice gates of the Zijpe, flooding the land surrounding the town and forcing the besiegers into a frantic retreat. The Spaniards could forget about besieging one of the towns on the Zuiderzee; they knew only too well that the rebels would repeat their tactic of drowning the land in case of need.[25]

---

one of the articles in his instructions to Juan Baptista de Tassis for his journey to Holland in October 1574: "Asimismo los diques y fuertes que es necesario guardar y asegurar desde Utreq hasta la Haya para que la estrada sia franca y segura yendo por Amsterdam y Harlem, y si sera necesario prevenir en esto y ganar algunos fuertes de nuevo y prevenir en esto por la mano a los enemigos." Biblioteca Francisco de Zabálburu, inv. no. 100/53.

[23] For the attack on the Barndegat see Bor, 617–20; Velius, 244–45; *DWJ*, 490; RH, 10 April 1575; *CP*, III, 312 (Requesens to the King, 10 May 1575); William of Orange to an unknown correspondent, 9 April 1575, KHA, inv. no. 1 11, XVI I 11, fol. 25; Amsterdam to Requesens, 19 April 1575 (ARAB, Aud., inv. no. 1731/3 fols. 137, 138, 144; 1715/3 (not foliated).

[24] Sonoy's fourth attempt to cut the Spanish supply lines near Muiden in May 1576 was also to be a failure, Velius, 250.

[25] See for example Caspar de Robles to Hierges, 25 May 1575, ARAB, Aud. inv. no. 1731/3, fol. 164: "vous veuillant bien avertir que si vous n'estes assurez de tous les digues,

Even without such deliberate inundations it was almost impossible for an army to enter North Holland by land. In a memorandum of 1569 on the strategic situation in Holland and Zeeland a committee set up by Alba had already given a gloomy appreciation of the region's inaccessibility. From Haarlem to Alkmaar and thence northward to Huisduinen the only possible route for cavalry was along the beach at low tide, or if need be through the dunes. If the object was to penetrate West Friesland from the belt of dunes, the countless ditches and channels that intersected the marshy meadows left only one possibility: the sea dikes. But these were so narrow that carts and wagons could only move in single file, while even horsemen could not ride in formation. The report concluded that the region was inaccessible for cavalry and wagons; only infantry could be sent there, and then only in the most extreme necessity.[26]

That left a landing from the sea as the only hope of subjugating the Northern Quarter, but this was impossible as long as the rebels controlled the sea-lanes. To break the maritime supremacy of the rebels, Philip II fitted out a gigantic armada in Spain in the summer of 1574.[27] The plan was for this fleet first to seize the island of Texel, and then to land large forces on the beaches of the Northland. But the fleet was never to leave port. When everything was ready, and only the signal to weigh anchor was awaited, the sailors and soldiers packed into the ships' holds were struck by a virulent epidemic of plague, which also carried off Admiral Pedro Menéndez. The king had no option but to call off the expedition.

In the final analysis, of course, the king's chief concern was not to free Amsterdam from its encirclement, or to secure the supply lines to his army in Holland, but to end the war, preferably by winning it. But in the autumn of 1574 the prospect of Spanish victory appeared remote. The military campaign that Alba had begun so vigorously in 1572 with the sacking of Mechelen, Zutphen, and Naarden, had become bogged down. The Spanish army had taken seven months (December 1572 to July 1573) to capture Haarlem, with heavy losses. It had then been forced to raise the siege of Alkmaar, while the government fleet had suffered a crushing defeat on the Zuiderzee, in which the rebels captured the king's Stadholder in Holland, Boussu (8 and 11 October 1573). The government knew very well that it could not defeat the rebels without a fleet, but its attempt to send an armada to the Netherlands began and ended in the harbor of

---

l'intention des rebelles est se voiants a l'extreme, les couper; ce que les pourront faire entre la susdite ville [Enkhuizen] et les Salmes [sic] et autres lieux pres de Hoorn et Medemblik en temps de trois heures et en moins de quatre jours inonder tout le Noordholland, de maniere que sans prendre ladite ville [Enkhuizen] vous ne vous en pouriez garder."

[26] "Zeeland en Holland," 159, 160, 167.

[27] Bor, 495, 523–30; Mendoça, *Commentaires*, 269–74; CCG, V, 172, 244; NHA, GNK, inv. no. 237, fols. 6v, 7v, 14; Parker, *Grand Strategy*, 139–40.

Santander (September 1574). At about the same time in the Mediterranean a Turkish fleet took the important Spanish fortress of La Goletta and the nearby city of Tunis. The Dutch rebels immediately understood the implications for their own cause of the Spanish debacle.[28] And as if that were not enough, the long drawn-out siege of Leiden ended in a fiasco. Once again the rebels cut the dikes and forced the Spaniards to retreat before the rising waters (3 October 1574). Immediately after this, a mutiny broke out in the chronically underpaid royal army, which lasted through the winter of 1574/75. The army turned its back on Holland and allowed the rebels to occupy its abandoned fortifications.

In these difficult circumstances the king was left with only two ways to end the war, and he tried both at the same time. The first was the way of negotiation.[29] The conference began in Breda in March 1575. The negotiators were able to reach agreement on many of the grievances of the Netherlands opposition, including the withdrawal of the Spanish army, but Requesens and the king would not yield on the point of freedom of religion in Holland and Zeeland. On 14 July 1575 the negotiations broke down. The second way to end the war was much grimmer. It was a counsel of despair: the total, and as it seemed permanent, destruction of Holland and Zeeland, beginning with the Northern Quarter. It was this plan for total war, strategic terror, the sixteenth-century equivalent of a modern nuclear war, that underlay Hierges's attack on the Northern Quarter.

In a letter to Requesens dated from Madrid on 22 October 1574, Philip carefully weighed the pros and cons of a plan to devastate the countryside and villages of "Waterland," by which he meant the whole peninsula of North Holland.[30] Such a scheme, the king wrote, had already been contemplated, but he had been restrained by the consideration that it was not an enemy territory but his own domains that would suffer, and he had preferred milder means. Now that they had failed he was prepared to inflict the ultimate penalty on the rebels. He could do this either by flooding the villages and the countryside or by setting them on fire. The advantages in both cases were abundantly clear, for as long as the rebels had their crops and herds, their commerce would thrive and they could pay the taxes that financed the war.

To flood Holland, turning the rebels' own tactic against them, would not present any technical problem. But such a drastic remedy had a disadvantage: once the dikes had been breached, the land would have to be written off permanently, to the detriment of the neighboring provinces.

---

[28] Parker, *Dutch Revolt*, 165–66; Bor, 572.
[29] Janssens, *Brabant*, 230–54; Fruin, "Prins Willem in onderhandeling."
[30] *CP*, III, 174–77; Waxman, "Strategic terror"; Parker, *Army of Flanders*, 134–35; Parker, *Grand Strategy*, 136–38.

"For all things considered, one may say that Holland at present is a dike that protects all the other provinces, and that if Holland were flooded, the other provinces would be exposed to manifest danger and forced to build their own dikes; and before they are built their territory will undoubtedly be lost." What was more, the idea had a "certain character of cruelty," which would damage the reputation of the Spaniards.[31]

Fire was open to none of these objections. The king believed that fire was a regular weapon of war. It could always be put out again. It was not so impossible to defend oneself against as water. If the villages and crops were burned, the soil would recover in time. With his characteristic enthusiasm, excited by the possibilities of the plan, the king expected success. In fear of going up in flames with the villages, the towns would make haste to capitulate. Deprived of their food supply—cattle, grain, hay, butter, fruit, and fish—the rebels would surrender of their own accord rather than starve to death. Even on the seas they would be ruined, because they would have no provisions to feed their ships' crews. Foreign states would cease their aid to the rebels, for who would have any reason to set foot in Holland once its trade was ruined? The only disadvantage that attached to this panacea was that Philip might lose the esteem of his good Netherlands vassals who had families, friends, and property in Holland, and perhaps even of the whole population. He would just have to accept this.

At the end of his letter Philip instructed Requesens to weigh all the arguments for and against and to make his decision accordingly. If threats no longer sufficed, he must invade Waterland with a force of ten to twelve thousand men and burn the villages and countryside to ashes. He must then make it clear to the rest of Holland that the same fate was in store for it. Fear might make the rebels reconsider. The best time to put the plan into effect would be at the first frost, when the ditches were frozen. Until then Requesens was to keep the plan top secret.

Requesens replied on 9 November. Given the mass evacuation of Holland by his mutinous army, he had in fact ordered his commanders in the field to breach the dikes, provided they were certain that most of the towns in rebel hands would be hit, but that Amsterdam and Haarlem would not suffer any damage.[32] The military leadership on the spot, however, had not seen much advantage in this plan. Hierges, a Netherlander himself, had announced that he could only support the cutting of the dikes if it would win the war, but that was not the case. The water would undoubtedly inflict heavy damage on the rebels and leave the area occupied by the royal army unharmed, but many of the rebel towns in Holland

---

[31] CP, III, 174–77.
[32] CP, III, 191.

would survive and would never be reconquered. Moreover, it was to be feared that in reprisal the Zeelanders would cut the dikes of Flanders, causing enormous devastation in that area and around Antwerp. This was the dilemma of mutual strategic deterrence in a sixteenth-century and peculiarly Netherlands context.

Even the loyal towns, for obvious reasons, were unenthusiastic.[33] The burgomasters of Amsterdam predicted that the North Holland towns, protected from the rising waters by their walls, would supply themselves with food from the Baltic, even after the countryside was under water. In the meantime, once the Spanish army had definitively moved out, the rebels would cut off Amsterdam and Haarlem from Utrecht and starve them into submission. The burgomasters proposed a better plan: a permanent military occupation of the countryside of North Holland. That would deprive the rebels of their revenue from taxes on dairy products and cattle, and also of the recruits who manned their fleet. An invasion would be possible in a hard frost or over open water in spring. Once the countryside was occupied, a way would have to be found to stop food supplies reaching Hoorn and Enkhuizen, so that the blockade of the Zuiderzee could be broken. The capture of the towns themselves, however, would remain impossible as long as the government was powerless at sea.[34]

Although there was a hard frost for a time in January 1575, nothing came of these plans then. The Spanish army was still mutinous and did not return to its colors until 3 March 1575,[35] after the chance to invade the Northern Quarter had already passed. But the king's plan still appeared to be relevant.

In the spring of 1575 the Spanish high command decided to adopt scorched-earth tactics. Shortly after Hierges had driven Sonoy away from the Barndegat, Requesens wrote to the king that the stadholder could have scored an even greater success if he had been able to carry out his orders "to burn the whole countryside up to the gates of Enkhuizen and Hoorn."[36] The preparations for such an expedition were under way. Requesens was discussing a new campaign with his advisers in Antwerp, but the counselors were divided. The Netherlanders among them urged him to be content with quartering troops on the villages, while the Spaniards

---

[33] *CCG*, V, 512.

[34] Cf. *CCG*, V, 508, Nicolas Polweiller to Requesens, 28 October 1574, for a similar view: "Il convient faire de grandz dégastz sur cest hyver, icy principalement au Waterlande sitost que la gelée viendra, assavoir ruyner tout le pays, villaiges, demeurances et batteaulx, joignans aux villes rebelles. Car c'est l'une des principales forces de l'ennemy. Et sans lesdicts villaiges c'est peu de leur forces, mesme en la marine. Avant toutes les choses le meilleur serait de faire l'entreprise d'Einchuisen."

[35] *CP*, III, 267.

[36] Ibid., III, 312.

and Italians argued for burning the whole country and putting to the sword everyone who fell into their hands. Requesens preferred the advice of the latter and gave Hierges orders to act accordingly.[37]

Such an invasion would be far from simple. Since 1572 Sonoy had transformed the Northern Quarter into a heavily defended stronghold, which would be difficult to capture. Nevertheless, the most important means of defense that Sonoy and the rebels possessed still lay in the natural features of the country. The rebels had ensconced themselves behind a wide water line, which extended from the flooded Zijpe polder in the north along the small River Rekere to Alkmaar, along the Schermer mere, the River Zaan, the Wormer and Purmer meres, reaching the Zuiderzee near Monnickendam. This meant they had abandoned large parts of North Holland to the Spaniards: the tract of sandy soil behind the dunes in Kennemer, and the southern flank of the Zaan area and Waterland.

Without ships the Spaniards had no chance of seizing the water barrier, but in the winter there would be nothing to stop them crossing the frozen lines, and a hard frost on the meadows would lay the country open to a large-scale military operation. To avert the threat of an invasion across the ice, in the early and hard winter of 1572/73 Sonoy mobilized the peasants of North Holland to cut a channel in the ice along the entire water line from Petten to Monnickendam.[38] The following winter, 1573/74, was mild, ruling out the Spanish plan for an invasion over the ice. Throughout the winter they kept horses shod with iron and sledges specially made for the occasion in readiness. When it froze for a few days in February 1574 they immediately crossed the frozen water line and took the village of Wormer.[39]

In January 1575 there was another hard frost, but because the Spanish army was still crippled by mutiny, the North Hollanders had little to fear. A few freebooters from the Spanish army appeared on skates before Graft, but were chased away by the inhabitants of Schermer island.[40] Sonoy's ordinance of 16 January 1575 to cut another channel in the ice shows what a massive undertaking this was.[41] The channel was not to be less than forty-two feet wide; each village was told exactly how many men, horses, and sledges it had to supply and what output was expected of it. Schagen for example had to provide 250 men and cut a channel of 1,125 rods in length; Barsingerhorn and Haringhuizen supplied 202 men for

---

[37] Ibid., III, 315.
[38] Velius, 198.
[39] Ibid., 235.
[40] Ibid., 243; Bor, 616.
[41] Bor, 616–17; see also NHA, GNK, inv. no. 237, fol. 129, 13 January 1575.

909 rods; Sint Maarten and Valkoog 159 men for 716 rods, and so on.[42] The village sheriffs had to conduct the peasants to the designated sites, equipped with banners, drums, arms, and food for several days. Anyone who shirked his duty to cut the ice would have his house burned down and be treated as an enemy of the country.

The villages must have been left almost entirely without their menfolk during this digging campaign. On 21 January 1575 the States of North Holland warned Sonoy that no watch was being kept in the villages along the Zuiderzee shore, because they were empty of people. These villages were now in grave danger of a sudden invasion; the Zuiderzee was frozen hard, so that the Spaniards could cross it on horses and sledges.[43] It goes without saying that the authorities could fall back on their experience in dike maintenance, in which each peasant who owned land was responsible for the upkeep of a particular section of dike.[44]

The most important gateways to the region under rebel control were Alkmaar in the west and Purmerend in the south. Alkmaar, which was regarded as "a fortress for the whole of North Holland," had modern bulwarks on its southern and western walls.[45] Purmerend, strategically situated on the canal that linked the Purmer, the Beemster, and the Wormer, was also provided with earth ramparts and bastions on its southern side.

Sonoy also had sconces built at seven points along the line of defense: at Petten on the secondary dike in the rear of the Hondsbosse Zeewering, at Krabbendam, Schoorldam, on the Rekerdijk, the Galgendijk, and on the River Zaan near Het Kalf.[46] A sconce was a fort that consisted of a breastwork enclosed on all four or more sides by earthworks. The earth required to build it was dug out of the surrounding moat, or if necessary carried in wicker baskets from the neighboring farmland. Each sconce had a drawbridge, a gate, a house for the officers, and simple shelters of palings and reeds for a few hundred men. The great sconce at Het Kalf on the Zaan was hexagonal in shape and had two moats on the landward side, the inner one being very wide and deep. On the outer moat there was a counterscarp, or defensive wall, four or five feet high. Within the sconce there were four or five rows of houses, and a start had been made

---

[42] The Alkmaar rod measured 12 Dutch feet (11 English feet) or 3.35 meters, Verhoeff, *Oude Nederlandse maten*, 2.

[43] NHA, GNK, inv. no. 237, fol. 132v, 21 January 1575.

[44] Van der Woude, *Noorderkwartier*, 41.

[45] Cited in Foreest, *Cort verhael*, 4.

[46] Bor, 478; Geus, "Schansen." During the siege of Alkmaar, Sonoy had also had sconces built on the Huigendijk near Rustenburg and at Broek op Langedijk (Bor, 452). In May 1574 a sconce near Ilpendam was proposed (Bor, 496).

on building a round tower, which however was never completed.[47] Most sconces were to be found in the north between Alkmaar and Petten, where the water line was narrower than elsewhere. The central fortress at Schoorldam was the most important of the sconces erected here. To complete the defensive line Sonoy had an earth breastwork built on the Rekerdijk and six watch posts erected between Alkmaar and Krabbendam.[48]

The defense of these lines was entrusted to the companies of soldiers quartered in North Holland, supplemented by companies of civic militia and the local peasantry. The core of the defensive force was rather grandly named the North Holland Regiment, but in practice it consisted of an indeterminate number of mercenary companies of varying size and composition.[49] We are not well informed about the size of these forces. Muster rolls have survived for thirty-one North Holland companies for the period 1572–77, but they were not all in existence at the same time. In November 1573, shortly after the Spanish army had abandoned the siege of Alkmaar but had also occupied most of Waterland, the companies were divided between the towns, with Hoorn, Alkmaar, Enkhuizen, Medemblik, and Edam each receiving two companies of three hundred men (on paper), and Monnickendam and Purmerend one each.[50] The remaining companies were moved to the threatened southern front. Ilpendam, Purmerland, and the sconce at Het Kalf each received one company, while Krommenie, Krommeniedijk, Wormer, and Westzaan shared four between them. In all, nineteen companies were quartered in North Holland.

At the time of mustering each company had an average strength of 175 men. At first they were larger, but later they were reduced in size. Each company was commanded by a captain, who was assisted by a lieutenant and a troop leader, and some junior officers and other specialists, such as drummers, a piper, a forager, a barber-surgeon, a provost (responsible for maintaining discipline), and in one or two cases a field preacher. Most of the ordinary soldiers were armed with arquebuses and pikes, and a smaller number with muskets, halbards, and swords. The captains of the companies that served in North Holland included a fairly large number of former Sea Beggars. Only a few captains came from the nobility, and a few from the well-off citizenry.

Apart from their names and places of origin, little is known about the rank and file. It is striking that in many cases they were recruited in the region itself. Of the 4,960 soldiers whose origin is known, 1,440 (roughly three in ten) came from North Holland north of the River IJ, compared

---

[47] Van der Aa, *Aardrijkskundig woordenboek*, s.v. Het Kalf.
[48] Geus, "Schansen," 132.
[49] Wijn, "Noordhollandse regiment," 245.
[50] Velius, 231.

with only 250 from the Southern Quarter and Zeeland. Most of the soldiers came from the northern provinces, with a remarkable number of Friesians (850). Apart from about 700 Germans there were few foreigners. The company of Claes Gijsbrechtszoon Aker, which was mustered on 1 August 1572, numbered 309 men in all, 192 of them North Hollanders, while in other companies Friesians predominated.

A few companies were quartered in the towns immediately after the outbreak of the Revolt of 1572, to help them defend themselves against the expected assault from the government army, but also to make sure that they did not forsake William of Orange's cause. The townsfolk had strong objections to the quartering of the troops, all the more so because in several towns, such as Enkhuizen and Hoorn, it was opposition to the quartering of government troops that had provoked them into revolt in the first place. In practice the companies were often quartered in the surrounding villages, where they were a grievous burden on the peasant population.[51] The soldiers, whose pay was often in arrears, preyed on the peasantry, and although the villagers could submit claims for compensation to the States, they rarely received any payment.

Professional soldiers looked down on the peasantry. The military revolution of the sixteenth century had led to a decline in the importance of the cavalry, made up of heavily armed noblemen, but it had also reduced the role of the armed peasantry as an element of the defensive force. Even so, all early modern armies continued to be largely dependent on the local peasants, though rarely on their capacity to bear arms. For quartering, foraging, and the performance of all manner of labor services, the peasants remained indispensable. Besides using them to keep open the frozen canals and meres, Sonoy also drew heavily on the locally available peasant labor force for the building of sconces and other fortifications. The inhabitants of the villages in the Zeevang were required to work every day in the spring of 1574 on the ramparts of Purmerend.[52] The peasants were also compelled to keep watch. A troop of Amsterdammers who appeared with ten boats before the dike between Hoorn and Enkhuizen in January 1575 did not dare to go on shore, because "the peasants were on the dikes in good numbers."[53]

With only a few companies of mercenaries at his disposal, Sonoy was forced to rely heavily on the military capacities of the local population to defend the Northern Quarter. This was not a new burden for them. When

---

[51] Ibid., 200; Wijn, "Noordhollandse regiment," 245.

[52] NHA, Archief Ruychaver, inv. nos. 89, 91, 99. The work was generally awarded to a local contractor and paid for by the villages that were considered to be protected by the sconce in question. Geus, "Schansen," 130–31.

[53] Bor, 616.

the countryside of North Holland was suffering from the raids of the Sea Beggars in 1571, Boussu had also entrusted its defense to the local peasantry, though with little success. The peasants had offered little resistance to the Beggars but denied passage to the Spanish soldiers sent to prevent the landings. Sonoy had also used armed peasants in the capture of Alkmaar.

To mobilize the peasantry Sonoy could fall back on an old tradition.[54] In the Middle Ages, in time of war, both the nobles and the ordinary peasants who did not possess fiefs had to perform military service. In Holland the military organization of the peasantry reflected the province's traditional maritime role. The country had long been divided into *ambachten* and these in turn into *koggen*; the inhabitants of each *kogge* had to supply a *heerkogge* (an oar-powered war galley for service on the inland waterways) with its crew and equipment. The *koggen* were further subdivided into *riemtalen*, their number being equal to the number of men that could be called up for military service.[55] This custom had fallen into disuse under the rule of the Burgundians, although in emergencies the tocsin was rung to call out the *lantwere*—every man who could bear arms. Whenever a dike was breached a "dike army" was similarly raised. During the feuds of the Hoeks and the Kabeljauws in the fifteenth century the peasants had also resorted to armed force.

Although the king had ordered Requesens to keep his sinister plans strictly secret, the report of the imminent campaign raced ahead of the army. "The enemy is informed of everything that happens in the council," Requesens complained to Philip on 16 April 1575, "either by the counselors themselves or by third parties to whom they report."[56] As early as 28 April, a day after Hierges had driven the North Hollanders from the Barndegat, William of Orange sent a warning to Sonoy, the States of the Northern Quarter, and Alkmaar, that "the enemy with all his force of people and also with a great quantity of artillery and a multitude of sconce diggers' planned to invade Holland, as he believed, to besiege Alkmaar.[57] The Spaniards were said to have taken on four hundred pioneers, to be fitting out ships in Antwerp, Amsterdam, and Harlingen, and to be gathering twelve thousand men to attack the Northern Quarter simultaneously

---

[54] Jansen and Hoppenbrouwers, "Heervaart"; De Graaf, *Oorlog*.

[55] De Goede, *Swannotsrecht*, 26, 31; De Goede, "Westfriesche grondwet," 641; De Graaf, *Oorlog*, 219.

[56] *CP*, III, 310.

[57] William of Orange to Sonoy, the States of the Northern Quarter and Alkmaar, 28 April 1575, KHA, inv. no. A 11, XIV 11, fols. 41v–2v. A few days later the prince feared a new siege of Leiden, RHG, 1 May 1575.

on three fronts.[58] Wouter Jacobszoon also wrote on 28 April that it was believed in Amsterdam that Hierges would invade the Northland.[59]

These reports caused feverish activity in North Holland. To keep the enemy out of the country Sonoy relied on the trusted methods of water, the sconces, the soldiers, and the armed peasants and townsmen. The water line was at its narrowest north of Alkmaar, along the little River Rekere. By breaching the sea dike in the north near the flooded Zijpe polder, and by cutting the Galgendijk in the south, Sonoy let the waters pour in from two sides at once. This left the sconces at Krabbendam and Schoorl and those along the Rekerdijk in the middle of a wider water line, and also inundated part of the Geestmerambacht. Sonoy also had the neglected sconces along this northern defensive line repaired.[60] Alkmaar took in another company of soldiers, and fifty men were hurriedly sent to reinforce the sconce at Het Kalf. In case of need, Hoorn and Enkhuizen would send their garrisons to the west. At Alkmaar a stock of munitions, weapons, and provisions was laid in to withstand a long siege. At Huiswaard, north of Alkmaar, huts of wooden planks and reeds were built to house the additional soldiers.[61]

Help was also on its way from Holland south of the IJ. At the end of May, while Hierges was assembling his forces in Beverwijk, and it was becoming obvious that he would attack North Holland, the Prince of Orange proposed to the States of Holland that he himself should leave for the Northern Quarter with eight or nine companies, to help in its defense. Such an expedition was not without risk, for an attack on South Holland was still a possibility, and in that case the companies would be needed in the South.[62] In the end the help from the South never material-

---

[58] Bor, 620. Twelve thousand men was also the number that Philip had suggested to Requesens in his letter of 22 October 1574, *CP*, III, 174–77.

[59] *DWJ*, 492; cf. above, p. 3.

[60] "Memoire touchant l'estat du pays d'Hollande" in "Onuitgegeven brieven Berlaimont," 291; Bor, 620; *RH*, 29 May 1575; NHA, GNK, inv. no. 236, 23 April and 24 May 1575; Sonoy to William of Orange, 25 August 1574, KHA inv. no. A 11, XIV C, S 29.

[61] Vroedschap resolution 2 May 1575, RAA, SA Alkmaar, inv. no. 92, fol. 234v; NHA, GNK, inv. no. 236, 24 May 1575.

[62] *RH*, 26 and 29 May 1585. The Spaniards too were unaware of the true intention of the campaign and believed the expedition was a diversionary maneuver. Mendoça wrote that the army remained at Beverwijk "to put fear into the rebels and to tempt them to withdraw their garrisons from [South] Holland and to reinforce the places in Waterland, because they believed that our men wanted to besiege some places there." Mendoça, *Commentaires*, 295. Pietge Pieterszoon Joncx, a native of Nibbixwoud who had left his village and served in Hierges's cavalry, later declared that he had not known the purpose of the campaign in the Northern Quarter, but had afterward understood that it was to draw soldiers out of South Holland, as the later capture of Schoonhoven and Oudewater showed. Statement of the burgomasters of Hoorn, 25 October 1577, NA, Hof, inv. no. 4592 (1577).

88 • Chapter Five

ized, because after his raid on the North Hierges returned to Beverwijk and then, as the States had feared, transferred the war to South Holland.

Sonoy counted on the armed peasantry as well as on the soldiers. In an ordinance on the watch issued on 9 May he organized their mobilization.[63] Watch houses were to be built at regular intervals around the entire rebel-held district, both along the water line and the sea dikes, equipped with signal masts from which a sail or a basket could be hoisted by day and a fire beacon by night. This would enable a report of an invasion to be passed rapidly across the region and troops sent to the place threatened. The village sheriffs were instructed to raise a specific number of villagers to man the watch at these posts. Each village was given a precise quota of men to stand watch at each post, the night watch being manned by three or four times more men than the day watch. The better-off peasants had to equip themselves with a firearm, gunpowder, lead, and fuses; the less well off had to bring a good pike or a long two-pronged pitchfork with a sidearm (a sword) or a sharp axe on their belt. The numerous Anabaptists, whose faith forbade them to bear arms, had to report with spades and baskets to be put to work digging fortifications. The peasants were ordered to bring enough food for three days and nights, after which they would be relieved by a fresh guard from their home village. Sonoy also paid particular attention to the weakly defended Rekere line. While most of the watch houses were manned by no more than a few dozen villagers, he sent more than two hundred men to Krabbendam and Schoorldam, where he expected Hierges's invasion.

On 6 May Requesens drew up detailed orders, in which he described precisely what Hierges was to do in the North.[64] He claimed that the inhabitants had richly deserved their punishment, for they had not only been the first to rise in revolt against the king, but most of them had been avowed heretics long before the people of the rest of Holland and Zeeland had forsaken the old faith. They clung so stubbornly and obdurately to their false religious convictions that it was futile to hope for their submission.

The timing of the invasion was intended to cause the failure of the hay harvest. The most important source of the Northern Quarter's prosperity, according to Requesens, was the grass on which the cattle lived summer and winter. The cattle yielded so much milk, butter, and cheese that the Quarter supplied Holland, Zeeland, and the adjoining provinces. This in turn enabled the rebels to levy taxes to finance the war. Hierges did not

---

[63] Bor, 621–23.
[64] Recuerdo de lo que execute mossiur de Hierges luego que vuelva a Utrecht por importar mucho al servicio de su md. Instituto de Valencia de Don Juan, Caja 93, envío 68, C, fols. 5–8.

need to hold the countryside later than mid-June. Once the first rains had spoiled the hay crop and ruined the chief source of the rebels' income, the war was half won.

Requesens left the choice of the actual point of entry of the Northern Quarter to Hierges's strategic insight. Because the governor estimated that the rebels could not raise more than 2,000 infantrymen and 150 cavalry, and these would be mostly "very wretched people" ("gente muy ruin"), it would be sufficient for Hierges to take nine companies in active service in the field under Valdéz, in all 1,200 to 1,300 men, reinforced by 1,800 Spaniards on garrison duty. Besides these 3,000 elite Spanish troops, he could also dispose of 1,200 Dutch and Walloons, divided into five companies of cavalry, three companies of arquebusiers, and two of pikemen.[65] He was to lead this force as far as possible in the direction of Hoorn, Enkhuizen, and Medemblik, while leaving a detachment to cover his rear against a possible sortie from Alkmaar. The cattle in the pastures were to be seized and transported to the rear.

The invasion force was not to be content to inflict only the damage usual in wartime; it was to leave not a man alive, not a house standing, "to wipe out the memory of such an unfortunate people." The orders said not a word about the possibility of help from pro-Spanish elements among the population.

On 10 May, Hierges was in Antwerp to receive his marching orders. A week later he was in Utrecht, which he left for Amsterdam on the 23rd. On 25 May he reached Amstelveen, and from there he made his way to Beverwijk, where his troops had already assembled on 24 May.[66] The force was much smaller than the ten or twelve thousand men the king had previously recommended. It had no heavy artillery, since it was not the intention to besiege any of the rebel towns.

Although his marching orders said nothing about them, it seems that there were plans for Hierges's expedition to be accompanied by seaborne landings. It was said that fifty flatboats had been loaded onto wagons and taken to the beach at Wijk aan Zee, ready to carry out landings near

---

[65] For the size of Hierges's expeditionary force see Mendoça, *Commentaires*, 295, and Bor, 623 (nine companies of infantry from the regiment of Don Fernando de Toledo and nine from the regiment of Valdéz, as well as "some" "German" and Walloon companies and cavalry). The States of Holland estimated the invasion force at 3,000 infantry and 125 cavalry (*RH*, 1 July 1575). The estimate made by the Beggar poet, of 6,000 foot and 700 horsemen, is exaggerated (*Geuzenliedboek*, 246). A company of Spanish infantry on paper numbered 250 men (Parker, *Army of Flanders*, 274) but according to a "summary statement of the King's troops in the Netherlands" of January 1575 (*CP*, III, 245–47), the eleven companies of Don Fernando de Toledo's regiment in reality numbered 1,100 men, and the twelve of Valdéz 1,000 men.

[66] *CP*, III, 315; several letters from Hierges to Requesens and Berty, ARAB, Aud., 1731/3, fols. 163–86.

Petten.⁶⁷ A landing led by the Stadholder of Friesland, Caspar de Robles, was also contemplated. Robles wanted to use small shallow-draft peat boats to land artillery on the dike at Broekerhaven south of Enkhuizen at dawn, with the aim of taking Enkhuizen by surprise. Hierges's correspondence with Requesens reveals that he was highly skeptical of this idea. "The Lord of Billy [Caspar de Robles] has written to me about the means that he has to assist us in North Holland . . . they are all impossible means, as Your Excellency will hear from those who know the country better than I do."⁶⁸ Evidently Hierges managed to convince Requesens, for the landings never took place.

Even without a risky invasion across the Zuiderzee, Hierges had enough to preoccupy him. He knew that the badly paid Spanish army, always on the brink of mutiny, had little chance of breaking through the defensive lines of North Holland. "Tomorrow all the men of war arrive in Beverwijk" Hierges wrote on 23 May to Requesens, "and the day after tomorrow they will march on the rebel-held region. There are more difficulties attached to this than those who proposed this undertaking to Your Excellency represented to You. I shall do what is humanly possible."⁶⁹

The Spanish army had a reputation as the most formidable fighting force in sixteenth-century Europe, but it had one weak point: it was very rarely paid. Apart from the rebels in the North, Spain was almost continually at war with the Ottoman Turks in the Mediterranean. Philip gave the Turkish war priority. His income from American silver was far from adequate to maintain a war on two fronts for such a long time. Ultimately, the financial weakness of the Spanish monarchy was the most important reason for the king's failure to win his war against the Dutch rebels.⁷⁰

These financial problems were the constant refrain of the letters Hierges wrote to Requesens almost every day during his campaign. On 25 May he wrote from Amstelveen: "The confusion in which I find myself here, without money in the midst of all these fighting men, forces me to write once again to Your Excellency, humbly begging you to provide a remedy,

---

⁶⁷ Bor, 620.

⁶⁸ Hierges to Requesens, 22 May 1575, with copy of missive from Robles to Hierges, incorrectly dated 25 May 1575 (15 May?), ARAB, Aud., inv. no. 1731/3, fols. 163–64. See also Bor, 620: Edam and Monnickendam warn Sonoy that the enemy intends to land four or five thousand men between Medemblik and Enkhuizen.

⁶⁹ Hierges to Requesens, Amsterdam, 23 May 1575, ARAB, Aud., inv. no. 1731/3, fol. 182: "Les gens de guerre arriveront tous demain a Beverwyck, et marcheront apres demain au pays occupé par les ennemys, et pour ce faire se trouve trop plus de difficulté, que ceux qui ont mis a votre excellence ceste entreprise en avant ne luy ont representé. Ce que humainement se peult faire se ferat, et ne fauldray journellement d'en avertir votre excellence."

⁷⁰ Parker, *Army of Flanders*, 139–57, 231–68.

and not to leave me thus in the lurch, otherwise I shall be forced to break up the army and let it turn back."⁷¹ On 6 June he wrote from the camp at Beverwijk: "I cannot omit to represent to Your Excellency once more that if you do not send the necessary sums to maintain the men of war each month, they will one of these days abandon their position, and the rage of hunger will ensure that they will tear me to pieces."⁷²

On 27 May, Hierges led his small force of unpaid, hungry, grumbling, and unruly troops out of the camp at Beverwijk to the North.⁷³ In Schoorl he left the infantry behind and rode ahead with the cavalry to the secondary dike north of Groet. Hierges could now see for himself that the country was inundated and the sconces in good repair and manned with soldiers and armed peasants. With his small invasion force he could achieve nothing. There may have been a few minor skirmishes, but they cannot have been very important.⁷⁴ Hierges had no choice but to abandon his expedition and return to base. Some time later Requesens wrote to Hierges, giving his opinion that the expedition had failed because the force was too small; he wished him success with the capture of Schoonhoven and concluded that an invasion of Holland was off the agenda unless a larger army could be assembled.⁷⁵

While the infantry in Schoorl awaited the return of Hierges and the cavalry, they amused themselves by pillaging and burning some houses and a corn mill at Schoorl. The flames of the burning mill were visible for miles around. The rebels behind the Rekere line were to draw completely mistaken conclusions from this sight, with far-reaching consequences.

---

⁷¹ Hierges to Requesens, Amstelveen 25 May 1575, ARAB, Aud., inv no. 1731/3, fol. 184: "La confusion en laquelle je me trouve icy sans argent au milieu de tous ces gens de guerre me cause de rechief escripre ceste a votre excellence et la supplier très humblement y vouloir pourvoir de remède sans me laisser ainsy a l'habbandon, aultrement je serai constrainct de separer tous les gens de guerre, et les laisser retourner."

⁷² Hierges to Requesens, Beverwijk, 6 June 1575, ARAB, Aud., inv. no. 1731/3, fol. 188: "Ne puis laisser derechief de remonstre a votre excellence que si elle ne renvoie tous les mois la somme qu'il convient pour les secours des gens de guerre qui sont par ici ordinaires, que ung de ces iours d'une part sans nulle doubte ils abandonneront les forts et d'aultre la rage de faing causera qu'ils me mectront en piece. Car ne vois qu'ils perdent la patience et la respect disants que ie ne fais que les entretenir de parolles. La suppliant très humblement que vouloir remedier."

⁷³ Unfortunately no report on this undertaking is to be found in Hierges's correspondence. On 29 May he sent his lieutenant Tambergen to Requesens to report in person: Hierges to Berty, Beverwijk 29 May 1575, ARAB, Aud., inv. no. 1731/3, fol. 186. There is a brief account of this mission in Bor, 623.

⁷⁴ On 10 June Captain Michiel Samplon at the sconce in Schoorldam approved an account that mentioned a payment to a boatman for bringing to Hoorn two soldiers "who had been shot by the enemy." Geus, "Schansen," 133.

⁷⁵ Requesens to Hierges, 31 August 1575, Biblioteca Francisco de Zabálburu, inv. no. 1004/49: "y que despues no se quedase en Olanda sin un buen golpe de gente suelta."

Hierges and his men returned to Beverwijk, where he spent two weeks in camp. That was the end of his ill-starred expedition to North Holland.

From Beverwijk, Hierges moved on via Utrecht to the small town of Buren, which had no modern fortifications to defend it. After it fell to a siege,[76] the soldiers plundered the buildings, while the population, which had taken refuge in the castle, surrendered in exchange for freedom to leave. Hierges then laid siege to Oudewater.[77] This small town was taken by storm on 7 August after fierce resistance, sacked and burned. Virtually the whole population was slaughtered. About twenty citizens still found alive were ransomed; some who could not raise the money were put to death, a few had their ransoms paid by others. Pieter Bor relates how his brother-in-law, who had come from Utrecht to witness the storming of the town, paid two *daalders* for a girl named Anna, who had been shot in the leg and who remained in his service for some time afterward.

It cannot have been long before the reports of the bloodbath in Oudewater penetrated to North Holland, perhaps through the Beggar song that was devoted to this event.[78] In any case not much imagination was required to envisage what the consequences would have been if Hierges had succeeded in breaking through the defenses of the Northern Quarter. In the meantime the North Hollanders' attention was turned elsewhere. The sudden departure of Hierges was a mystery to them; why had he first assembled a force in Beverwijk and then done nothing with it? Why had he not attacked the sconces? Could there have been treachery involved?

---

[76] Bor, 643–44.
[77] Ibid., 644–46
[78] *Geuzenliedboek*, I, 251–52 (no. 109).

CHAPTER SIX

# Treason

REPORTS REACHING the Northern Quarter in May of the year 1575 suggested that the advance of the Spanish army was not the only threat. Warnings poured in from all corners that treason was afoot. Sonoy's right-hand man Willem Baerdesen, or Bardesius, received an alarming letter from Amsterdam. It claimed that "vagabonds and enemies" planned to burn the villages of North Holland as soon as the Spanish army appeared before the sconces. When they saw the fires, the peasants who had been pressed into service to defend the country would leave their posts and hurry to protect their homes and farms. The Spanish army would then be able to enter North Holland unopposed.[1] The magistrates of Hoorn, Edam, and Monnickendam wrote to Sonoy with similar warnings. They had heard that "certain vagabonds, being foreigners," were roaming the Northland waiting to set fire to the villages on the enemy's orders.[2] The plot was said to be led by a certain "Colonel" Pieter van Hoef, and the plotters were alleged to wear "red silk ribbons" on their clothing to be recognized by the enemy.[3] Pieter van Hoef was no figment of their imagination but the captain of a Beggar company, which was quartered in Grootebroek and had been sent to Alkmaar in July 1573. Later this company was disbanded, and Van Hoef lived in Hoorn. But no one had seen him since the rumors of treason began to circulate, and that alone was highly suspect.[4] How far these reports had any basis in truth is not relevant now; the point is that the authorities believed them.

Sonoy did not hesitate for a moment. On 25 May he sent out a circular letter ordering all the sheriffs in the countryside to read out a proclamation at 8 a.m. "to the sound of the tocsin," forbidding the people to shelter "strangers, unknown persons or those who have come from the country

---

[1] *RH*, 1 June 1575. According to the resolution of the States of Holland this letter was dated 25 April, but the States probably meant 25 May, because they refer later to "an edict of the 27th of the same" [month]; this can only mean the ordinance of 27 May discussed below. Bor, 623, and NHA, GNK, inv. no. 236, 27 May 1575.

[2] Bor, 620, 24 May 1575.

[3] *Geuzenliedboek*, I, 246–49.

[4] Note of the cost of feeding the soldiers quartered in Grootebroek, 1572–73, 1576, WFA, OA Grootebroek, inv. no. 765; "Rekening Maerten Ruychaver," 81; *Brieven en andere bescheiden*, 51; Velius, 246. Also Wouter Jacobszoon had heard that "certain Beggar captains" wanted to deliver the sconces to the enemy. *DWJ*, 500.

of the enemy."[5] Above all "those who had left this country," the so-called *glippers*, or sneakers, were suspects. Sonoy made an exception for those who could show a current passport issued not more than three weeks earlier, but the sheriffs had to make sure that these papers were not forged. Anyone who gave shelter to a foreigner must report him to the authorities at once, on pain of death on the gallows.

The proclamation was immediately followed by mass house-to-house searches throughout the Northern Quarter. Assisted by the village magistrates the sheriffs searched all the houses in their districts to the sound of the tocsin bell on 28 May. All the strangers they found were arrested and held in the churches.[6] The villagers were obliged to cooperate in these searches "on pain of fire," that is, the burning of their houses and goods.

By chance, the ordinance against the strangers was proclaimed on the very Friday that Hierges's invasion force appeared before the sconces on the Rekere line. It is hardly surprising therefore that many interpreted the burning of the corn mill at Schoorl, which was seen for miles around, as a signal from the Spaniards: their army had arrived, and it was now time for the conspirators to act. Only Sonoy's decisive intervention, so it seemed, had foiled the plot. The enemy evidently realized that its plan had failed, and returned empty-handed to Beverwijk.

When the house searches were completed, it appeared that the authorities had arrested more than twenty "vagabonds, vagrants and beggars," called *kalissen* in North Holland. They were taken on wagons to Sonoy's headquarters in Alkmaar.[7]

The Prince of Orange was delighted. He wrote to Sonoy to congratulate him on his "particular zeal and good diligence," and encouraged him to proceed vigorously with the questioning and punishment of the fire raisers. That would be an exemplary deterrent to anyone who might contemplate such action in the future.[8] He urged him above all to find out

[5] Sonoy to the sheriffs of the Northern Quarter, 25 May 1575, Bor, 623; see also the relevant Resolution of the States of the Northern Quarter, NHA, GNK, inv. no. 236, 24 May 1575.

[6] The churches are named in *RH*, 1 June 1575.

[7] *DWJ*, 501, 4 June 1575: Wouter Jacobszoon reports that in Alkmaar seven wagons of "Beggar soldiers" had been brought in. Register of extraordinary expenditure of the burgomasters, 1574–75, WFA, OA Hoorn, inv. no. 2498; 1 June 1575, paid to Dirrick Puthaeck and Claes Dijckgraeff each two guilders ten stuivers for riding to Alkmaar with "Master Joost and his vagabonds"; 27 July 1575, paid to Claes Dijckgraeff thirty-six stuivers for riding to Alkmaar with a vagabond. See also 25 May 1575, to Heynrick Schoorstienveeger ("chimney sweep") twelve stuivers, for going to the governor in Alkmaar with a missive about the vagabonds who roam the country; 26 May to the same, fourteen stuivers for going to the peacemakers in the neighboring villages to warn them to stay in their villages and keep a good watch for vagabonds; 17 June to the same, ten stuivers for going to Enkhuizen to warn them to keep a good watch.

[8] William of Orange to Sonoy, 6 June 1575, KHA, inv. no. A 11, XIV I 11, fols. 61–61v.

exactly what the enemy's intentions had been. The prince also expressed his satisfaction with the good will and courage of the North Holland peasants, and advised Sonoy to

> always animate them therein more and more, and hold out to them the freedom of their fatherland; and that the Spaniards seek nothing else than to make away with them and all their property, and besides to bring and keep them and their wives and children in intolerable and perpetual slavery.

Sonoy hardly needed this advice from the prince. The day before William of Orange wrote to him, he had already set up a special commission of inquiry to get to the bottom of the matter.

The members of this body derived their authority from a letter of commission that Sonoy drew up on 5 June, and from which they took their title of "commissioner." It is worth examining this document in more detail.[9] The letter states that Diederik Sonoy, in his capacity as lieutenant and governor of North Holland and Waterland and commander of the army for the Stadholder and captain-general of Holland, Zeeland, and Utrecht, Prince William of Orange, had learned that "diverse traitors, arsonists and others" had plotted to burn the whole Northern Quarter. He therefore authorized four persons "sharply to examine" the delinquents who were already in custody or would later be arrested, and to record their confessions in writing. If necessary the commissioners were allowed to compel the suspects to confess "by strict examination and torture." Sonoy then retrospectively authorized everything that the commissioners had already done in this matter; evidently they had set to work before 5 June. Finally, he promised them a salary, to be paid by the States of the Northern Quarter, "with fairness and discretion." The investigation was entrusted to four experienced court officers: the sheriffs of Alkmaar and Hoorn, the bailiff of Waterland and Zeevang, and the bailiff of Brederode and Bergen. The town clerk of Alkmaar acted as secretary of the commission.

This letter of commission is a remarkable document for more than one reason. In the first place it betrays not the slightest doubt of the fact of the intended treason or of the guilt of the suspects. The commissioners were not required to determine whether or not a crime had been committed, or if the persons arrested were guilty of it. Both the crime and the guilt were assumed in advance. Sonoy explained the reason for the appointment of the commission as follows:

> Diverse traitors, arsonists and others, led by the enemy of the common fatherland and the inducement and persuasion of some husbandmen,

---

[9] The letter of commission of 5 June 1575 is in Bor, 624.

burghers and other persons of ill will, and inclined more to the enemy than to their own fatherland, were brought and bought thereto by money and fair words, on a certain day and time fixed beforehand by them, to set the whole Northern Quarter on fire.

The investigation commission had two tasks. The first was to make the suspects confess. Given their explicit permission to use torture, this was not expected to present any difficulty. In sixteenth-century criminal procedure a confession was essential, for a suspect could not be sentenced to death until he had admitted his guilt for the crime with which he was charged. If he did not confess of his own free will, the judge could decide to put him to torture. A confession extracted under torture was not legally valid until the accused had repeated it "without pain and bonds," that is, without torture and outside the torture chamber. The judge could then pronounce the final sentence. In view of the gravity of the charge this would undoubtedly be a sentence of death.

The second task of the investigating commissioners was to find out who had given the accused their orders. Sonoy was convinced from the outset that the vagabonds had not acted on their own initiative. The terms in which he justified the formation of the commission assume that they must have received their orders from unknown others.[10]

The most remarkable thing about this investigating commission, however, was that it existed at all. Such an extraordinary commission, invested with far-reaching judicial powers and standing outside and apparently above the normal existing courts, was highly unusual in the legal practice of the sixteenth century. The judicial system of Holland and the other provinces of the Netherlands was extremely decentralized and fragmented.[11] Each town, each lordship, and each bailiwick (a rural district that comprised several lordships) had its own court. The organization and functioning of these courts and the laws they applied were determined by local custom (customary law), bylaws, and privileges.

Nevertheless, these courts displayed some common features. The judges were an odd number (often seven or nine) of *schepenen* (justices), recruited from the wealthier inhabitants of the town or lordship. They sat for a term of one year, in most cases had no legal training, and received no pay. This bench of lay justices was chaired by the sheriff or bailiff, an officer who was appointed by or on behalf of the ruler. This official was

---

[10] The second task was not explicitly stated in the letter of commission, but it was obvious from what followed that the commissioners did their utmost to discover the identity of the persons who had given the orders. The Prince of Orange also urged this in his letter to Sonoy, referred to above.

[11] Egmond, "Fragmentatie."

also responsible for hunting down and charging suspects. After the bench of justices had pronounced a verdict, it was his job to enforce it. The sheriff or bailiff thus combined the roles of a modern police chief and prosecutor. He did not need to be a trained jurist either.

An important distinction was drawn between "low" and "high" justice. In the former category the bench of justices only tried less serious criminal cases punishable by a fine; in the latter, capital crimes also fell within its competence. No appeal to a higher court could be lodged against a death sentence pronounced by the local court; after all, the convicted prisoner had already confessed his guilt in all cases. Another essential principle was the right of citizens of a town to be tried exclusively by their own court (that is, their fellow citizens, who knew the accused and the local circumstances), and not to be handed over to another court. This was called the *ius de non evocando*.

Above these independent and in principle equal local courts stood the Court of Holland and Zeeland in The Hague. The counselors of the Court of Holland were trained jurists, who were appointed by the ruler of the province, the count of Holland, that is, Philip II, and who administered justice according to "learned," that is, Roman Law. The Court acted as a court of appeal for judgments pronounced by the lower courts, except, as we saw, for death sentences. In a few cases it was a court of first instance, for example in matters in which the sovereignty of the count was at stake, called *enormous* or *reserved* cases, such as lese majesty (*crimen laesae majestatis*), high treason, and counterfeiting of the coinage. Cases of heresy, which was regarded as a special form of (divine) lese majesty, could also be heard in the first instance by the Court of Holland. A judgment of the Court could be appealed to the highest court of the Netherlands, the Great Council of Mechelen, but of course this was not possible in time of war.

The Court of Holland was therefore the obvious body to carry out a thorough investigation of the treason in the Northern Quarter. Since so many suspects were said to have been at work all over North Holland, it was not appropriate to entrust the case to one of the local courts in the Quarter. Not one of them was equipped for such a task, and, more importantly, no single town could claim jurisdiction over the whole district. Moreover the crime in question, high treason, was clearly a reserved case for which only the Court of Holland was competent. In previous cases of foiled treasonous plots in the Southern Quarter, the investigation had been left to the Court.[12]

---

[12] See for example William of Orange to the Court, 25 April 1575 (with a request of Joost Janszoon of Gouda), NA, Hof, inv. no. 4592.

But the Court of Holland was far away. While Sonoy was trying to get to the bottom of the plot, the Spanish army was still at Beverwijk, and no one in the North knew if it would make another attempt to overrun the Northern Quarter, with or without the aid of the local population. Since 1572 it had been all but impossible to refer North Holland cases to the Court, but in May and June 1575 it was totally out of the question.[13]

Sonoy therefore had to improvise. A comparable episode had occurred at Gouda in the summer of 1572. A notorious plot to deliver the city to the Spaniards had involved members of the *vroedschap*. For that reason alone it had been impossible to leave the matter to the bench of justices in Gouda. But the Court of Holland could not have dealt with it either, for in July that year most of its members had fled to Utrecht with the Spanish army, and the Prince of Orange did not appoint new officials until February 1573. The hearing of the accused was therefore entrusted to an ad hoc investigating commission of the States of Holland.[14]

Sonoy's commission was therefore not an extraordinary court or tribunal.[15] It was called into being for a single clearly defined purpose. Its task was simply to hold an investigation and to make a written report to Sonoy, not to pronounce judgment on the accused. The addition to an existing court of delegated commissioners, men who had received a special "commission," was not unusual. Inquisitors appointed by the central government were often added to the courts in heresy cases. The ecclesiastics questioned the prisoners in the presence of some of the justices, but it was the court that pronounced the final verdict.[16]

One may wonder what the proper course of the proceedings would have been after the commissioners had submitted their report. Who was competent to pass judgment on the arrested vagabonds? The archives of the investigating commission, which were still available for Pieter Bor to consult, have been lost, and therefore cannot provide the answer. Only one judgment, pronounced later in the same affair, has been preserved.

---

[13] The Court's correspondence for 1575 not only makes no reference to this case but also does not mention a single other case in North Holland.

[14] Boeree, "Verraad," 216. The Gouda commission consisted of the governor of Gouda, Jonkheer Adriaen van Swieten; Master Dirck van Bronckhorst, a counselor of Count van der Marck (Lumey), Master Claes Camerlingh, advocate; and Cornelis van der Wolff, secretary of the Court of Holland, both the latter as delegates of the States.

[15] Motley, *Rise*, III, 31: Sonoy "improvised, on his own authority, a tribunal in imitation of the infamous Blood Council." Motley's charge that Sonoy acted on his own authority is incorrect, since he not only invoked his authority as Orange's lieutenant but also was explicitly supported by the prince.

[16] For example in the trial of Jan de Bakker (Johannes Pistorius) in 1552, where the inquisitors were referred to as "commissioners," *CD*, IV, 452–96. On the Inquisition see Goosens, *Inquisitions*; Scheerder, "Werking van de Inquisitie"; Van de Wiele, "Inquisitierechtbank."

This was signed by Diederik Sonoy in his capacity as lieutenant and governor of North Holland and Waterland on behalf of the Prince of Orange.[17]

Because Sonoy acted as judge, it was strictly speaking a case of "princely justice," however unlikely that may appear in the context of revolt and rebellion. The prince or ruler (in this case Philip II as Count of Holland) was regarded as the ultimate fount of all law and justice and thus the highest judge.[18] As the deputy of the Prince of Orange, who in his turn claimed to be the rightful deputy (stadholder) of Philip II, Sonoy was competent to exercise princely justice without the intervention of courts or councils. In a reserved case such as high treason it was axiomatic that the ruler or his deputy could pronounce judgment without involving one of his judicial councils, which, after all, only derived their authority from him. In 1540, for example, Charles V had given judgment in person on the city of Ghent after it rebelled against him.[19]

The extremely doubtful legitimacy of Orange's claim to be Stadholder of Holland in 1575 made no difference. In the region under rebel control no one doubted, at least openly, that the rebel regime had such authority.

No formal written charge against the arrested vagabonds has been preserved. Indeed, such a document may never have existed. The letter appointing the commissioners refers to the vagabonds as "traitors and arsonists." Treason and arson must therefore have been the crimes of which they were accused. What exactly was meant by these words?

In the sixteenth century the Netherlands did not have a single uniform criminal code on the grounds of which a prosecutor, that is, a sheriff or bailiff or the prosecutor-general of the provincial court of justice, could bring a prosecution. Proceedings could be based on the (unwritten) customary law and the various local bylaws. In addition, the Constitutio Criminalis Carolina proclaimed by Charles V at Regensburg in 1532 for the entire Holy Roman Empire also applied throughout the Netherlands. In 1570 Alba had replaced this "criminal code" by a new code, the Criminal Ordinances, which also applied in all seventeen provinces of the Netherlands.[20] How far did the commissioners choose to be guided by these new Criminal Ordinances? The Revolt in Holland had begun as a protest

---

[17] Judgment on Nanning Coppenszoon, 30 September 1575, WFA, ORA Hoorn, inv. no. 4515, fol. 202r–v, and in Bor, 627. The judgment was pronounced by Sonoy, but in the sentence book of Hoorn it is entered among other judgments pronounced by the bench of justices in Hoorn. As an inhabitant of Wognum, Nanning Coppenszoon fell under the jurisdiction of Hoorn. See Sonoy to Heukesloot, 22 September 1575, WFA, ORA Hoorn, inv. no. 4515, fol. 203, in which Sonoy asks for four justices of Hoorn to be sent to Alkmaar for the confirmation of Nanning Coppenszoon's confession.

[18] For the idea of the "rex iudex" see De Schepper and Cauchies, "Justicie."

[19] Decavele, *Keizer*, 176.

[20] De Vrugt, *Criminele ordonnantiën*.

against the unconstitutional rule of Alba, who thought he could govern the country from Brussels without heeding the local and provincial privileges. In practice, however, the question is not very important, for the Criminal Ordinances in most cases did not differ from the Carolina.

Filips Wielant, a counselor of the Great Council of Mechelen, had written a manual, the *Practijcke criminele*, dealing with the most common criminal offenses, for the guidance of the many local court officers and lay justices in the Netherlands who had no legal training. The Bruges jurist Joos de Damhouder brought out a new edition of this work under his own name in 1555.[21] In this form the book must have been familiar to Sonoy's commissioners, who were all sheriffs or bailiffs. It is therefore worth looking at what it had to say about treason and arson.

Treason or crime against the majesty of the ruler of the time (lese majesty), according to De Damhouder, could take many forms.[22] They included assisting the enemy with goods, money, advice, or otherwise. The intent to commit a crime was as liable to punishment as the deed. The offense was punished by confiscation of property and death by the sword, at the stake or by quartering. In this case women were regarded as more culpable than men, and were always burned at the stake. However vague and general this definition, there would certainly be no difficulty in making it cover admitting a foreign army. The same applied to arson (treacherous, secret fire raising resulting in death). This crime too was punished by death by the sword or at the stake, and here too the intent was as criminal as the deed.[23]

Yet in this case the notion of treason or lese-majesty was certainly not without problems, for those who accused the vagabonds of these crimes were themselves rebels in revolt against their lawful ruler, or at least against the governor he had appointed. In the eyes of the king and of those who remained loyal to him, therefore, the accusers themselves were guilty of high treason and lese-majesty. Who was the traitor here? Could a subject commit treason against a regime that was itself in treasonable revolt against its lawful ruler?

The authorities had solid grounds to fear treason. In 1575 most of the inhabitants of Holland and Zeeland longed for an early end to the war. Above all those who felt most strongly attached to the Catholic Church hoped that such an end would be achieved by the victory of the rightful government. The boldest or the most desperate among them were prepared to lend a hand to hasten such a result. As early as August 1572, shortly after Gouda had opened its gates to a Beggar company, one Cap-

---

[21] Wielant, *Practijcke*; De Damhouder, *Practycke*.
[22] De Damhouder, *Practycke*, fols. 85–86.
[23] Ibid., fols. 182–85.

tain Maerten Schets tried to deliver the city to the government army, probably with the cooperation of several members of the *vroedschap*.[24] The plan leaked out, and Schets was arrested and executed.

As the war dragged on there were several further attempts at treason. In March and February 1574 Gouda witnessed two more bids to admit the royal army under Noircarmes. The plotters must have been influenced by Noircarmes's promise to pardon the citizens and to quarter his troops in the castle, and not in their homes. This plot, too, was betrayed and the ringleaders were executed, but the matter was never investigated thoroughly, because most of the conspirators were among the leading citizens of the town, some of them even being relatives of members of the *vroedschap*.[25]

In July the same year some citizens of Delft tried to hand over their city to a Spanish detachment under Valdéz. That plot, too, ended in failure, because the conspirators could not find the keys when the time came to open the gates.[26] At about the same time some citizens of Dordrecht conspired to deliver their city to the Spaniards. Their letters were intercepted, and thanks to the Prince of Orange's intervention this plot was nipped in the bud. A few burghers were banished, and one of the wealthiest was imprisoned on suspicion of high treason.[27]

The Northern Quarter had had its own earlier mutterings of treason. In March 1574 it was rumored that a plot was afoot in Hoorn, led by Boussu, who had been held in prison in the town since his capture in the battle on the Zuiderzee. Two hundred firearms were supposed to have been smuggled into the town and distributed among the people; the rising would coincide with an attack from several warships sent from Amsterdam. The rumor was probably baseless, for mass house-to-house searches discovered nothing.[28]

The countryside of the Northern Quarter was just as unreliable. Wouter Jacobszoon had heard reports that in January of the same year, 1574, between twenty and thirty villages around Alkmaar had conspired to submit to the Spanish army and had offered to help it seize the town. This plot had also failed. The Beggars threw up sconces around the villages to prevent a possible advance of the government army and threatened to kill the peasants, to burn their houses, and to seize all their property.[29]

[24] Hibben, *Gouda*, 70–71; Boeree, "Verraad"; Bor, 410–11; Walvis, *Beschryving Gouda*, I, 349.
[25] Hibben, *Gouda*, 210; Walvis, *Beschryving Gouda*, I, 361–65; *DWJ*, 360–71.
[26] *DWJ*, 429; Smit, *Den Haag*, 243.
[27] Swart, *William of Orange*.
[28] Velius, 237.
[29] *DWJ*, 362, 366.

Sonoy and the other leaders of the Revolt therefore had very cogent reasons to fear betrayal. The war had now lasted three years. The collapse of the peace conference at Breda, which finally broke up for good on 13 July, only deepened the mood of despair among the people. In May 1575, Sonoy received reports from several sources (Bardesius, Hoorn, Edam, and Monnickendam), which all told more or less the same tale of an imminent treasonous conspiracy. Those who still had doubts were convinced by the burning of the mill at Schoorl, the arrest of the vagabonds, and the sudden withdrawal of the army, which was inexplicable in any other way.

The question of treason was far from academic for those who had stuck their neck out in the spring of 1572. The people of the Northern Quarter were engaged in a life and death struggle with an implacable enemy. It makes little difference whether or not they knew the details of Hierges's grim orders to burn their country to ashes and slaughter the inhabitants. The fate of Mechelen, Zutphen, Naarden, and Haarlem had already left them in no doubt of the retribution that lay in store for them if the Spanish army reconquered their Quarter. Traitors who sought to aid the enemy had to be ruthlessly suppressed.

The four men to whom Sonoy entrusted the investigation were Jan van Foreest, sheriff of Alkmaar; Willem van Sonnenberg, bailiff of Brederode and Bergen; Master Joost Heukesloot, sheriff of Hoorn; and Willem Maertszoon Calff, bailiff of Waterland and Zeevang. All four were professionals (Heukesloot's title of "Master" indicated that he had a law degree), skilled and experienced in detecting, judging, and punishing miscreants. Sonoy had tried to recruit his team from a widespread geographical area. The commissioners came from the two largest towns and two of the rural areas on the front line, where the alleged treason was to have been perpetrated. But their personal qualifications were as important as their place of origin: all four men had thrown in their lot with the Revolt. Who were these commissioners who were to earn such a reputation for ruthlessness in the following months?

The most distinguished member of the commission was the sheriff of Alkmaar, Jan van Foreest (1540–1580).[30] He came from a noble family, which had been settled in Alkmaar for a long time, had married into the town patriciate, and had served in its magistracy for many years. Jan's father Jorden was among the wealthiest inhabitants of Alkmaar, where he had served as a justice, a *vroedschap* member, and burgomaster. Jan was the youngest son in a huge family of sixteen or seventeen children. In 1560 he matriculated at the University of Leuven, where he studied medicine.[31] After his return to Alkmaar he married Jannetje Bollen Jansdochter, a girl from a leading Alkmaar patrician family.

[30] Foreest, *Oude geslacht*, 157–68.
[31] *Matricule*, IV, 596.

Jan van Foreest first came to notice in the Wonder Year 1566, when he and his brothers Dirck and Nanning were among the leaders of the Reformed congregation that was founded in Alkmaar in that year. With some others the three brothers submitted a petition asking to be allowed to use the church of the Franciscan monastery for Reformed preaching. In the same year Jan and his wife Jannetje, who was also "greatly of the sect," had a child baptized in the barn where the Calvinists held their services.[32] Jan's eldest sister Geertruijt was another early convert to the new ideas. She was a follower of the evangelically inspired pastor Cornelis Cooltuyn, who organized clandestine Bible reading meetings in Alkmaar until the town became too hot to hold him.[33] In the spring of 1559 Geertruijt followed her spiritual guide into exile in Emden, where they married. Socially, Geertruijt was marrying far beneath herself by becoming the wife of the ex-pastor Cooltuyn. Their son was born in April 1560, but mother and child died of an infectious disease only a month later.

Foreest left the country when the repression began. The Council of Troubles sentenced him and his brothers to banishment for life and confiscation of their property. When the authorities arrived to make an inventory of his goods, Foreest's wife had already followed her husband into exile. Their two small children were entrusted to the care of family members, and one of them, who had been baptized by the Calvinists and therefore illegally, was again presented for baptism in the Catholic Church.[34]

The three Foreest brothers returned to Alkmaar in the spring of 1572. As early as 3 May, some time before Alkmaar went over to the Revolt, the town magistrates had Jan's house on the Mient repaired.[35] It is a safe assumption that Jan and other returned exiles were active in bringing the town over to the rebel side. In June he became a confessing member of the Reformed Church, and in March 1573 was appointed sheriff.[36] He also played an active role in the defense of the town during the Spanish siege in September and October 1573.

Jan van Foreest was thirty-four years old when he was appointed to Sonoy's investigating commission. He had deep roots in the community of Alkmaar and was a man of culture and standing, a Protestant and a

---

[32] Van Vloten, "Noordholland," 306, 316.

[33] See above, pp. 41–42. For his marriage see Vis, *Cooltuyn*, 36.

[34] *Sententiën*, 118; Van Vloten, "Noordholland," 316. For Foreest's seized goods and the children he left behind, see NA, Grafelijkheidsrekenkamer, rekeningen, inv. no. 683 B, Alkmaar, fols. 5v–8.

[35] *Vroedschap* resolution 3 May 1572, RAA, SA Alkmaar, inv. no. 92, fol. 173. See also fol. 179: the burgomasters must settle accounts with Jan van Foreest for the repair and letting of his house in 1571–72.

[36] Membership register, RAA, Archief van de kerkeraad van de Nederlands-hervormde gemeente Alkmaar, inv. no. 137, fol. 4; register of political commissions, NA, Staten van Holland, inv. no. 1788, fols. 20–22v (undated); Fasel, "Ontzetviering," 86.

firm adherent of the new ecclesiastical and political order. His fate was inseparable from that of the Revolt. If the government should succeed in the reconquest of Holland, he could expect no mercy.

Yet Foreest took little or no part in the hearing of the prisoners. His name is not mentioned in the depositions later made by witnesses about the conduct of the hearings, nor was he summonsed in the proceedings that were later brought against the commissioners. Was this cultivated man repelled by the unlawful use of force against the accused, or did he simply not believe in the existence of the plot? There is no evidence that he made any protest against the procedure, or that he officially laid down his post. In day-to-day practice his place appears to have been taken by the provost marshal of the army in North Holland, one Michiel Heugelcke, of whom nothing more is known.[37] This Heugelcke, as far as we know, never received an official letter of commission from Sonoy.

We know little about Willem van Sonnenberg, the bailiff of Bergen and Brederode, but it is clear that he too matched the profile of the Calvinist rebel.[38] A native of the Land of Vianen and in the service of Hendrik van Brederode, he, like Foreest, first appears in the sources in 1566. Although not a nobleman himself, with many others in Brederode's service he signed the Compromise of the Nobility.[39] The Council of Troubles called him a "great favorer of the ministers and sectaries." In July he arranged for Brederode's country house Te Kleef near Haarlem to be used for open-air preaching. He forbade the village priests in Brederode's lordships to say mass, and even forced one of them to marry within the forbidden degrees, and assaulted a monk in the abbey of Egmond.[40] Brederode owned extensive estates in the dune belt between Zandvoort and Callantsoog, where Sonnenberg acted as his steward. On 26 August 1566, as we saw, Brederode ordered him to remove the valuables from the churches in his lordships in Kennemerland for safekeeping.[41]

The brutal energy with which Sonnenberg performed this task says a great deal about his feelings toward the Catholic Church. In Bergen he seized the Holy Blood of Miracles, a relic that was kept in a silver ciborium. "How long have you deceived the people?" he asked the terrified priest. He is also said to have polished his boots with the consecrated oil kept for the sacrament of extreme unction, a distant echo of the material-

---

[37] Bor, 624, calls him Michiel Vermertlen, but the executioner Jacob Michielszoon refers to Michiel Heugelcke. Deposition of Jacob Michielszoon, 20 March 1577, NHA, Aanwinsten, inv. no. 1185, fol. 12v.

[38] Te Water, *Verbond*, III, 295–97.

[39] Ibid., IV, 22, appendix C. His name is not mentioned by Bonnevie-Noel, "Liste critique."

[40] *Sententiën*, 58–59.

[41] Van Vloten, "Noordholland," 333.

ism of Wendelmoet Claesdochter forty years earlier. The Council of Troubles, which did not know about his membership of the Compromise of the Nobility, sentenced Sonnenberg in his absence to lifelong banishment and confiscation of property for his activities during the Wonder Year.[42] We do not know where he spent the years 1567 to 1572, but presumably he followed Brederode to Germany. He returned to Holland on the outbreak of the Revolt. He was never a member of the newly created Reformed community in Alkmaar in 1572. His importance to the cause of the Revolt in the Northern Quarter became apparent in 1573, when he was appointed to deputize for Sonoy, who was temporarily incapacitated by an illness.[43]

Master Joost Heukesloot was a rebel of a quite different stamp. He had been a loyal servant of Alba's government, but remained in his post after the revolution of 1572. Heukesloot was born in Delft in 1524 or 1525 to a prominent but non-noble family.[44] In 1549 he matriculated at the University of Orléans, where he studied civil and canon law.[45] After his return to the Netherlands he married a daughter of the secretary of the Court of Holland, Master Rombout van Steynemolen, a learned humanist.[46] One of Heukesloot's wife's sisters was married to the scholarly physician of Hoorn, Dirck Hendrickszoon Hogerbeets, whose father and grandfather had served many times as burgomaster of Hoorn, and who himself was nominated to the *vroedschap* in 1562.[47] Presumably thanks to his connections with Hogerbeets, Heukesloot was appointed pensionary, or legal adviser, of Hoorn in 1556, without even taking the trouble to acquire citizenship. When the central government appointed him sher-

---

[42] Ibid., 333–35. Hearings of Alba's commissioners in Alkmaar and surrounding villages, NHA, Kopieën, inv. no. A 518, fols. 5v–6; 17v–18v; *Sententiën*, 58–59; not in Verheyden, *Conseil des Troubles*. The inventory of his seized property: NA, Grafelijkheidsrekenkamer, rekeningen, inv. no. 683 B, Haarlem, fols. 50v–2v.

[43] Sonnenberg's name does not appear in the register of members of Alkmaar, RAA, Archief van de kerkeraad van de Nederlands-hervormde gemeente Alkmaar, inv. no. 137. For his appointment as stand-in for Sonoy, see Foreest, *Cort verhael*, 21.

[44] Van Vloten, "Noordholland," 145; on 14 July 1567, when Heukesloot gave evidence before commissioners of the Council of Troubles, he was forty-two years old. For the Heukesloot family see *De Wapenheraut*, 42 (1892), 565–69. One Maria Heukesloot, whose relationship to Joost is not clear, was married to a rather distant relative of Jan van Foreest. Several members of the Heukesloot family married nobles. In the seventeenth century the family settled in the Holy Roman Empire, where they were raised to the nobility.

[45] *Deuxième livre*, 100.

[46] Bijleveld, "Gegevens Hoogerbeets." Joost Heukesloot and Maria van Steynemolen had five children, of whom only one daughter survived to adulthood and had descendants.

[47] In 1566 Dirck Hogerbeets joined the reform movement in religion, in 1568 he fled and was banished by the Council of Troubles, but returned to his native town of Hoorn after it went over to the Revolt in 1572. On him see Velius, 350, 375, 379–80, 393, 396; *Sententiën*, 142–43, *NNBW*, IX, 384.

iff of Hoorn in August 1562, the burgomasters rightly objected, for according to the privileges of their town only a citizen of at least three years standing could hold the office of sheriff. Heukesloot summonsed the town before the Court of Holland, which ruled in his favor.[48]

It is not clear why the government should have wished to flout the privileges of Hoorn by appointing an outsider, but whatever the background to the case a difference of policy between The Hague and the tolerant magistracy is not likely. As sheriff, Heukesloot treated dissent with a remarkable leniency, which was entirely in harmony with the tolerance the town magistrates had practiced for years. A typical instance of his attitude to religious dissenters occurred in 1564, when the Bishop of Haarlem ordered him to arrest six Anabaptists in the village of Beets, which was under the jurisdiction of Hoorn. Heukesloot ignored the order until the Dean of West Friesland, who resided in Hoorn, became involved. The dean challenged the authority of the bishop, but then issued his own orders to arrest the Anabaptists. Heukesloot complied, but released the Anabaptists after a brief hearing.[49] Thanks to the moderate policy of the sheriff, the Anabaptists in Hoorn were allowed to continue to profess their faith undisturbed, as long as they did not do so too overtly.

In 1556 Heukesloot had to deal with the Reformed, who organized their first open-air preaching in Holland just outside the town's jurisdiction. At the same time that Jan Arentszoon was conducting a service in a meadow near the monastery of Westerblokker, the sheriff, undersheriff, and burgomasters of Hoorn were dining in the same monastery. Heukesloot, a few monks, and two of the nobles who were present went out to investigate and tried to intimidate the preacher, but because the sermon was being given outside his jurisdiction he could do nothing.[50]

Once the government had restored order in 1567, and most of the adherents of the Reformation had fled abroad, Heukesloot assisted in the repression. He gave evidence on events in Hoorn before the commissioners sent to the Northern Quarter. Evidently the Council of Troubles saw nothing to distrust in the sheriff's conduct.[51] On 3 March 1568 (Shrove Tuesday) the castellan of Medemblik, the undersheriff, and some of the burgomasters of Hoorn raided the houses of the leading suspects in the

---

[48] Judgment pronounced by the Court in the case of *Heukesloot v. Hoorn*, WFA, OA Hoorn, inv. no. 2496 A; Velius, 158. Heukesloot was appointed on 12 August 1562 and swore the oath two weeks later: NA, Grafelijkheidsrekenkamer, registers, inv. no. 495, fol. 34r–v. On 27 July 1565 he took the oath to extend his office for a further six years: register of political commissions, NA, Staten van Holland, inv. no. 1788, fol. 1r–v. The lease payment was increased on that occasion from six Flemish pounds to 131 Flemish pounds.

[49] Voets, "Hervorming," II, 32.

[50] Velius, 162; Sol, 134.

[51] Van Vloten, "Noordholland," 145.

town, among them Heukesloot's brother-in-law Hogerbeets. But because they had all been warned in advance, they managed to escape.[52] Was it Heukesloot himself who tipped off the suspects?

Heukesloot's tolerant attitude in religious matters did not persuade him to support the Prince of Orange's plans for an armed uprising. In October 1568 the people of the Northern Quarter were alarmed by a band of about forty "vagrants, exiles, vagabonds and malefactors." Led by a burgher of Alkmaar, Dirck Maertszoon van Schagen, they roamed the countryside of West Friesland, robbing and plundering.[53] They had a letter of commission from the Count of Hoogstraten, who had empowered them, apparently in a fit of optimism, to seize several towns in Holland for the Prince of Orange. These desperadoes could not count on the support of the peasantry. Their campaign of plunder ended beneath the walls of Hoorn, where the militia, led by Heukesloot and two of the burgomasters, routed the miserable little band. The leader Dirck Maertszoon and a few others were taken to The Hague and executed, while the rest were hanged in the marketplace at Hoorn. When Heukesloot was commissioned to investigate the rogues and vagabonds who were once again believed to threaten the safety of the Northland in 1575, his attitude toward the suspects must have been prejudiced by his recollections of the earlier marauders.

Immediately before the revolution of 1572 there was nothing to suggest that the sheriff of Hoorn would shortly find himself on the side of the rebels. In March 1572 some citizens of Hoorn who had been appointed to collect the Tenth Penny refused to do so, fearing that an attempt to levy the tax would provoke a riot.[54] Their refusal led to a fierce clash with Heukesloot, who threatened to hold them personally liable for the loss the town suffered as a result of their recalcitrance. But when the town went over to the Revolt shortly afterward, the Tenth Penny became a dead letter, and the question had no further consequences.

After Hoorn had declared for William of Orange in June 1572, Heukesloot remained in office. Nothing is known about his behavior during the transition. Did financial considerations determine his decision to stay? Not long before, he had paid a considerable sum to renew the lease of his office. In any case he must have sworn the new oath of loyalty to the prince after the town went over. Three years later, in May and June 1575,

[52] Velius, 170–71.
[53] Ibid., 172; Van Vloten, *Nederlands Opstand*, I, 281–87 (the citation on 281); the judgments are in *Sententiën*, 335, 340. Most of the documents are published in "Rooftocht." A few unpublished documents on this affair, including a letter from Louis of Nassau, in RAA, ORA Alkmaar, inv. no. 3.
[54] Velius, 179; Jan Jeroenszoon to Jan Corneliszoon Spranger, 15 February 1577, RANH, Aanwinsten, inv. no. 1186.

when Hierges menaced the Northern Quarter, Heukesloot was active in arresting suspects. On 1 June the burgomasters paid two carters for conveying "Master Joost and his vagabonds" to Alkmaar.[55]

Joost Heukesloot was thus a different type of rebel from Foreest and Sonnenberg. They had been actively committed to the ecclesiastical and political opposition movement since 1566, and had had to pay for their zeal with exile and the loss of their property; but Heukesloot did not join the rebels until 1572, perhaps for no better reason than to keep his office and protect his investment in it. Unlike Foreest in Alkmaar, Heukesloot was regarded as an outsider in Hoorn and had already clashed with the town authorities as a result. He was to be involved in further bitter quarrels with the burgomasters while serving on the commission of investigation. Before the revolution of 1572 Heukesloot had shielded religious dissenters, though he is not known to have joined the Reformed community after 1572. But he too could not have expected mercy if the Spaniards were victorious. He was to be no less ruthless than his fellow commissioners in dealing with the vagabonds.

The fourth commissioner, Willem Maertszoon Calff, was another who did not join the rebels until 1572. Calff had been born at Alkmaar in 1533, but grew up in Amsterdam.[56] His father Hendrick Gerritszoon Pecklap died when Willem was eleven or twelve. His mother remarried a widower with ten children, and Willem, his mother, sister, and younger brother moved into the house of his stepfather. When Willem was seventeen his mother and stepfather died of an infectious disease at almost the same time. Willem was thus free to dispose of his inheritance at an early age, and in 1556, aged twenty-one or twenty-two, he married a woman from a respected Amsterdam family.

In Amsterdam Calff held the post of substitute sheriff under Master Willem Dirckszoon Baerdesen, the father of Sonoy's later collaborator. Baerdesen in Amsterdam treated religious dissenters with the same leniency as Heukesloot in Hoorn.[57] In 1564 Calff was also appointed Bailiff of the district of Amstelland for a six-year term.

The year of the iconoclastic riots was a turning point for Calff, as it was for many others, though he did not join the opposition at that time. Later he was wrongly suspected of being involved in bringing the ex-basket maker Jan Arentszoon into the city after Jan had preached outside

---

[55] Extraordinary expenditure of burgomasters, 1574–75, WFA, OA Hoorn, inv. no. 2498, 1 June 1575. On 19 July the burgomasters paid the sheriff's servants thirty stuivers for a prisoner (Jan Driemunt?) who had been sent to the governor. Burgemeestersrekening 1575, WFA, OA Hoorn, inv. no. 219, 19 July 1575.

[56] Elias, *Vroedschap*, I, 134–36.

[57] Woltjer, "Conflict."

St. Anthony's Gate.⁵⁸ Calff just managed to escape prosecution by the Council of Troubles by offering to purge himself before the Court of Holland. This was a procedure that gave anyone the opportunity to clear his name by demanding that his accuser should prove certain charges. If he failed, the person who had asked to be purged was declared innocent by the Court.

Calff's position became awkward when he was also accused of acting on his own initiative as substitute sheriff to release a number of persons arrested for iconoclasm.⁵⁹ In September 1566, during the looting of the Carthusian monastery, which stood just outside the Haarlem Gate, the sheriff had arrested four of the ringleaders and taken them in custody to the city. This had provoked disturbances. To prevent the situation from getting out of hand the burgomasters had ordered Calff to go to meet the sheriff and release the prisoners. In spite of another purge, Calff was now arrested and held in a "thieves' pit" in Amsterdam. The written instruction from the burgomasters to set the prisoners free, which would have exonerated him, was nowhere to be found. Calff asserted that the new sheriff had removed the document from his house. For two years, from February 1569 to February 1571, Calff languished in solitary confinement. He was not released until one of the Amsterdam exiles in Emden sent a copy of the order, showing that the substitute sheriff had indeed acted on instructions from above. Calff's lease of his office of Bailiff of Amstelland had expired while he was in prison, and another man had been appointed to it. To compensate him for his long imprisonment and the loss of income, Calff was appointed Bailiff of Waterland and Zeevang on 2 April 1572, the day after the Beggars seized Brill.

Calff was not to enjoy his new post in peace for long. In the last week of June, Edam, Monnickendam, and the surrounding countryside capitulated to the rebels. Like Heukesloot in Hoorn, Calff remained in office. Not long afterward he had his commission as Bailiff of Waterland and Zeevang confirmed by the new regime. When the rebels briefly besieged Amsterdam in August 1572 he served as captain of a company of soldiers.⁶⁰ What motivated him to choose to side with the rebels? There is nothing to indicate that he was inclined to the cause of the Protestant Reformation. By remaining in office he at least avoided losing his official incomes once again. And we may assume that he was also driven by a deep rancor after his long imprisonment for an offense he had not committed.

---

⁵⁸ Ter Gouw, *Geschiedenis van Amsterdam*, VI, 268.
⁵⁹ Ibid., 116–17, 280–82; ruling of the Court of Holland in the case of *Calff v. the Prosecutor-General*, NA, Hof, inv. no. 552.
⁶⁰ Declaration of Calff's expenses, 14 May 1575, WA, OA Edam, inv. no. 48. His commission was confirmed on 16 July 1572 by Sonoy, on 18 September 1572 by the States of

Calff had little luck with his offices. In the last days of August 1573 the Spanish army invaded the northern bank of the River IJ, and the greater part of Waterland was lost to the rebels and its Bailiff Calff.[61] As if that were not enough, Calff now became embroiled in an acrimonious conflict with Edam over what was left of his official territory.

The occasion of the dispute was the office of Bailiff of Zeevang, that is, the right to exercise justice in that district and to enjoy the associated incomes. Like other Holland towns in this period, Edam was trying to exploit the chaotic conditions to tighten its grip on the administration of justice in the town and its surrounding countryside.[62] Naturally it faced stiff opposition from the sitting bailiff. The first tensions became apparent on 4 November 1572, when Calff sent a halbardier to the town to demand that the burgomasters repay certain sums advanced to them.[63] The dispute became so fierce that in June 1573 the burgomasters persuaded William of Orange to appoint a former burgomaster of Edam, Pieter Thomaszoon, to replace Calff as Bailiff of Zeevang.[64] Calff would not stand for this and lodged an appeal with the Court of Holland.[65]

Pieter Thomaszoon died only a few months later in December 1573, so that Calff's appeal was no longer admissible. The burgomasters of Edam immediately proposed a new candidate to the prince.[66] Calff refused to yield and traveled to Flushing, where William of Orange was staying at the time. The prince passed over Edam's candidate and granted Calff a new commission, but the winter weather prevented the new bailiff from returning in triumph to the Northern Quarter until 11 March 1574.[67]

It was not long before the bailiff and the town were once again at loggerheads, this time over the appointment of the sheriff of Edam, the official who was responsible for administering "low" justice in the town. Formerly the appointment of the sheriff had been reserved to the Stadholder or the Court of Holland. Since 1572 that meant either the Prince of Orange or, in the absence of the Court, the States of Holland. The confusion of the summer of 1572, however, had given the burgomasters

---

Holland, and on 24 October by Orange. His role in the siege of Amsterdam is described in Ter Gouw, *Geschiedenis van Amsterdam*, VII, 52.

[61] See above, p. 76

[62] See also Van der Gouw, "Schieland."

[63] Calff to Jan Pieterszoon Smit, 4 November 1572, WA, OA Edam, inv. no. 48. This contains all the documents on this conflict.

[64] Copy of a deed of the Commissioners of Accounts at Delft, 12 June 1573.

[65] Copy of an affidavit of the notary Pieter Janszoon Poulunburg at Hoorn, 22 July 1573. Heukesloot acted as witness.

[66] Burgomasters and magistrates of Edam to the Commissioners of Accounts, 22 December 1573.

[67] "Since he was frozen in there," statement of Calff's expenses, 14 May 1575.

the chance to gain influence on the appointment. After the progovernment sheriff fled in June 1572, they appointed the ex-justice Jan Pieterszoon Smit, who received a letter of commission from the States of Holland a few months later.[68] Smit died in October 1574, and the burgomasters on their own authority nominated a new sheriff, Lambrecht Janszoon, also a citizen of the town. The Chamber of Accounts reminded them that this was beyond their powers, and in the name of the Stadholder, William of Orange, it granted a commission to an outsider, Claes Corneliszoon van Oostland. Bailiff Calff had backed his candidacy and demanded that the burgomasters should dismiss their own nominee.[69]

Now the people of Edam intervened in the conflict. The militia remonstrated with the burgomasters, claiming that the appointment of a "strange man" would lead to discord and mutiny, "to the great detriment of the Prince of Orange and the destruction of the common cause and our home town," and urged them to appoint a citizen of Edam.[70] Thus assured of support from below, the burgomasters and the heads of the militia now appealed to William of Orange to free them from Calff, for "the aforementioned burghers cannot abide him or bear him." If the prince should not grant their request, they added with a sense of dramatic effect, the Edammers humbly begged permission to leave their town and move to other towns obedient to the prince, where they could live in peace under his protection.[71]

For all its humble tone this was fighting talk, which got their petition heard. For the second time William of Orange dropped Calff in favor of the town. On 13 December 1574 he granted a commission to the Edam candidate Lambrecht Janszoon, not only as bailiff, sheriff, and dike-reeve of Edam, but also of the whole bailiwick of Zeevang.[72] On 22 April 1585 the Prince of Orange issued further regulations, detaching the high and low justice of the towns of Edam and Monnickendam from the bailiwick of Zeevang. Calff remained bailiff of the villages of Waterland and Zeevang, and in that capacity was allowed to appoint the justices in the Zeevang villages each year. To compensate him for the loss of his judicial powers in Edam and Monnickendam, Calff was to receive four

---

[68] Request of Jan Pieterszoon Smit to the States of Holland, August or September 1572; request of Jan Pieterszoon Smit to Sonoy, with apostille, 22 August 1572; deed of magistracy of Edam, 23 September 1572.

[69] Commissioners of Accounts to the Bailiff, burgomasters and magistrates of Edam, 19 October 1574; deed of Calff, 1 November 1574.

[70] Request of captains and lieutenants of the militia to the burgomasters and aldermen of Edam, undated.

[71] Magistrates and captains of the militia to Orange, 18 October 1574.

[72] Commission of the Council and Finances of His Excellency to Lambrecht Janszoon, 13 December 1574.

hundred Carolus guilders a year, two hundred from each town, for the remainder of his lease.[73]

This ought to have said the last word on the matter, but the Prince of Orange had unwittingly sown the seeds of yet another dispute. Since 1413 Edam had enjoyed the privilege that the villages of the Zeevang, Middelie, Warder, and Kwadijk were united with the town in a single citizenship.[74] This meant that the villagers enjoyed the benefits of the town law of Edam, but also, and more important, that the jurisdiction of Edam extended over the surrounding villages. By granting the bailiff the right to appoint the justices in the villages, and thus detaching them from the jurisdiction of the town, William of Orange had clearly violated its privileges. The burgomasters immediately protested and had the backing of the deputies of the Northern Quarter.[75] Confronted by the privilege of Edam the prince had no choice but to sacrifice Calff again. On 29 June 1575—when Calff had already spent four weeks investigating the alleged treason—the prince revoked his commission as bailiff.[76] Calff did not acquiesce in this humiliation. The last we hear of the affair is that on 2 July he arrested his rival, the new bailiff Lambrecht Janszoon, at the Moor's Head tavern in Alkmaar. Two days later Calff's colleague on the commission, the sheriff of Alkmaar, Foreest, explicitly distanced himself from Calff's action in a statement before an Alkmaar notary.[77]

Although Calff had made himself impossible in Edam and had suffered a serious loss of face, the rebel leaders continued to make use of his services.[78] In March 1575 they appointed him steward of the confiscated ecclesiastical estates in Waterland, Zeevang, and Katwoude, where rents were not being collected in "several burned and destroyed villages."[79] Evidently they saw the intransigence that made him so hard to stomach for the citizens of Edam as an indispensable quality for winning the war.

The intrigues around the bailiwick of Zeevang were important for the light that they throw on Calff's character. The documents in the case reveal him as ambitious, but also rancorous and pitiless, quarrelsome and quick to anger. At the very moment when Calff was about to lose his post

---

[73] Deed of William of Orange, 22 April 1575.

[74] Charter of Count William VI of Holland, 13 March 1413, WA, OA Edam, inv. no. 19.

[75] Request of the magistracy of Edam to the deputies of the towns of North Holland (May 1575) with apostille of 21 May 1575.

[76] Request of the magistracy of Edam to the Prince of Orange, with apostille of 29 June 1575.

[77] Affidavit of Jan van Foreest on request of Lambert Janszoon, 4 July 1575.

[78] States of the Northern Quarter to Sonoy, 21 September 1574, NHA, RNK, inv. no. 237, fol. 47v: the States send Sonoy some Spanish letters, which no one can translate; they suspect that Calff will be able to do so.

[79] "First white register," NA Grafelijkheidsrekenkamer, registers, inv. no. 25, fols. 165–66.

as bailiff for good, Sonoy appointed him to his investigating commission. After the succession of reverses he had suffered, Calff must often have been in an irritable mood.

The tableau of the commissioners whose task it was to investigate the treason would not be complete without a sketch of the man who had called the commission into being, who kept himself constantly informed of its progress, ultimately pronounced judgment on the prisoners, and as such was held responsible by many for the commission's activities (plate 2). Jonker Diederik Sonoy was born in 1529 at Kalkar in the Duchy of Cleves.[80] His father died of the plague in the same year. Young Diederik was brought up by his mother, grandmother, and aunt, all three of whom were natives of the Bishopric of Utrecht. His elder brother Joost matriculated at the University of Leuven, but the turbulent Diederik chose a military career. He served in a company of ordonnance, a heavily armed cavalry force consisting chiefly of noblemen that formed the core of the standing army in the Netherlands, and distinguished himself in the wars against France. After the peace of Cateau-Cambrésis in 1559 he returned to the Netherlands, where he had married Maria van Malsen, a noblewoman who owned rich estates in South Holland. The couple settled in The Hague. Like most noblemen in Holland, Sonoy held no offices and was passionately devoted to hunting.

For Diederik Sonoy, as for so many others, the Wonder Year was the turning point of his life. He signed the Compromise of the Nobility against the Inquisition and revealed himself as an enthusiastic adherent of the movement for religious reformation. He allowed followers of the new faith to meet in secret in his house, and in July 1566, with others, he organized hedge preaching near The Hague.[81] He was close to Brederode, and in December 1566 he subscribed four hundred guilders to recruit troops for an armed uprising, refused to swear the new oath of unconditional loyalty to the king in 1567, and went into exile after the collapse of the opposition movement.[82] The Council of Troubles sentenced him in his absence to perpetual banishment and confiscation of his property.

In exile Sonoy became one of the Prince of Orange's chief collaborators in the organization of his military campaigns. He was active in planning the first expedition in 1568, and after its failure in fitting out the Sea Beggars' fleet, of which he was appointed admiral. In 1570 he was engaged in collecting funds and preparing for the unsuccessful assault on

[80] Jonckheer, "Dirk Sonoy"; *NNBW*, V, 773.
[81] *Sententiën*, 51–53; Smit, *Den Haag*, 27, 31–32, 35.
[82] Sonoy's letter to the Court, in which he refuses to swear the new oath of loyalty, in Bor, 148.

Enkhuizen. In the following year he led an embassy to the kings of Denmark and Sweden that sought to win support for William of Orange.

It was natural, therefore, that the prince should appoint the former professional soldier Sonoy to head the revolt in Enkhuizen in May 1572. His letter of commission was drawn up on 20 April 1572, two weeks before Enkhuizen declared for the prince.[83] In it William of Orange appointed Sonoy as his lieutenant and governor of the villages and towns of North Holland, which had not even been taken yet. The instructions attached stated that Sonoy was to free the region from "tyranny" and restore its old privileges. He was to ensure that the true word of God was proclaimed, but without hindering the Catholics in the practice of their religion. As William of Orange's lieutenant, Sonoy was also invested with the power to exercise all the sovereign prerogatives that belonged to the stadholder as the ruler's deputy: the supreme command of the army, the fortresses, and the fleet; the right to appoint and dismiss the town magistrates; and the right to confiscate the possessions of those who resisted him. It is remarkable that the Prince of Orange had framed a complete set of regulations for the government of the Northern Quarter before a single town had fallen into his hands.

From the start Sonoy was the undisputed leader in the region and answered to William of Orange alone. He was assisted by an improvised administration of several counselors, who placed scarcely any restrictions on his power. In an attempt to acquire some influence on policy in North Holland the States of Holland sent two delegates to join Sonoy's council. They were to discuss all matters concerning the conduct of the war with Sonoy and were not required to refer them back to the States. Both men were pillars of the Revolt, the nobleman Jan van Woerden van Vliet, who had been burgomaster of Haarlem during the siege, and the Amsterdam merchant Reinier Cant, a returned exile.[84] After disputes with the towns the Prince of Orange added Charles de Boisot as Sonoy's commissioner-general for the Northern Quarter. With three representatives of Alkmaar, Hoorn, and Enkhuizen, Boisot formed a second college, with which Sonoy was supposed to discuss all matters that concerned the waging of the war.[85] His other advisers included the Amsterdammer and returned exile Willem Baerdesen; the steward of the Vroonlanden Jonkheer Frederik van Zevender; and the military governors who were placed in command of the towns in 1572, Jacob Cabeliau in Medemblik, Josua van

---

[83] Bor, 375. See above, p. 61.
[84] Bor, 413. On Van Woerden van Vliet see Van Nierop, *Nobility of Holland*, 193; Verwer, *Memoriaelbouck*, vii, 13, 18, 22, 26, 54, 88, 99, 117, 122, 129, 142, 161; Wijn, *Beleg*, 19, 32, 139, 143. For Cant see *NNBW*, VI, 265.
[85] Velius, 213; for Boisot see *NNBW*, V, 42.

Alveringen, Lord of Hofwege, in Hoorn (an old comrade of Sonoy, with whom he had already carried out missions for Brederode in 1567), Guillaume Mostaert in Alkmaar, and Willem de Grave in Edam.[86] Maerten Ruychaver was appointed as treasurer of the war chest.[87]

Sonoy's colleagues were, like him, rebels who had been in at the beginning of the Revolt, for the most part noblemen who had signed the Compromise and petition against the Inquisition, had been banished by the Council of Troubles and stripped of their estates. Many of them were former captains of the Sea Beggars and virulently anti-Catholic.

The towns of the Northern Quarter were not at all happy to be placed under Calvinistic military rule. As we have seen, they were fiercely attached to their autonomy. In 1572, for the first time, they had been admitted to the States of Holland, assembled at Dordrecht, but since the Spanish army had cut the rebel region in two the States had had very little opportunity to intervene in the affairs of Holland north of the River IJ. Even so, it was crucially important to William of Orange and Sonoy that the towns should remain actively committed to the continuance of the war. The walled towns and their armed inhabitants were vital to the war effort, while as long as Amsterdam remained loyal to the government, the ports were indispensable as bases for the rebel fleet and to secure imports of grain and other foodstuffs. Finally, the towns paid the lion's share of the taxes that financed the war.

In February 1573 Sonoy therefore summoned delegates from the six largest towns of the Northern Quarter to a meeting in Alkmaar, intended to implement a resolution previously adopted by the States of Holland to levy a special tax.[88] In June these assemblies were given more permanent form by the creation of the Council of Deputies of the Northern Quarter, a standing committee that was to sit at Hoorn, centrally situated between the other towns. Shortly afterward, at the Prince of Orange's insistence, Purmerend was added as the seventh voting town. Gradually, Governor Sonoy began to discuss other important matters besides taxes with the delegates.

The administrative organization of the Northern Quarter was an almost exact copy of that in Holland and Zeeland as a whole, where the Stadholder, William of Orange, and his counselors stood alongside—and sometimes opposed to—the States of Holland and Zeeland.[89] Although the towns had no formal right to debate military policy, in practice they held the purse strings and could not be denied a say.

---

[86] Geus, "Bewoners," 104; Bor, 377.
[87] His instructions in "Rekening Ruychaver," 50–55.
[88] Persman, "Bestuursorganisatie," 142.
[89] Koopmans, *Staten van Holland*, 119–23.

This dualistic model of government could hardly fail to provoke bitter recriminations between Sonoy and the representatives of the towns.[90] There was similar friction between William of Orange and the States of Holland and Zeeland, but Sonoy lacked the prince's tact. The towns held Sonoy responsible for the fiascos in which every one of his attacks on the Spaniards had ended. In the background, they were always seeking to gain more influence on the civil government and on the conduct of the war. Twice the conflicts reached such a pitch that Sonoy offered his resignation, but William of Orange believed the Northern Quarter could not do without a single strong leader, at least for as long as the war continued.

In the summer of 1574 relations between the towns and Sonoy were so near breaking point that the prince offered to send his own brother-in-law, Count Willem van den Bergh, to replace him. The towns reacted with shock. In 1572 the count had made himself notorious by failing to defend Zutphen against the Spanish army and thus allowing it to be sacked and destroyed. The remedy appeared worse than the disease. Rather than submit to Van den Bergh's authority, the towns reconciled themselves to Sonoy, but their relations with him remained tense. Sonoy blamed the lack of cooperation from them for the failure of his assault on the Barndegat in April 1575, and they in turn bitterly reproached him for failing to hold Muiden in May 1576.

Sonoy was equally brusque and tactless in his dealings with individual towns. In September 1572 he was embroiled in an acrimonious quarrel with the citizens of Hoorn over who should be master in the town. In November of that year the citizens of Medemblik resorted to arms in protest against the authoritarian methods of the new rulers.[91]

Sonoy was unlucky indeed in his military ventures. After the undefended Northern Quarter had fallen into his hands without resistance in May and June 1572, he never scored another military success. Twice he was chased away from the Diemerzeedijk (March and June 1573); he had to surrender the Barndegat (April 1575); and after a successful attack on Muiden he withdrew prematurely, and in the opinion of many observers unnecessarily, in May 1576. This seriously compromised his authority in the towns of North Holland, but his personal degree of responsibility for these failures is debatable. The Beggar companies were wholly inadequate for a direct engagement with the experienced Spanish units. Sonoy could only hope to damage the Spanish army by repeatedly attacking its Achilles' heel, the long and vulnerable supply line between Utrecht

---

[90] Bor, 437–38; 571; NHA, RNK, inv. no. 237, fol. 36 (8 September 1574); William of Orange to the States of the Northern Quarter, 3 July 1574, WFA, OA Medemblik, inv. no. 1239.

[91] Velius, 193; Bor, 415.

and Haarlem. And so he did, but in the end he had too little equipment and too few men to drive the Spaniards away from the dikes along the River IJ permanently.

Sonoy was more successful in defense. By flooding the land in October 1573, over the bitter opposition of the local peasantry, he forced the Spanish army to retreat from Alkmaar. Given the weakness of his mercenary companies, he made the best use he could of the two resources the countryside of North Holland offered in abundance: water and local manpower. The water line between the Zijpe and the Gouwzee remained an impregnable barrier for the Spanish army. Sonoy had Alkmaar and Purmerend reinforced with modern fortifications and heavily fortified sconces built at strategic points along the water line.

Sonoy revealed his talent as an organizer in the defense of the Northern Quarter. When reading the ordinances he issued on the cutting of the channel in the ice in January 1575 and on the watch in May 1575, one is impressed by his capacity to create an almost impassable defensive line with the most limited and simple means in such a short time.[92] His extensive correspondence testifies to his boundless energy and feverish activity. The letters he wrote to Captain Nicolaes Ruychaver between 21 February and 10 May 1574 show him constantly on the move between the various places where his presence was required.[93] That the Northern Quarter was able to withstand the Spanish army was largely thanks to Sonoy's talent for organization and ability to improvise.

Sonoy was one of the few Beggar leaders who was not only anti-Catholic but also was a confessing member of the Reformed Church. He took an active part in synodal assemblies and tried to promote the preaching of God's word in a variety of ways. He proclaimed days of prayer and fasting, on which visiting taverns and other worldly amusements were forbidden on pain of strict penalties. He was convinced that the Revolt was the unfolding of God's plan for salvation.[94] This was not likely to endear him to the majority of the local population who remained attached to the old Church.

In the early months of the Revolt Sonoy's soldiers had been guilty of serious outrages against Catholic clergy. Six monks from the Franciscan

---

[92] See above, pp. 82–83, 88.
[93] Sonoy to Ruychaver, NHA, Ruychaver, inv. nos. 75–103. On 21 and 22 February 1574 Sonoy was in Alkmaar, on 24 February in Purmerend, on 17 March in Alkmaar, on 25 March in Purmerend, on 27 March in Alkmaar, on 30 March in Enkhuizen, on 17 April in Hoorn, on 23 and 27 April in Enkhuizen, on 5, 6, and 10 May again in Purmerend.
[94] Membership register Alkmaar, RAA, Archief van de kerkeraad van de Nederlands-Hervormde gemeente Alkmaar, inv. no. 137, fol. 7v. For days of prayer and fasting see Bor, 457; proclamation of days of prayer, fasting, and thanksgiving for the victory of 12 October

monastery outside Alkmaar were assaulted and hanged a few days after the town went over, and there were other victims in the countryside.[95] Of course, Sonoy can be held responsible for the misdeeds of soldiers under his command, but he quickly restored discipline in his army. After one of his captains, Michiel Crock, had cruelly tortured and murdered a priest in Langedijk, Sonoy had him arrested, tried, and executed.[96] This put a stop to outrages against the clergy, presumably also because so many of them had since fled to safety in Amsterdam and other loyal towns.

Sonoy has earned himself a bad name in historical literature, partly through the cruel mistreatment of the Catholic clergy by his men, partly through the brutal conduct of the commission that investigated the "traitors" of 1575, which is the subject of this book. His numerous conflicts with the towns of the Northern Quarter have done his posthumous reputation among Dutch historians no good. Finally, he put himself even further in the wrong by siding with Leicester in the conflicts of 1585–87 and refusing to submit to the authority of Maurice of Nassau, Oldenbarnevelt, and the States of Holland. Sonoy belonged to the school of thought that stood for a relatively strong central authority and a dominant position for the Reformed Church. After the departure of Leicester and the rise of Oldenbarnevelt this was the side that lost the argument in the politics of Holland.

Several historians have alleged that Sonoy, who was born in Cleves, was not a Netherlander, but this is to apply a criterion that was irrelevant at the time.[97] It was relatively fortuitous that the Duchy of Gelderland had ended up in the Habsburg Netherlands while Cleves remained outside them. If one adopts the criterion of birthplace, William of Orange was a foreigner. Sonoy came from the Cleves branch of a noble family that was also settled in Utrecht and Gelderland. His mother came from the Bishopric of Utrecht, where he spent most of his youth. He served in the Netherlands cavalry and fought under the command of a Netherlands nobleman in the campaigns of Charles V and Philip II. By taking a wife in the Netherlands he acquired estates in Holland, where he lived for a fairly long time before the Revolt. His letters were written in the eastern variant of Dutch.

William of Orange protected Sonoy and kept him on as governor of North Holland, even after the Spanish army had left the province in 1576,

---

at Alkmaar, 17 October 1573, WFA, OA Hoorn, inv. no. 55, fol. 161v; ordinance of Sonoy, 16 October 1575, WFA, OA Medemblik, inv. no. 1238.

[95] Opmeer, *Martelaarsboek*, 19–31, 94–99, 198–209.

[96] Bor, 434; Opmeer, *Martelaarsboek*, 100.

[97] Although Sonoy himself invoked it in 1576, when he had to swear an oath of unconditional loyalty to the king. His claim that he owned no estates in the Netherlands was untrue. Cf. Bor, 148; Hooft, *Nederlandsche historiën*, 425; Wagenaar, *Vaderlandsche historie*, VII, 61.

and there was no longer any need for a separate administration in the peninsula. It is remarkable that he dismissed Lumey, his lieutenant who held the same post in South Holland as Sonoy in the Northern Quarter, and whose troops had been guilty of similar outrages against Catholic clergy.[98] Was this because Lumey had been personally implicated in the murders of priests and monks, while Sonoy had ultimately called his captains to order? In any case, military talent was too rare to waste. However much he relied on the towns to support his rebellion, the Prince of Orange knew he could not win the war without professional officers.

The group portrait of the members of the investigation commission and the man who stood behind them shows that several groupings can be distinguished in Holland during the war years. The men who held military and political power were largely rebels who had joined the Revolt at the beginning: Calvinists, confessing members of the Reformed Church, most of them already in the opposition in 1566, men who had been banished and stripped of their property by the Council of Troubles, had served in Orange's armies or with the Sea Beggars, and were embittered and hardened by exile. Other members of the revolutionary elite had chosen to stay at their posts in the new circumstances of 1572; although these men were less pugnacious than the returned Calvinist exiles, for them too there was no going back.

The men of 1572 came into repeated conflict with the magistrates and citizens of the towns, who formed another element in the interplay of forces in Holland. The towns had only admitted Sonoy's troops in the summer of 1572 because that appeared to be the lesser of two evils. When Alba began his campaign they could not go back on their choice. To be sure, most of the sitting magistrates in 1572 were replaced by new men who were regarded as supporters of the Prince of Orange's cause, but these men were much more moderate than Sonoy and his followers. Even though some of them joined the new Reformed Church communities, and there were returned exiles among them, nevertheless they were always obliged to take account of the prevailing mood in their towns, where the majority of the people wanted little or nothing to do with religious innovations. The magistrates had to steer a course between the demands of the political and military administration backed by William of Orange and their fellow townsfolk whom they represented. The careers of Sonoy, Calff, and Heukesloot were punctuated by continual clashes with the citizenry. Was it by mere chance that the only member of the commission who was firmly rooted in his town community, Foreest, took no part in its activities?

[98] Oosterhuis, *Lumey*, 186.

Another group has gone unmentioned up to now: those who stayed out of the conflict because they had no voice of their own in politics and no one else to speak for them, namely the peasantry and the other dwellers in the countryside. Finally, on the very bottom rung of the social ladder were the wayfarers with no fixed abode who roamed the highways and byways as vagrants and vagabonds. It is time to turn to the victims of Sonoy's commissioners.

CHAPTER SEVEN

# Vagabonds

VAGABONDS, VAGRANTS, or whatever they were called, the wayfaring folk who roamed the roads in large bands had an evil reputation in sixteenth-century Europe.[1] To be sure, official Roman Catholic theology still offered a fairly positive image of the poor. They were supposed to confront believers with the Christian ideal of poverty and enable them to win eternal salvation by performing works of charity. In orthodox Catholic circles, and naturally above all among the mendicant orders, this ideal had not yet lost its force, but most town magistrates and other officials who were responsible for maintaining public order in practice took a much less rose-tinted view.

Since the second half of the fifteenth century Europeans had come to feel increasingly fearful and hostile toward vagrants and beggars. They perceived the poor as a menace to public order, with the result that vagabonds and wayfarers were criminalized and marginalized. This negative approach to the problem of poverty was linked to the surge in population throughout Europe, with which employment opportunities and the standard of living had failed to keep pace.[2] Peasants driven from their land, workless day laborers, discharged soldiers, and craftsmen in search of work traveled singly or in groups from place to place, earning a living by performing all manner of marginal services. An ordinance of 1586, for example, spoke of "tinkers, peddlers, glass sellers, spindle sellers, sulfur thieves, serge sellers, ink sellers, cloth sellers, chalk sellers, quacks and the like vagrants."[3] There was only a fine line between these humble trades and outright begging. Many gave up the search for honest work and tried to keep themselves alive by begging for alms or, unavoidably, by theft, robbery, or extortion.

The fear and distaste for the poor felt by the elite is evident in literature. Such popular works as Sebastian Brandt's *Ship of Fools* were translated into many tongues, including Dutch.[4] In colorful language these books

---

[1] For perceptions of the poor see Geremek, *Les fils de Cain*; Chartier, "Elites"; Burke, "Perceiving a Counter-Culture."

[2] Lis and Soly, *Poverty*, chapter 3.

[3] Ordre op 't schouwen en bedelen der Leprosen [order on the begging of lepers], 13 October 1586, *Groot Placaet-Boeck*, I, 470–71.

[4] Brant, *Narrenschiff*. Dutch translations appeared in 1500, 1504, 1548, and 1584. Pleij, *Gilde*, 307.

depicted a world of nefarious practices, and what was believed to be the hierarchical organization and esoteric jargon of the people on the margins of society. The *Liber Vagatorum* contained a long catalog of various types of deceitful beggars, each with its own name in thieves' slang.[5] The chief message of this book was that most beggars could work, but did not want to. Picaresque novels such as *Lazarillo de Tormes* and the Dutch *Tyl Ulenspieghel*, a genre in vogue at this time, displayed a similar attitude. The hero, a young rogue, was implicitly held up to readers as a negative model, an example of how one ought not to live.

The humanists concerned themselves intensively with the question of poverty. Some of them offered practical suggestions, but all of them unanimously rejected begging. In Thomas More's *Utopia* (1516) begging was forbidden and work obligatory for the work-shy poor. Erasmus devoted one of his *Colloquies* to the problem and concluded that begging was antisocial, dangerous, and harmful to public order.[6] Not long afterward the Spanish humanist Juan Luis Vives published in Bruges his influential treatise *De subventione pauperum* (On the support of the poor, 1526), in which he set out a complete social program for the suppression of poverty. It was based on a strict ban on begging, the obligation to work for everyone who could, without distinction of sex or age, and the centralization of all local charitable funds under the supervision of the town authorities. His ideas were put into effect in numerous towns in the Netherlands. Luther, Zwingli, and Calvin were just as eager to condemn paupers and beggars. They argued for the absolute prohibition of begging, a duty to work for all able-bodied persons, and the centralization of support funds, which were to be kept to a bare minimum.[7]

In the pictorial arts satirical and allegorical depictions of beggars and vagrants were popular subjects.[8] In many prints and paintings of beggars the link between begging and human failings and sin is prominent. The poor had only themselves to blame. While a pious Christian would lead an industrious life, a beggar owed his misery to his own idleness. Poverty was palpably the work of the Devil.

The authorities attempted to put such ideas into practice in their legislation. A Draconian edict proclaimed in 1513 and 1514 at Hoorn and other towns of Holland prescribed that beggars must be nailed by the ear to the

---

[5] Boehncke and Johannsmeier, *Buch der Vaganten*.

[6] Erasmus, *Colloquies*, 248–54. In this dialogue the rogue Misoponus [Work-Hater] relates his deceitful practices. At the end he declares that beggars should no longer be allowed to roam freely, that each town should care for its own beggars, and that sturdy beggars must be put to work.

[7] Gutton, *Société*, 97–115; Bonenfant, "Origines."

[8] Tóth-Ubbens, *Verloren beelden*; Vandenbroeck, *Over wilden*; Vandenbroeck, *Jheronimus Bosch*.

pillory and remain there until they had torn themselves free.⁹ In 1531 the central government in Brussels, inspired by Vives's proposals, issued an edict against begging, which would remain in force until the time of the French revolutionary invasion in 1795.¹⁰ The text drew a distinction between the "rightful" or deserving poor and fraudulent beggars. The former category, which included invalids, orphans, widows, and others who through no fault of their own were unable to earn their bread, deserved support. The second category, those who had "turned to idleness (which is the principle of all evil)," were to be forced to work. Begging was forbidden under virtually all circumstances. Only the mendicant orders and lepers were exempted. The latter were to make themselves recognizable by their special clothing and carry a rattle with which they loudly proclaimed their approach. Poor people were forbidden to wander the roads and settle in other places, except in time of war or inundation. On the positive side, all the existing charitable funds were centralized in a "common purse," a local poor relief fund under a single administration. Offertory boxes were to be placed in the churches and a register of receipts kept. It goes without saying that the edict of 1531 offered no solution at all for those who took to the roads in search of work.

All the legislation distinguished on principle between the local needy and outsiders. While the former were eligible for relief if they fell into distress through no fault of their own, the latter were definitely ruled out. They were to be kept under strict surveillance. An Amsterdam bylaw prescribed that outsiders who arrived by boat from Gouda, Leiden, or Utrecht must land outside the Regulars' Gate and only enter the city on foot. They were to be registered and issued with a passport, which they had to surrender when they left. Those who had no urgent business in the city were limited to a maximum of two nights' stay on pain of whipping and banishment. Those who slept in the open or in the cheapest lodging houses always ran the risk of being expelled from the city.¹¹ The judicial archives of Amsterdam show that outsiders were far more liable to come before the courts. A hundred and fifty persons were sentenced for begging and vagrancy in the second quarter of the sixteenth century, but only three of them were from Amsterdam.¹²

In criminal proceedings suspects who were beggars and vagabonds suffered from a very unenviable discrimination. Whereas normal suspects could only be subjected to torture under precisely defined conditions—

---

⁹ After this they were banished from the country for life, Velius, 101; Boomgaard, *Misdaad*, 118.
¹⁰ *Groot Placaet Boeck*, I, 470–76.
¹¹ Boomgaard, *Misdaad*, 119.
¹² Ibid., 120.

the judge had to rule in an interlocutory judgment that there was sufficient circumstantial evidence of their guilt—vagabonds could be put to torture immediately and without any legal impediment.[13] Town justices were very reluctant to apply torture to their own citizens in particular. In some cases a suspect had to be stripped of his citizenship before he could be tortured. Vagrants were liable to torture for the mere fact of not having a fixed abode or employment; even an interlocutory judgment was not always necessary. Unemployment, idleness, and leading a wandering life were regarded as sufficient signs of criminality in themselves.

In times of crisis and war vagrants and beggars were feared as an even greater threat to public safety than usual. People were all too ready to believe that such sinister characters would sell their services to anyone. In the revolutionary year 1572 the magistrates of Gouda appointed a special officer to ensure that the countless beggars who were prowling around outside the city did not enter its gates.[14] When one town after another admitted the Sea Beggars in June 1572 Amsterdam gave all beggars who were not citizens, unless they were sick or mutilated, a day to leave the city, on pain of whipping and banishment.[15]

While we are well informed about how the elite saw beggars and vagabonds, the lives of these unfortunates themselves are obscure.[16] Their voices echo frequently but faintly through the pages of the confession books of local courts, where their words were recorded and often garbled by the court clerks. The defendants only answered the questions that were put to them by the judges. Yet here too it is evident that the fears of the elite were not simply the consequence of negative stereotyping. In the countryside above all, bands of vagrants often extorted money from the peasants by burning their property.

Perhaps the life of the vagrant Willem Maertenszoon, also known by the remarkable alias "the Waterland *Landwijf*" ("country woman"), who was interrogated by the justices of Alkmaar in March 1571, is representative of the other vagabonds who roamed the countryside of North Holland.[17] The *Landwijf* had been without work for three years and had kept himself alive in that time by begging and stealing in Waterland and the dune belt. He admitted stealing clothes and linen: a cloak, skirts, a fur, a mantle, a cap, men's and women's shirts, a pair of shoes, bedclothes, pillow slips, a sheath with a knife. He had sold the linen "in a little house outside Heiloo, near the mill, to a woman whose husband was called

---

[13] Van Heijnsbergen, *Pijnbank*, 55–57.
[14] Van Deursen, *Mensen*, 64.
[15] Bylaw of 26 June 1573, SAA, Archief Burgemeesters, inv. no. 5020/10, fol. 66.
[16] For marginal people at a slightly later period see Egmond, *Underworlds*.
[17] Confession of Willem Maertenszoon, 15 March 1571, RAA, SA Alkmaar, inv. no. 48.

Drunken Pieter." He had tried to set fire to houses at Heiloo and Uitgeest, because the occupant had struck his comrade Witcop (White-Head) a blow. In Bakkum he had joined in an attack on a farmhouse, in which he had tied up a married couple and their daughter with sheets torn into strips. The *Landwijf* had committed these offenses in the company of varying groups of vagrants. He had stolen clothing "from the bleach-green by the Poor Clares' convent with Jan van Wormer, Hansgen Pieter alias Deelbecker of Antwerp and Jet from Friesland." His accomplices in the attack at Bakkum had been "Geerloff and Minne, Rootgen, Monnik (Monk) and Thomas." Other fellow offenders were Louris de Pelser (the Furrier), Harman Witcop, and Harman Geelcous (Yellow-Stocking).

Most of these criminals met an early death. The *Landwijf*'s comrade Witcop, alias Harman van Emden, alias Jacob Folkertszoon van Leeuwarden, was arrested at Amsterdam in November 1571, examined under torture, and sentenced to be burned at the stake because he had "for three years and more roamed and conversed with thieves, extortionists and other evildoers."[18] He too confessed to numerous thefts and extortions and named his accomplices. His friend Harman Geelcous (from Cologne) proved to have been executed at Muiden in the meantime, two other mates, Schipper from Flushing and Aelbert from Texel, had been burned alive in Haarlem.

These groups of vagabonds were not the hierarchically organized bands of robbers that the author of the *Liber vagatorum* had imagined. They came together in their wanderings, shared their booty, and after a while went their own way. It is no coincidence that both the *Landwijf* and Witcop admitted that they had not practiced any trade for three years (that is, since 1568), for those were the very years when the country was in a deep economic crisis. On 24 March 1572 Morillon wrote to Granvelle about the lamentable situation in Holland: In several towns and villages, where previously there had not been a beggar to be found, their numbers had now risen to six or seven hundred, for the most part unemployed sailors and fishermen.[19]

Of the twenty-three vagrants who were arrested on Sonoy's orders on 27 May 1575, we know little more than their names and places of origin.[20] Jan Driemunt came from Hoorn; three brothers Michiel, Jan, and Gerrit Joosten came from Beverwijk; Gerrit Pieterszoon and Jan Coek from Krommenie; the brothers Pieter and Jan Janszoon from Buiksloot; six vagrants, Dammas Correliszoon, Pieter Ariszoon, Jan Alewijaszoon, Jan

---

[18] His confession in SAA, RA, Confessieboeken, inv. no. 273, fols. 31–33; judgment in SAA, ORA, Justitieboeken, inv. no. 568, fol. 131.

[19] CCG, IV, 148.

[20] Bor, 624, cited from a lost letter of Sonoy to Orange, 30 May 1575.

Keeszoon, Quirijn Dirkszoon, and Cornelis Pieterszoon came from Haarlem; and Roelken Gerritszoon alias Nooschert hailed from Naarden. Friesland contributed Roomken or Reynken Symons and Claes Roeloffszoon from Dokkum, Pieter Janszoon alias Geelcous from Koudum, and Ysebrant Janszoon from Echte. From Groningen and the Ommelanden came Pieter Jacobszoon de Vries of Groningen and Jacob Janzsoon of Midwou (presumably Midwolde in the West Quarter or Midwolda in the Oldambt, and not Midwoud in North Holland). Jacob alias Blaurok came from "Engien," perhaps Enghien in Hainault.[21] Jan Clouk's place of origin is unknown.

However little to go on the personal names offer (in spite of the exotic sounding aliases), the places of origin are revealing. Only one of the arrested vagrants is known to have come from the region under Sonoy's command, namely Jan Driemunt of Hoorn, the official territory of Joost Heukesloot.[22] Seven vagrants originated in three small places in the Northern Quarter, Beverwijk, Krommenie, and Buiksloot, which were occupied by the Spaniards. Another seven came from the towns of Haarlem and Naarden, which had suffered at the hands of the Spaniards. Six prisoners came from the northern provinces of Friesland, Groningen, and the Ommelanden, which were also firmly under Spanish rule. None of them was from the areas of South Holland or Zeeland that were under the Prince of Orange's control.

All but one of the vagabond prisoners were "strangers," outsiders in both senses of the word: in the figurative sense of the marginal vagrants and beggars in the paintings of Bosch and Brueghel, but also in the very real and dangerous sense of people from the territory of the enemy. That is not surprising, since the towns of North Holland had warned Sonoy to be on his guard against "certain vagabonds, being strangers." The raids of 27 May had not been targeted at vagrants as such but at outsiders, people who came from the area under enemy control and who did not possess the required papers.

The alarm felt by the North Holland authorities at the presence of strangers and contacts with the enemy was not new. Although from a military viewpoint the peninsula was isolated, traffic between it and the area in Spanish hands was certainly possible. The rebels did their utmost to control such trade with the enemy. Shortly after it had gone over to the Revolt Monnickendam issued a bylaw forbidding the citizens to leave the town without a passport issued by the burgomasters, denying strangers access to the town, and prohibiting trade with Amsterdam and correspondence with the inhabitants of the city. Hoorn, too, forbade its inhabitants

---

[21] Perhaps Enghien-les-Bains, a village just north of Paris; or was Anjum in Friesland meant?

[22] Two if Jacob Janszoon came from Midwoud in West Friesland.

to have any dealings with Amsterdam.²³ In August 1573 Sonoy warned the towns of North Holland that many "redeemed prisoners" (possibly released prisoners of war) were secretly attempting to leave without entering the service of the Prince of Orange. He gave orders for a strict watch to be kept, and for no one to be allowed to leave unless he was provided with a passport signed and sealed by Sonoy. Those who were caught without a valid passport must be put in irons at once and punished as "dishonorable and faithless rogues and scoundrels." Should anyone nevertheless manage to enter the villages without a passport the peasants were to "strike the same on the head and treat them as public enemies." The inhabitants of the Quarter were forbidden to carry such people in their boats on pain of forfeiture of the vessel. Moreover they were to be prosecuted as public enemies of the Prince of Orange.²⁴

The waterways that penetrated into every corner of North Holland made it both unavoidable and necessary for its communications with the outside world to remain open. Since the beginning of the blockade of Amsterdam the towns of West Friesland and Waterland had drawn all the city's trade to themselves. They were permitted to trade with the enemy, but only in goods for which permits were issued. High export duties, called licenses, were levied on these goods and applied to finance the rebellion.²⁵ However advantageous it might be, the licensed trade posed new problems for the authorities, because it made it essential for the local merchants to have frequent dealings with the enemy. The authorities supervised the trade by issuing passports to North Hollanders whose ships sailed to enemy-held ports. For each voyage the ship's master had to state his destination and promise that he would return to his home port and not enter the service of the enemy. For added certainty he had to deposit a surety.²⁶ The States of the Northern Quarter frequently debated "too lightly granted" passports, which had allowed confidential information to leak out, to the great danger of the common cause.²⁷ The frequency with which this item appeared in the States' resolutions shows that their attempts to control the movements of the inhabitants were largely in vain.

---

²³ Bylaw of 10 August 1572, WA, OA Monnickendam, inv. no. 61. At the end of this register is a list of passports issued to citizens who left the town, 1574–75; Ordinance on the militia, undated (after 23 August 1572), WFA, OA Hoorn, inv. no. 55, fol. 130.

²⁴ Sonoy to the magistrates of Hoorn, 16 August 1573, WFA, OA Hoorn, inv. no. 55, fol. 2. The same letter to the magistrates of Alkmaar, *Brieven en andere bescheiden*, 67.

²⁵ Kernkamp, *Handel*.

²⁶ Ordinance of Sonoy forbidding ships to sail until they have deposited a surety, 27 June 1574, WFA, OA Hoorn, inv. no. 55, fol. 182; sureties on behalf of merchants and shippers who sail to enemy territory, WFA, OA Hoorn, inv. no. 166.

²⁷ For example the deputies of the Northern Quarter to the burgomasters of Alkmaar, 10 February 1575, NHA, GNK, inv. no. 236, 10 February 1575.

The origins of the imprisoned vagabonds reveal a second common feature: many of them must have been refugees driven from their homes, trades, families, and friends by the violence of war, who had no option but to join the great army of vagrants that made the roads hazardous. One of those arrested came from Naarden, a town that had been razed to the ground and its people massacred by the Spaniards in December 1572. Six came from Haarlem, which after the long siege had been forced to pay a heavy fine and bear the costs of the Spanish garrison. Its trade and industry were at a standstill. Three of the prisoners came from Beverwijk, from where two companies of Spaniards, quartered on the village since the beginning of the siege of Haarlem, were ravaging the countryside.[28] The fact that Hierges's army was encamped at Beverwijk must have thrown even more suspicion on these two men. Buiksloot, from where the brothers Pieter and Jan Janszoon came, had been occupied by the Sea Beggars in the autumn of 1572 but had been recaptured by the Spaniards in October 1573.[29] Krommenie, the home of Gerrit Pieterszoon and Jan Coek, lay in the middle of the front line and had changed hands several times between Spaniards and rebels. Its people had suffered from plundering and exactions by both parties. In late 1573 Krommenie was partly burned down by the Spaniards, but the rebels managed to drive the enemy away after heavy fighting. In February 1574 several days of frost allowed the government army to cross the frozen waterways and retake the village. A month later the Spaniards abandoned it again, to march off to fight the rebel army under William of Orange's brother Louis of Nassau at Mook Heath, but before they moved out they reduced what was left unburned of Krommenie to ashes.[30] Where could its inhabitants turn?

The Hoorn chronicler Velius gives a striking picture of the stream of refugees who fled from the nearby village of Wormer when the Spanish army overran it in February 1574. Thick fog, which persisted during several hours of fighting between the Spaniards and the rebels, allowed the peasants to flee to safety with their wives and children

> although with very great difficulty, for there was no other opening but the channel cut in the ice, and then they had to make their way in winter weather and with wet clothing for a long way before they came to a place of safety, which was near Purmerend. Thus the dike between the two places was black with people, often so much so that they pushed one another down off the dike. Truly it was a pitiful spectacle to see so many women and innocent children fleeing from their comforts, wet

---

[28] Mendoça, *Commentaires*, 188–89; *DWJ*, 141.
[29] Velius, 193, 216.
[30] Ibid., 228, 231, 232, 235, 236.

and almost stiff with cold, with such wailing as anyone may think, and coming to the houses of strangers, in the winter time, and without bringing any of their goods with them.[31]

These then were the prisoners whom Sonoy's commissioners were to interrogate: refugees forced to take to the roads by the war; strangers without friends or family who could bear witness or stand surety for them; vagabonds who could not invoke town privileges and who could be tortured without the flimsiest pretext; vagrants and beggars, the very lowest strata of society, feared and despised by settled townsfolk and peasants. All of them were outsiders, who did not possess the required papers, who came from areas in the hands of the enemy, and who might well have been in touch with the enemy. They certainly had to be considered capable of betraying the country for a few coppers. For Sonoy and the commissioners their guilt was a foregone conclusion.

It was not long before the commissioners were able to take down the first statements from the terrified vagabonds.[32] To begin with the suspects confessed to a variety of minor offenses. One admitted stealing a chicken; another had taken linen. But once they were put to torture, the confessions the commissioners were looking for soon followed. Michiel Joosten of Beverwijk, who had been arrested with his two brothers at Petten, confessed to seeking to set fire to the villages of Wognum, Zwaag, Westerblokker, and Oosterblokker. His brother Jan admitted that he had targeted Spanbroek, Benningbroek, Berkhout, Grootebroek, Wervershoof, and Oude Niedorp. Their brother Gerrit had sought to reduce the villages of Nieuwe Niedorp, Hoogwoud, and Opmeer to ashes. Jan Keeszoon of Haarlem confessed to seeking to do the same for Westerblokker and Oosterblokker, Zwaag, Sijbekarspel, and Benningbroek. Pieter Jacobszoon de Vries from Groningen and Cornelis Pieterszoon from Haarlem admitted their intention to raise fires in the two Blokker villages, Binnenwijzend and Zwaag, while Quirijn Dirckszoon of Haarlem did the same for Wervershoof, Twisk, Oostwoud, Midwoud, Hauwert, and Berkhout; and Gerrit Pieterszoon of Krommenie for Ooster- and Westerblokker, Zwaag, Binnenwijzend, Sijbekarspel, and Benningbroek.

The commissioners had made up their minds before they set to work that the vagrants could not have acted on their own initiative. Their questions were therefore designed not just to elicit confessions from the suspects, but also to force them to reveal the names of those who were behind the plot and had given them their orders. The accused named several peas-

---

[31] Ibid., 236.
[32] Bor, 624–25.

ants from the West Friesland villages of Wognum, Benningbroek, and Hoogwoud, who had given them alms and shelter recently. These peasants were immediately seized from their beds and brought to Alkmaar.

The confessions and accusations of the vagrants largely agreed with one another. That must have satisfied the commissioners and convinced them that they were on the right track. How is the uniformity of the statements to be explained?

Undoubtedly the use of torture played some part. Nowadays torture is no longer regarded as an acceptable means of finding the truth. Besides the humanitarian objections, it is believed that pain or the fear of pain will lead an accused to admit offenses in which he had no share. The principles of humanity generally accepted today were alien to sixteenth-century justice, which was nevertheless well aware of the risk that false confessions might be extorted. The use of torture was therefore governed by strict rules. The Constitutio Criminalis Carolina, the Criminal Ordinances of 1570 and the authors of manuals of judicial practice all went into detail about the conditions in which torture might or might not be applied. All of these authorities issued emphatic warnings against asking leading questions. Wielant and De Damhouder warned that the judge might not "indicate and persuade" the "patient" to admit anything incriminating himself, nor threaten him with extra pain.[33]

It is safe to assume, however, that the rules laid down from above were not always observed in practice. Because the accused was not permitted to appeal in cases where a sentence of death or other physical punishment was imposed, few suspects were in a position to complain to a higher court of procedural abuses during their questioning.[34] In principle the provincial courts were charged with supervising the lower courts, but they did not have the means to make this control effective. In practice the local officers and benches of justices were almost always left to go their own way undisturbed. It goes without saying that in the war years after 1572 the Court of Holland was in no state to exercise any supervision whatever.

In nearly all cases the actual conduct of the hearings and the unlawful methods the courts employed to extort the most unlikely confessions do not appear in the records. The North Holland treason case, however, was an exception. During the proceedings that some of the suspects later brought against Sonoy and his commissioners, several of those who

[33] Van Heijnsbergen, *Pijnbank*, 40, 78; De Damhouder, *Practycke*, 51.

[34] De Waardt, *Toverij*, 101, mentions some cases in which suspects successfully appealed against the interlocutory judgment by virtue of which they had been ordered to be tortured. In that case the torture did not take place, and no charge was made. See also Egmond, "Strafzaken."

had been directly involved made notarized depositions before witnesses. These give us a revealing and often shocking picture of the way the interrogations were conducted. They form a unique document, which gives us an insight into the practice of the "sharp examination." That practice evidently deviated widely from the juridical rules that were supposed to regulate it.[35]

On 20 March 1577 "Master" Jacob Michielszoon, the public executioner, appeared before the notary Guillaume van Triere the younger, in the presence of witnesses, and deposed

> that he well remembered that once Jan Driemunt was hung from a ladder by him, deponent, and left hanging there for four and a half hours, with his arms behind him above his head, and weights of two hundred pounds on both his big toes. He was brought by this to such great torment that the sweat ran from him in fear and dripped onto the floor. While he was so hanging, the commissioners questioned him and called out to him by name and surname several peasants, reading their names from a booklet or paper, especially one Coppen and his son from Wognum, and especially Pieter Nannincxzoon and others; holding out to him what they would have him say, saying, "You shall speak and accuse the same, or we shall do the like every day"; which peasants he deponent did not know at that time, but later thought that they were the peasants who were later caught; but the aforenamed patient, while he was hanging thus, did not confess or answer. Then the commissioners, that is Master Joost Heukesloot, sheriff of Hoorn, Willem Maertenszoon Calff, Willem van Sonnenberg and the secretary Adriaen Corneliszoon Texel, went and made good cheer in the Moor's Head in the Langestraat, at the house of Pieter Pieterszoon Heilichdach; and after the aforenamed Jan Driemunt had hung so for three hours, he called to him deponent, "Master Jacob, can you read or write? I shall tell you something." Whereto he deponent answered, "No, but I shall fetch someone who can write, or the commissioners." The aforenamed Driemunt said, "Run quickly, for I cannot hold out any longer." And he deponent went to the aforesaid inn and gave this message through

---

[35] Depositions before notary Willem van Triere at Alkmaar in favor of the prisoners at Schagen, 1576 and 1577, copy of 1581, NHA, Aanwinsten, inv. no. 1185. The original documents and the protocols of the notary Van Triere have been lost. This manuscript once belonged to Jan Jeroenszoon himself, according to a letter in the hand of his descendant Maria Clomp preserved under the same inventory number. The document is in poor condition. There is a second copy in UA, OBC, inv. no. 248. It is undated (possibly a copy from the above) and in good condition. The document in the NHA has been used as the source for the passages cited below; where words have become illegible because of wear, the document in the UA has been used to supplement or correct them.

the commissioners' servant. They remained sitting drinking for a good half hour. After that, practically drunk, they came to the patient and asked him what he wanted to say. To which the patient replied, "What do you want to know from me?" To which they said, "That you shall tell us the truth, who your accomplices and comrades in the treason are; then we will take you down and not torture you any more." The patient said, "Let me down and I will tell you." After he was let down, the commissioners held out to the patient and made him false promises that if he would tell the truth about what they had asked, his life would be spared, and he would become a *claudijt* (servant) of the provost.[36] The commissioners said to the patient, "We have our eyes on you, you know everything about the treason";[37] whereupon the patient then betrayed and denounced several peasants. The aforenamed deponent further declared that he knew that the aforesaid commissioners held out to Jan Driemunt and other beggars who were killed, saying these words: "If you will say what we hold out to you of such peasants and that before the gentlemen of Alkmaar [the bench of justices], then we assure you of your lives, and all the foregoing facts, for which you have deserved to die three deaths, will be forgotten and forgiven, and we shall give you letters of grace, signed by the Governor himself [Sonoy], so that no sheriff or bailiff will make difficulties for you now or at any time"; and he deponent also noticed that the aforesaid beggars and especially the aforenamed Jan Driemunt all said of one Pieter Nanningszoon and other peasants what the aforesaid commissioners wanted and held out to them.[38]

The unanimity of the confessions and accusations made by the vagabonds is sufficiently explained by the nature of the procedure. It is also clear that the commissioners flagrantly violated the rules for interrogation. The judges and secretary of the court were supposed to be present throughout the hearing and were forbidden to compel the accused to admit facts that incriminated himself. They were not permitted to urge him to denounce accomplices whose names they themselves had put forward.[39]

Furthermore, the vagrants were all locked up in a single room, and thus had ample opportunity to coordinate their evidence. Several witnesses declared that the prisoners in their communal cell told one another how

---

[36] New members of a neighborhood community in Utrecht were called *claudíten*. Kaplan, *Calvinists*, 280.

[37] The text reads "wij hebben den rechten voghen aen u"; the copy in UA, OBC, has "wij hebben den rechten voghel aen u." The reading "ooghen" [eyes] may be presumed.

[38] Deposition of Jacob Michielszoon, 20 March 1577, NHA, Aanwinsten, inv. no. 1185, fol. 8r–v.

[39] Van Heijnsbergen, *Pijnbank*, 40, 43, 48, 78; De Damhouder, *Practycke*, 51.

the commissioners had treated them, and what they had said. "Let us speak with one voice," they said, "and rather die than be tortured so." Before they died, they agreed to proclaim their innocence and that of the peasants they had denounced, "screaming and groaning often, and lamenting the poor peasants and themselves."[40]

Jan Driemunt declared that he had received three guilders from Coppen Corneliszoon, a peasant of Wognum, in the presence of Coppen's son, so that he and four other prisoners should set the villages on fire on 27 May, the day when the enemy appeared before the sconces. As prescribed, the accused repeated their confessions within twenty-four hours "without pain and bonds." Confronted with the peasants, who had by now been arrested, they told them to their face that they were the ones who had bribed them to burn the villages. This gave the commissioners enough grounds to subject the peasants in their turn to questioning.

The commissioners' promise to free the prisoners in return for the confessions demanded was as worthless as one might expect. If they wanted to put the treasonous plot beyond doubt, they could not avoid inflicting a severe and exemplary punishment on everyone who had been involved in it. Nor could they run the risk that the vagabonds, once released, would publicly denounce the way in which the commissioners had forced them to confess. For the commissioners personally and for the further course of the proceedings the vagrants had to be silenced permanently.

All the vagabonds were sentenced to death at the stake on the grounds of their confessions, the usual penalty for arson. The judgment was presumably pronounced by the justices of Alkmaar in the case of Jan Driemunt, and by the justices of the other places where the sentences were executed for the other vagabonds.[41] In most cases this was one of the villages they were alleged to have tried to burn down. Jan Joosten was put to death at Spanbroek, Gerrit Joosten at Hoogwoude, Gerrit Pieterszoon of Krommenie at Nieuwe Niedorp, Quirijn Dirczxoon of Haarlem at Wervershoof, Cornelis Pieterszoon of Haarlem at Grootebroek, Roelken Gerritszoon and Claes Roeloffszoon at Enkhuizen. At Hauwert and Nibbixwoud three men, Jan Clouk, Jan Coek, and Ysbrant Janszoon, and a woman whose name is unknown, were executed. Some of the vagabonds managed to escape from prison before the sentence was carried out, and no further trace of them was ever found.[42]

---

[40] Bor, 625.

[41] The commissioners asked Jan Driemunt to confirm his confession before "the gentlemen of Alkmaar." The criminal judgments of Alkmaar for this period have been lost.

[42] Bor does not name the place of execution for nine of the twenty-three arrested vagrants; probably they escaped. They were Michiel Joosten of Beverwijk; Dammas Corneliszoon of Haarlem; Jacob van Engien alias Blaurok, Roomken, or Reynken Simonszoon of Dokkum;

As agreed, all of those who were sentenced to death proclaimed their innocence and that of the peasants they had denounced before they were put to death. On 8 February 1577 the former servant of the sheriff of Alkmaar, Cornelis Janszoon, and his wife, Baertgen Hermansdochter, deposed before the notary Guillaume van Triere

> that one Roelken and Claes, who were burned at Enkhuizen, sitting on the wagon at Alkmaar to be carried out, openly cried out in the hearing of all the burghers and bystanders that all the peasants whom they had denounced—they named Pieter Nanningszoon, Coppen [Corneliszoon] and his son Nanning by name—were innocent of the crimes of which they had accused them, and they called out that they had confessed under torture.[43]

Pieter Janszoon of Koudum was executed at Sijbekarspel. Sitting at the stake, his neck in the belt with which he was to be strangled before being burned, and weeping bitter tears, he told the preacher Jan Ambrosius, who had to comfort him in his final hours, "that he was no more guilty of the treason than the rye that stood flowering in the field."[44]

Jan Driemunt was conveyed on a wagon to the place of execution outside the Kennemer gate at Alkmaar, where he knelt on a raised platform and addressed the crowd:

> "Ye good people, since I shall die the death that neither the peasants I accused nor I myself deserve, I am not guilty of any treason, yea, no more than the stones in the street or the youngest child that was born in the night"; and standing up to sit on the stool: "Here I could get no justice, but I hope that God will have mercy on me and will do justice."[45]

Such public denials could still embarrass the commissioners. To avert the danger the provost Michiel Heugelcke threatened the condemned prisoners that he would take them back to Alkmaar and torture them for as long as necessary to make them stand by their confessions and accusations. The condemned men complained, "with weeping eyes," to the executioner:

---

Pieter Ariszoon of Haarlem; Jacob Janszoon of Midwoud, Midwolde, or Midwolda; Jan Keeszoon of Haarlem; and Pieter and Jan Janszoon of Buiksloot.

[43] Deposition of Cornelis Janszoon and Baertgen Hermansdochter, 8 February 1577, NHA, Aanwinsten, inv. no. 1185, fol. 6v.
[44] Bor, 625–26.
[45] Ibid., 625.

Is it not a hard thing that we must confess our innocence as guilt to the provost? Oh Master Jacob, help us to a quick death! We shall be children of eternal life, for we will rather die ten deaths than let ourselves be tortured again.[46]

For the peasants who were now in prison the recantations of the executed vagrants were too late.

[46] Deposition of Jacob Michielszoon, 20 March 1577, NHA, Aanwinsten, inv. no. 1185, fol. 12v.

CHAPTER EIGHT

# Peasants

As soon as Sonoy heard that the vagrants had confessed and revealed the names of the alleged instigators of the plot, he ordered the peasants they had denounced to be arrested and brought to Alkmaar. Sheriff Joost Heukesloot seized Jacob or Coppen Corneliszoon, his wife, and their son Nanning and daughter Hillegont in Wognum, which was within the jurisdiction of Hoorn.[1] Mother and daughter were soon released, but Coppen Corneliszoon and Nanning Coppenszoon remained in custody. The arrest of these peasants followed quite shortly after that of the vagrants, not later than 6 or 7 June, perhaps a few days earlier.[2] The letter of commission written on 5 June explicitly gave retrospective authorization to the commissioners' previous actions. About six weeks later, in mid-July, the sheriff of Benningbroek arrested a certain Pieter Nanningszoon.[3] The vagabonds had named him too.

Why had these peasants in particular been denounced as the instigators of the treason? We know from the depositions made before notary Van Triere that the commissioners had read out the names of the peasants "from a little book or letter." It might be inferred from this that the com-

---

[1] Opmeer, *Martelaarsboek*, 248. The daughter, who is not named by Opmeer, must be the same as Hillegont Coppens, who is named in a register of landowners of Wognum: Notitie van de schade die Wognum heeft geleden (Note of the damage that Wognum has suffered) 1572–73, WFA, GA Wognum, inv. no. 212.

[2] Cornelis Janszoon and Baertgen Hermansdochter later deposed that they had cared for Nanning Coppenszoon "for about twelve and a half weeks" in the jail at Alkmaar before he was taken to Schagen. The date of the removal of the prisoners to Schagen is not precisely determined, but must have been about 1 or 2 September, for on 4 September the commissioners wrote from Schagen that they had questioned the prisoners there over the last three days. Cornelis and Baertgen must therefore have looked after Nanning for about eighty-seven or eighty-eight days before 1 or 2 September, that is, from about 6 June. Bor dates Coppen's death to 2 June; this could mean that the peasants were arrested a week earlier. Opmeer, however, puts his death on 14 June. Deposition of Cornelis Janszoon and Baertgen Hermansdochter, NHA, Aanwinsten, inv. no. 1185, fol. 6v; for the removal to Schagen, see also Bor, 640–41; for the dating of Coppen's death, Bor, 626, and Opmeer, *Martelaarsboek*, 249.

[3] Cornelis Janszoon and Baertgen Hermansdochter deposed that they had cared for Pieter Nanningszoon in Alkmaar for seven weeks. Besides this trio, another unnamed peasant was held at Hoogwouden, of whom nothing more is known. Probably he was soon released, or it may be an error. Bor, 625.

missioners themselves were the first to suggest the names of the unfortunate peasants. In that case they must have suspected them for some time.[4] It is more likely, however, that the initiative came from the vagrants, since they were locked up in the same cell and had agreed to accuse the same persons. They had unanimously named Coppen Corneliszoon of Wognum and Pieter Nanningszoon of Benningbroek, who were known to them because they had often given them shelter.[5] The names of the peasants must have been mentioned several times by one or more prisoners before the commissioners questioned Jan Driemunt. What the commissioners wanted and got from him was merely a confirmation of the charges already made by the other vagabonds.

More is known about the arrested peasants than about the vagrants. Coppen Corneliszoon must have been a fairly old man at this time.[6] If we are to believe his hagiographer Petrus Opmeer he was "a very honorable, mild-mannered man of integrity, modest in his way of life," who excelled in his hospitality to poor wayfarers. If this is true, he paid a high price for his charity. His son Nanning was a young single man, perhaps still a boy, with a minor physical handicap. As a result of an unspecified illness he suffered from "swollen legs," and was "quicker in his wits than on his legs." Opmeer also relates that the peasants were richer than the average, and he emphasizes their piety. Bor, too, writes that those arrested were "well to do husbandmen," and adds that "the people" were more willing to believe them guilty because they were Roman Catholics.[7] Well-off and Catholic: two facts that can be tested to a certain extent, the first more easily than the second.

The assessment register of the tenth penny of 1561 (a 10 percent tax on real property, not to be confused with Alba's notorious Tenth Penny sales tax) names Coppen Corneliszoon as the owner and occupier of a house in Wognum assessed at an annual value of four guilders ten stuivers. The farmhouses in Wognum ranged between two and six guilders in value, which means that Coppen's farm must have been of average size. He also owned two parcels of land; a meadow of reasonable quality within the dike, six *morgen* one *hont* in area, and 5.5 *morgen* of hay meadow of lesser quality outside the dike, altogether 11.5 *morgen*, or

---

[4] This is the interpretation of Velius, 246.

[5] Bor, 624.

[6] He is named as an owner of land and a house in the assessment register for the tenth penny in Wognum in 1553, twenty-two years before his arrest: NA, SvH, inv. no. 842, fols. 11, 17, 20; Coppen's daughter Hillegont was already married in 1575, as her brother Nanning spoke of "my brother-in-law Allert" during his interrogation. Deposition of Cornelis Janszoon and Baertgen Hermansdochter, NHA, Aanwinsten, inv. no. 1185, fol. 5.

[7] Opmeer, *Martelaarsboek*, 248–49, 256; Bor, 625.

twenty-six acres.[8] In Wognum in 1561, 148 householders and some ecclesiastical institutions and townsfolk together owned 1,600 *morgen* of land, an average holding of 10.8 *morgen* each, roughly the same as Coppen's property.[9] On such a limited area, half of which was outside the dike, he cannot have grazed more than three cattle. If even a farmer with an average herd of five or six animals could not live on the proceeds and had to depend on ancillary activities, Coppen must certainly have been in the same position. According to the *Informacie* of 1514 most of the inhabitants of Wognum earned their living by "working the land and going to sea."[10] Pieter Nanningszoon of Benningbroek also had an average sized, that is, fairly modest, property. In 1558 he owned a house and hayloft assessed at four guilders a year. Most of the houses in Benningbroek were taxed at three or four guilders, a few at rather less, but none was valued at more than four guilders. Pieter therefore belonged to the better-off householders in Benningbroek, but did not stand out from his fellow villagers. Nor was he distinguished from his neighbors as a landowner. Most of them owned about seven *morgen* per household. Pieter could boast at least one parcel of eight *morgen* one hundred *roeden*, which he cultivated himself.[11] Like the rest of the villagers he must have relied on second jobs to make ends meet. The *Informacie* names "farming . . . and diking" as the most important sources of income in Benningbroek.[12] We cannot rule out the possibility that Coppen and Pieter owned other parcels of land outside their home villages, or that they had inherited or otherwise acquired more property in the intervening years. But in the tax assessments of 1558 and 1561 neither man stands out as unusually wealthy. For the moment we must assume that they were small, at the most average, peasants, who scraped a hard living from the waterlogged soil. How well they made out with the help of a variety of sidelines is impossible to discover,

---

[8] Tenth penny register of Wognum, 1561, NA, SvH, inv. no. 1489, fols. 16v, 47v, 61. This was Jacob Corneliszoon alias Coppen. Another Jacob Corneliszoon ("of Spierdijk") owned six *morgen* two *hont* of pasture and 8.5 *morgen* two *hont* of hay meadow; fols. 54v, 55. See also inv. no. 1175 (tenth penny register of Wognum, 1558), fols. 14v–15; Jacob Corneliszoon (alias Coppen) and fols. 35, 37v (Jacob Corneliszoon van Spierdijk), and inv. no. 842 (tenth penny register of Wognum, 1553), fols. 11, 17, and 20.

[9] Naber, *Terugblik*, 33, 36. In 1514 Wognum comprised 1,600 *morgen* and numbered eighty-five houses and 350 communicants. In 1561 according to the tenth penny register the village had 148 households.

[10] *Informacie*, 99; cf. above, p. 18

[11] Tenth penny register of Benningbroek, 1561, NA, SvH, inv. no. 1435, fols. 2, 4v. The register is badly damaged at the edges, and it is therefore not impossible that Pieter Nanningszoon owned more land, for which the register entries have been lost. Pieter Nanningszoon is not mentioned in the registers for 1553 and 1556. In 1558 Benningbroek had an area of 634 *morgen* and numbered ninety-one households.

[12] *Informacie*, 113.

but they are not likely to have prospered during the economic recession from 1568, the floods of 1570, and the outbreak of the Revolt in 1572.

Were the arrested peasants Catholics? Opmeer's description of Coppen's piety cannot be accepted as reliable without reservations. His *Martelaarsboek* belongs to the genre of Catholic hagiography, in which martyrdom must form the apotheosis of a life that was pious by definition. Yet it may be presumed that the arrested peasants had remained loyal to the old Church. In this, however, they were no different from the majority of the villagers. All the evidence shows that the Protestant Reformation aroused little enthusiasm in the countryside of Holland during the early years of the Revolt.

As we saw earlier, isolated North Holland offered fertile soil for the Reformation. But before 1572 there are no reports of dissident priests leading their flocks astray from the path of orthodoxy in either Wognum or Benningbroek. That does not mean that all the parish clergy were strictly orthodox in all respects, or that they lived spotless lives in accordance with the rules of the Church. In the Northern Quarter many clergy lived with a woman and their children, and in other respects they differed little from their fellow villagers. Most of them would not have been so scandalous as the priest of Zwaag, whose own parishioners demanded his removal. This Anthonis Laurenszoon lived with Emme, "a whore ... by whom he has a certain number of children, and who urges him to all kinds of wickedness and lewdness." He lived outside the village next to a barn "where his cows stood." His parishioners complained that he had not said mass during Holy Week because he had been herding the sheep before the mass, and did not serve the community. The priest of Obdam, a son of the priest of Monnickendam, was a drunkard who was always to be found in the tavern, where he was once stabbed in the cheek during a brawl. "Our priest studies in his tankard," said his parishioners.[13]

No such stories are told of Wognum or Benningbroek. This may suggest that the ecclesiastical authorities had nothing to worry about, but it may also mean that the villagers did not complain to the authorities, because they were satisfied with a priest who was well integrated in the community. As long as the parishioners were content, and the clergy did not come under the notice of the Inquisition, there was little cause for concern. In 1566 and afterward both villages remained calm, with no iconoclasm, no priests who turned Protestant, and no investigation by the Council of Troubles. In 1572, so far as is known, the parish priests did not go over to the new Church.

---

[13] Voets, "Hervorming," I, 75, 77; *Bronnen kerkelijke rechtspraak*, VII, 46–47, 162; *BBH*, 26, 117–20.

Lenaert Bouwenszoon's list of baptisms shows that there were sizeable Anabaptist communities in several of the North Holland villages, namely Barsingerhorn, Bovenkarspel, Durgerdam, Grootebroek, Hoogkarspel, Kolhorn, Landsmeer, Middelie, Nieuwe Niedorp, Ransdorp, Watergang, and Zaandam.[14] But it makes no mention of Anabaptist activity in Wognum or Benningbroek. The itinerant preachers either made no converts there or simply never visited the two villages. Apparently the peasants were satisfied with the old Church and had never asked for its reform.

Nevertheless, in the summer of 1572 the Reformation movement in its most drastic form was to be imposed on them. At the beginning of July several Beggar captains arrived in Wognum to seize the gold- and silverwork in the church, as well as the chasubles, missals, candelabra, and all the other requisites of the mass. The soldiers stripped the church of its ironwork—two wagonloads of it—and took down the church bells to cast cannon from them. The villagers were allowed to ransom their fire bell for twenty-five guilders. Anything that could not be used for the war effort, such as a valuable tabernacle worth seven hundred guilders and the stained glass windows, was smashed to pieces by the soldiers. In all they caused damage estimated at 2,680 guilders to the church at Wognum.[15]

Although William of Orange had given explicit orders in 1572 that Catholics were not to be victimized and not to be prevented from practicing their religion, in the event these good intentions came to nothing.[16] The undisciplined soldiers attacked ecclesiastics and stole their property. Most monks, nuns, and parish priests fled to Amsterdam or Utrecht. Others disappeared into lay society. In many places, including Sint Maarten, Zwaag, Winkel, Aartswoud, Sijbekarspel, Purmerend, Opmeer, Langedijk, Schermer, Petten, Huisduinen, and Schardam, the priest went over to the new religion.[17] Political and military developments also worked against the Catholics. After the bloodbath at Naarden and the long siege of Haarlem they were mistrusted as a potential fifth column. In these circumstances an official ban on Catholic services soon followed. Since the resolutions of the States of Holland for this period have been lost, the exact date of this prohibition is not known. On 8 May 1573 Wouter Jacobszoon mentioned an edict of the Beggars that required all priests to swear an oath to the new Reformed religion or leave the country within three days. On 22 February 1573 an informant in Delft reported

---

[14] Vos, "Dooplijst."

[15] Notitie van de schade die Wognum geleden heeft, 1572, WFA, GA Wognum, inv. no. 211.

[16] Instruction from the Prince of Orange to Sonoy, article 2, 20 April 1572, in Bor, 375.

[17] *Acta*, I, 8, 24, 25; see also Voets, "Hervorming," II, 65.

[1]
The village of Den Ilp in Waterland, aerial photograph KLM ca. 1921–39
(photo Noord-Hollands Archief, Haarlem).

[2]

Diederik Sonoy (1529–1592). Etching in Pieter Bor, *Oorsprongk, begin en vervolgh der Nederlandscher oorlogen*, 3rd ed., 1621 (photo Library of the University of Amsterdam).

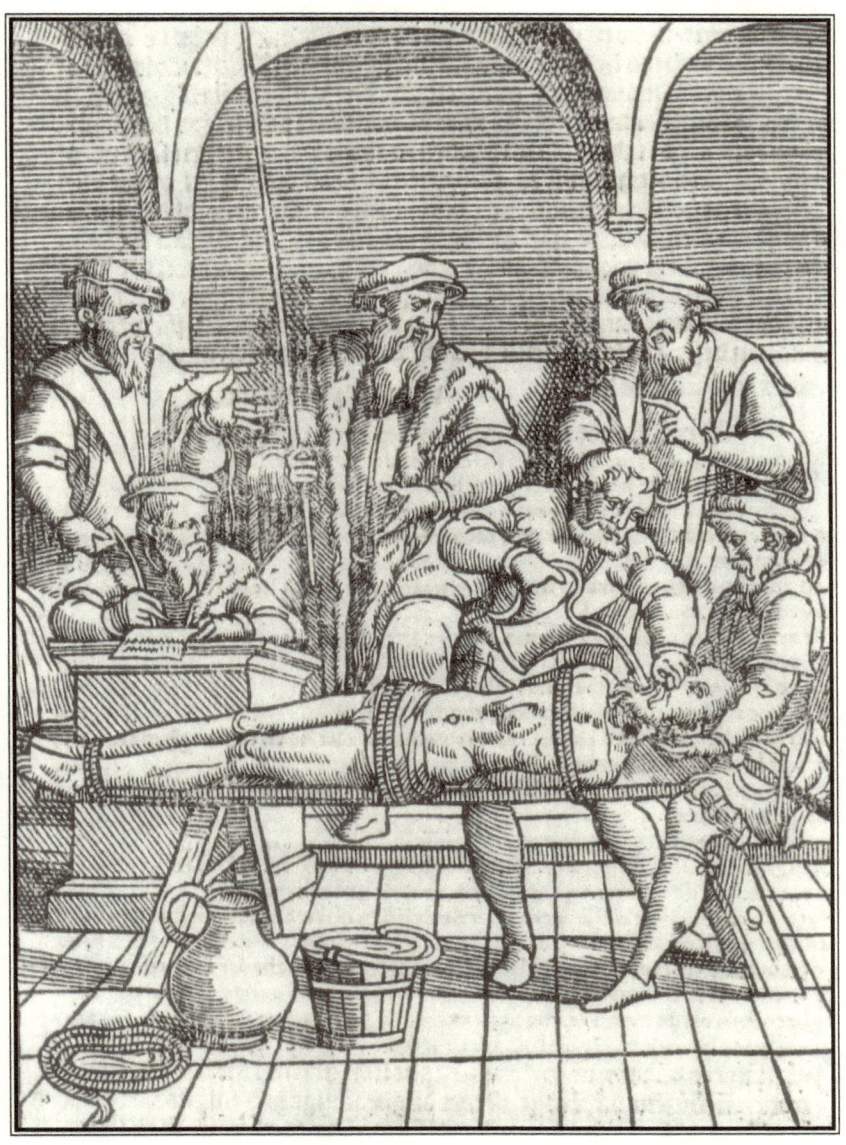

[3]

The rack. Legal instructions prescribed that the sheriff (with mace),
two judges, and a secretary be present while the accused was being tortured.
Woodcut in Joos de Damhouder, *Practycke ende handbouck in criminele zaken*, 1555
(photo Library of the University of Amsterdam).

[4]

Torture. The "patient" is being racked while the executioner tightens several ropes around his legs and chest using a toggle. Woodcut in Joos de Damhouder, *Practycke ende handbouck in criminele zaken*, 1555 (photo Library of the University of Amsterdam).

[5]

*Martyrium Jacobi et Nanningi et aliorum* (martyrdom of Coppen and Nanning and others). The anonymous artist shows the execution of Nanning Coppenszoon as well as the torturing of Coppen Corneliszoon taking place in public. The foreground scene is apparently inspired by the illustration in Richard Verstegan, *Theatre des cruautez* (ill. 13). Etching in Petrus Opmeer, *Martelaarsboek ofte Historie der Hollandse martelaren*, 1700 (photo Library of the University of Amsterdam).

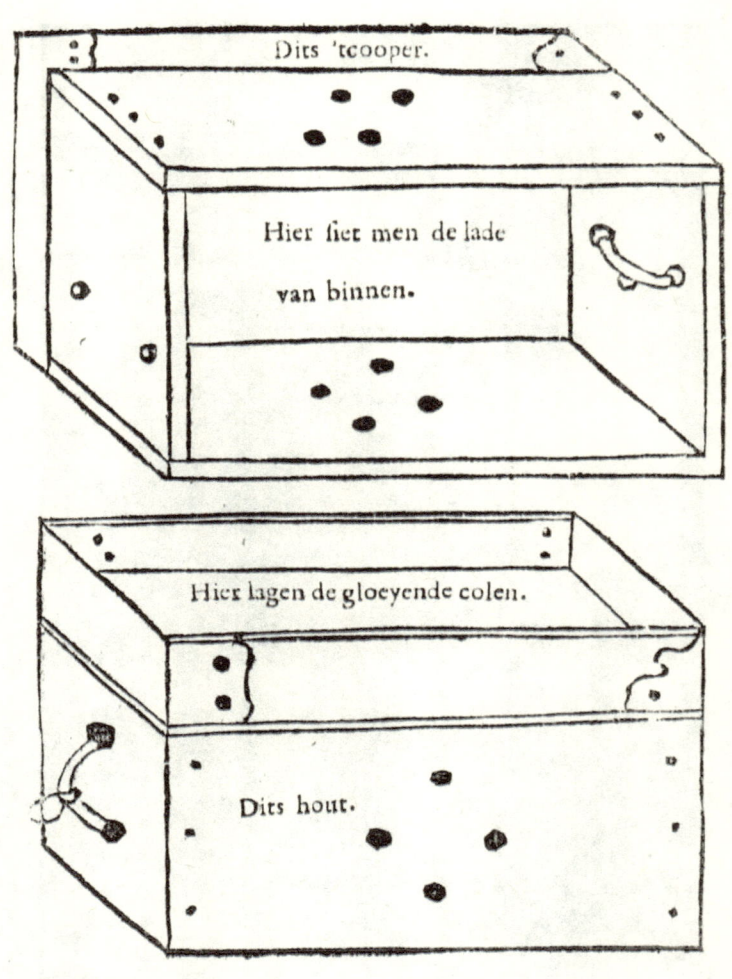

[6]
The box used for torturing Pieter Nanningszoon, Jan Jeroenszoon, and others. The inscriptions read, from top to bottom: *This is copper; Here one sees the drawer from the inside; Here were burning coals; This is wood.* The instrument was the property of Jan Jeroenszoon's descendant Maria Clomp. Engraving after Hendrik Goltzius in Pieter Bor, *Oorsprongk, begin en vervolgh der Nederlandscher oorlogen*, 3rd ed., 1621 (photo Library of the University of Amsterdam).

[7]
The castle of Schagen, Sonoy's headquarters in the Northern Quarter. Nanning Coppenszoon and Pieter Nanningszoon were imprisoned here around 1 September 1575. The building also served as a prison for Jan Jeroenszoon, Piet El, and Sybout Janszoon.
Etching by J. Schijnvoet, 1737
(photo Noord-Hollands Archief, Haarlem).

[8]

Map of North Holland, dated 1575, reprinted in 1609, etching and engraving by Joost Janszoon Beeldsnijder alias Bilhamer. Hierges made use of a version of this map during his failed invasion of the Northern Quarter (photo Library of the University of Amsterdam).

Map of North Holland, engraving by Jacob van Deventer, 1558 (photo Library of the University of Amsterdam).

[10]

Map of North Holland, etching by Christiaen Sgroten, 1573
(photo Library of the University of Amsterdam).

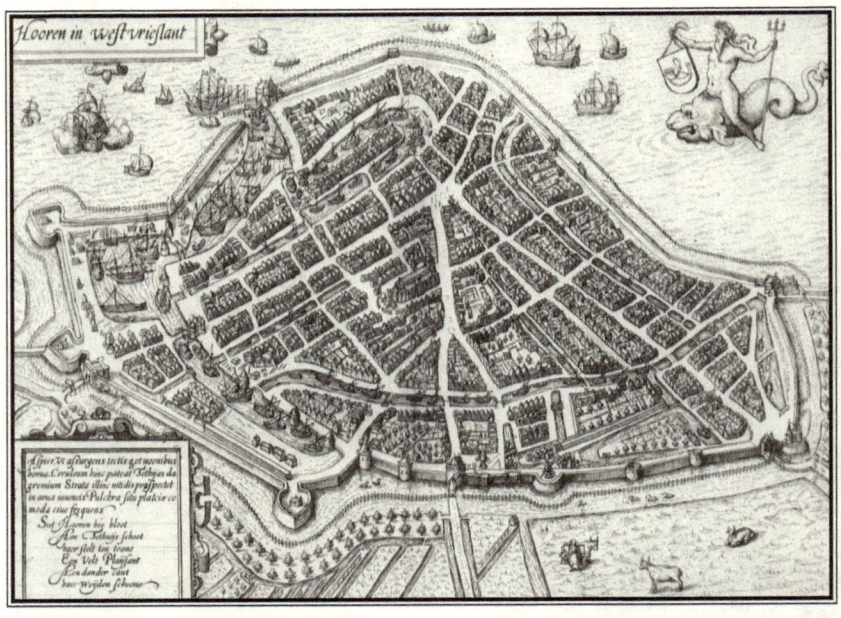

[11]
Bird's-eye view of Hoorn, late sixteenth century, etching in
Lodovico Guicciardini, *Beschrijvinghe van alle de Neder-landen,
anderssins genoemt Neder-Duytslandt*, 1612
(photo Noord-Hollands Archief, Haarlem).

[12]

Session of the Court of Holland in The Hague, etching, title print in
Hugo Grotius, *Inleiding tot de Hollandsche rechtsgeleerdheid*, 1631
(photo Library of the University of Amsterdam).

[13]
Torturing of Jan Jeroenszoon. Engraving in Richard Verstegan,
*Theatre des cruautez des heretiques de nostre temps*, 1587
(photo Library of the University of Amsterdam).

[14]
Theodoricus Velius (Dirck Volckertszoon Seylmaker, 1572–1630).
Engraving in his *Chroniik van Hoorn*, 3rd ed., 1648
(photo author).

[15]

Pieter Christiaenszoon Bor (1559–1635). Engraving by A. Zylveldt after Frans Hals in
*Oorsprongk, begin en vervolgh der Nederlandscher oorlogen*, 4th ed., 1679–84
(photo author).

to William of Orange's brother John of Nassau that the mass had been abolished in "the whole Waterland," that is, in the Northern Quarter.[18]

That in effect cut the majority of the population off from every organized form of religious life. On 22 March 1573, Easter Sunday, Wouter Jacobszoon in his exile in Amsterdam lamented the fate of his oppressed fellow Catholics:

> We saw the good people everywhere in such a plight, without the practice of any good religion. They were denied the invaluable sacraments. No one might preach God's holy word to them. They were wholly deprived of the services of the priests, since they [the priests] had mostly fled and could not use the streets openly.[19]

Catholic life was at a complete standstill. An old woman of Wognum complained to Wouter Jacobszoon in April 1578 that for six years, that is, since the beginning of the Revolt, she had not been to confession or received the sacrament.[20] The official ban on the mass, which had been proclaimed at the end of 1572 or early in 1573, had long made no difference for the peasants of Wognum, and the situation in Benningbroek cannot have been very different.

For the time being there was little to take the place of the mass. The Prince of Orange's instructions to Sonoy to protect the Catholics also declared that God's word was to be preached everywhere. That was easier said than done. Planting the Reformed Church in the Northern Quarter was an extremely laborious process. The village magistrates, who had not been deposed in 1572, showed little sympathy for the new church order. In Nieuwe Niedorp, for example, only one of the twenty-six members of the "wealthy" had joined the Reformed Church. To the great irritation of the local magistrates the Reformed often appealed over their heads to the military authorities to gain possession of church buildings and other provisions.[21] This happened in Purmerend and Warmenhuizen, for example.

The new Church had to recruit its followers from a population that had been more or less intensively exposed to a variety of unorthodox ideas for half a century. This did not mean that it would convert to the Reformed Church en masse. The core membership of the new communities was drawn from those who had already converted as early as 1566. When they returned from exile to North Holland in 1572, they became the most zealous fighters for the new faith.

---

[18] *DWJ*, 250; *Archives*, IV, 62; Duke, *Reformation*, 207.
[19] *DWJ*, 210.
[20] Ibid., 713.
[21] Duke, *Reformation*, 217, 205–6; Duke, "Nieuwe Niedorp," 69.

Before 1572 the Anabaptists formed the largest group of defectors from the Catholic Church, and they continued to outnumber the Reformed for many years after 1572. Even in 1570, during the regime of Alba, they had founded two new congregations, at Bovenkarspel and Nieuwe Niedorp.[22] The Reformed Church held little attraction for the inward-looking Mennonites. These simple people, who refused to swear oaths and bear arms, played no significant role in politics.

There were far from enough preachers to give every village its own minister. In Nieuwe Niedorp the young congregation was reinforced by brethren from Barsingerhorn, Winkel, and Langedijk, who had no minister of their own. Of the fifty-nine parishes comprised in the former deanery of West Friesland, three received a preacher for the first time in 1572 (one in Hoorn and two in Enkhuizen), sixteen in 1573, twenty in 1574, four in 1575, and one in 1576. By the time of the Pacification of Ghent in 1576, three out of four former parishes had their own minister, but sometimes only on paper. Gerardus, the preacher of Graft and De Rijp, was absent until 1576, because of the continual invasions of the Waterland by the enemy. Nor did all the new preachers have the gift of preaching God's word. In Winkel, Ulricus was dismissed in 1579 "because no one could understand what he said, and very few profited by his teaching."[23] Jan Michielszoon, a former monk from Flanders, but now the preacher of Grootebroek and Sonoy's messenger boy, had served the Sea Beggars and the Wood Beggars before he was called to the Northern Quarter. In that capacity he had played a sinister role in the murder of priests in the West Quarter of Flanders. His curriculum vitae cannot have endeared him to the peasantry of North Holland.[24]

It is not clear when Wognum and Benningbroek received preachers of their own. In March 1573 the villages were attached to the *coetus* (preachers' meeting) of Hoorn, but the first we hear of preachers in the two villages is in April 1574: Cornelis van Ravesteijn in Wognum and Gijsbertus Zythopeus in Benningbroek. The former was largely an absentee, because the synod sent him to Texel "to let his gifts be heard there" (to preach on invitation). Was he chosen for this missionary work because there was little for him to do in Wognum?[25]

All the evidence suggests that the Reformed were not very popular. The Lord of Obdam and Hensbroek issued a bylaw in circa 1575, which

[22] Voets, "Hervorming," II, 22.

[23] Duke, *Reformation*, 208, 217, 218, 220.

[24] *NNBW*, VIII, 1153; Backhouse, "Beeldenstorm," passim; "Documenten betreffende de godsdiensttroebelen," passim; *Troubles religieux*, passim; De Meij, *Watergeuzen*, 44, 162, 229.

[25] *Acta*, I, 13, 23, 26. Zythopeus ("Brewer") was a former priest of Schagen who had turned Protestant in 1566. Vis and Woltjer, "Predikanten."

threatened heavy fines for everyone who abused the preacher "maliciously" or called someone a "papist" or a "Beggar."[26] In September 1574 the court of Hoorn issued a bylaw forbidding the breaking of the church windows at Wognum "with stones, clods or otherwise."[27] And in April 1578 Wouter Jacobszoon attended the baptism in Amsterdam of a four-year-old girl from Wognum "who was still a heathen." The villagers present said that there were more than a hundred unbaptized children in the village, "since they could not get a priest and they were not inclined to the Calvinist sect."[28]

The most important reason for the slow progress of the Reformation in Holland was the war. No one could have suspected that the ultimate result of the war would be a new state, in which the Reformed Church would enjoy a privileged position. As long as the reconquest of Holland by the government army appeared to be only a matter of time, it seemed safer to watch events from a distance. But even after the war had moved a long way from the frontiers of Holland, the Reformed Church never made up for this slow start. In 1605 the Reformed in Hoorn were still complaining of "the great license of the Papists, not only in meeting, but also in holding funeral ceremonies, public burning of incense, lighting candles in the churches, as has happened for example at Berkhout, Wognum and Grosthuizen."[29] In 1610 the Catholics in Hoorn organized clandestine services in Wognum, where a Roman Catholic priest was permanently stationed from 1622.[30] In this respect Wognum was no different from most of the other villages in the Northern Quarter, where 65 to 75 percent of the population was still Catholic as late as the middle of the seventeenth century.[31]

Neither did the new political regime command the respect of the villagers. The roots of its unpopularity went back before 1572, to 1568, when Dirck Maertszoon van Schagen and his marauding band of vagabonds and exiles had attacked the village. In the name of William of Orange they had drunk a barrel of beer at the priest's house and extorted money from a poor widow.[32] After Enkhuizen went over to the Revolt the rebels

[26] Bylaw of Gijsbrecht van Duvenvoerde, ca. 1575, SWG, Archief Huis Weldam, inv. no. 28.
[27] Bylaw of 19 September 1574, WFA, OA Hoorn, inv. no. 55, fol. 183v.
[28] *DWJ*, 713.
[29] *Acta*, I, 381.
[30] "Papisticque vergaderingen," 316–18; Rogier, *Geschiedenis van het katholicisme*, 387, 753–55, 762. In 1839, 63 percent of the population of Wognum was still Catholic.
[31] De Kok, *Nederland op de breuklijn*, 183–87. In the area around Schagen, Broek op Langendijk, and Bergen in 1656 Catholics outnumbered Protestants ten to one. The Baptist village of De Rijp and Protestant Graft were exceptions to this pattern. For the ecclesiastical situation in Graft see Van Deursen, *Dorp*, 24–28, 81–99.
[32] *Sententiën*, 340; "Rooftocht," 361, 364, 372.

made themselves masters of the villages in the Streek without firing a shot. Villagers who did not live on the front line in Waterland, the Zaan district, or Kennemerland were not directly exposed to the war, but they suffered all the more from the roaming bands of soldiers who, against Sonoy's wishes, were kept outside the town gates and quartered on the peasants. In 1572 the company of Captain Nicolaes Ruychaver was quartered at different times in the villages of Avenhorn, Grosthuizen, Berkhout, Beets, Nibbixwoud, and Hauwert, all under the jurisdiction of Hoorn.[33]

Two long itemized accounts for the years 1572 and 1573 give a depressing picture of what the presence of the soldiers meant to Wognum.[34] As early as 16 May 1572, only five days after Enkhuizen went over, two captains arrived with their troops and took sixty guilders worth of food without payment. When the church valuables were seized in July the captains lodged with the innkeeper Cornelis Thijszoon, whose loss amounted to forty guilders. When Captain Jan Otszoon and his men came to collect the *morgengeld* (a land tax), they consumed one hundred guilders worth of food. Captain Jan Taemszoon Schaft and the militia of Hoorn confiscated all the weapons, three hundred guilders worth, and devoured thirty guilders worth of food and drink at the inn.

To these costs were added the expenses of the soldiers quartered in the village: Captain Van Triere with 350 men for nine days, six hundred guilders; Wigbolt Ripperda with 225 men for eight days, 540 guilders; Koenraad van Steenwijk with eighty men, for one night, twenty-four guilders and a further twelve guilders "freely consumed" in the tavern; Jaep Thaemszoon van Hoorn with two hundred men for twenty-four hours, sixty guilders and twenty-five guilders in the inn; Pieter Vrerickzoon van Grootebroek "with the great galley" and its crew of forty men for four days, three hundred guilders; and so it went on.

The inhabitants of Wognum also had to pay for soldiers, sailors, and sconce diggers quartered elsewhere. They were assessed at five stuivers per *morgen* of land, in all 317 guilders and ten stuivers, to pay for the garrison in Medemblik; at 554 guilders five stuivers for boatmen and sconce diggers during Sonoy's unsuccessful campaigns on the Diemerdijk; at 2,100 guilders for beer and wages for the sconce diggers who built the fortifications at Hoorn, Enkhuizen, and Medemblik. In all, adding up the damage to the church, the *morgengeld*, the other taxes and forced loans they were made to pay, plus the horses and equipment the soldiers took without payment, their costs for the year 1572 came to a total of 8,261

---

[33] Velius, 200–202.

[34] "Notitie van de schade die Wognum geleden heeft, 1572 en 1572–73," WFA, Wognum, inv. nos. 211, 212. A similar account is found in WFA, OA Stede Grootebroek, inv. no. 765. The accounts were drawn up following a resolution of the States of Holland, see Bor, 413.

guilders. That was an enormous sum for a community of around 150 households to bear.

The villagers tried desperately to avoid the hated quartering of soldiers. Whenever a company was billeted on them the magistrates immediately petitioned Sonoy, pleading the poverty of the local people and the many good services they had already rendered to the prince's cause. If Sonoy responded positively, the company moved on to the next village, which in its turn submitted a petition in the same terms. The result was that the soldiers were constantly on the move from one village to another, and the burdens of the war were spread more or less equally over the whole country, as Sonoy must have intended.

On 25 March 1574 Sonoy gave orders to Nicolaes Ruychaver to leave Ilpendam with his men at once and proceed to Oosthuizen and Hobreede, "since more and more complaints reach me about your men, yea that they ruin everything."[35] This was promptly followed by a petition from the burgomasters of Oosthuizen, who pointed out that the common people and residents were "very humble" folk who could not bear the costs, because "they had long lain next to the sea" and their land was still largely under water. Sonoy took into account their willing cooperation in fortifying Purmerend, and ordered Ruychaver to leave for Schardam or Beets, villages that had been less cooperative. Apparently Ruychaver ignored this order, for on 17 April he was at Oudendijk, where Sonoy sent him another order to move on to Beets. On 23 April Sonoy ordered the magistrates of Grosthuizen to receive Ruychaver's company. This immediately provoked the burgomasters of Hoorn (in whose jurisdiction Grosthuizen lay) to write to Sonoy, reminding him that this was a breach of their earlier agreements. The tactic worked. Sony reflected that Grosthuizen was a small village, whose inhabitants had to work every day on the fortifications of Purmerend, and on 27 April he commanded Ruychaver to quarter his men in Wognum.

Now it was turn of the burgomasters of Wognum to petition the governor. They claimed that their village had just had to bear the burden of Hans von Cremnitz's company, which had only left a week ago; could the soldiers not be sent on to a village that had not yet had to pay so dearly?[36] Once again, and undoubtedly to the great relief of the villagers of Wognum, Sonoy granted the petition. He ordered the troops to be sent to Nibbixwoud and Hauwert, two villages in the jurisdiction of Hoorn. Yet

---

[35] Sonoy to Ruychaver, 25 March 1574, NHA, Ruychaver, inv. no. 86. The route of the company is reconstructed from inv. nos. 86, 87, 91, 95, 96, 99, 100, 102, and 103.

[36] The petition of the burgomasters of Wognum to Sonoy, 30 April 1574, NHA, Ruychaver inv. no. 100, calls him "hopman [Captain] Hans van Crijmen." For his identification see Wijn, "Noordhollandse regiment," 259.

again Hoorn intervened, though only in favor of Hauwert. On 6 May the troops quartered there were ordered to join their comrades in Nibbixwoud. Fortunately for the villagers the Prince of Orange needed Ruychaver's company in South Holland at just that time, and on 10 May Sonoy issued him a passport to leave for the South. In six weeks the company had been quartered in ten villages, consuming everything in its path like a swarm of locusts.

Raising the very substantial costs incurred by the quartering of the troops was even more difficult now that trade in the countryside had come almost to a halt as a result of the war. Since the All Saints' Day flood large tracts of the country had lain under water, and as if that were not bad enough, Sonoy had twice breached the dikes to halt the Spanish army, during the siege of Alkmaar and before Hierges's attempted invasion. The governor had faced stubborn resistance from the peasants, who tried to stop up the breaches in the dikes, forcing the army command to mount a guard on the opened sluice gates.[37] A memorial of 1576 complained that two-thirds of all of Holland was under water. In the Northern Quarter the Geestmerambacht, Waterland, the Zeevang, and parts of Kennemerland were the heaviest hit.[38] The tenants of the Vroonlanden, north of Alkmaar, complained to the Chamber of Accounts in 1573 that the inundations had made land scarcer and leases dearer, and that their income from the herring fishery, estimated at more than five thousand guilders a year, had fallen almost to nothing, that most of their stocks of butter and cheese had been stolen by the soldiers, and that the rest had been spoiled by being kept too long, because the markets were no longer being held.[39]

To prevent the enemy living off the peasantry if it should occupy the countryside, the peasants were forbidden to keep more than two weeks' stock of food in their houses. They had to bring the rest to market in the towns, where they were not allowed to buy more than two guilders worth of provisions for themselves. These rules were strictly enforced by the sheriffs, who carried out house-to-house searches, seizing any stocks they found in excess of the permitted maximum.[40]

The military and labor services the peasants had to perform have already been mentioned: digging duties on the sconces and the town ramparts, guard duty, cutting channels in the icebound water line, and manning the fleet. Naturally the inhabitants of Wognum and Benningbroek

---

[37] Bor, 291–92, 454.

[38] "Mémoire touchant l'estat du pays d'Hollande," in "Onuitgegeven brieven Berlaymont," 291–93.

[39] Geus, "Bewoners"; account of Frederik van Zevender of the office of *rentmeester* [treasurer] of the Vroonlanden, NA, Rekenkamer, rekeningen, inv. no. 1263, fol. 244.

[40] Velius, 202.

did their fair share of these duties. In the ordinance on the cutting of a channel in the ice around the Northern Quarter of 16 January 1575, Wognum was assessed at ninety-one men, who were to keep open 230 rods (842 yards) between Spijkerboor and Purmerend. Benningbroek and Sijbekarspel together had to send 114 men to cut 285 rods (1,088 yards) on the same reach of the waterway. This was a heavy burden for such small villages.[41] When Sonoy attempted to force the townsmen to take a share in cutting the channel, he was met by indignant opposition from the States of the Northern Quarter.[42] The ordinance on the watch of 25 May 1575, Sonoy's response to the threat from Hierges's army assembled at Beverwijk, stipulated that the inhabitants of Wognum and the nearby village of Wadway had to provide thirty-eight men by night and eight by day to stand guard on the north side of the West Friesland sea dike between Lambertschaag and Twisk. Benningbroek supplied twenty-two men for the watch on Krabbendam, the very place where Hierges's army appeared before the sconces.[43]

Every third adult male inhabitant of the Northern Quarter was called to arms.[44] Many of them were sent to man the fleet, in many cases as oarsmen on the galleys. Anyone who failed to report could face sentence of death. The sheriff of Westwoud, which comprised the villages of Westwoud, Binnenwijzend, Oosterblokker, and Westerblokker, charged two villagers, Jacob Claeszoon Gons and Jan Does, on 2 October 1573, a week after the battle on the Zuiderzee. They had been chosen by lot to serve on the ships, but had not reported for duty and had thus forfeited their lives and their property. Jacob Gons claimed that he had been ill; Jan Does's defense was more principled: he asserted that he could not serve two masters, but he added that he already had three sons in the fleet and thought that was quite enough.[45]

In his chronicle of Hoorn, Velius describes in detail how the poorly paid soldiers terrorized the countryside.[46] They were not satisfied with simple peasant fare and forced the peasants to pay a sum for each man. Those who refused were visited by a platoon of soldiers, who drank a

---

[41] Bor, 616–17. In 1561 Wognum had 148 households, Benningbroek ninety-one. A rod has been taken as the Alkmaar rod of 12 Dutch feet, or 3.35 meters. Verhoeff, *Oude Nederlandse maten*, 2.

[42] States of the Northern Quarter to Sonoy, 13 January 1575, NHA, GNK, inv. no. 237, fol. 128v. Unlike the villagers the townsfolk were to be paid for their services, according to the proposal.

[43] Bor, 622.

[44] *DWJ*, 112, 143.

[45] "Registers van criminele en civiele rollen," 20 October, 17 November, 1 December 1573, WFA, ORA Stede Westwoud, inv. no. 4713. The justices' judgment is not known.

[46] Velius, 200–201.

couple of barrels of beer dry or broke open the chests and cupboards, and took away whatever they fancied. Peasants who resisted were beaten up or killed. The soldiers entered a village, several platoons at a time, dragged the richest peasants from their houses and threatened that they would be taken to the army or the sconces and hanged, if they did not pay a ransom. The soldiers also used all kinds of slanderous charges to extort money from the peasants: one was accused of having dug sconces for the enemy, another of illegally transporting food, a third of concealing his property, a fourth of uttering disloyal words about the Prince of Orange.

Nor were the soldiers the only ones the peasants had to fear. Many of the new men in power, the sheriffs, bailiffs, and other officials who had received their commissions from the rebels, some of them returned exiles, others turncoats, were a match for the soldiers in their arbitrary behavior. The deposition of Lijsbeth Bouwens, the widow of Fop Claeszoon, made in September 1585 before the notary Evert Meliszoon in Hoorn, illustrates the misery of the countryside in wartime. Lijsbeth declared that in August 1576, when she was thirty-one years old,

> when she deponent was living at Benningbroek, Gerrit Jacobs the officer of Sijbekarspel and Benningbroek, with certain soldiers, came to the house of her deponent; closing all the doors and saying to the soldiers, "This woman has money, and she will have to pay the costs due in May, seize her and torture her until she shows you where the money is." Whereupon the soldiers said, "Sir sheriff, how are we to do that, will we not be punished for it?" To which the aforesaid sheriff replied, "Leave that to me, she is a papistical whore, I give you my word for it, whatever happens to you." She also says that the aforesaid sheriff opened her well and said to the soldiers, "She is a sturdy woman, hang her in this well until she shows us where the money is." To which the soldiers said, "She will cry out grievously, and that may bring a crowd into the village. We know a better way." With that they seized her deponent, hanging her by the hair on a certain ladder. And as she deponent still did not reveal the money to the aforesaid sheriff, they tore her clothing in front and tied her up with certain ropes and stretched her out, and then set her shift on fire, and treated her so that she was quite out of her wits. And the soldiers then brought her outside the house and held vinegar in front of her nostrils, and when she came to herself a little the aforesaid sheriff then demanded that she deponent should show him the money, and she deponent was then fetched by the neighbors and taken to a neighbor's house. And the said sheriff and soldiers forced a peasant who came riding by with his cart to fetch a barrel of beer from Oostwoud, which they drank at her, deponent's, house, where they remained a night and two days until such time as the court ordered them to leave. And after the deponent was again in her house,

she found that all her food and victuals had been eaten and taken away and her chests, household utensils and other things smashed to pieces.[47]

The burgomasters of Hoorn and some of the preachers wrote letters to Sonoy, pleading with him to take pity on the miserable state of the countryside and the suffering of the peasantry, but in vain. The preachers' letter was deeply pessimistic; they wrote that the arbitrary violence of the soldiery was damaging the common cause and

> that such a burden on the peasantry was not to be borne. If they carried on like this they would drive them to desperate counsels, of which mutterings were already being heard, such as to slay the soldiers by night, to set the villages and houses on fire and then to go their way, each as best he could, wherever God and his fortune might lead him.[48]

Perhaps Sonoy recalled these words when the affair of the treason of the Northern Quarter burst upon him. The vagabonds had denounced three peasants—Coppen Corneliszoon, his son Nanning, and Pieter Nanningszoon—as the men who had given them their orders, and they had repeated these charges in the presence of the accused. Sonoy knew that the peasants of Wognum and Benningbroek had little reason to be enamored of the political and ecclesiastical revolution that William of Orange and he had set in motion. The peasants were evidently ready to run any risk.

For the three peasants their arrest began a nightmare from which they were only released by death. Like the vagrants who had been arrested earlier, they were required to confess their guilt of a crime of which they had known nothing. Moreover they had to accuse others who were completely unknown to them. Compared with the case of the vagabonds, the commissioners needed much longer to extort useable confessions from them. The steadfast endurance of the peasants compelled the commissioners to resort to a degree of force that was extraordinary even by the harsh standards of the sixteenth century. It is recalled in detail in the depositions before notary Van Triere.[49]

Coppen Corneliszoon was the first victim. The commissioners mentioned to him the name of Pieter Nanningszoon, who had been accused by the vagrants but had not yet been arrested. "You shall accuse him," they urged the terrified peasant, "and say that he gave money to those rogues to raise fires for that treason, or we shall torture you to death." In a few days they put the old man to torture eight or ten times. The execu-

---

[47] Deposition of Lijsbeth Bouwens, 26 September 1585, WFA, Not. A Hoorn, inv. no. 2048, fol. 281r–v.

[48] Velius, 201.

[49] Unless otherwise stated, the following is based on the depositions made before notary Van Triere, NHA, Aanwinsten, inv. no. 1185.

tioner flayed the soles of his feet "to the nerves," and burned a shirt soaked in brandy on his body. Three *mengelen* (about six pints) of brandy had been fetched, the executioner later declared, of which he had burned eight tankards on Coppen. He and the other personnel had drunk the rest.[50]

Coppen died soon, only a few days after his arrest.[51] When the old peasant was brought to the hearing room in the afternoon and saw the instruments with which his son had been tortured that morning, he fell on the table at which the commissioners were seated. "What do you want to know from me?" he asked. "What we held out to you today," they answered. "I cannot say it," said Coppen, as he collapsed and died. The sheriff's servant Cornelis Janszoon later deposed

> that the said Coppen, before he [Cornelis] brought him to the torture bench where he gave up the ghost as stated, had done nothing else the whole night and that day also but speak of God, saying that he was innocent and free of that charge they sought to make him bear. He further deposed that when the aforenamed Coppen collapsed and died, the commissioners ordered him to go out of the room to Nanning, Coppen's son, forbidding him deponent to say that Coppen was dead. But when he deponent came to the aforesaid Nanning, who was lying in his shirt with his hands between his legs bound to a bench, and who asked him how his father was, he whispered to him that he could be at ease; and immediately afterward the commissioners followed him and when they came in they said to Nanning, "You scoundrel, you traitor, your father has confessed and accused you too."[52]

Coppen's death dismayed the commissioners. "What can we do now?" they asked one another. They had put themselves in precisely the unfortunate predicament the handbooks of judicial practice warned them to avoid. They ordered the executioner to quarter Coppen's body in secret, but what they hoped to achieve by this is not entirely clear. Hanging up the quartered bodies of executed criminals in a public place was supposed to be a deterrent, but that could hardly apply when the quartering took place in secret and the body was not exposed. Perhaps the commissioners could not stomach the way in which Coppen had cheated his proper punishment by dying first?[53]

[50] Deposition of Jacob Michielszoon, fols. 1, 9v; deposition of Cornelis Janszoon and Baertgen Hermansdochter, fol. 4v.

[51] Bor, 626, places Coppen's death on 2 June; Opmeer, *Martelaarsboek*, 249, on 14 June, the "feast of the Holy Trinity." Neither Bor nor Opmeer quotes a source for the date; cf. above, note 2.

[52] Deposition of Cornelis Janszoon and Baertgen Hermansdochter, fol. 5.

[53] Bor, 626. Opmeer, *Martelaarsboek*, 249, however states that after the quartering Coppen's head was displayed above one of the gates of Alkmaar and that his possessions were confiscated. This was not possible without a (posthumous) sentence.

In any case, the facts of Coppen's death could not remain hidden for long. For the time being they did not lead to criticism of the commissioners' actions. On the contrary, Hierges and his army were still at Beverwijk at the beginning of June, and most of the people of the Northern Quarter were firmly convinced that the rumors of treason had a foundation of truth. A Beggar song that was sung in the towns and villages of the Northern Quarter at this time presented the unfortunate Coppen as the leader of the traitors ("they chose as their captain a peasant born in Wognum, a knave of Jezebel") and his death as a well-deserved punishment.

> Hear what they did
> With this false traitor.
> The Captain's body was quartered,
> The Devil broke his neck first:
> This truly happened,
> Many people stood by,
> Such are the wages that all those who betray
> their fatherland can expect.[54]

Only in a later verse did the song mention the executions of the vagabonds (Then all the fire raisers together / were bound to the stake / each in his village by name). Coppen must have been the first victim of the investigation into the plot.

Now that the prime suspect had died prematurely, it became all the more important to extract a confession from his son Nanning. During his twelve weeks' imprisonment at Alkmaar Nanning was tortured no fewer than fourteen times. Pieter Nanningszoon, who was arrested around the middle of July, was also subjected to fourteen sessions of torture, but even this excessive cruelty did not produce the confessions demanded.

Around 1 September both prisoners were taken to Sonoy's headquarters in the castle of Schagen, at the extreme northern tip of the peninsula, where the castellan was Gerrit Hendrikszoon Calff, the younger brother of commissioner Willem Maertszoon Calff (plate 7).[55] Here the commissioners, shielded from prying eyes, questioned them another ten times. In total, therefore, the two prisoners were interrogated under torture on twenty-four separate occasions. Such an intensive recourse to the sharp examination was highly unusual and completely unlawful. It is almost unimaginable that the accused should have been able to resist their questioners for so long.

---

[54] *Geuzenliedboek*, I, 246–49. For this Beggar song see also pp. 239–42.

[55] Bor 627; Elias, *Vroedschap*, I, 134–36. In spite of their different patronymics Willem Maertszoon and Gerrit Hendrickszoon were full brothers.

Before he was tortured again, all Nanning's body hair was shaved off, presumably in an attempt to emphasize his defenseless nakedness.[56] The usual repertoire of techniques in the torture chamber also included binding the victim to the bench with exceptional force. Seven cords were bound so tightly they burst apart, and "one could see the bare bone and the hole of the shank [of Pieter Nanningszoon] from within, and the sinews of the hands and fingers clenched so that he could not use his hands."[57]

The use of fire, such as was applied to Coppen's body, was equally normal. Two flagons of brandy were burned on Nanning's body, so that "all his skin from his throat to his navel was burned off, such that there was not a finger's-breadth still whole." Both Nanning and Pieter were burned under the armpits and on the soles of their feet with candles and sulfur, so that Nanning "had to crawl on his knees for six weeks and could not walk or stand." Burning fat was dripped on to the prisoners' skin, "which made holes the size of stuivers on their bodies."[58]

The commissioners also tried to extract confessions by exhausting the prisoners.[59] Nanning was laid on a bare floor without a mattress or blanket, and kept awake for thirteen nights by the use of a bucket of water and rods. When even this did not yield the desired results, some servants were stationed permanently by him, to keep him awake for fourteen days and nights. The prisoners were denied all drink for five or six days and nights, and given only pickled herring and other salty food to eat, so that both men "cried out very bitterly for drink."[60]

But the depositions also referred to new and unheard-of tortures, which exceeded any cruelty shown before. Besides inflicting pain, these appear to have been intended above all to humiliate the victims. Air was blown into Nanning's body through a reed stuck in his penis, and he was then struck on the groin. The use of a variety of animals must have been simi-

---

[56] Heinsbergen, *Pijnbank*, 84, 92, says that the patient's hair was sometimes shaved off to see if he or she was wearing a remedy that made him or her insensible to pain. This treatment appears to have been normal above all in witchcraft trials.

[57] Deposition of Cornelis Janszoon and Baertgen Hermansdochter, fol. 6v. Cf. Van Heijnsbergen, *Pijnbank*, 83, and De Damhouder, *Practijcke*, chapter 37.

[58] Deposition of Cornelis Janszoon and Baertgen Hermansdochter, fol. 6; deposition of Stijn Jansdochter, fol. 3v.

[59] Cf. De Waardt, *Toverij*, 99–100.

[60] Deposition of Cornelis Janszoon and Baertgen Hermansdochter, fol. 6; deposition of Jacob Michielszoon, fol. 10v. Cf. Bergsma, *Wereld*, 35, 120: the supporters of the Prince of Orange tortured some Groningen peasants by forcing them to eat salt herrings and denying them water. The source is Eppens, *Kroniek*, II, 74: "Thus some peasants were tortured by being fed salt herrings and given nothing to drink, and they extorted money [from them], and one of them died." Is this a parallel case, or had Eppens in Groningen heard about the peasants in the Northern Quarter?

larly intended to strip the suspects of all dignity. The executioner Boeckgen had a number of "beetles" (digger wasps?) dug out of the ground; Baertgen Hermansdochter, the wife of the sheriff of Alkmaar's servant, later deposed that "she deponent herself had drawn the sting of one of the insects from Nanning's navel, which was as long as a finger joint." The commissioners paid nine stuivers for a calf, which was made to suck Nanning's penis, which had been smeared with cream.[61]

The most depraved cruelty involved the use of a rat. The animal was laid on the victim's belly under an earthenware bowl made especially for the purpose, with a partition. A small fire was lit on top of the bowl "to terrify the rat, which being in the bowl, standing on the patient's body, would bite into his body, the said rat being bound fast by a small chain."[62]

The depositions made before notary Van Triere reveal the sinister company that joined the commissioners in this orgy of cruelty. The leading role was played by the executioner or hangman, "Master" Jacob Michielszoon. He was a young man of twenty-two, who could neither read nor write. He came from Luxemburg and may have spoken and understood little Dutch. Master Jacob and his wife Stijn Jansdochter lived at Alkmaar with a landlady, in rooms in the Oudhof near the church.

Master Jacob was thus as much a foreigner and outsider as the vagrants he had tortured and executed. That was no accident. The profession of executioner or hangman was regarded as infamous and its practitioners despised.[63] Some people even shunned the place where the executioner lived, considering it unclean simply because of his presence. Nevertheless he fulfilled an essential function in criminal procedure and the judicial system as a whole, and therefore enjoyed the special protection of the authorities. Executioners were regarded as rough, brutal men, who often used more force than was necessary. Joos de Damhouder warned that they

> do not perform their office with such compassion and such humanity to the patients as is proper, but they often handle the miscreants, rack them, kill them, murder them, execute them, as irreverently as if they were dealing with beasts, glorying in their cruel and tyrannical execution, so that sometimes they blame the patients for their pain and misdeeds, often putting them to death too severely and quickly, as if

---

[61] Deposition of Stijn Jansdochter and Anna Barentsdochter, fols. 2v, 4; deposition of Cornelis Janszoon and Baertgen Hermansdochter, fol. 5v.

[62] Deposition of Stijn Jansdochter and Anna Barentsdochter, fol. 3v; for the use of rats, cf. George Orwell, *Nineteen Eighty-Four*, 907–10.

[63] De Damhouder, *Practycke*, 289–91; See also Vanhemelryck, *Misdadigers*, 36–44 on torture, and 45–68 on the hangman. Blok, "Over de infamie"; Blok, "Infame beroepen."

they were indulging their own whims rather than the commands of reason and justice.[64]

Although Master Jacob plays a far from sympathetic role in this story, he does not emerge from the depositions as a mere sadist without a conscience. Stijn Jansdochter related that

> her, deponent's, husband was often very ill tempered and weary when he came home in the evening, and the skin could come off his hands through the great heavy work he had to do in racking and torturing the prisoners; ... and her husband Master Jacob many times cried out in compassion, saying "I cannot torture the prisoners any longer; but I have to do it or I will be dismissed."[65]

Stijn herself claimed to have done her modest bit to thwart the process of justice. A man she did not know had knocked on her door and asked her for a rattrap. He wanted to take it to Sonoy's lodgings, to put a rat in it that the sheriff's servant had just bought for twelve stuivers. Stijn had replied that

> the wife of Master Jacob—concealing that she was the same—had gone out and would not come home before evening; and even if she were at home and had the rattrap, he could fetch it from the town hall.[66]

Another macabre character who took part in the interrogation of the suspects was the second executioner, one Boeckgen. The absence of a patronymic suggests that he must still have been young, perhaps no more than a child, possibly a former soldier and presumably scarcely less marginal than the condemned vagrants. His subordinate role is evident from the commissioners' promise to clothe him "in red velvet" if he succeeded in forcing the prisoners to confess. Boeckgen appears to have been involved in the more unusual tortures, using the calf, insects, and rats, that Master Jacob, or his wife, may have felt beneath him. It was Boeckgen who borrowed a bowl from Stijn Jansdochter, who in turn borrowed it from her landlady, in which to keep the cream for the calf. Boeckgen's own landlady Anna Barentsdochter of Amsterdam gave evidence that the youth had brought the rest of the cream back, saying "Look, Nanning's balls have been hanging in that"; whereupon she had fed the cream to the dogs. "We'll teach that scoundrel, that traitor a lesson," Boeckgen was supposed to have said, laughing.[67]

---

[64] De Damhouder, *Practijke*, fol. 290.
[65] Deposition of Stijn Jansdochter, fols. 2v–3.
[66] Ibid., fol. 3
[67] Deposition of Anna Barentsdochter, fols. 2v–3.

The third executioner was the provost of the army, a certain Michiel Heugelcke (whom Bor calls Michiel Vermertlen). He may have been a German, and may have taken the place of the absentee Foreest among the commissioners. He seems to have been active mainly in the executions of the vagabonds.[68]

Very different figures were the thirty-four-year-old servant of the sheriff of Alkmaar, Cornelis Janszoon, and his ten-years'-older wife, Baertgen Hermansdochter. While the prisoners were in custody at Alkmaar, Cornelis acted as their jailer, and was therefore able to supply the notary with many details. Baertgen assisted him in this function. The couple deposed that they had fed and cared for Nanning and Pieter during their imprisonment in Alkmaar and

> had put food in their mouths and given them drink like young children, for seven weeks; and also had to hold the pot for them to make their water in, since they were so crippled in the hands by the aforesaid torture that they could not help themselves.[69]

Baertgen had also "constantly smeared, salved and plastered" Nanning and Pieter whenever they were being tortured, sometimes assisted by Sonoy's medical orderly (barber-surgeon). Apparently this treatment was merely intended to patch up the victims for the next session as quickly as possible. Cornelis and Baertgen declared that their costs had been met by the prisoners' families. The commissioners had never paid them a penny.

It appears amazing that the prisoners held out so long before they admitted involvement in the plot and denounced others. The commissioners themselves were baffled and could think of only one explanation: there must be witchcraft at work. When Coppen Corneliszoon died in the torture chamber, they were convinced that the Devil must have had a hand in it. "See, he will not tell us the truth," they cried, "the Devil breaks the rogue's neck and rides off to hell." This interpretation was echoed in the Beggar song devoted to the plot. The idea that the death of a suspect during his questioning was caused by supernatural forces was very common. Buchelius related how an advocate had once told him that he had seen how the Devil had broken a witch's neck during her trial.[70]

Diabolical intervention was the only possible explanation of the stubbornness of Coppen's son. On 4 September Calff and Heukesloot wrote

---

[68] Deposition of Jacob Michielszoon, fol. 12v; Bor, 624.

[69] Deposition of Cornelis Janszoon and Baertgen Hermansdochter, fols. 6v–7.

[70] Deposition of Jacob Michielszoon, fol. 9v; Van Buchell, *Diarium*, 262: "advocatus Cockius quandam [sc. maleficam] se vidisse in juditio a daemone collo fractam [sc. narrabat]." This case occurred in 1591. The *Woordenboek der Nederlandse taal* gives the expression "iemand of iets de hals breken" [to break someone's or something's neck] in the sense of to damage or spoil, but not in combination with the Devil.

from Schagen to tell Sonoy how they had struggled vainly for three days to wrest a confession from Nanning. The executioner had lashed him with "freshly soaked sharp birch rods," but could not make him bleed. During the torture Nanning had remained deathly still,

> and after the cord was loosened, and he began to come to his senses again, the master let burning fat drip all over his body, which he [Nanning] brushed off with his hands as if it were cold water, and he did not utter a sound during the said torture; nor did his body show any blisters or bruises, by which we were much amazed and do not doubt that it is a trick of the Devil, as it was with his father.[71]

Witchcraft may have satisfied the commissioners as an explanation for the unimaginable power of endurance displayed by the peasants, but we must look for something more rational.

Like all their contemporaries the peasants were convinced that they would have to account for their deeds after their death. They dreaded the prospect of appearing before the highest judgment seat burdened with the unredeemed sin of denouncing innocent persons for a capital crime. They might fear that the tortures they underwent here on earth were merely a pale foreshadowing of the eternity of torment they could expect after death. This was why all the vagabonds loudly and publicly recanted their confessions at the place of execution: that was the only way they could hope to save their souls at the eleventh hour.

The depositions recorded by notary Van Triere give us an insight into the horrible dilemma that faced the prisoners. Master Jacob recalled Pieter Nanningszoon's reply to the commissioners when they put several names to him: "If you want my goods, then take them; if you want my blood, kill me and do not force me to say what I do not know, so that I can save my soul."[72] The sheriff's servant Cornelis and his wife Baertgen told how Nanning Coppenszoon,

> through the many great tortures was at one time so desperate that he said to them deponents, "I will denounce Teunis Joosten and Allert my brother-in-law, and they will have so much do with them that I shall have peace in the meantime"; to which they deponents then answered him, "Honorable man, will you do such a thing and denounce innocent people? Don't do it for the whole world, for your salvation depends on it." To which the aforenamed Nanning replied: "Yes, I am going crazy, I don't know what to do." And so she deponent fetched a New Testament from Cornelisgen in the Valck, and put it in his hand, saying that

---

[71] Bor, 640.
[72] Deposition of Jacob Michielszoon, fol. 11.

he must read of Our Lord's passion, and see if it said there that he might slander innocent people.[73]

The depositions were intended to serve as evidence against the commissioners, a purpose they amply fulfilled, for they formed a damning indictment. As in their earlier interrogation of the vagabonds, the commissioners had tried to compel the prisoners to accuse certain persons, whose names they themselves had suggested. "You shall tell us the truth," they cried to Pieter Nanningszoon, "and accuse those whom we shall tell you, or we shall torture you and tear you apart every day for a year, until you confess or are dead."[74] As in the case of the vagabonds, they also promised to spare the prisoners' lives and property if they were prepared to accuse certain persons.

According to Master Jacob the commissioners were "for most of the time well tipsy and drunk" whenever they had the prisoners tortured. "If you want to torture us," pleaded the prisoners, "then turn up sober in the morning." Were the refinements of cruelty the result of excessive drinking, or did the commissioners drink precisely to deaden their more humane instincts? At any rate a degree of fanaticism in their behavior cannot be denied. Whenever her husband was tired of torturing, Stijn Jansdochter declared, "then Master Joost, the sheriff of Hoorn, himself wound the rack and lent a hand therein."[75]

It is easy enough to condemn the commissioners for their merciless cruelty. Many historians, both Catholic and Protestant, have done just that.[76] But the historian's job is not to pronounce a moral judgment, but to make the acts of historical characters as understandable as possible, by interpreting them against the background of the norms, values, and expectations that applied at the time. Those who attempt to do this must answer two questions: was the commissioners' action lawful, measured by the law of the time? And second, what were they trying to achieve? Why did they choose a procedure that must undoubtedly lead sooner or later to the conviction of the suspects, but certainly would not reveal the true background and course of the plot?

In civilized countries today the use of torture is forbidden both on humanitarian grounds and because its effectiveness is doubtful. In the sixteenth century, however, torture was a completely accepted part of criminal procedure, in which the suspect was not a party but only the object

---

[73] Deposition of Cornelis Janszoon and Baertgen Hermansdochter, fol. 5r–v.

[74] Ibid., fol. 6v.

[75] Depositions of Jacob Michielszoon, Cornelis Janszoon and Baertgen Hermansdochter, Stijn Jansdochter, fols. 13, 7, 3.

[76] See below, chapter 12.

of an investigation.⁷⁷ Those who seek to explain the harshness of the commissioners must first realize that they had all earned their living for years as officers of the courts. Each of them had already compelled dozens of suspects to speak by applying torture. In their eyes the questioning of the vagabonds and peasants would have been no different from their everyday work. Most of the tortures to which the suspects were subjected were not unusual, but belonged to the standard repertoire of the torture chamber. Only the enormity of the crime with which the prisoners were charged made the case exceptional for the commissioners.

What was truly exceptional was the long time it took to extort confessions from the accused. Whereas in most cases a single session or even the mere threat of torture was enough, the dogged endurance of the peasants led the commissioners to apply torture far more often and far more rigorously than usual. Above all the sadistic acts of the young executioner Boeckgen suggest that the commissioners must have been near despair.

The use of torture was defined and restricted by many legal rules.⁷⁸ Suspects could only be tortured following an interlocutory judgment given by a judge. In this case no such judgment applied, because the commissioners were not judges and therefore had no authority to pronounce judgment. The legal basis for their actions was formed by their letter of commission from Sonoy, in which the use of "sharp examination" was explicitly permitted.

A suspect could only be sent for torture when there were enough indications of his guilt, based on the testimony of two "good" witnesses or at least one eyewitness of the crime. To be sure, the vagabonds had admitted receiving money from the peasants, but these confessions had been extracted on the rack, and the vagabonds could hardly be regarded as well-known and reputable witnesses. Their personal shortcomings and the way in which their confessions were wrung from them made it highly doubtful that the use of torture in this case was lawful.

We have already seen how the rules for torture were interpreted more loosely or even ignored altogether when the suspects were vagrants or other dishonorable persons. But this did not apply to the peasants, who pointed out time and again that they were honest villagers. "Ask in our villages and our officers, and you will find what sort of people we are" they begged, "and how we have always behaved, and let us have justice and prove our case." The sarcastic reply of the commissioners was only,

---

⁷⁷ Van de Vrugt, *Criminele ordonnantiën*, 131–40; Monballyu, "Onderscheid."
⁷⁸ The legal basis for torture was laid down in Roman law, the Carolina and the Criminal Ordinances. The manuals of practice by Wielant and De Damhouder dealt with the matter in detail for the guidance of court officers and lay justices. Van Heijnsbergen, *Pijnbank*, chapter 2; De Damhouder, *Practycke*, fol. 12.

"Yes, there is your justice," pointing to the rack, and, "Yes, look, there is your spokesman," pointing to the executioner.[79]

It was a violation of the rules of criminal procedure to put leading questions during interrogation. The way in which the commissioners urged the peasants to accuse certain named persons was therefore unlawful. The method of torture, however, was not defined by rules but left to the discretion of the judge. It had to be appropriate to the seriousness of the deed and the suspect's power of endurance. In general, torture was not supposed to leave any permanent injury. This explains why judges preferred to rack the victim, as the commissioners did with Jan Driemunt. This was assumed to be extremely painful but not fatal. It was never permitted to inflict lasting injury, and a fortiori to cause the death of the patient.

If the legality of torture in this case was doubtful, the frequency with which it was inflicted on the prisoners was illegal beyond a doubt. A suspect who confessed under torture but then denied the confession could be tortured once more, and then had to be returned to jail. Only after new indications of his guilt had been found could he be tortured again. The commissioners were perfectly well aware that repeated tortures were unlawful. Calff and Sonnenberg warned the executioner Jacob Michielszoon that if he were later to be summoned for questioning by the Prince of Orange, his commissioners, or the Court of Holland, he must insist that none of the prisoners had ever been tortured more than three times, and that he had only threatened them at other times.[80]

It is therefore abundantly clear that the commissioners acted unlawfully on several points. Yet the legal terms to which they could turn for guidance were very vague. It was not even established beyond dispute that the Criminal Ordinances of 1570, which might have provided the firmest legal basis, had the force of law in the rebel-held territory.[81] Only Heukesloot had gained any experience in applying them in the years from 1570 to 1572. Moreover, it had always been the custom to leave a great deal to the judge's discretion, over which there was no effective control. It is not unlikely that the tortures inflicted on the peasants were more or less what the commissioners had been accustomed to employ in their careers as sheriffs or bailiffs; the reality may have been quite a long way from what the formal legal rules required. Certainly, such disreputable persons as vagrants and vagabonds could not expect any written law to confer many rights on them.

---

[79] Deposition of Cornelis Janszoon and Baertgen Hermansdochter, fol. 14.
[80] Deposition of Jacob Michielszoon, fol. 12.
[81] Van de Vrugt, *Criminele ordonnantiën*.

The question of the legality of the commissioners' actions is less interesting than that of their motives. What were they trying to achieve? Even if they were originally convinced of the reality of the treason plot and the guilt of the accused, they must have begun to feel doubts at some point. The way in which they had wrung confessions from the vagrants ought to have made them more suspicious. The public recantations of the vagabonds and the stubborn denial of the peasants must sooner or later have made them wonder if they were not on the wrong track. No sign of such an insight is to be found in the sources. On the contrary, the commissioners tried to continue the proceedings long after public opinion had largely turned against them.

The motives of the commissioners can only be guessed at. It is obvious that they feared losing face. No one likes to admit that he was wrong, certainly not when his error has claimed more than a dozen lives. Loss of prestige could easily lead to loss of influence and power. Such a rancorous and embittered man as Willem Calff, who had just suffered a painful defeat at the hands of the burgomasters of Edam, would not have been eager to admit his fault.

Political considerations must have weighed even more heavily in the balance. Even if the guilt of the arrested suspects was highly doubtful, no one doubted the reality of the crime. Independent reports of the alleged plot had come in from various sides, and the theory of attempted treason, foiled in the nick of time, seemed to be the only satisfactory explanation for the baffling behavior of the enemy before the sconces at Schoorldam and Krabbendam. The lack of enthusiasm for the new regime in Church and State displayed by the population of North Holland also persuaded Sonoy and his colleagues in power that such a plot was entirely plausible. It was crucial to punish the guilty. If that was impossible, then a terrifying example had to be set, which would crush any idea of treason for good. The national interest mattered more than the individual rights of the accused, certainly if they were only wretched vagabonds or rude peasants.

The commissioners' persistence becomes easier to understand when it is placed against the background of contemporary political and military events. On 14 July, about the time when Pieter Nanningszoon was arrested, the peace negotiations in Breda, long at an impasse, were broken off, and the chance of peace seemed more remote than ever. After breaking up his camp at Beverwijk, Hierges was now menacing the eastern frontiers of Holland. For the first time since it had abandoned the siege of Leiden, the Spanish army was scoring remarkable successes. On 26 June Hierges took Buren, on 7 August Oudewater, on 24 August Schoonhoven. He quickly followed up these victories by capturing the sconces at Krimpen and Papendrecht, and laid siege to Woerden, thereby also threatening

Gouda.⁸² On the southern front at the same time the Spanish commander Mondragon seized the islands of Klundert, Ruigenhil, and Fijnaart. At the end of September the Spanish army made its famous crossing of the Zijpe channel, a feat of arms that brought the islands of Schouwen and Duiveland under its control, threatened Zierikzee, and drove a wedge between the islands of Holland and Zeeland.⁸³

The rebels had no successes to set against these Spanish victories. Sonoy's attempt to bring Amsterdam over to the rebel side by a subterfuge was a miserable failure. Sixteen Beggar soldiers who had been smuggled into the city on peat barges were arrested on 19 August, tortured, and executed.⁸⁴

The successes of the Spanish army were in part the result of war-eariness among the Hollanders.⁸⁵ Although it had a strong and well-manned castle, Buren surrendered without a shot being fired, because the soldiers would not fight. Schoonhoven capitulated after a short siege, because the citizens were unwilling to defend themselves. Mondragon only began his attack on Klundert and the other islands after he heard that the inhabitants were willing to come over to his side. The citizens of Zierikzee also sought to yield their city to the Spaniards because they could not believe that the enemy troops would treat them any worse than the soldiers of William of Orange. Only the decisive intervention of one of the garrison commanders, who arrested seven of the leading citizens, prevented the surrender of the town.⁸⁶ Only the small town of Oudewater chose to defend itself to the utmost, and the result of its warlike spirit was the murder of its entire population and the sacking and burning of the town. In these circumstances there were some who hoped for an early Spanish victory, and if need be were ready to lend a hand to hasten it. In Dordrecht, where the Prince of Orange was residing at the time, some prominent citizens conspired to hand over their town to the Spaniards.⁸⁷ The majority of the population still saw little hope of relief in a government victory, but despaired of any other solution. "All Holland is like to be gone," an English merchant wrote to Elizabeth's minister Burghley. "Out of Holland the people prepare to fly into England, both men, women and children, not only those of the religion but also the Papists, for none dare abide the government of the cruel Spaniards."⁸⁸

---

⁸² Bor, 643–48; Swart, *William of Orange*, 89.
⁸³ Bor, 649.
⁸⁴ Ter Gouw, *Geschiedenis van Amsterdam*, VII, 143–45.
⁸⁵ *CCG*, V, 327 (Morillon to Granvelle, 3 July 1575).
⁸⁶ Swart, *William of Orange*, 90–91.
⁸⁷ Ibid., 89.
⁸⁸ *Calendar of State Papers, Foreign*, no. 389 (George Soutwicke to Burghley, 4 October 1575).

These worrying developments occurred at the very moment when the commissioners were busy investigating the treason plot in the Northern Quarter. It is understandable that the rebels still felt far from secure even after Hierges had moved away. The mood in the Northern Quarter was as panic-stricken as ever. In August it became known that the Stadholder of Friesland had assembled a fleet of 150 ships to transport troops across the Zuiderzee for a landing in West Friesland.[89] The guard on the watch houses built in May was doubled again. On 17 and 18 August the States of the Northern Quarter again ordered the arrest of all vagabonds and aliens without a recent passport, a well-tried tactic, which this time yielded no new suspects in the investigation of the plot.[90] Sonoy considered the commissioners' inquiry to be an essential weapon in his struggle against defeatism and treachery, but he may not have been aware of the dubious methods they used to extract confessions from the prisoners.[91]

Ultimately no one can stand up to prolonged and continual torture, and the unfortunate peasants were no exception. On 6 September Calff and Sonnenberg were able to write to Sonoy from Schagen that Nanning Coppenszoon had confessed. They reported with satisfaction that his confession agreed entirely with those of the executed vagabonds.[92] Nanning had admitted and confirmed "without pain and bonds" that he had paid several persons to set fire to various villages such as Nieuwe Niedorp when the enemy attacked. He himself had intended to reduce the village of Zwaag to ashes. He had also planned to burn two stacks of reeds on the Noorderdijk, to serve as beacons to guide the invasion fleet from Friesland. Presumably this was to be done at the place that had been assigned to the people of Wognum to guard in the previous May. Nanning named his fellow prisoner Pieter Nanningszoon as his accomplice.[93]

On the grounds of these grave crimes Sonoy condemned Nanning to death and the confiscation of his property. Because Wognum was within the jurisdiction of Hoorn, Sonoy summoned four justices from the town to Schagen to confirm the sentence and execute it at Hoorn.[94] The judg-

---

[89] Velius, 248.

[90] Resolution of 17–18 August 1575, NHA, GNK, inv. no. 236.

[91] Bor, 640, thought that the commissioners deliberately misled Sonoy.

[92] Calff and Sonnenberg to Sonoy, 6 September 1575, in Bor, 627.

[93] Bor, 628.

[94] Judgment on Nanning Coppenszoon, 30 September 1575, in Bor, 627, and WFA, ORA Hoorn, inv. no. 4515, fol. 202r–v. See also Sonoy to Heukesloot, 22 September 1575, ibid., fol. 203, where Sonoy writes that he has ordered the burgomasters of Hoorn to send four justices to take the confirmation of Nanning's confession. See also the register of extraordinary expenses of the burgomasters for 1574–75 in WFA, OA Hoorn, inv. no. 2498: "27 September, paid to burgomaster Jan Corneliszoon Loeff 7 guilders 13 stuivers for costs of travel and meals when he was summoned to the castle of Schagen with four justices by the

ment prescribed that the death sentence was to be carried out by cutting Nanning's heart from his body while he was still alive and striking him in the face with it, the barbarous but traditional punishment for treason.

On 29 September a platoon of soldiers escorted Nanning on his last journey to Hoorn. The next day he was led to the scaffold. A public execution was a spectacle stage-managed by the authorities, but in which the condemned man had a certain freedom in playing his part. It was customary for him to address the onlookers as his last act. As the condemned vagabonds had done before, Nanning cried out "very loudly" to the crowd that neither he nor Pieter Nanningszoon, whom he had denounced, was guilty of treason; he had only confessed because he had been tortured and given fair but false promises. "If they want to kill me," he added, "then they might as well kill the whole of Hoorn."[95]

These words, which he repeated while the executioner stripped him and bound him to the bench, did not fail to produce an effect. The spectators who had flocked to the scene became uneasy, while the burgomasters too began to doubt that justice was being served. Fearing a riot, they ordered the prisoner to be untied and the execution to be delayed. They wrote to Sonoy requesting further instructions and asking for the commissioners to be sent to Hoorn. In the meantime Nanning was locked up in the town hall.

We know what happened there thanks to the detailed deposition of the executioner Jacob Michielszoon:

> And being there the sheriff of Hoorn [Heukesloot] spoke very harshly to him [Nanning], asking him why he made such difficulties, since he had confessed everything and must die; threatening that if he said any more to exculpate himself, they would tear him limb from limb; whereupon Nanning answered, "Everything I confessed, I confessed through pain and on orders, because you held it out to me and wanted me to say it; and so you promised me that if I persisted therein, I should keep my life and goods, and now you do not keep your word, but want to kill me."[96]

The next morning, 1 October, the other commissioners and the secretary arrived to carry out the delayed execution. Master Jacob found Nanning in a small room in the town hall, accompanied by the town preacher and "well drunk with sweet wine." By producing him drunk the authorities

---

governor; 3 October paid to Thijs Stoffelaer 2 guilders 10 stuivers for traveling to the governor in Alkmaar with a missive concerning the justice of Nanninck Jacobszoon, whether it was to be proceeded with or not."

[95] Bor, 627–28.
[96] Deposition of Jacob Michielszoon, fol. 10.

hoped to avoid scenes like those of the previous day. It may not be a coincidence that Nanning's last words were almost the same as those of the vagabonds executed earlier:

> That he was guiltless of the matter; and if he must die, then he was a child of eternal life, and he and all those whom he had accused were as free [of guilt] as the child that was born that night.[97]

For the second time Nanning was brought to the scaffold, "very drunk"; he shook Master Jacob's hand firmly and asked him for a quick death. Once again he wanted to protest his innocence, but Heukesloot ordered the executioner to strangle him and stop him speaking. The preacher Jurriaen Ypeszoon, whose task it was to console the victim in his last hours, spoke to him so loudly that Nanning's words were lost. The sentence was executed at four in the afternoon in the prescribed manner.[98] Nanning's lifeless body was quartered, and the quarters displayed above the gates of Hoorn. His head was stuck on the tower of Wognum church but removed the same night by unknown hands, and we may assume buried in consecrated ground.[99]

So died Nanning Coppenszoon after four months of imprisonment. His execution evoked memories of those of the vagabonds in the villages, who had also publicly recanted their confessions. But a great deal had happened since then. The execution did not provoke the riot the burgomasters of Hoorn had dreaded, but many now began to have serious doubts about the commissioners' methods. From now on the people began to call Sonoy's commission the Blood Council, a nickname echoing that given to Alba's hated Council of Troubles.

The story had an unexpected sequel. Jurriaen Ypeszoon had warned Nanning not to deny his misdeeds, which he had confessed before the commissioners. When the preacher tried to prevent him speaking on the scaffold, Nanning challenged him to justify himself before God's judgment seat in three days. Troubled by the curse of a condemned man, Jurriaen went home after the execution and took to his bed. In three days he was dead.[100]

---

[97] Ibid., fol. 10v.

[98] Velius, 247.

[99] "Kohier van extraordinarisuitgaven van burgemeesters 1574–75," WFA, OA Hoorn, inv. no. 2498: "on 4 October paid Master Jacob the executioner 26 stuivers for hanging up two quarters of Nanning Jacobszoon, one on the East Gate and one on the Cow Gate." For the removal of Nanning's head the only source is Twisck, *Chronijck*, II, 1318.

[100] Velius, 247. Velius bases this story on oral tradition of the inhabitants of Hoorn. Some believed that the term fixed for the preacher to justify himself was not three days but five. Jurriaen Ypeszoon was active as a preacher in Leiden in 1566–67. Blok, *Geschiedenis eener Hollandsche stad*, III, 38–40. For his career in the Northern Quarter see *Acta*, I, 19, 23, 25.

CHAPTER NINE

# Citizens

Now that Nanning Coppenszoon was out of the way, only Pieter Nanningszoon remained in the hands of the commissioners. He had been named by Nanning as his accomplice, and only he could put the commissioners on the track of the instigators of the plot. In the end the peasant from Benningbroek was no more able than Nanning to resist repeated and ever-crueler tortures. A new and frightful instrument, called the *running windlass*, was especially contrived for him. The earthenware bell jar used to place the rat on the victim's belly was replaced by a specially produced wood and copper box, which was later drawn at Pieter Bor's request by the famous Haarlem printmaker Hendrik Goltzius (plate 6).[1]

Broken in body and mind, Pieter Nanningszoon finally gave the commissioners everything they had so long been urging him to reveal. He named three men who had allegedly given him his orders: Jan Jeroenszoon and Piet El, both from Hoorn, and Sybout Janszoon from Medemblik.[2] He confessed to being in touch with Pietge Pieterszoon Joncx, an inhabitant of Nibbixwoud who had fled to Amsterdam. Pietge, he said, had sent him money and letters, which Pieter Nanningszoon had shown to Jan Jeroenszoon and Piet El. They in turn had promised financial help if he could not get enough money from Amsterdam in time. With the funds received from Amsterdam Pieter had hired some vagrants to set the North Holland villages on fire, namely "Pieter de Boer" (presumably the wayfarer Piet Janszoon of Buiksloot), Reyntgen de Vries (Roomken or Reynken Symons of Dokkum) and Jan Clouk. None of the vagrants named could confirm or deny Pieter's story. The first two had escaped from jail in Alkmaar and vanished without trace, the last had been executed at the stake in Nibbixwoud or Hauwert.

It is obvious that this forced confession was worthless, but the commissioners were elated. "Praise God, we have got Pieter Nanningszoon to confess as well," they reported to Sonoy, "without torture [*sic*], so that we will without doubt get to the bottom and the truth of this whole matter."[3] Now that Pieter's resistance was broken, renewed tortures quickly

---

[1] Bor, 628.

[2] Ibid., 628–29; and also one Wouter Symonszoon, of whom nothing more is heard, and "some others."

[3] Bor, 629.

produced a flood of names: Wigger Allertszoon of Medemblik, the former dike-reeve of the Zijpe polder, and Barent Roest of Enkhuizen, both of whom had also received letters from Pietge Pieterszoon Joncx in Amsterdam; these letters also named the citizens of Hoorn, Willem Pieterszoon Schijtgelt, Dirck Jezus, and Gerbrant Verduyn. Ben Pieterszoon, Jacob Pieterszoon Pillis,[4] and Willem Jan Garbrantszoon also knew of the plot. Fop Claeszoon had procured a safe-conduct from the enemy, and Jacob Sweerszoon had confided to him that he had received money from Coppen Corneliszoon of Wognum.

Pieter Nanningszoon also claimed that in May the villagers of Benningbroek and Sijbekarspel had asked the authorities to be exempted from guard duty on the Krabbendam, because they knew that this was where the enemy would try to break through the lines. He named burgomaster Adriaen Pieterszoon of Benningbroek and the justices Aris Hermanszoon, Cornelis Adriaenszoon, and Marten Pieterszoon as the conspirators behind this treasonable plot. Once again it was Jacob Pieterszoon Pillis of Hoorn who had got in touch with them, through the burgomaster's brother-in-law.

Unlike the vagrants and peasants held in the first wave of arrests, the commissioners now had a group of suspects who were more than a mass of anonymous faces in a crowd. They displayed a clear common profile, and all the evidence pointed in the same direction. The instigators of the plot must be sought among the *glippers*, or sneakers, that is, those who had sneaked away to enemy-held territory.[5] Most of them came from Hoorn. Jan Jeroenszoon, Piet El, Willem Pieterszoon Schijtgelt, Dirck Jezus, Gerbrant Verduyn, and Jacob Pieterszoon Pillis were all established citizens of the town.[6] Wigger Allertszoon of Medemblik and Barent Roest of Enkhuizen also belonged to the better-off refugees.[7] Pietge Pieterszoon Joncx of Nibbixwoud had even served as a cavalryman in the Spanish

---

[4] According to Bor "Jan Pieter Pillis." He can be identified as Jacob Pieterszoon Pillis; see "Remonstrantie over het onvermogen van de stad lasten te betalen" [Remonstrance on the town's inability to pay charges], ca. 1573, WFA, OA Hoorn, inv. no. 2530; bylaw of 16 January 1574, ordering the return of those who had been expelled from the town, WFA, OA Hoorn, inv. no. 55, fol. 165v; Velius, 199.

[5] See *Woordenboek der Nederlandse taal*, s.v. *glipper*. The term was probably first mentioned in Bor, 531.

[6] See above, note 4, and resolution of the *vroedschap* of 13 November 1574, WFA, OA Hoorn, inv. no. 91, fol. 72.

[7] On Wigger Allertszoon, see a register of names of persons who have left Medemblik and are said to be staying in Amsterdam, 14 March 1573, WFA, OA Medemblik, inv. no. 1478. It names Wigger Allertszoon Dijkgraaf, his wife Maritgen, and daughter Magdaleen, and the two children of their dead son. On him see Noordeloos, "Fugitieve personen," 82–84; Belonje, "Polderregering." On Barent Roest, see Noordeloos, "Fugitieve personen," 85.

army during Hierges's attack on the Northern Quarter.⁸ The commissioners now had a clear track to follow, even if it was one they themselves had laid down.

They could therefore press ahead energetically with their investigation, but there was one problem: most of the suspected refugees were still in the enemy zone and out of their reach. Two suspects, Jan Jeroenszoon and Piet El, however, had returned in December 1574. They had lived in Amsterdam for two years, and the treason plot was discovered shortly after their return. In the eyes of the commissioners all this was highly suspect.

By chance, on 25 September, six days before the execution of Nanning Coppenszoon, Piet El was making his way, all unsuspecting, from Huisduinen to Hoorn. He passed through the little town of Schagen, where the commissioners were still staying.⁹ They immediately had him arrested and brought to the castle. Piet El denied the charges against him, but admitted that he had lived for a time in Amsterdam as a refugee. Around Christmas 1574 he had returned to Hoorn and had been pardoned by the burgomasters, after paying a heavy fine of 166 guilders. The commissioners then confronted him with Pieter Nanningszoon. The exhausted and utterly broken peasant must have been a ghastly sight for Piet El, above all when he declared that El was the man who had promised to supply the money needed for the conspiracy.

The confrontation gave the commissioners enough grounds to interrogate Piet El. Three times he was put on the rack, while Heukesloot and the castellan of Schagen, Calff's brother Gerrit Hendrickszoon, promised to put in a good word for him if he confessed to everything his interrogators demanded of him. The executioner Jacob Michielszoon later deposed that it was clear that El had been led by these promises to confess everything the commissioners held out to him.¹⁰ It was therefore not long before they had a full confession from him. Piet El and Pieter Nanningszoon unanimously denounced Jan Jeroenszoon as the chief conspirator.

Now that everything pointed to Jan Jeroenszoon, the commissioners asked Sonoy to arrest this citizen of Hoorn. There was much that was still murky in this case; only now had they stumbled on the "main branches" of the conspiracy. Sonoy must "show courage" to purge the country of traitors. Jan Jeroenszoon was a "sly and cunning man," who could tell them a great deal.¹¹ On the insistence of the commissioners

---

⁸ Statement of Pietge Pieterszoon Joncx before burgomasters and counselors of Hoorn, 25 October 1577, NA, Hof, inv. no. 4592.
⁹ Bor, 629.
¹⁰ Deposition of Jacob Michielszoon, fol. 11v.
¹¹ Bor, 629.

Sonoy instructed the sheriff of Hoorn (that is, Heukesloot), to arrest Jan Jeroenszoon and bring him to Alkmaar.

But now it was to prove that in Holland, even in wartime, it was much more difficult to lay hands on a burgher than on a defenseless peasant or a vagabond without rights. One of the most important privileges the townsfolk of the Netherlands enjoyed was the right to be brought to trial before a court in their own town, in which their fellow citizens sat in judgment on them. The towns had fought several bitter battles with the central authorities to defend the *ius de non evocando* in connection with the antiheresy laws, and had not infrequently emerged victorious.[12]

The legal procedures customary in the towns also offered the citizens some protection. In criminal procedure the accused was not a party but the object of an investigation. His guilt was assumed; the aim of the proceedings was merely to extract a confession from him, and preferably also the names of any accomplices, if necessary with the aid of torture. A suspect might not have the assistance of an advocate and could not appeal against a death sentence. It was thus of the greatest importance for an innocent person to avoid being put on trial in criminal proceedings, for once one was accused the outcome of the trial was practically a foregone conclusion. Citizens therefore enjoyed the right to a preliminary investigation, to protect them against false accusations and judicial arbitrariness. This was called the *informatie precedente*. The sheriff had to investigate the reputation of the suspect and convince himself that there was a prima facie case against him; only after the burgomasters had given their consent could he then proceed to make an arrest.[13] The magistrates of Hoorn invoked this privilege, and on 26 September they resolved not to hand over Jan Jeroenszoon without a thorough preliminary inquiry. He was, however, placed under house arrest, under the guard of three servants of the court, and had to deposit a surety.[14]

Sonoy was highly offended by the uncooperative attitude of the magistrates, and told them that while he was happy to respect their privileges, this was a "reserved" matter, a case that fell under the direct jurisdiction of the provincial authorities, so that the privileges simply did not apply. The burgomasters therefore were duty bound to surrender Jan Jeroens-

---

[12] De Monté Ver Loren, *Hoofdlijnen*, 138; Duke, *Reformation*, 165.

[13] Duke, *Reformation*, 159; Monballyu, "Onderscheid," 127.

[14] Bor, 629, states that the magistrates of Hoorn began to distrust the action of the commissioners after Nanning Coppenszoon's public recantation on 1 October. But the burgomasters and *vroedschap* had already decided five days earlier on 26 September not to hand over Jan Jeroenszoon, on the grounds of the town's privileges. *Vroedschap* resolution of 26 September 1575, WFA, OA Hoorn, inv. no. 91, fol. 78. Nanning's recantation must have confirmed the magistrates in their resolve. Jan Jeroenszoon was locked up in his own house on 27 September. Velius, 248.

zoon to the sheriff, who was to keep him under close guard.[15] To put even more pressure on the town Sonoy also asked the States of the Northern Quarter to add another company or even two companies of soldiers to the one that was already quartered in Hoorn.[16] The delegates of the other towns of North Holland supported the governor's proposal, with the result that Hoorn not only had to bear the burden of even more soldiers but was also compelled to yield up its citizen. To show some consideration for Hoorn, however, the States stipulated that the sheriff and two justices of the town must be present at the hearings.

Sonoy was right to argue that treason was a reserved matter, but it is surprising that he won the unanimous support of the other six towns, which might have been expected to join in the common cause of defending their privileges. Their complaisance in this case shows how deep the fear of treason had penetrated. They can hardly have objected to placing a heavier burden of troops on Hoorn, for that would only lighten their own.[17]

Under such intense pressure Hoorn was forced to yield. On 16 October Jan Jeroenszoon was conveyed to Schagen.[18] Two burgomasters, four justices, and the town clerk accompanied him, at least to be present at the confrontation with Pieter Nanningszoon and Piet El. As a citizen of Hoorn he was not altogether alone, but his future appeared very bleak. Who was this Jan Jeroenszoon, for whom Hoorn was prepared to make such an effort?

Jan Jeroenszoon was born in 1545 at Middelie, a village of 173 households, or about 865 inhabitants, on the Purmer dike, which fell within the jurisdiction of Edam.[19] There he grew up as the youngest of the four or five children of Jeroen Claeszoon and Neel Jansdochter.[20] Jan's father

---

[15] Bor, 629.

[16] Resolution of the States of the Northern Quarter, 6 and 7 October 1575, NHA, GNK, inv. no. 236.

[17] On the lack of solidarity between the towns of North Holland see Aten, *Als 't gewelt komt*.

[18] Bor, 629.

[19] Number of houses in Middelie: Van der Woude, *Noorderkwartier*, 622. The birth year of Jan Jeroenszoon is inferred from the statements of his age in several notarized deeds: on 26 February 1584 he gave his age as thirty-eight, on 7 August 1591 as forty-five, on 31 October 1592 as forty-seven, on 26 September 1602 as fifty-eight, on 18 January 1605 as fifty-nine, and on 24 June 1606 as sixty-one. WFA, Not.A Hoorn, inv. nos. 2048, fol. 141; 2036, fol. 288; 2037, fol. 157; 2043, fol. 242v; 2045, fol. 266v; and 2046 fol. 244v. Jan Jeroenszoon's birthplace Middelie is revealed in "Papisticque vergaderingen," 316.

[20] Jan's father Jeroen Claeszoon was, according to the tenth penny register for Edam, the only Jeroen living at Middelie or Edam at this time. He was born around 1507 (hearings of Alba's commissioners, NHA, Kopieën, inv. no. A523, fols. 49 and 35v). In the register for 1530 "Jeroen's wife" is named as the owner of a few parcels of land written in the margin, perhaps an indication that Jeroen and Neel married at about this time. Register van de

Jeroen appears in the tax assessment registers as a simple peasant, who rose to prosperity and a position of some standing over the years and exchanged the countryside for the town.[21] In 1530 he and his sister Aecht owned a modest farm of half a farmhouse and a few parcels of land, on which they grazed three cattle and a heifer, but by 1554 he had become the largest landowner in Middelie and could also boast a large house in Edam, where he had settled with his family. In 1563 he invested in another house in Edam, which he rented out. In 1561 he was considered sufficiently notable to be appointed as assessor of the tenth penny tax. That did not mean he was an educated man, for he signed the assessment register with a cross, as indeed did his fellow assessors.[22] In the following year he donated the munificent sum of 150 guilders to the newly opened Edam orphanage, and in 1564 he acted as one of the three "orphan-masters," or administrators of the institution.[23]

It is unlikely that Jeroen Claeszoon made his fortune from the three cows he owned in 1530, or the five he could call his own in 1554. The *Informacie* of 1514 states that the villagers of Middelie "made their living from the sea, like their neighbors," that is, they earned their bread by going to sea.[24] Possibly Jeroen Claeszoon invested in the Edam timber trade, or he may have been engaged in shipbuilding, the chief industry of the little town.

Edam and its surrounding villages in those years offered ample opportunity to become familiar with the new religious ideas that were circulating in the Netherlands. Since 1537 or 1538 Jan de Haen, a priest who came

---

inbreng, WA, OA Edam, inv. no. 238, fol. 103. This Neel was the daughter of one Jan Melis, see "Schotboek 1569," WA, OA Edam, inv. no. 239 c, fol. 103. Jan's brothers and sisters are known from the will of 17 May 1582 of the sixteen-year-old Claes Janszoon, alias Claes Jeroenszoon of Edam, WFA, Not.A Hoorn, inv. no. 2048, fols. 2v–3v. Since the testator had no parents, brothers, or sisters but only collateral relatives, he instituted as his heirs his uncle Gerbrant Jeroenszoon, Gerbrant's daughter Griet Jeroensdochter or Griet Gerbrantsdochter, his aunt Garberich Jeroensdochter and any children she might have in the future, Anna Claesdochter, the daughter of his late uncle Claes, and his uncle Jan Jeroenszoon and his children. The fact that Jan Jeroenszoon was named last, after his brothers and sister, suggests that he was the youngest. The relationship between Claes Janszoon or Jeroenszoon and his uncles and aunt is not entirely clear; he may have been the son of Jeroen Claeszoon, but he could also have been the son of a daughter of Jeroen Claeszoon whose name is not known. For more on the family relationships see Looijesteijn, "Geslacht."

[21] Register van de inbreng, 1530, 1546, 1554, 1563, WA, OA Edam, inv. no. 238, fols. 8, 31v, 103. In the register for 1554 Jeroen Claeszoon is not named under Edam but under Middelie. Tenth penny registers of Edam 1543, 1544, 1553, 1556, 1561, NA, SvH, inv. nos. 195, 462, 598, 932, fol. 36, and 1248, fol. 150v.

[22] Tenth penny register of Edam, 1561, NA, SvH, inv. no. 1248, fol. 84.

[23] *Register burgerweeshuis Edam*, 24; Kwijtscheldings-register [register of discharges], WA, ORA Edam, inv. no. 3813, 23 May 1564.

[24] *Informacie*, 189.

from the Leper-House in Amsterdam, had been preaching in Edam and had "brought many people to the sect of Luthery by his wicked sermons." When Edam became too hot to hold him he continued his activities at Middelie, where he had obtained a living as parish priest. After the Court of Holland began an inquiry he disappeared without trace, but his successor Arent Graet or Arent van Collen was no more orthodox in his doctrine.[25] Waterland and the Zeevang were notorious for their strong Anabaptist presence, and Middelie, too, had a sizeable Anabaptist community. Between 1563 and 1565 Lenaert Bouwenszoon baptized twenty-five persons there, a large number for a village with only 173 households. By that time, however, Jeroen Claeszoon and his family had already moved to Edam, where the Mennonites were less active, performing only fifteen baptisms between 1563 and 1565.[26] The town was also visited several times between 1558 and 1566 by a Reformed preacher sent from Emden, Nicolaes Carineus, a native of Edam, by Jan Arentszoon and probably also by Cornelis Cooltuyn himself. In the deepest secrecy they preached to small groups of sympathizers with the Reformation and performed baptisms.

Jeroen Claeszoon and his family were certainly not among those who went to hear these religious dissenters. They were and remained good Catholics. In 1547 Edam received an outstanding priest in Meinert van Enkhuizen, who was as orthodox as he was popular among his parishioners.[27] It was probably through his influence that Edam offered less attraction to those who were open to new ideas in religion than its neighbors Monnickendam and Hoorn.

Jan was an intelligent youth, and so his parents sent him to the Latin School, probably the institution attached to the library of the parish church of Edam.[28] This was the necessary first step on the path to a university education. By allowing his son to study, Jeroen Claeszoon confirmed his own rise in society. Jan was not only the first of his family to go to university, but also was unusual among the town population as a whole. Only eleven Edammers matriculated at the University of Leuven between 1528 and 1569, in spite of the existence of two bursaries, which provided funds for bright but poor boys from the town to study there.[29]

On 3 June 1563 "Joannes Hieronimi, Edamensis" and five others swore the oath before Rector Augustinus Hunaeus.[30] By chance the little group

---

[25] Driessen, *Waterland*, 185–86.
[26] Vos, "Dooplijst," 65, 67. In Axwijk, a hamlet that belonged with Middelie, Lenaert baptized eight more persons between 1568 and 1582.
[27] Driessen, *Waterland*, 159–62.
[28] For the Latin School in Edam see Driessen, *Waterland*, 149–50 and 180–81.
[29] *Matricule*, passim; two deeds of foundation for a bursary at Leuven, WA, OA Edam, inv. nos. 360 and 361; Driessen, *Waterland*, 163–64.
[30] *Matricule*, 655, no. 78.

included one "Henricus de Catsenellenboge ex comitibus de Nassau," no less a person than Henry of Nassau, the youngest brother of William of Orange, the king's Stadholder in Holland. Henry, still a minor, was accompanied by his *pedagogus* George Clant, who took the oath on his behalf. One can imagine the peasant's son from Middelie, impressed by the many new and strange sights he saw in Leuven, humbly doffing his cap while the expensively dressed nobleman and his retinue strode by. Both freshmen, each in his own way, were to become victims of the conflict that was soon to break out: Jan as a Catholic refugee would be suspected of high treason, while Henry would fall on the rebel side at the battle of Mook Heath in April 1574.

The University of Leuven, where Jan Jeroenszoon studied, was in the autumn of its sixteenth-century flowering. The Revolt would inaugurate a period of decline, in which the university would attract far fewer students. Like most undergraduates, Jan would first have followed a two and a half year *propaedeusis* in the faculty of arts, attending lectures in logic, physics (natural philosophy), metaphysics, and ethics. After completing this preliminary course he entered himself in the faculty of law, where he presumably mastered both laws, Roman and Canon. In both branches of legal study, which could be followed at the same time, the first three years were concluded by the bachelor's examination and the next three by the licentiate. Lectures were offered on Roman and ecclesiastical law, but no attention was paid to the living law, that is, customary and feudal law. Graduates in "learned" law were of course considered capable of working in them.[31]

Jan Jeroenszoon therefore did not experience the political and religious tensions of the Wonder Year in his home town, but Leuven was a suitable vantage point from which to observe at close quarters the presentation of the Compromise of the Nobility and other exciting, but from a Roman Catholic point of view alarming, events. The religious peace and quiet of the orthodox Catholic University were not disturbed. The faculty of theology and the countless clerics attached to the university kept a sharp eye on religious life, so that no hedge preaching was organized in the neighborhood, and the city was spared iconoclastic rioting.[32]

Jan's parental home Edam did not escape the Wonder Year so lightly. The Alkmaar basket maker Jan Arentszoon preached to four thousand eager listeners in the open air between Edam and Monnickendam on 4 August 1567. Fourteen days later he addressed an even larger audience outside the North Gate of Edam. There was no iconoclasm in the town, but a guard had to be mounted on the church, which remained closed for

---

[31] Lamberts and Roegiers, *Universiteit van Leuven*, 69–71, 86–92.
[32] Van Uytven, "Protestanten," 258.

six months, seriously interrupting Catholic religious life. Once the government had restored order in the spring of 1567, Reformed activities ceased in Edam as they did elsewhere. Twenty-seven inhabitants, among them the town clerk, went into exile and were sentenced in their absence to perpetual banishment and confiscation of their property by the Council of Troubles.[33]

The restoration of normality created new possibilities for Jan's father, the good Catholic Jeroen Claeszoon. On Easter Sunday 1567 he was appointed to serve for a year as one of the four burgomasters of Edam. It is unlikely that the illiterate "new man" would have risen so high but for the troubles of 1566. In the new political circumstances the town needed burgomasters whose orthodoxy was beyond reproach. As burgomaster, Jeroen Claeszoon gave evidence that was damaging to his fellow townsmen before the commissioners of the Court of Holland who came to inquire into the troubles.[34] In 1568 his year of office was already over, but the new town fathers sent his promising young law graduate son to Brussels to discuss matters concerning water control with the government.[35]

After completing his studies—the exact date is not known—Jan Jeroenszoon settled in Hoorn, perhaps because the larger town offered better prospects to an advocate just starting his career. He acquired citizenship of Hoorn by marrying Griet Frederiksdochter, the widow of Jan Claeszoon.[36] She may have been a little older than her new husband. The marriage made Jan a member of a widely ramified network of families in Hoorn, a fact that was to prove of great importance during his captivity.

Little is known about Griet Frederiksdochter, but a letter that Jan Jeroenszoon later wrote from his prison cell in Delft sheds some light on her social background. He asked her to give his greetings to "my relations who are now being put to the test in our case, to wit Coomen Vreerick, Pieter schipper Aris, Claes Dijckgraeff, and the carpenter on the North [Street] Lammert Melissen and all the friends who are lovers of justice."[37] "Coomen" [*koopman* or merchant] Vreerick was not the father of Griet Frederiksdochter, but the same "comen" Frederick Gerritszoon Kannegieter who witnessed the will of Jan Jeroenszoon's nephew Claes Janszoon or Jeroenszoon in 1582, signing with his mark. Jan Jeroenszoon later

---

[33] *Sententiën*, 35–36; Driessen, *Waterland*, 187–88.
[34] Hearings of Alba's commissioners, Edam, NHA, Kopieën, inv. no. A523, fols. 35v, 49.
[35] Town account for 1568–69, WA, OA Edam, inv. no. 184, fol. 314.
[36] Schepenrollen [justices' rolls], WFA, ORA Hoorn, inv. no. 4165, 4 October 1574: "Jan Claeszoon Veen, having married Griete Vrerixdr"; and inv. no. 4184, 12 June 1591: "Jan Jeroenszoon as husband and guardian of Griet Vrerix, former wife of the late Jan Veen." For the acquisition of citizenship at Hoorn, *Westfriesche stadsrechten*, 96–97.
[37] Jan Jeroenszoon to Jan Corneliszoon Spranger, 15 February 1577, NHA, Aanwinsten, inv. no. 1186.

declared that he had "good knowledge and conversation" with him.[38] Pieter schipper Ariszoon was a beer merchant whom Sonoy expelled from the town as an unreliable, that is, Catholic, element in December 1572. Like Jan Jeroenszoon he spent the years of the Revolt in exile and did not return to Hoorn until after the Pacification of Ghent, renewing his oath as a citizen on 28 December 1576.[39] The carpenter on the North Street (the main street of Hoorn), Claes Dijckgraeff, earned a living as a carrier as well as a carpenter. Payments by the town for the use of his services appear frequently in the burgomasters' accounts. From the driver's seat of his wagon Claes Dijckgraeff could observe the excitement stirred up by the alleged plot to betray the Northern Quarter: he conveyed the burgomasters and justices to Schagen to confirm the judgment on Nanning Coppenszoon, and on 16 October he took Jan Jeroenszoon to Schagen after he had been handed over to the commissioners.[40]

These details suggest that Griet Frederiksdochter came from a milieu of Catholic middle-class tradesmen and small merchants, economically independent but below the level from which the burgomasters, justices, and orphanage masters of Hoorn were recruited.[41] As a widow Griet may have had a fortune of her own. Jeroen Claeszoon must also have died at about this time, allowing Jan to take possession of his portion of the inheritance.[42] In any case his practice in Hoorn seems to have prospered, despite the difficulties that Alba and the Sea Beggars caused to the town.

In March 1572 Alba decided to introduce the Tenth Penny despite the years of resistance from the towns, the States, and the nobles. Eight citizens of Hoorn were designated to collect the new tax, of whom Jan Jeroenszoon was one. Although he had only recently graduated and was no more than twenty-six, he was evidently already considered to belong to the notables of the town. It was a doubtful honor, for the new tax was both extraordinarily unpopular and hard to collect, because it had to be calculated retrospectively on all goods sold since the edict was first proclaimed. The eight designated assessors, who themselves admitted that they feared provoking a riot among the population, therefore refused to cooperate.[43]

---

[38] Deposition of Jan Jeroenszoon, 24 June 1606, WFA, Not.A Hoorn, inv. no. 2046, fol. 244v.

[39] Velius, 199, and appendix (unpaginated); remonstrance on the inability of the town to pay charges (ca. 1573), WFA, OA Hoorn, inv. no. 2530.

[40] Register of extraordinary expenses of the burgomasters, 1 June, 27 July, 19 September, and 29 November 1585, WFA, OA Hoorn, inv. no. 2498.

[41] The names of burgomasters, justices, *vroedschap* members, and orphanage masters in Velius, 361–99.

[42] Register of the hundredth penny, 1569, WA, OA Edam, inv. no. 241, fol. 1v. In the register Jeroen Claeszoon's house is valued, but the item and the amount payable are crossed out by the clerk.

[43] Velius, 178–79.

Their refusal involved them in a bitter battle of wills with the burgomasters and Sheriff Heukesloot, who at this time was still a loyal supporter of the central government in Brussels. The burgomasters and sheriff threatened to recover the town's lost revenue from the recalcitrant citizens. The citizens of Hoorn supported the eight reluctant tax collectors and offered to mount a guard of thirty men on their homes at night, to prevent Heukesloot from arresting them. Jan Jeroenszoon later declared that the "great enmity" between him and the sheriff dated from this time, "in particular because I, being indignant for the aforementioned reason, called him a 'lantern without light.' "[44] Three years later this enmity was to have disastrous consequences for Jan Jeroenszoon.

Alba's Tenth Penny was never introduced, because the Revolt broke out before it could be collected. We have seen how Enkhuizen's adherence to the Revolt on 21 May 1572 placed Hoorn under great pressure to follow suit; how an attempt of the burgomasters to bring in government troops was frustrated by the citizens; and finally how a majority on the Broad Council, which represented the citizenry, resolved on 18 June to open the gates to the rebels. What Jan Jeroenszoon thought of all these events is unknown. His experience as an unwilling collector of the Tenth Penny cannot have made him enthusiastic about admitting government forces. Although the religious question played no explicit role in the transition, as a Catholic he could expect no good from the notoriously antipapist Sea Beggars. All we know is that at a certain moment he decided to leave the town.

The exact date of his departure is unknown, but three of the four sitting burgomasters and several of the wealthiest and most prominent citizens went into exile on 18 June, immediately after the revolution.[45] Jan Jeroenszoon is unlikely to have been among this first group of émigrés, since he had only recently been in conflict with the burgomasters and was not a member of the Hoorn patriciate. Like many others he must have decided to wait and see.

What he saw was not encouraging. The day after the revolution a violent thunderstorm burst over Hoorn. Hailstones "as big as lapwing's eggs" tore the leaves off the trees "like razor blades" and ruined the vegetation in the fields. Many regarded this as a portent of evil to come. Indeed on the same rainy, stormy day a band of Beggars under Jacques Hennebert entered the town. The undisciplined and unruly soldiers were quartered in the houses of the citizens, a violation of earlier agreements to the contrary.[46] The town now had to accept a military commander appointed by

---

[44] Jan Jeroenszoon to Jan Cornelis Spranger, 15 February 1577, NHA, Aanwinsten, inv. no. 1186.
[45] Velius, 188.
[46] Ibid., 188–89.

Sonoy alongside its own burgomasters, and on 3 July the citizens were required to swear a new oath of loyalty to the Prince of Orange as the lawful Stadholder. According to Velius there were "many" who could not reconcile this oath with their conscience. They too left the town to join the exiles in Amsterdam.[47]

The same jealous attachment to their autonomy that had led the citizens to choose for the Prince of Orange and against Alba in June now brought them into conflict with the new regime. In September tensions ran high between the population and Sonoy, who was in the town at the time. The governor wanted to quarter a second company of soldiers in the town, against the will of the citizenry, which was already suffering grievously from the presence of the existing garrison. In the end Sonoy got his way, to the great discontent of the townsfolk. When he also demanded that the keys of the town gates, which had always been controlled by the burgomasters, should in the future be entrusted to him or one of his men, this was the last straw. The militia closed the gates, collected the keys, and kept them at the town hall.[48] There was no real riot, as there was at Medemblik on 16 November. There the citizens were so dissatisfied with their new rulers they disarmed the company garrisoned in the town and drove it from the castle.[49]

The Revolt brought changes in the Church that were hard for Jan Jeroenszoon and the Catholic majority in the town to swallow. Most citizens of traditionally tolerant Hoorn must have hoped for a certain degree of latitude to be shown to those who thought differently on religion. But the Reformed assumed that their faith, the only true one, must take over the monopoly of the Catholic Church. On the same day that the citizens swore the new oath to the Prince of Orange, the Reformed requested the magistrates to make the Great Church available to them for their services. The response was that in view of their small numbers they would have to be satisfied with the smaller church of Our Lady. The leaders of the Reformed threatened to bring their followers on to the street to show just how many supporters they really had. Were they counting on help from Sonoy and the Beggar garrison in the town? At any rate the burgomasters gave way to the intimidation and allowed them to use the Great Church, provided that the altars and images were removed in an orderly fashion.

The removal was anything but orderly, however; the workmen who were given the job, although deliberately chosen from among Catholics

---

[47] Ibid., 189. The governor of the town was Josua van Alveringen, Lord of Hofwegen. Bor, 377. On him see Te Water, *Verbond en smeekschriften*, 148–51, and *Sententiën*, 53–54.

[48] Velius, 193–94.

[49] Bor, 415.

as well as supporters of the Beggars, were "no lovers of images," and went about their work with such zeal that at the end of the day nearly all the images had been vandalized. All the ecclesiastical silver in Hoorn was sent to Dordrecht to be melted down for coin to finance the war effort.[50] Mass was still said outside the Great Church for a time, but it ceased in the winter of 1572/73, probably as early as December 1572.

The clergy who lived in or around Hoorn suffered most. In December 1572 the inhabitants of Hoorn, both Protestant and Catholic, were compelled to demolish the nearby monastery at Westerblokker, to prevent the rapidly approaching Spanish army fortifying it.[51] All the regular clergy were also expelled from their monastic houses in December and forced to settle in a single house.[52] The ecclesiastical property was given to the town in March 1573 to compensate it for the expenses it had incurred in the war. Presumably to avoid the resulting obligation to maintain the clergy, the town magistrates now expelled all fifty residents in the beguinage from the town. The women were herded onto two ships and put ashore near Amsterdam. Eight of them later found shelter in the convent of St. Agnes at Amsterdam, where Wouter Jacobszoon was also living. They told him their story. The soldiers who had escorted the beguines on board had done them "much injury and insult with blows, pushing and evil speech," and had raped five of them.[53]

The mood in Hoorn was not improved when the town began to feel the pinch of the grain shortage in the autumn of 1572. Winter set in exceptionally early, so that the Zuiderzee was already frozen in December.[54] "It was another bitterly cold day today" wrote Wouter Jacobszoon in his journal on 22 November. "It froze very hard, it hailed, it snowed and the wind blew very fiercely, and it has lasted from All Souls' Day [2 November] to today."[55] Yet it was not the cold weather or hunger that divided the people of North Holland into two camps, but the changing political and military situation in Holland.

Some of them had hoped—naively as it later proved—that by admitting the Beggars they could put the government under pressure. Others had secretly hoped to ride out the storm without getting involved. The successful offensive of the Spanish army in the autumn of 1572, and above all the massacre of nearly the entire population of Naarden on 1 December,

---

[50] Velius, 190, 192.

[51] Velius, 203, wrongly dates the demolition of the monastery in January 1573, but Wouter Jacobszoon had already mentioned its destruction on 13 December (*DWJ*, 100).

[52] *DWJ*, 98.

[53] Ibid., 204–5; Velius, 204.

[54] Velius, 196.

[55] *DWJ*, 75.

forced them to face the harsh reality.⁵⁶ When the Spaniards began to besiege Haarlem, the people of the Northern Quarter realized they were in a trap. The bloodbath at Naarden had made it clear to them that even good Catholics could not expect mercy. The wave of panic that swept over the Northern Quarter polarized attitudes. Many now resolved to join the émigrés in the relative safety of Amsterdam. Others, many Catholics among them, decided to defend themselves to the utmost. In this tense atmosphere fear of treason could easily take root.

The war hysteria claimed its first victims in Hoorn. On 5 December a large number of "half suspect" citizens were summoned before Sonoy and the burgomasters to renew their oath to the Prince of Orange and the town as an extra precaution.⁵⁷ It was generally felt that this was only a pretext to eliminate a potential fifth column. When the first group of eighteen citizens summoned to the town hall raised objections, they were all promptly thrown out of the town by the soldiers. Although it was freezing and snow lay thick on the ground, they were not even given the opportunity to go to their homes first. The citizens expelled included many who had served the town as burgomasters or justices, as well as Jan Jeroenszoon's relative, the beer merchant Pieter Ariszoon, and Jacob Pieterszoon Pillis, who would be denounced as a traitor by Pieter Nanningszoon.⁵⁸ Sonoy had a list of the names of 150 citizens he wished to expel; only the protests of the militia officers forced him to renounce the plan. The eighteen already expelled, however, were not allowed to return. Jan Jeroenszoon was not among them. Had he already left the town, or would he soon follow them?

A second wave of panic engulfed the country after the capitulation of Haarlem on 13 July 1573, which left the Northern Quarter open to the Spanish army. It was obvious that Alkmaar would be the next town to face a siege. Three days later its magistrates issued a bylaw summoning all fugitive Alkmaar citizens in Hoorn to return to the town, on penalty of loss of their clothing and all the money they had on them.⁵⁹ A week later Sonoy wrote to William of Orange about the defeatist mood that had gripped the people of the Northern Quarter. Even those who were most favorable to "our cause" were so fearful they thought only of how

---

⁵⁶ For the political significance of the massacre at Naarden see Bor, 420.

⁵⁷ Velius, 199, erroneously says 15 December, but adds "St. Nicholas's Eve." Wouter Jacobszoon had already referred to the affair on 7 and 12 December. *DWJ*, 94, 98.

⁵⁸ The names of twelve of those expelled are in Velius, 199; all eighteen are named in the bylaw of 16 January 1574, in which they are told to return to Hoorn. WFA, OA Hoorn, inv. no. 55, fols. 155v–156.

⁵⁹ Wytzema, "Alkmaar," 100. A day later the court of Hoorn issued a bylaw ordering citizens of Alkmaar residing in Hoorn to leave the town. Bylaw of 17 July 1573, WFA, OA Hoorn, inv. no. 55, fol. 150, published in *Brieven en andere bescheiden*, 54.

to make their escape. The ordinary man in the street felt that if the prince did not come to his aid, he, his wife, and children would have to board ships with what few possessions they could carry and abandon the country. Anything was better than watching one town after another fall to the enemy and being executed as willful and obstinate rebels.[60]

Among the many citizens of Hoorn who left their homes in 1572 and 1573 there was a remarkably large number of wealthy merchants and entrepreneurs. A memorandum from the town magistrates, probably drawn up in 1573, reported that "all the wealthy people who had any fortune" had left the town, and that those left behind "were not a fourth part of the wealth of the aforesaid fugitives." Trade and employment had collapsed with their departure. The document listed forty fugitive citizens by name, including both Jan Jeroenszoon and Piet El.[61]

Yet the departure of many wealthy citizens was not a pure loss for the rebels. The property confiscated from the fugitives yielded an essential source of finance for the war effort.[62] As early as 23 August 1572 the Prince of Orange had issued an ordinance that laid the legal basis for this measure.[63] It claimed to seek to put an end to the unbridled license of the troops, who had been seizing the property abandoned by the clergy and other fugitives. The property was to be inventoried, and the owners were given fourteen days to return to reclaim it. If they did not appear by the deadline, the incomes from their property would be used in the service of the common cause. Given the extremely unstable situation in the rebel-held area, it is very unlikely that William of Orange expected many fugitives to heed his call. It is safe to assume that he always intended to confiscate the property of the clergy and others who had gone into exile.

This was not a simple matter. Many had placed their property in the hands of friends and relations. Nor was it always easy in such uncertain times to find tenants for the confiscated lands and buildings. The magistrates to whom the administration of the property was entrusted were in many cases reluctant to cooperate.[64]

---

[60] Sonoy to William of Orange, 24 July 1574, in Bor, 446–47. In the same letter Sonoy informed the prince that he considered success impossible, unless the prince made an alliance with some "great and powerful Potentates." William of Orange gave his famous reply that "we have made such a firm alliance with the supreme Potentate of Potentates that we are wholly assured that we and all those who trust firmly therein shall in the end be relieved by his powerful and mighty hand." Ibid., 448.

[61] Remonstrantie over het onvermogen van de stad lasten te dragen, WFA, OA Hoorn, inv. no. 2530. The document may have been written to support the request for financial help submitted on 6 March 1573. Velius, 203–4.

[62] Tracy, "Émigré and ecclesiastical property."

[63] Bor, 399–400.

[64] Sonoy asked the Prince of Orange to give orders to Cornelis Boom "that the fugitive and enemy property be inventoried, the incomes received by him, and employed for the

A few registers of leases of confiscated property for the year 1576 have survived at Alkmaar.[65] They give an indication of the number of fugitives. In the towns and villages of West Friesland and in Edam and Monnickendam the property of 241 persons was leased, but the total number of fugitives must have been much greater. In Hoorn, for example, the property of forty-five persons was leased, but after the Pacification of Ghent 153 citizens (heads of households) returned, so that there must have been at least that many émigrés.[66] Those who returned included hardly any names of priests. By striking contrast, only 133 persons had been recorded as abandoning their property in the same places in the troubles of the Wonder Year. If these figures are in any degree representative of the numbers of fugitives, they imply that those who fled from the Prince of Orange and the Beggars were at least twice as numerous as those who went into exile to escape from Alba and the Council of Troubles.

Most of the fugitives from the Northern Quarter settled in Amsterdam, where, like exiles in all ages and places, they spent many hours in one another's company planning and dreaming of their return.[67] The city's attitude to these asylum seekers was ambivalent. On the one hand the citizens saw it as their duty to help their persecuted co-religionists and fellow loyalists; on the other their resources were stretched, particularly after the rebels began their economic blockade. In January 1572 the city magistrates ruled that fugitives who wished to settle in Amsterdam must supply a *mud* of wheat, rye, or barley per head at a fixed price.[68] But above all the city had to keep a watchful eye open to ensure that no suspect elements who might seek to betray Amsterdam to the enemy from within slipped into the city among the genuine refugees.

Numerous bylaws testify to this suspicion.[69] All incoming fugitives had to submit a certificate signed by the parish priest and civil authorities of their former home, guaranteeing that they were good Catholics and loyal

---

common use, as those of Enkhuizen do nothing at all for this"; Sonoy to William of Orange, 24 July 1573, in Bor, 447. See also Noordeloos, "Fugitieve personen," 84–85 (Enkhuizen and Medemblik).

[65] Noordeloos, "Fugitieve personen," 85–90; Condities en voorwaarden voor de geannoteerde goederen van geestelijke, fugitieve en andere gelatiteerde personen [Terms and conditions for the inventoried property of ecclesiastical, fugitive, and other émigré persons], RAA, SA Alkmaar, inv. nos. 2902, 2903, 2904.

[66] Velius, appendix (unpaginated), names 180 persons, of whom twenty-seven came from elsewhere.

[67] Velius, 227.

[68] *Vroedschap* resolution, 15 January 1573, SAA, Archief Burgemeesters, inv. no. 5026/2, fol. 231v.

[69] Bylaws of 21 June, 1 July, 8 July, 10 July, 25 August, and 31 December 1572 and 17 April 1573, SAA, Archief Burgemeesters, inv. no. 5020/10.

subjects of the king. Within a few days of their arrival they had to swear an oath before the burgomasters or their delegates, whose office was open for this every morning or afternoon. Inhabitants of Amsterdam were forbidden to rent rooms to strangers who could not show a certificate or who had not taken the oath. Innkeepers were required to report the names of their guests to the city authorities. Mass house-to-house searches, during which the tocsin was rung and the entire population was ordered to remain indoors, ensured that these measures were put into effect. The rules were strictly enforced. Many refugees, among them some Catholic clergy, were implacably sent back home. On 5 January 1573 Wouter Jacobszoon and the prior of the Zijl monastery in Haarlem presented themselves before the burgomasters. The prior, however, was ordered to leave, "however humbly we begged them."[70]

The industrious pen of Wouter Jacobszoon, himself a fugitive, gives us detailed information on the hardship in which his fellow sufferers lived. The first problem was to earn a living. That was far from simple, since their possessions had been seized and there was very little employment to be had in Amsterdam, now that trade and industry had been crippled by the blockade, and the city was bursting with refugees. Sometimes the war itself offered the chance of work: on 1 July 1573 forty ship's carpenters, all Catholic exiles from Edam, went to the Spanish lines before Haarlem to build storming bridges and other siege engines. The presence of so many ships' carpenters says something about the number of Edammers who must have fled to Amsterdam.[71]

The monasteries and other church institutions did what they could, but the poor relief funds could not cope with such a mass of fugitives. In September 1573 Wouter Jacobszoon mentioned a report that two people had been found dead on the street, "who had died of great distress of hunger and want," and added that the hospices were refusing to admit strangers.[72]

The grain shortage and general dearth only exacerbated the problem. Sometimes there was no bread at all to be had; sometimes it was only to be had with great difficulty.[73] For many fugitives there was nothing for it but to swallow their pride and beg on the street.[74] Even priests, monks, and nuns were forced to resort to begging to stay alive.[75] Epidemics regularly broke out in the overcrowded city, where Wouter believed that the

[70] *DWJ*, 43, 123, 129, 134.
[71] Ibid., 270.
[72] Ibid., 299.
[73] Ibid., 131; see also 105.
[74] Ibid., 386.
[75] Ibid., 364.

air had been corrupted by poverty. In 1573 and 1574 plague raged in the city.[76] Many of the fugitives, who had hoped to be away from their homes for only a short time, died in misery and squalor.[77]

> On this Holy Easter Day [1573] two parish priests died in Amsterdam, one from Medemblik and one from that neighborhood. Both had become fugitives as a result of the Revolt, and almost perished through want, because they had been stripped of all their property and they had no incomes. The priest of Medemblik could not find a roof over his head, but at last found shelter in a corner of a warship. There he was found dead in his bunk, without anyone knowing of his illness before. But one could easily see that he had wasted away of hunger and other want.[78]

The misery to which they were reduced was bound to depress the fugitives. Many of them "disappeared into themselves" as Wouter inimitably put it.[79] Wouter claimed that the oppression of the good Catholics, who had fled their homes because they wanted nothing to do with the ungodliness of the Beggars, was beyond the power of any pen to describe. And yet he filled more than four hundred folios of his journal with variations on that theme. The core of the problem was that the fugitives, who had once had a fixed place in society, had sunk to the status of outsiders. In their former homes they had been "people of honor," accustomed to prosperity, citizens of their native towns. Now they had been driven out of their homes as exiles, even as miscreants, and had little hope of seeing their friends and relations in the near future. They lacked the means to survive, and could not fall back on their own families now that they were among strangers. Because of the scarcity of food and the great number of fugitives, they were not welcome anywhere. "Anyone of good understanding can easily comprehend from this, what oppression and fear these good people must have experienced at this time. But nevertheless everyone had to bear patiently whatever burden God placed upon him."[80]

The fugitives sought desperately to find a deeper meaning in their misery. The only solution they could find was to put their trust in the same God who had apparently forsaken them. Wouter wrote that the exiles, "good people" who had fled from the towns because of the "dissoluteness" of the godless, saw no hope of redemption except in the miraculous power of God, who can do what in our eyes is impossible.

---

[76] Ibid., 233, 419; Noordegraaf and Valk, *Gave Gods*, 226, 230.
[77] *DWJ*, 55, 187, 233; Velius, 227.
[78] *DWJ*, 211.
[79] [79]Ibid., 158, 233.
[80] Ibid., 158–59.

We grieved for this, and grew even more oppressed whenever we meditated on outward events; but we took courage and strength whenever we thought, on the other hand, that we were in the care of the Lord, who never slumbers or sleeps and shows His goodness most when it has formerly seemed as if He was most deeply angered.[81]

Jan Jeroenszoon and Griet Frederiksdochter shared the lot of the fugitives in Amsterdam, where they lived on the "Burchwal" on the Oude Zijde, the eastern parish of the city. On 1 August 1574 they presented their newborn daughter Anna for baptism in the Old Church. The godparents were Jan's elder brother Gerbrant Jeroenszoon and his niece Anna, the daughter of his deceased brother Claes. Both had fled from Edam. Jan's sister Garberich had also joined the Catholic exodus from their native town.[82] All the children of Jeroen Claeszoon had remained loyal to the old Church and supported one another in their exile.

Only eleven weeks later, on 18 October, Jan Jeroenszoon again appeared in the Old Church "with a child under his arm." Was it little Anna, or an earlier child who was buried in a cheap grave?[83] In any case, the brief laconic entries in the burial registers of the Old Church show that life in Amsterdam was not easy for Jan and Griet. Their confidence that the war would yet take a turn for the better must have been shaken at this time, for on 3 October the Spanish high command had raised the siege of Leiden. The mutinous army evacuated the countryside of South Holland, plundering as it went, and left the fortifications to be occupied by the Beggars. It seemed as if the war would continue for a long time. On 11 October Wouter Jacobszoon wrote of the mood among the fugitives:

On the eleventh we saw the people, one more oppressed than the other, completely inconsolable, and heard them say openly that no one could now withstand the Beggars, since they were masters on land and sea. The country folk ran like sheep being chased, fleeing their farms, leading their beasts and bringing their hay into town as if it were hay-harvest time.[84]

In these circumstances Jan Jeroenszoon gave up the struggle. In a request to the magistrates of Hoorn he humbly pleaded to be allowed to return

---

[81] Ibid., 190–91.
[82] Baptismal register of the Old Church, SAA, DTB, inv. no. 7714, I, 112. On Jan's brothers and sisters see the will of Claes Janszoon, alias Claes Jeroenszoon, WFA, Not.A Hoorn, inv. no. 2048, fols. 2v–3v (above, note 20). The lease of the property of the fugitive Gerbrant Jeroenszoon and "Jeroen's daughter" in the terms and conditions for inventoried property, Edam account, 8 March 1576, RAA, SA Alkmaar, inv. no. 2904.
[83] Burial register of the Old Church, SAA, DTB, inv. no. 1041, 100.
[84] DWJ, 447.

to the town. On 13 November the burgomasters and *vroedschap* resolved that "Jan Jeroenszoon, formerly a fugitive, shall be allowed to come into the town, provided that he gives a good surety that he will not go to the enemy again, and he shall also make a donation to the town, at the discretion of my lords."[85] The same permission was granted to Piet El and the other fugitives who would apply for permission to return, but Willem Pieterszoon Schijtgelt, Gerbrant Verduyn, Dirck Jezus, and some others, the persons who would be named as leaders of the plot a year later, were refused admission.

Around Christmas 1574 Jan Jeroenszoon and Piet El returned to Hoorn, where they again swore an oath of loyalty to the town and to the Stadholder, the Prince of Orange.[86] Almost immediately there was disagreement over the fine that Jan was to pay the town. On 26 December the *vroedschap* decided that returned émigrés must pay seventy-five Carolus guilders, but in practice the fines varied greatly, evidently according to ability to pay.[87] Jan Jeroenszoon was considered capable of paying a large sum, but he would not stand for this and again submitted a petition to the magistrates and probably also to the Prince of Orange. On 22 January 1575 the *vroedschap* discussed "the petition of Jan Jeroenszoon and the missive from [His] Excellency," and decided that "he shall be given good advice, and shall pay a reasonable sum into the hands of our burgomasters."[88] The question had still not been resolved on 9 April, when the *vroedschap* decided that Jan Jeroenszoon must comply with the terms of an earlier agreement between the burgomasters and one Pieter Claeszoon of Westwoud, concerning the incomes "from the enemy's country" that he enjoyed in Hoorn. Only after he had done so would he be reinstated in the possession of his property.[89] It was not until 24 May—while Hierges was assembling his army at Beverwijk and the Northern Quarter was buzzing with rumors of treason—that the treasurer, in the presence of all the burgomasters, received 250 guilders from the hands of Jan Jeroenszoon as "half of his fine." The penalty that Jan Jeroenszoon paid was thus significantly higher than that imposed on the other returned fugitives. It

---

[85] *Vroedschap* resolution, 13 November 1574, WFA, OA Hoorn, inv. no. 91, fol. 72.

[86] Ibid., 26 December 1574, WFA, OA Hoorn, inv. no. 91, fol. 73: "that an oath of loyalty shall be taken from those who were expelled from this town."

[87] Ibid., 26 December 1574, WFA, OA Hoorn, inv. no. 91, fols. 72v–73: Pieter Ariszoon and Jacob Symonszoon Potgen ten guilders each, Thonis Cuyper fifty guilders, Jan Dirricxzoon seventy-five guilders, Anthonis Cat one hundred guilders. Bor, 629: Piet El paid 166 guilders.

[88] *Vroedschap* resolution, 22 January 1575, WFA, OA Hoorn, inv. no. 91, fol. 84v.

[89] Ibid., 9 April 1575, WFA, OA Hoorn, inv. no. 91, fol. 76.

also represented an enormous sum in absolute terms, five hundred times the daily wage of a master mason.[90]

Jan Jeroenszoon could not enjoy his returned property for long. On 27 September he was placed under house arrest as the chief suspect in the treason plot. On Sunday 16 October, in spite of an appeal by the burgomasters of Hoorn to the privileges of their town, he was taken in custody to Schagen, where the commissioners were waiting for him.

---

[90] Burgomasters' account, 24 May 1575, WFA, OA Hoorn, inv. no. 219. It does not appear from the sources that the second installment was ever paid. For the wages of a master mason in Holland see Noordegraaf, *Hollands welvaren*, 67–74.

CHAPTER TEN

# Law against Terror

THE ARREST OF JAN JEROENSZOON opened a new phase in the affair of the treason plot. Unlike his predecessors, Jan Jeroenszoon was not a defenseless victim, but an intelligent and extremely tenacious man, a trained jurist with a highly developed sense of justice, firmly resolved to defend himself to the utmost.

To the pious Calvinist Sonoy the arrest of the leader of the plot was yet another sign of God's direct intervention in the course of history. The Lord had punished the Netherlanders for their unbelief by inflicting many disasters on them. Only those who submitted to His will could hope to see their efforts crowned with success. The same day, Sonoy proclaimed a day of prayer and fasting to be observed in all the towns and villages of the Northern Quarter on the following Sunday.[1] On that day it would be forbidden to drink in taverns or other public places, to play games and sports, or commit other unseemly acts. Those who violated the ban, as well as the innkeepers who allowed them to do so, were threatened with a heavy fine of three Carolus guilders. The strong arm of the Lord of Hosts, Sonoy wrote, had miraculously brought the rebels into these countries and, as in the time of Joshua, opened the towns to them by rumor alone. But now He was punishing them for their disobedience and delay in converting to His Holy Word, by sending pestilence, treason, and military defeat. There was only one hope of relief from these visitations of divine wrath: turning humbly to the Lord God. A government that claimed to know Christ was bound to enforce His law. Sonoy's explanation for the disasters that had struck the Netherlands was almost the same as that of Brother Wouter Jacobszoon; only the remedy differed.

At the same time as Jan Jeroenszoon, two other inhabitants of Hoorn were transported to Schagen: an old woman named Guerte van Spaarndam, or "Old Guerte," and the chambermaid whose job it was to make the bed for the Count of Boussu, who had been held as a prisoner of war in Hoorn for two years since his capture on the Zuiderzee.[2] The women

---

[1] Sonoy to the magistrates of Medemblik, 16 October 1575, WFA, OA Medemblik, inv. no. 1238. On days of prayer and fasting see Van Deursen, *Mensen*, 269–70, and Van Rooden, "Dissenters."

[2] Bor, 623; NHA, GNK, inv. no. 236, 6 October 1575; WFA, OA Hoorn, inv. no. 91, fol. 78v; inv. no. 2498, 29 November 1575; see also Boon, "Boussu's gevangenschap."

were suspected of involvement in a frustrated attempt to smuggle Boussu out of his captivity, dressed as a peasant. Further investigation was to find out if this attempt was connected with the treason plot. Hoorn had been unwilling to hand over these women and had invoked its privileges in their case also. But the same resolution of the States of the Northern Quarter that ordered the magistrates to surrender Jan Jeroenszoon also commanded them to deliver the two women to the commissioners.[3] Sybout Janszoon, the man from Medemblik who had been denounced by Pieter Nanningszoon, was also imprisoned at Schagen at around this time, though it is not clear precisely when.[4]

A deputation of two burgomasters, four justices, and the town clerk of Hoorn accompanied the prisoners, to be present when Jan Jeroenszoon was confronted with Pieter Nanningszoon and Piet El. This was a larger body than the States had prescribed (they had only referred to the sheriff and two justices), but to avoid further recriminations the commissioners decided not to make difficulties about it.[5]

The sight that awaited the magistrates was not edifying. Pieter Nanningszoon and Piet El were brought from their cells. They unanimously declared that they recognized Jan Jeroenszoon as the man who had shown them letters from Amsterdam about the plot. It was he, they said, who had promised to provide them with the money they needed for the attempted treason. Jan Jeroenszoon was given no opportunity to defend himself. When he tried to speak, the commissioners shouted him down, saying "Be quiet, traitor, traitor, chief of traitors!" They cried so loud that Jan Jeroenszoon could not make himself understood and asked in amazement, "What is this? Mustn't I justify myself against everything you say, when my neck is at stake?" The commissioners' response was to have him forcibly removed.[6]

What the deputation from Hoorn was not shown was even more shocking. The executioner would later depose before the notary Van Triere and explain how, shortly before the confrontation, while he stood concealed outside the window of Pieter Nanningszoon's cell, he had heard the commissioners threatening him:

---

[3] NHA, GNK, inv. no. 236, 6 October 1575.

[4] His imprisonment is first mentioned on 7 July 1576 (Bor, 637). The executioner Jacob Michielszoon deposed, however, that Sybout Janszoon had been tortured twice, which means that he must have been in captivity before 26 November 1575, when the Prince of Orange forbade the commissioners to continue the investigation. On 19 September 1575 the burgomasters paid Claes Dijckgraff fourteen stuivers for conveying to Hoorn a prisoner who had "got over the wall at Medemblik." Was this Sybout Janszoon? Nothing more is known about him. His name does not appear in a list of fugitives from Medemblik. WFA, OA Medemblik, inv. no. 1478.

[5] Bor, 630.

[6] Ibid., 630.

188 • Chapter Ten

See, Jan Jeroenszoon will shortly be brought before you in the presence of the gentlemen from Hoorn; if you do not say "yes" to what we have written and will read out to you, we shall immediately torture you again so long that you will be glad to say it; so look to it, you have to say the right thing for the gentlemen from Hoorn.[7]

Once the confrontation was over the commissioners could therefore report to Sonoy, to their satisfaction, that it had gone off as planned. Both prisoners had persisted in their confessions. Because the commissioners foresaw that Jan Jeroenszoon would continue to deny the charge, they asked for permission to question him under torture. They also asked Sonoy to add several new members to the investigating commission, because it had become clear that they had only now stumbled on the "main branches" of the plot, and there was "much more still hidden." On Monday 24 October, the day after the day of prayer and fasting, Sonoy gave them leave in a private deed to proceed against Jan Jeroenszoon using "torture and sharp examination." He added the sheriff of Nieuwe Niedorp, Pieter van Rhoon, and the military governor of Alkmaar, Guillaume Mostaert, to the commission.[8]

Little is known about Pieter van Rhoon, a Holland nobleman. He was not one of the first converts to Calvinism, had not been an adherent of the Compromise of the Nobility, and as far as is known he played no part in the troubles of 1566–67, and therefore was not banished by the Council of Troubles. Yet he must have chosen the rebel side in 1572, for in that year the Prince of Orange appointed him bailiff of Putten, and later sheriff of Nieuwe Niedorp.[9]

Guillaume Mostaert perfectly matched the profile of the Calvinist rebel typified by the original commissioners.[10] He was born at Antwerp around 1537, and matriculated in 1557 at the University of Leuven and in 1560 at Orléans. It was probably in the latter year that he converted to Calvinism.[11] After completing his studies Mostaert settled in Alkmaar, perhaps

---

[7] Deposition of Jacob Michelszoon, 20 March 1577, NHA, Aanwinsten, inv. no. 1185, fols. 10–11v.

[8] Bor, 630.

[9] Van Nierop, *The Nobility*, 195; see also 137, 159. He was probably the father of Pieter van Rhoon Jr., who matriculated at Leiden in 1583 and at Orléans in 1587. Pieter senior was said to have been married first to Maria, the daughter of Master Willem van Diemen, and second to his cousin Catharyne van Rhoon. Van Kuyk, "Lijst van Nederlanders," 341 (no. 201); *Deuxième livre*, 156.

[10] Bodel Nyenhuis, "Iets over Guillaume Mostaert"; *NNBW*, II, 946.

[11] Mostaert studied in Orléans at the same time as Jan van Stralen (a half-brother of the burgomaster of Antwerp Antoon van Stralen and procurator of the German nation at Orléans), Matheus de Lanoy, Peter van Aelst, and Joris Hoefnagel, all leaders of Calvinism in Antwerp. See Ridderikhoff, *Deuxième livre*, 325. For Van Stralen, de Lanoy, and Van Aelst,

hoping to find a safer refuge in the isolated Northern Quarter than in Antwerp, the center of emerging Calvinism in the Netherlands. His choice of the Northern Quarter must also have been influenced by the fact that his father, a diamond polisher, was one of the largest landowners in the recently reclaimed Zijpe polder, in which many wealthy Antwerpers had invested. In 1565 Guillaume became a member of the board that administered the Zijpe polder.[12]

In the Wonder Year 1566 Mostaert was among the leaders of the recently formed Calvinist community in Alkmaar. With Jan van Foreest and others he submitted a petition calling for the Franciscan monastic church to be turned over to Reformed worship. In 1568 the Council of Troubles sentenced him in his absence to perpetual banishment and confiscation of his property. After his return in 1572 he became a confessing member of the Reformed community in Alkmaar.[13] Sonoy appointed him governor of the town, and a year later he married the daughter of one of its patricians. When Alkmaar was forced to admit Beggar troops after the fall of Haarlem, this provoked disturbances among the citizenry, during which Mostaert was shot in the leg, so that he subsequently walked with a limp. As governor and Sonoy's right-hand man he regularly clashed with the citizens and magistrates of Alkmaar, who in April 1574 resolved that they would no longer take the watchword from him, but from the burgomasters.

Like Sonoy and Sonnenberg, Mostaert belonged to the Calvinist hard core of the rebels, and as a returned exile he had nothing to lose. As a representative of the new political order he, like the other investigating commissioners, had clashed with the townsmen, who were deeply attached to their autonomy. He was no more a native of North Holland than the commissioners or Sonoy himself. The appointment of the new commissioners did not appear to promise any improvement for the prisoners under arrest for treason.

On 1 November the commissioners had all the windows of the castle of Schagen closed and ordered the personnel there to leave.[14] They could now proceed to question the prisoners without being disturbed. Four times, over two successive days, they placed Jan Jeroenszoon on the

---

see Marnef, *Antwerp*, 16, 95, 109–10, 113, 115, 149, 151–52, 256 n. 92; for Hoefnagel see Tanis and Horst, *Images*, 11–25.

[12] In 1561 5,000 *morgen* out of a total of 8,400 behind the dikes were in the hands of inhabitants of Antwerp. Belonje, "Polderregering"; Baart de la Faille, "Beurs," 43.

[13] *Sententiën*, 118; the inventory of his property, including a large humanist library, in NA, Grafelijkheidsrekenkamer, rekeningen, inv. no. 683B, Alkmaar, fols. 18–23, 50–51. Membership register, RAA, Archief van de Nederlands Hervormde Gemeente Alkmaar (archive of the Dutch Reformed congregation at Alkmaar), inv. no. 137, fol. 5.

[14] Bor, 630.

rack. Once again it was the executioner Master Jacob whose deposition reveals what went on. He explained how Jan Jeroenszoon repeatedly but vainly protested his good reputation and how he demanded to be confronted again with Pieter Nanningszoon and Piet El, so that he could defend himself:

> Listen to me, listen to me, and make enquiries everywhere whether I am such a man as you claim, and how I have behaved in my conduct and conversation; and stop torturing me until you have got this information, and bring the witnesses who slander me into my presence![15]

The commissioners' answer was brief: "Be quiet, traitor!" They put the names of several others to him: "We shall not cease to torture you until you have denounced the same, or we shall torture you to death."

Master Jacob's wife Stijn heard from her husband that Jan Jeroenszoon cried out the following on the rack: "I cannot bear this pain any longer, help me to die!" The commissioners had replied: "You must suffer even more, and you shall acknowledge the names that we shall name to you, that you shall charge and accuse, or we shall torture you so much more that you will die in our hands."[16]

It was a tried and trusted procedure, which appeared to assure success. In the same way, sooner or later, the commissioners had already wrung confessions from Jan Jeroenszoon's predecessors, Jan Driemunt and the other vagrants, Nanning Coppenszoon, Pieter Nanningszoon, and Piet El. There can be no doubt that they would eventually have succeeded in breaking Jan Jeroenszoon's resistance, if his friends and relations in Hoorn had not intervened.

Griet Frederiksdochter and some *friends* (a term that included relatives by blood and marriage as well as friends in the modern sense) had followed Jan Jeroenszoon to Schagen in deep disquiet.[17] As soon as they realized the drama that was being played out behind the ominously closed doors and windows of the castle, they immediately returned to Hoorn and complained to the magistrates that Jan Jeroenszoon was being interrogated without justices from Hoorn being present, as the resolution of the States of the Northern Quarter had stipulated. The burgomasters, who were under pressure from the whole citizenry as well as from Jan's wife and relatives, called a meeting of the *vroedschap*, which resolved to fight for their privileges. They at once wrote to Sonoy and sent a delegation of two burgomasters, some justices, and the town clerk to Schagen.

---

[15] Deposition of Jacob Michielszoon, 20 March 1577, NHA, Aanwinsten, inv. no. 1185, fol. 12.

[16] Deposition of Stijn Jansdochter, 27 November 1576, NHA, Aanwinsten, inv. no. 1185, fol. 3v.

[17] Bor, 630.

The magistrates of Hoorn gave the commissioners notice that they would regard as null and void any proceedings that were conducted without their presence, and thus in violation of the States" resolution.[18] For their part the commissioners pointed out that no one had officially informed them of the contents of the resolution. Sonoy had not given them instructions to question Jan Jeroenszoon "sharply" until 24 October—after the resolution had been passed. They also emphatically disclaimed any responsibility for the harm that might befall the country if their investigation was delayed. Nevertheless they stopped their activities and asked Sonoy for further instructions.

Sonoy reacted with predictable irritation. The burgomasters of Hoorn were trying to shield a traitor. What could that mean, except that they were implicated in the treason? The burgomasters, for their part, invoked their privileges and the resolution of the States of the Northern Quarter, but they also declared quite plainly that they had no confidence in the impartiality of the commissioners. Everyone was talking about the way in which the vagabonds had recanted their confessions and denunciations in the face of death at the stake. And they had witnessed the unsavory scenes that accompanied the execution of Nanning Coppenszoon.

Sonoy and the burgomasters disagreed on three points.[19] In the first place they took different views of the correct interpretation of the States' resolution, and therefore of the procedure followed so far and to be followed in future. Secondly, they disagreed on the lawfulness of the use of torture. And thirdly, they were at odds on the importance and scope of Hoorn's privileges.

On the first point the burgomasters complained that their sheriff and justices had not been admitted to the hearing, in spite of the resolution. Sonoy riposted that Sheriff Heukesloot certainly had been present, but the burgomasters insisted that since he had been there in his capacity as one of Sonoy's commissioners he could not represent their town. One of the burgomasters ought to have been allowed to attend in Heukesloot's place. Sonoy however maintained that the sheriff also represented Hoorn, and had only been appointed to the commission because the plot had first come to light in the town, where, he added menacingly, new revelations were still being made.

---

[18] *Vroedschap* resolution of 11/12 November 1575, WFA, OA Hoorn, inv. no. 91, fol. 78v: the *vroedschap* agreed with the declaration of the burgomasters of 7 November. It was a sign of the mood in the town that the commissioners were referred to in this resolution as "the commissioners of blood."

[19] The correspondence between the burgomasters of Hoorn and Sonoy is in Bor, 630–32. Hoorn wrote to Sonoy on 3, 12, and twice on 15 November; he replied on 6 and 14 November.

As for the presence of the two justices Sonoy twisted the text of the States' resolution, claiming that it had only required the two justices to be present at the first confrontation between Jan Jeroenszoon and his accusers, and not at the later hearings. To accommodate the burgomasters he offered to admit two justices from Hoorn, but first they must swear an oath to him to keep what they heard secret, and they must remain at Schagen until the case was closed. This was unacceptable to the burgomasters, for swearing an oath to Sonoy would make the justices answerable to the governor and not to the town.

On the second point, the lawfulness of torture, Sonoy insisted that there were sufficient indications of guilt to put Jan Jeroenszoon to the "sharp examination," because he had been accused by two separate witnesses. Sonoy was invoking the current procedural law, which prescribed that a suspect could be tortured on the accusation of two "good" witnesses.[20] The burgomasters objected that Pieter Nanningszoon had been "alone and singular" when he made his accusation; that his charges were extremely improbable; and that he had not "confirmed his charges by his death." They attached all the more weight to this last point, because several of those condemned in the case had recanted their confessions in the face of death. As for Piet El's accusation, they could be brief. It should be disregarded, "since the same has always been reputed a fool and a jester."[21] Finally they emphasized time and again that Jan Jeroenszoon was a man of quality in both person and property, who ought not to be put to torture.

The third point, which concerned the privileges, was the most important issue of principle. Did Sonoy have the authority to override Hoorn's privileges for the sake of the country's safety? For Sonoy the answer was obvious: in such a case as this, freedoms or privileges did not apply.[22] The burgomasters countered by claiming that not all their privileges and rights had lapsed, only the right that Jan Jeroenszoon enjoyed as a citizen, to be released on bail. The suspect ought to have been held in custody in the town, just as the practice had been, they pointed out acutely, under Alba's tyranny. Then, two commissioners of the Court of Holland had come to Hoorn to question some persons suspected of treason against king and country, and had passed judgment on them with the assistance of the town's sheriff and justices.[23]

This comparison between his own procedure and that of Alba was just too much for Sonoy. Furious, he wrote that as "one who knew an ass by

---

[20] Van Heijnsbergen, *Pijnbank*, 38–39.

[21] Bor, 631.

[22] Ibid., 630.

[23] The reference was to the trial of the followers of Dirck Maertenszoon van Schagen at Hoorn in the presence of two commissioners of the Court. Velius, 172.

its ears," he understood who was behind these shameless words. While the burgomasters were using every means at their disposal to protect the traitors, he, Sonoy, was trying to track down and punish these malefactors. Others would have to judge, at the proper time, who had been right. "And also your fine bringing in of what happened under the Albanese tyranny, which is a stew that I can smell all too well."[24] The burgomasters could now send two justices, from whom he would take an oath. If not, he would resume the investigation without them.

Sonoy's "piquant words" placed the magistrates of Hoorn in a very disagreeable predicament. They were under suspicion of at least passive involvement in the treason plot, not only from Sonoy but also from the magistrates of the other towns of the Northern Quarter. The burgomasters' role in the frustrated attempt to free Boussu, for which Hoorn had already had to surrender two women, contributed not a little to the bad odor in which they stood with their fellow magistrates.[25]

That affair bore some resemblance to the case of Jan Jeroenszoon. One Frans Gijsbertszoon of Amersfoort had spread a rumor that two burghers of Hoorn, Claes Hermanszoon and Jacob Corneliszoon, who had licenses to trade with enemy territory, were implicated in a plot to bring about Boussu's escape to Amersfoort. Boussu was to have arrived there on 1 October, the very day on which Nanning Coppenszoon was executed in public at Hoorn.[26] On these grounds Sonoy had had the two licensed traders arrested in their hometown. Backed by their friends and relations, the two men spared neither money nor effort to prove their innocence. The case grew even more serious when Claes Hermanszoon's wife went to plead with Sonoy for her husband's release. In circumstances that were never cleared up, her wagon was overturned on the return journey and she was murdered in cold blood.

Just as they did in the case of Jan Jeroenszoon, the burgomasters had sprung into the breach for the rights of their fellow citizen. They were convinced that the whole story was a fantasy, and on the application of the licensed traders and their friends they ordered the arrest of Frans Gijsbertszoon. It was a murky business, but in the eyes of the magistrates of the other towns, even on the most charitable interpretation, the burgomasters of Hoorn seemed to care more for the defense of their privileges than for clearing up the alleged plot. In the worst case, they themselves were involved in it.

---

[24] Bor, 630.
[25] Ibid., 632.
[26] Bor, 632 and 634, calls him Jan Gijsbertszoon and Frans Gijsbertszoon. The latter is correct; cf. resolution of the States of the Northern Quarter, 21 November 1585, NHA, GNK, inv. no. 236.

Squeezed into a tight corner by pressure from Sonoy and the other towns of the Northern Quarter on the one hand, and from the friends and relations of Jan Jeroenszoon on the other, who insistently reminded them of their duty to defend the town's privileges, the burgomasters saw only one way out: a direct appeal to the highest authority in the land. At the request of the magistrates the friends of Jan Jeroenszoon drew up in his name a petition to the Stadholder, which several magistrates of Hoorn personally handed to the Prince of Orange with their recommendations. The petition begged the prince to send a committee of members of his council or the Court of Holland to Hoorn to investigate whether or not the prisoners were guilty of the charges against them.

The form of words used in the petition, which asked for the Stadholder's commissioners to take information "both on his accusation and his innocence," was significant.[27] Up to this point the commissioners had been following what was known as "extraordinary" criminal procedure, in which the guilt of the accused was assumed from the beginning, and the purpose of the questioning was merely to elicit a confession and the names of his accomplices. If the possibility of the accused's innocence were now left open, then a criminal trial would have to be held in the "ordinary" or "civil" manner. This meant the accused could defend himself and had the right to inspect the documents and have an advocate.

William of Orange decided to respond positively to the petition, and "stayed the hand" of the commissioners. He ruled that the investigation could only be continued in the presence of two justices of Hoorn, as the States of the Northern Quarter had stipulated, and of two delegates of the Stadholder. The prince named as his own commissioners *jonker* Johan van Woerden van Vliet and the lawyer Sebastiaen Loosen, two of his counselors who happened to be in the Northern Quarter at the time on other business.[28]

But Sonoy was not the man to take such a rebuff lying down. He sent Sonnenberg to the Southern Quarter to persuade the prince to revoke his promise to Hoorn.[29] To achieve this, Sonnenberg put the burgomasters of Hoorn in the worst possible light, accusing them of completely misrepresenting the true facts of the case to the prince. He told him of the bitter quarrel between Hoorn and the other towns in the States of the Northern Quarter. Those towns had given proof of their patriotism, and would never have invoked their privileges in a case in which *crimen laesae patriae*

---

[27] Bor, 633.

[28] Their commission for the matters on which they had to gather information in the Northern Quarter is in *RH*, 3 October 1575; see also resolution of the States of the Northern Quarter, 10 and 20 October 1575, NHA, GNK, inv. no. 236.

[29] The remonstrance presented by Sonnenberg is in Bor, 633–34.

was at stake.³⁰ All that mattered to them was to see the traitors punished. They would rather join forces against Hoorn than have anything to do with traitors and those who protected them. If they themselves had had burgomasters or fellow citizens who were conspiring with traitors, the towns had added, then they would have "seized them by the scruff of the neck" and thrown them out of the town gates "on a hurdle." Moreover, they accused Hoorn of punishing the poor while leaving the rich undisturbed. The burgomasters of Hoorn had played an extremely suspect part in the foiled escape of Boussu. They had ordered the arrest of Frans Gijsbertszoon, the man who had brought the plot to light, but released the two suspected licensed traders; and they continually allowed "sneakers" to return to their town.

Sonnenberg's mission was successful to the extent that the prince did not permit the proceedings to be continued in Hoorn. On 3 January 1576 he issued a new commission to his own counselors Van Woerden van Vliet and Loosen, to the five previously named by Sonoy (Heukesloot, Calff, Sonnenberg, Mostaert, and Rhoon) and to two justices to be designated by Hoorn.³¹ In future the commissioners would derive their authority directly from the Prince of Orange and not from Sonoy.

On 12 January Sonnenberg returned to the Northern Quarter. Hoorn immediately designated two justices to attend the hearing, of whom one, Matheus Matheuszoon de Clerck, had been one of Jan Jeroenszoon's colleagues in the collection of the Tenth Penny tax in 1572.³² There appeared to be no obstacle to the resumption of the investigation.

But now a new difficulty presented itself. The Prince of Orange's commissioners, Van Woerden van Vliet and Loosen, suddenly showed a great haste to leave the Northern Quarter. They said they feared the investigation would take too long, and they wished to return to make their report to the prince on the problems that had originally brought them to North Holland. The real reason for their eagerness to be gone was that they had no wish to get their fingers burned in this affair. By now they knew the strength of popular feeling on the matter, but they had no intention of laying themselves open to suspicion of involvement in the plot.³³ Sonoy

---

³⁰ The use of the term *crimen laesae patriae* (harming the fatherland or betraying the country) is remarkable. The usual term for high treason was *crimen laesae majestatis* (lese majesty). Apparently for Sonoy it was already anachronistic to invoke the person of the king, and he replaced him by the more abstract concept of the *patria*. See also Duke, *Reformation*, 139 and Swart, *William of Orange*, 61.

³¹ Bor, 635. Foreest, who held a commission from Sonoy but appears never to have taken part in the investigation, was no longer named.

³² Velius, 179. Justice De Clerck had also been present earlier at the confrontation between Jan Jeroenszoon and Pieter Nanningszoon and Piet El.

³³ Bor, 635.

now tried to continue the investigation, if necessary without the prince's commissioners, but the justices of Hoorn would not accept this. Once again the investigation was at a standstill.

Sonoy, the States of the Northern Quarter, and the commissioners failed in all their attempts to push the proceedings forward. The towns of the Northern Quarter, except for Hoorn, all pointed to the great dangers and costs the country would incur through any further delay. The old commission must resume its work, with the justices of Hoorn if they were willing, but if need be without them.[34] The commissioners drew up a document in which they stated that the only explanation they could see was that "some private individuals" in Hoorn were protecting the traitors. They were prepared to resume their investigation at once.[35] Sonoy sent his regular secret envoy Jan Michielszoon, the preacher of Grootebroek, to the Prince of Orange to urge him in the governor's name to press ahead with the investigation.

The prince, however, was reluctant. On 17 February, "for certain reasons moving us," he explicitly forbade Sonoy to act in the matter of Jan Jeroenszoon.[36] By now, thanks to the efforts of Jan Jeroenszoon's friends and the magistrates of Hoorn, the prince was better informed about the previous conduct of the commissioners. Even so, he could not halt the proceedings, for he had urged Sonoy at the time to hold a thorough investigation, and he could not openly drop the governor and the other men who ruled the Northern Quarter in his name. Nor was it prudent to side openly with Hoorn in the quarrel between it and the other towns of North Holland. The most sensible course appeared to be to continue the investigation, but without presuming the guilt of the accused from the start, while his men and those of Hoorn would offer a guarantee against arbitrary excesses.

This left the case at an impasse. Jan Jeroenszoon's friends lobbied vigorously for the prisoners to be released or at least given a fair trial, while their opponents urged the dramatic argument that if they were not punished, the Northern Quarter would be brought down by its internal divisions.[37] It was not until 23 March that a solution appeared to be in sight, when the prince as Stadholder issued a commission to a burgomaster of Hoorn, Jan Maertenszoon Visscher, and a burgomaster of Enkhuizen, Jacob Pieterszoon Maelson or Maekschoon, to join the commissioners on his behalf.[38]

---

[34] Resolution of the States of the Northern Quarter, 14 February 1576, in Bor, 635. The registers of resolutions for this period have been lost.

[35] Bor, 635–36.

[36] William of Orange to Sonoy, 17 February 1576, ibid., 636.

[37] Ibid., 626.

[38] Ibid., 635.

For Jan Jeroenszoon's supporters the nomination of a burgomaster of Hoorn was extremely advantageous. But the other camp took a very different view. Baerdesen wrote to Calff that Sonoy, he himself, and many others found it "improper," because Visscher had already shown himself to be too partisan. Yet the knot had to be cut.[39]

The burgomaster of Hoorn accepted his commission, but Maelson excused himself on the grounds of his "sickness and incapacity, as not being sufficiently versed in such weighty matters, to which his nature and temper were wholly abhorrent." But when he was put under pressure, he declared that he would not be a "cat's-paw or do the dirty work of others." He would not serve on a commission that was being called the "Blood Council" on the streets. On 29 May Griet Frederiksdochter waited on him in person to beg him to accept this commission. Maelson made the same excuse of illness to her, but added that even if he had been in good health he would not clean up the mess made by others. His brother, the physician François Maelson, a leading member of the prince's council, had warned him not to get involved in this business.[40]

On 2 June the prince replaced Maelson with Master Jacob van Thoorenburg, a lawyer from Alkmaar.[41] Unfortunately the prince's earlier commission to Visscher and Maelson had given Sonoy the right to appoint a replacement if one of the Stadholder's nominees should refuse. On the previous day Sonoy had therefore already filled Maelson's vacant place by appointing his follower Claes Reyerszoon, an Amsterdam merchant who had been exiled by the Council of Troubles as a leader of the Reformed, and who now lived in Alkmaar. This threw another wrench into the works, this time because there were too many commissioners rather than too few.[42]

The burgomasters of Hoorn pressed Sonoy to drop Claes Reyerszoon in favor of the prince's candidate Thoorenburg, but now yet another obstacle cropped up. Mostaert was appointed receiver of ecclesiastical property in the Northern Quarter, and applied to the prince for leave to resign from the commission; this was granted on 7 July.[43] The attempts to fill this new vacancy failed. The advocate Gerrit Doedeszoon declined the honor, as did the ambitious young Rotterdam advocate Johan van

---

[39] Baerdesen to Calff, 31 March 1576, KHA, inv. no. A 11, XIV C, B 4: "doch is best eens op een eynde."

[40] Deposition of Pieter Proost and Jacob Walravenszoon, made at the request of Griet Frederiksdochter, 29 May 1576, WFA, Not.A Enkhuizen, inv. no. 814, no. 541. For Frans Maelson see Brouwer, "West-Friezen."

[41] Deed passed at the request of Jan Jeroenszoon, prisoner at Schagen, RH, 4 June 1576.

[42] Bor, 636. For Claes Reyerszoon see Ter Gouw, *Geschiedenis van Amsterdam,* VI, 58, 107, 172; Van Nierop, *Beeldenstorm,* 34, 130.

[43] Bor, 637.

Oldenbarnevelt, who already showed that he had too much political insight to get mixed up in this affair.[44] Meanwhile the prisoners were languishing in their cells, until the Pacification of Ghent transformed the whole face of things.

The royal governor of the Netherlands, Requesens, had died in March 1576, with no provision for his successor. The government had been in desperate financial straits for a long time. It had not a penny to pay its armies, especially since September 1575 when the king had declared that he could no longer pay his creditors. On 30 June the Spanish army had captured Zierikzee, but then mutinied and turned aside to plunder the countryside of Flanders and Brabant. On 25 July it took Aalst, a loyal small town within its "own" territory, and sacked it. The Council of State declared the mutineers enemies of the country. The States of Brabant and the States of Flanders raised troops to defend themselves against the Spaniards. The States of Brabant called the States-General together, and the Council of State upheld this after a miniature coup d'état within its membership. The rebel States-General made overtures to the two rebel provinces of Holland and Zeeland to resume the peace negotiations broken off in July 1575. The parties quickly agreed to live in peace and friendship with one another in future and to join forces to drive the Spaniards from the country. This peace treaty, which was proclaimed on 8 November 1576, is known as the Pacification of Ghent.[45]

The first and ninth articles of the Pacification directly concerned the fate of the prisoners. Article I determined that "all offenses, injuries, misdeeds and other damage" caused by the troubles between the inhabitants of the provinces included in the treaty should be forgiven and forgotten. In future they were to be considered not to have occurred. Article IX prescribed the release of all prisoners who were held captive "by reason of the troubles." They need pay no ransom, but only the costs of their imprisonment.[46] Thanks to these two articles the gates of the prison at Schagen were thrown open, and the prisoners were told to return home.

To the bewilderment of the commissioners the prisoners refused to leave. They declared that they had never been guilty of any crime whatsoever. They were not enemies but loyal subjects of the Prince of Orange. The articles of the Pacification simply did not apply to them. Article I of the treaty referred explicitly to misdeeds committed between the inhabitants of the two contracting parties "by reason of the troubles," while

[44] Ibid., 637; Den Tex, *Oldenbarnevelt*, I, 85–87.
[45] Parker, *Dutch Revolt*, 169–78; Woltjer, *Tussen vrijheidsstrijd*, 71–72; Baelde and Van Peteghem, "Pacificatie van Gent."
[46] The Dutch text of the Pacification of Ghent is in Bor, 739; *Opstand en Pacificatie*, 351–59. There are English translations in Kossmann and Mellink, *Texts*, 126–32, and Rowen, *Low Countries*, 58–64.

article IX also referred solely to the release of those imprisoned "by reason of the troubles." The terms thus covered only events that had taken place between those who stood on different sides in "the late civil or internal war," and did not extend to "fellow citizens and members of a town or province who lived under the same government." Without any right or reason and without a prior investigation they had been held in close confinement for a long time and "unnaturally and inhumanly tortured."[47] Their honor, persons, and property had been damaged. If they were now to leave the prison because of a general amnesty, a permanent stain on their honor, good name, and reputation would result. They demanded a trial in which they could prove their innocence. Until such time they were determined to remain in prison.

The attitude of Jan Jeroenszoon and his fellow prisoners was not merely highly principled but was also extraordinarily courageous. They had lain in prison for more than a year (in the case of Pieter Nanningszoon for sixteen months) in appalling conditions, far from their homes and trades, their friends and families. They had been cruelly tortured and must have been physically near the end of their tether. Although they felt they had a strong case, they had no guarantee whatever that a trial would in fact end in their acquittal. Even so, their attitude made sense. If they were to leave their cells by virtue of the terms of the Pacification, the stain of treason would cling to them forever. No one knew how long the peace between the two sides would hold. If the war should break out again, they would certainly be among the first to be dragged from their beds. It did not take much imagination to foresee how that would end.

At the same time the prisoners' attitude put Sonoy, the commissioners, and the whole political community in North Holland in a very awkward position. A peace treaty could only succeed if it was accompanied by an amnesty. In every civil war the opposing sides inflict damage, grief, and injustice on each other. Peace can only be maintained if both sides are prepared to bury the past and start with a clean slate. If the prisoners in Schagen were allowed to have their way, the fear was that many others would claim that they did not fall under the provisions of the Pacification of Ghent either; they too would demand their rights. Such a development could undermine the fragile edifice of peace. Such trials would above all be extremely damaging to the prestige and authority of Sonoy and his colleagues in political and military power. Under extremely difficult circumstances they had tried conscientiously and in good faith to resist the assault of the enemy. Against all expectations their efforts had been

---

[47] Their arguments are stated in the petition of Jan Jeroenszoon and others to the States of Holland, with apostille, 28 December 1576, NA, Hof, inv. no. 4592 (a file of documents on the prisoners in the Northern Quarter, 1576).

crowned with success. Who could blame them if they had not always observed the letter of the law in performing their difficult task? It was a war, after all; and war sometimes justified unpopular measures.

The prisoners did not wait passively, but actively organized their defense from their cells. Although all the petitions and other documents that were written in this case over the ensuing months bore the joint names of Jan Jeroenszoon, Piet El, and Pieter Nanningszoon, it is not hard to identify the sharp-witted and indomitable advocate from Hoorn as the brain behind all these activities. With the help of his friends outside the prison, Jan Jeroenszoon addressed a stream of petitions to the Stadholder, the Court, and States of Holland, in which he analyzed in finely argued detail just why he and his fellow prisoners could not be included under the terms of the Pacification of Ghent. They demanded a fair trial. This could not be entrusted to Sonoy's commissioners, who had so shamefully abused them, but must be put in the hands of members of the States and the Court whom the Prince of Orange should commission.[48]

Their enemies were not idle, however. The deputies of the Northern Quarter persuaded the States of Holland to pass a resolution advising the prince to include the prisoners at Schagen under the terms of the Pacification of Ghent.[49]

Finally Jan Jeroenszoon and his friends prevailed; on 28 December the States of Holland resolved, on their petition, that they must be released from prison after promising to remain at the disposal of the judicial authorities. Armed with this resolution and yet another petition Jan Jeroenszoon's friends from Hoorn immediately traveled to Middelburg in Zeeland, where the prince was residing at the time. The Stadholder was willing to approve the release of the prisoners and designated some of the counselors of the Court of Holland to deal with the matter.

It is at the very least remarkable that Jan Jeroenszoon should have persuaded the authorities in South Holland that he was in the right. William of Orange would have preferred to free the prisoners under the terms of the Pacification and to hold a further inquiry only if they refused to accept this. Thanks to the tireless efforts of Jan Jeroenszoon and his friends, the prince and the States had by now been convinced that the commissioners had acted unlawfully. For once political opportunism had to yield, and the law had to be allowed to take its course.

---

[48] Petitions of Jan Jeroenszoon to the States of Holland with apostille of 28 December 1576; to the Prince of Orange with a request to confirm the apostille of the States, with apostille of the prince, 19 January 1577; to the Court, to send some counselors to the Northern Quarter to act in this matter, NA, Hof, inv. no. 5492 (1576).

[49] *RH*, 26 December 1576. On 22 December the States of the Northern Quarter advised Sonoy to transfer the prisoners to Medemblik castle, evidently to prevent their release. Reso-

Something of the feverish activity among Jan Jeroenszoon's friends and relations in Hoorn is revealed in a letter that one Pieter Classzoon Flors wrote to a former burgomaster, Jan Corneliszoon Spranger, and Jan Jeroenszoon's wife Griet Frederiksdochter. The writer had traveled to Delft to approach Artus van Brederode, a counselor of the Court of Holland, who was about to leave for Schagen with yet another proposal to the prisoners that they should leave their cells under the terms of the Pacification. Pieter Classzoon Flors wrote that he had not been able to do much, because Brederode was ill; but Brederode had promised him that as soon as his health permitted he would go to Alkmaar. Burgomaster Jan Maertenszoon Visscher and the justices must hold themselves in readiness. The writer said that he hoped to be home soon and that everything would turn out for the best; and he encouraged the "friends" to keep their spirits up.[50]

At the end of January 1577, authorized by the prince's decision, his counselors Artus van Brederode and Pelgrom van Loon traveled to Schagen and once again pleaded with the prisoners to leave the prison on the grounds of the Pacification of Ghent. As expected, the prisoners refused and demanded justice. The counselors then required the commissioners to hand over all the relevant documents. On 1 February, at Sonnenberg's house in Alkmaar, they took possession of the commission's neatly inventoried papers: the letters of commission, the reports of the interrogations, the confessions of the executed vagrants, and the sentences. All these documents would be filed in the dossier that the Court compiled about the case.[51] Using these records and the information they had acquired in North Holland, the counselors drew up a report to the Court. Acting on this the Court ordered the prosecutor-general, Master Bernard van Wely, to bring the prisoners to Delft, where the Court was still sitting since the war had only just ended.

On 9 February the prosecutor-general arrived at Schagen, where his coming caused great excitement. The commissioners and the castellan Gerrit Hendrikszoon had left for Hoorn, to seek further instructions from the States of the Northern Quarter. In the absence of their chief the castle guard did not dare hand over the keys of the prison to the prosecutor-general. An express messenger was sent to Hoorn to find the castellan, but when he had still not returned by noon the next day the prosecutor-general decided to take matters into his own hands.

---

lution of the States of the Northern Quarter to Sonoy, 22 December 1576, NHA, GNK, inv. no. 238, fol. 9v.

[50] Pieter Classzoon Flors to Jan Corneliszoon [Spranger], Delft, dated 9 [January 1577], NHA, Aanwinsten, inv. no. 1186.

[51] Bor evidently saw this dossier of the proceedings while he was writing his history, but since that time the documents have been lost without trace.

The ensuing scenes were not without their theatrical side. The prosecutor-general impatiently ordered the castle gates to be broken open by force. The four prisoners, Jan Jeroenszoon, Piet El, Pieter Nanningszoon, and Sybout Janszoon, emerged blinking into the fierce daylight. In the words of Pieter Bor:

> This took place with a great concourse of people, to the great joy of the common man and the whole citizenry of Schagen and the other villages thereabouts, who watched it in their hundreds, so that it was a wonder where all these people came from. Everyone had his say, but in general they cried, "Where are the blood councils now? If they were right, they should dare to come out in the open!"[52]

Now that the prisoners were to be transferred to Delft and their case was to be heard before the Court of Holland, they were in a much more favorable position. But they did not remain in Delft for long; at the end of April 1577 the Court definitively returned to The Hague with the prisoners, who were housed in the Gevangenpoort (Prisoners' Gate).[53] Their relief shines through a letter Jan Jeroenszoon wrote to his friends and relations in Hoorn immediately after his arrival in Delft:

> Honorable and sorely tried friends, after all thanksgiving for all the foregoing things, too long to relate now because of the shortness of time, this is to let you know that we have all arrived (God be praised) in Delft, and because of the treatment in food and drink and the freedom that we have and the freedom that our friends have to act for us, we feel that we are in another world; except that we are now lawfully imprisoned, we shall be able to make our own defense (as we ought to have been from the beginning), wherefore we are so overjoyed that, knowing our innocence in this matter and trusting therein, we have no doubt whatever that everything will turn out for the best, and that soon. In such a way that justice and truth and all those who are zealous for them may triumph, and other wicked persons, being oppressors of the truth for their own scandalous profit, must bow their heads, yea peradventure it may go worse with them.[54]

But Jan Jeroenszoon was not the man to be content with expressions of thanks and relief. In the same letter he requested a certificate from those who had served with him as assessors of the Tenth Penny in 1572. They were to declare how their refusal to collect the hated tax had brought

---

[52] Bor, 638.
[53] Smit, *Den Haag*, 288–89.
[54] Jan Jeroenszoon to Jan Corneliszoon Spranger, 15 February 1577, NHA, Aanwinsten, inv. no. 1186.

them into conflict with the sheriff, and above all they were not to forget to mention the enmity between the two men that had existed since Jan Jeroenszoon had mocked Heukesloot as "a lantern without light." Jan Jeroenszoon also asked for the originals or copies of all letters concerning him that Sonoy or Heukesloot had written to the burgomasters during his imprisonment.

In his cell Jan Jeroenszoon carefully prepared his defense and that of his fellow prisoners. Sybout Janszoon, the man from Medemblik, was no longer among them. He did not have the means to pay for his defense as the others had; he had been crushed by his long captivity and followed his friends' advice to accept release under the terms of the Pacification of Ghent.[55] Jan Jeroenszoon, though, had been working intensively on his own case long before the Pacification. He had first demanded new commissioners, who he hoped would be better disposed to the prisoners, after Van Woerden van Vliet and Loosen had refused to join the commission. When Griet Frederiksdochter failed to persuade Maelson, the burgomaster of Enkhuizen, to accept his commission, Jan Jeroenszoon himself had petitioned the States of Holland to appoint the Alkmaar jurist Thoorenburg in Maelson's place.[56] Finally, he had submitted a series of petitions to the Stadholder, the Court, and the States of Holland after the Pacification.

The most spectacular tactic that Jan Jeroenszoon organized from his prison cell was to have the notary Guillaume van Triere take the depositions so often cited here. The inexplicable way in which the commissioners had exceeded their authority during the questioning of suspects was his strongest trump card. Even so, it would not be easy to prove their misdeeds, for what judge would believe the claims of the prisoners against the unanimous denials of the commissioners?

The statements taken down by the notary, in the presence of witnesses, from the executioner and others directly involved had to convince the counselors that the suspects indeed had a case, and that they had good reason to refuse release under the terms of the Pacification of Ghent. These documents offered the suspects their only chance to be heard by a judge, but the time factor was crucial, since the witnesses might leave

---

[55] Bor, 638; Resolution of the States of the Northern Quarter, 19 January 1577, NHA, GNK, inv. no. 238, fol. 14v: "Sybout Janszoon of Medemblik, prisoner in the house at Schagen was released from imprisonment following the Pacification, provided he lodged a surety and undertook to come before the court or to go to prison again if required, *sub poena confessi et convicti*" [on pain of confession and conviction]. Given the date of this resolution, it is unlikely that Sybout Janszoon was in the party that traveled to Delft on 10 February as Bor says.

[56] *RH*, 4 June 1576, a deed in which the States declare at the request of Jan Jeroenszoon that Jacob Pieterszoon Maekschoon is relieved of his commission, and that the States commit Master Jacob Thoorenburg in his place, 2 June 1576, NA, Hof, inv. no. 1093, fol. 59v.

or die at any time. Moreover it was not at all fanciful to fear that the commissioners would use every trick up their sleeves to put them under pressure, as they had already tried in the case of Master Jacob.[57]

Jan Jeroenszoon had therefore begun to organize the collection of incriminating statements while still in the castle prison at Schagen. On 27 November 1576, not quite three weeks after the Pacification of Ghent had been proclaimed, Stijn Jansdochter, the wife of the executioner, and Anna Barentsdochter, the landlady of his assistant Boeckgen, had appeared before the notary Van Triere in Alkmaar. They did so "at the instance and request" of Claes Nanningszoon of Zwaag, the brother of the prisoner Pieter Nanningszoon. It seems very unlikely that one of these two peasants would have taken the initiative for such a bold step. We may wonder why the legally necessary request for the depositions to be taken did not come from Griet Frederiksdochter or one of Jan Jeroenszoon's friends. Presumably he felt that the depositions, which were taken virtually under Sonoy's nose in Alkmaar, stood a better chance of being kept secret if the obscure peasant from Zwaag took the responsibility for them. On 8 February 1577 Cornelis Janszoon, the former servant of the sheriff of Alkmaar, and his wife Baertgen Hermansdochter made their depositions, once again at the request of Pieter Nanningszoon's brother. Three days later the deponents added an additional statement. The form of words they used, "They deponents declared that since their deposition they had thought of . . ." suggests that they gave their evidence perfectly freely.[58]

It was not until 20 March 1577 that the star witness Master Jacob Michielszoon made his deposition. This time he did so at the request of Claes Nanningszoon and also of "Maritgen Pilgroms of Hoorn and other

---

[57] Deposition of Stijn Jansdochter, NHA, Aanwinsten, inv. no. 1186, fol. 2: "the commissioners had spoken very harshly to him [her husband], wishing to reproach him with what he had told and revealed to the people about the actions, manner and manifold occasions of pain and torture done to the prisoners. The which her husband answered by denying that he had ever revealed such things to anyone; whereupon the same commissioners ordered him to see to it that he never revealed to anyone what had been done by him, for if they ever heard or learned of him [doing so], they would treat him in such a way that another man would have more sense." Deposition of Jacob Michielszoon, ibid., fol. 12: "That the six commissioners being met at Alkmaar in the house of Sonnenberg, he deponent came there to ask for payment of his wages, and Willem Calff and Sonnenberg said to him deponent harshly: why had he divulged and revealed the treatment and torture of the prisoners?; whereto he replied that this was untrue; and among other things he said that the commissioners said that his testimony was of no value or credit, and if he should ever be summoned before His Excellency or any commissioners or before the Court, he should no longer admit that he had ever tortured any one of the prisoners more than three times, and that the rest was only threats."

[58] Ibid., fol. 14.

friends" of Piet Nanningszoon, Jan Jeroenszoon, Piet El, and Sybout Janszoon. Maritgen Pilgromsdochter came from the same milieu of well-to-do Catholic émigrés to which Jan Jeroenszoon belonged.[59] Meanwhile, from the safety of Delft, Jan Jeroenszoon could now appear more openly as an interested party in the depositions. On 18 April Master Jacob made a second deposition, in which he corrected and amplified his earlier statements. This time he gave his testimony at the instance of Claes Nanningszoon and "the wife and friends of Jan Jeroenszoon, Piet El and Sybout Janszoon."

Guillaume van Triere was a rather surprising choice as notary.[60] He remains a rather shadowy figure. He was an uncle of Guillaume Mostaert, and like his nephew he came from the South. He belonged to the same group of early converts to Calvinism as Sonoy and most of the commissioners. In 1566 he and Mostaert had been among those who demanded the use of the Franciscan chapel in Alkmaar for Reformed services. Again in company with Mostaert he had been involved in staging the gesture of the parish priest of Petten, who publicly laid aside his vestments and introduced the Reformation in the village (see above, 46–47). In 1568 Van Triere had also left the country, after which the Council of Troubles sentenced him to perpetual banishment and the confiscation of his property. He returned to Alkmaar in 1572, and became a member of the Reformed Church.[61]

---

[59] She must have been a daughter of Pilgrom Janszoon Houtkoper, justice in 1571, who was named in 1573 as one of the wealthy émigrés. Burgomasters and *vroedschap* resolved that Arian Maertes, wife of Pilgrom, "shall not have a passport to travel to and fro to our town"; resolution of the *vroedschap*, 15 April 1575, WFA, OA Hoorn, inv. no. 91, fol. 76v. Pilgrom Janszoon returned to Hoorn after the Pacification of Ghent, and on 28 December 1576 he swore a new oath. Velius, 377 and appendix. Maritgen Pilgromsdochter made a will on 23 September 1584, and was then a widow; Jan Jeroenszoon is named in her will as a business relation. Will of Marie Pilgromsdochter, WFA, Not.A Hoorn, inv. no. 2049, fol. 79v.

[60] Willem or Guillaume van Triere called himself "the younger" to distinguish himself from his father Guillaume van Triere the elder, who came from Mechelen and later settled as a merchant in Antwerp. The elder Guillaume van Triere had four children: Joseph, Anna, Barbara (who was the mother of Guillaume Mostaert), and Willem Jr. The latter was thus the uncle of Guillaume Mostaert. His wife was probably buried at Alkmaar in 1574; he remarried Jacquemina Michiels. Belonje, "Polderregering," 52; *NNBW*, II, 946. In the Northern Quarter at this time there was also a Jan Baptista van Triere, who commanded a mixed company of Dutch and English troops. Wijn, "Noordhollandse regiment," 247, 259; for him, see also De Meij, *Watergeuzen*, 118. For Willem van Triere Jr., see also Duke, "Arnold Rosenberger."

[61] *Sententiën*, 118; the inventory of his confiscated property is in NA, Grafelijkheidsrekenkamer, rekeningen, inv. no. 683 B, Alkmaar, fols. 51v–52. Membership register, RAA, Archief van de kerkeraad van de Nederlands Hervormde gemeente te Alkmaar, inv. no. 137, fol. 4 ("Gwilliaen de jonge").

Shortly after his return Van Triere must have resumed his practice as a notary. In the register of notaries admitted to practice by the Court of Holland, however, his name does not appear.[62] Probably normal registration was impossible in those turbulent times. The old loyalist Court had fled to Utrecht, and the Prince of Orange did not appoint new counselors until early 1573, when communications between North and South Holland were broken.[63] Strictly speaking, therefore, Van Triere was practicing irregularly and had no right to describe himself in his deeds as a "notary public admitted by the Court of Holland."[64]

On 26 June 1577, while Jan Jeroenszoon and his fellow prisoners were still in the Prisoners' Gate at The Hague, the name of Willem van Triere suddenly appeared on the roll of the Court of Holland, where the prosecutor-general, as "plaintiff on a criminal report," demanded the chopping off of his right hand or some other exemplary punishment and provisional close arrest.[65] This was a Draconian demand, the background to which remains obscure, as indeed does its outcome. The penalty called for appears to suggest that the unfortunate Van Triere was suspected of falsifying documents; the date points to the affair of the treason plot in the Northern Quarter. Only two months earlier the notary had taken the last deposition made by the executioner. Is it too far-fetched to see the long and vengeful arm of Sonoy and his commissioners behind the prosecutor-general's demand?

We cannot tell how far the Court's counselors were influenced in their inquiry by the depositions, which were extremely damning for the commissioners. In any case the counselors immersed themselves in a great many other witness statements, some of them collected in the Northern Quarter by the counselors Brederode and Van Loon, others gathered during a second official journey to the North made by the counselors entrusted with the case.[66] The secretary of the investigating commission, Adriaen Corneliszoon Texel, made a statement with Master Jacob Michielszoon and others, describing how the vagabonds and vagrants held in the cellar of the town hall at Alkmaar had agreed to harmonize their confessions and denunciations. Others gave an account of the frightful scenes they had witnessed when Jan Driemunt was burned at the stake

---

[62] Register of names of notaries admitted by the Court, NA, Hof, inv. no. 5929.

[63] The first meeting of the new Court took place on 12 February 1573, Fruin, *Geschiedenis der staatsinstellingen*, 163.

[64] Van Triere was buried at Alkmaar on 10 January 1593. On 25 June 1595 his widow married the widower Jacob Jacobszoon Kistenmaker. Marriage registers of the Reformed Church, RAA, SA Alkmaar, DTB, 20, fol. 28.

[65] Roll of the prosecutor-general, NA, Hof, inv. no. 5801, 26 June 1577.

[66] Bor, 638. These statements have been lost, but are cited in several places by Bor.

outside Alkmaar.⁶⁷ The minister, the captain of the company of armed peasants, and some inhabitants of Benningbroek and Sijbekarspel made a statement on the execution of Pieter Janszoon, alias Geelcous, of Koudum. The preacher of Wadway and three peasants from that village related the end of Jan Alewijnszoon.⁶⁸ The burgomasters and justices of Hoorn recalled the events at the execution of Nanning Coppenszoon and the confrontation in Schagen between Jan Jeroenszoon and Piet El and Pieter Nanningszoon.⁶⁹

On the grounds of these statements and the dossiers the counselors had taken over from the commissioners in Alkmaar, on 15 July 1577 the Court released Jan Jeroenszoon, Piet El, and Pieter Nanningszoon on their promise to remain at the disposal of the judicial authorities.⁷⁰ After nearly two years in captivity the prisoners returned to their homes, where not surprisingly they were greeted "with great friendship" by the citizens.⁷¹

The release of the prisoners might have been the end of the treason affair, but Jan Jeroenszoon and his fellow suspects had other ideas. Their release had not cleared them of the suspicion of treason, nor had anyone been punished for the wrong done to them. Both these wrongs had to be remedied. Whereas previously they had been the objects of a criminal investigation, they now turned the tables and instituted civil proceedings against their persecutors.

The procedure they chose was that of "purge."⁷² In such a procedure the plaintiff, or "*impetrant* in a case of purge," summonsed the person or persons who had accused him, in his view wrongly, of a given offense. The standard procedure was to summons the judicial officer of his place of residence and the prosecutor-general (as the highest prosecuting instance in the province), as well as all those who had joined in the original case against the plaintiff. Those summonsed were expected to make good their accusations at the hearing or forever keep silent. On the day fixed for the hearing the plaintiff appeared bareheaded before the Court. If the

---

⁶⁷ Ibid., 625.

⁶⁸ Ibid., 636.

⁶⁹ Ibid., 627, 630; burgomasters Jan Maertenszoon Visscher and Tonis Jacobszoon, and justices Cornelis Grote Claes, Jan Pierszoon, Coman Vrerick Gerretszoon, Jacob Corneliszoon, Pieter Hermanszoon, Pieter Willemszoon, and Pauwels Jacobszoon. Coman Vrerick Gerretszoon is named by Jan Jeroenszoon as one of his "blood friends" in his letter from Delft. However the names cannot be reconciled with the list of magistrates in any year; cf. Velius, 378ff. Vrerick Gerritszoon Schilder was a justice for the first time in 1583; Jan Maertenszoon Visscher was burgomaster for the second time in 1572, but Tonis Jacobszoon is nowhere to be found.

⁷⁰ Bor, 639.

⁷¹ Ibid., 638.

⁷² De Waardt, *Toverij*, 103–4; Van der Linden, *Verhandeling*, II, 241–46; Van Apeldoorn, *Uit de practijck*, 190–92.

defendants persisted in their charges, the Court investigated the facts. If it concluded that the accusations were unfounded, it declared the plaintiff pure and innocent, and condemned the defendants to perpetual silence.

As in every trial before the Court the defendants could defend themselves by raising procedural objections (exceptions), that is, by arguing that the case was inadmissible.[73] They could for example challenge the jurisdiction of the judge (declinatory exception), or try to spin out the proceedings by demanding a postponement (dilatory exception). The latter could be particularly useful, because proceedings often dragged on for a very long time and became ruinously expensive for the plaintiff. If a defense by objections was not possible, or the objections raised were dismissed, the defendants had to answer on the principal, or substantive, matter.

Both parties had to appear in person before the Court, but had to be represented by a solicitor. If the defendant did not appear at the hearing, the plaintiff was granted a "default."[74] He or she was then summonsed again, but in such a case the "profit of the default" accrued to the plaintiff. In each successive default the defendant lost the right to raise certain objections. If the defendant had still not appeared after four summonses, the Court gave judgment against the defendant in his absence, in conformity with the plaintiff's demand, and also ordered him to pay the costs of the proceedings. The judge assumed that by failing to appear the defendant had implicitly admitted that his charge was baseless.

The course the proceedings took after the application for a purge had been submitted depended on the attitude of the defendants. If they took up the challenge to produce actual proof of the alleged offense, the case was heard as an ordinary criminal trial. The plaintiff who sought to be purged then became the defendant and ran the risk of being found guilty of the alleged crime and sentenced by the Court. If the defendants offered no proof of their charges, the case could take the forms of proceedings for slander or a claim for compensation, which were dealt with as civil matters.

The roll on which cases pending before the Court were recorded allows a fairly complete reconstruction of the proceedings.[75] Jan Jeroenszoon, Piet El, and Pieter Nanningszoon made an application for purge against the governor of the Northern Quarter, Diederik Sonoy, and the commissioners Heukesloot, Calff, Sonnenberg, Mostaert, and Rhoon; Foreest's name was not mentioned. They also summonsed, *ex officio*, the prosecutor-general and the court officers of their home towns, that is,

---

[73] Wedekind, *Bijdrage*, 80–91.

[74] Ibid., 60–70.

[75] Roll of the prosecutor-general, NA, Hof, inv. no. 5801. The procedure is clearly described by Verhas, *Beginjaren*, 76–99.

Joost Heukesloot as sheriff of Hoorn and the sheriff of Benningbroek, Gerrit Jacobszoon. In Heukesloot's case this made no difference, since he was already included in the summons as a commissioner.

Sheriff Gerrit Jacobszoon has already appeared as the man who had cruelly mistreated the widow Lijsbeth Bouwens in August 1576 (see above, p. 148). Other shady practices had earned him a reputation as a man of "a very evil, ungodly and irregular life, drinking, wenching and the like, and thereby wasting, dissipating and running through his property, so that he is involved in many debts."[76] All the towns of the Northern Quarter except Hoorn later joined the defendants.

The court process server served Sonoy, the commissioners, the sheriffs, and burgomasters of the towns of the Northern Quarter with summonses to appear before the Court of Holland on 25 September 1577. At this hearing the prosecuting counsel for the plaintiffs demanded that his clients be declared "pure, clear and innocent of the pretended treason and of having an understanding with the enemy," and that the defendants be sentenced to keep perpetual silence on the matter. Counsel for the defendants asked for three months "continuation" (deferment) to prepare their defense; the Court granted deferment of six weeks.[77]

Sonoy was not the man to sit and wait to be found guilty. A few days before the hearing he and the States of the Northern Quarter had already made a written application to the Court for the case to be held over for three months "for certain great and pregnant reasons moving us thereto."[78] What were these reasons? Undoubtedly they hoped to turn delay into abandonment; if they could not manage this, they would try to prevent the case from being heard by raising objections. Their chief defense was still the argument that the Pacification of Ghent had drawn a line under all injuries (unlawful acts), committed during the troubles.

The defendants had to allow for the possibility that the judge would dismiss their objections, and that they would have to defend themselves on the principal charge. In that case they would have to provide proof that the plaintiffs were indeed guilty of treason. Now that the tried and tested method of torture was no longer available to them, this might well give them some trouble. What the commissioners needed was a witness, preferably one who had seen the treason plotted with his own eyes. It did not take them long to find a suitable candidate for this role.

---

[76] WFA, Not.A Hoorn, inv. no. 2050, 9 May 1586. See also WFA, GA Sijbekarspel, *regest* no. 22, 21 March 1579.

[77] Roll of the Prosecutor-General, NA, Hof, inv. no. 5802, 25 September 1577 (continued session of 23 September).

[78] Sonoy and the States of the Northern Quarter to the Court, 20 September 1577, NA, Hof, inv. no. 4592 (1577).

Among the many refugees who had returned to their homes after the Pacification of Ghent was one Pieter Pieterszoon, "otherwise named Pietge Pieter Joncx," from Nibbixwoud. He was the man from whom Pieter Nanningszoon had earlier admitted, under duress, receiving letters and money.[79] This Pietge, a thirty-three-year-old, was called on one day in early October 1577 by Willem Willemszoon, the preacher of Nibbixwoud. The minister spoke to him about a homicide that Pietge had once committed, an offense for which he had still not received letters of remission (a form of pardon). In passing, the preacher asked him if he knew anything about the treason plot in the North in the year 1575. Had he not been in the army before the sconces at the time? Pietge admitted that he had served as a cavalryman under Hierges, but insisted he knew nothing about any treason.

The preacher now made a remarkable proposal. If Pietge would declare that he had sent letters and money in connection with the treason to Pieter Nanningszoon, Nanning Coppenszoon, Jan Jeroenszoon, or anyone else, then he would be granted immediate remission for his homicide. He, the preacher, could even arrange for Pietge to receive the letters of remission before he made his declaration. He added that he was not asking this for his own sake, but for the commissioners, who had requested him to get in touch with Pietge. Pietge would be doing the commissioners and the prince a great pleasure if he accepted the proposal.

Pietge Pieterszoon, however, was not willing to play the commissioners' game. He indignantly denied that he had ever written a letter to any of the persons named, either during the troubles or at any other time in his life. "I thought that there must be some foul deed or other lurking behind it, for the preacher to wish to speak to you," remarked a fellow villager whom Pietge told of the proposal.[80]

It is not clear how Jan Jeroenszoon got wind of this secret conversation, but it is a fact that he persuaded Pietge to make a statement on oath before the burgomasters of Hoorn on 25 October. The burgomasters in turn informed the Court of Holland, which ordered the prosecutor-general to investigate this attempt to suborn a witness.

At the same time, Sonoy and the commissioners were exerting all their political influence. They managed to persuade the States of the Northern Quarter, as usual over the opposition of Hoorn, to draft a petition to the States of Holland and Zeeland. Once again the towns of North Holland explained how damaging it would be to the common interest to allow the case to proceed. All the injustice and suffering to which the Pacification

---

[79] Statement of the burgomasters of Hoorn, 25 October 1577, NA, Hof inv. no. 4592 (1577). Cf. above, p. 165.
[80] Ibid.

had just put an end would be raked up once more. Secret information on conspiracies and attacks of the enemy would now be brought out into the open, with the names and surnames of those involved. Would everyone who had held office during the troubles now have to justify himself as soon as a complaint was made? All this was not only in conflict with the Pacification, but also would inevitably stir up hatred and bitterness among the people and lead to new unrest and the ruin of the country. For that reason the States must forbid the Court to admit Jan Jeroenszoon's case.[81]

These arguments were certainly not without weight and must have appealed to the members of the States. Nevertheless, the delegates, presumably on the insistence of the representative of Hoorn, chose first to give Jan Jeroenszoon the opportunity to put forward his view.[82]

Jan Jeroenszoon had not been waiting passively for the States to deign to hear his side. He had presumably heard through the burgomasters of Hoorn that the States of the Northern Quarter were trying to prevent his case coming before the Court. Diligent as always, he had meanwhile submitted his own petition to the States of Holland and Zeeland, in which he once more set out his case in detail and pleaded that justice be permitted to take its course.[83]

In his petition Jan Jeroenszoon once again invoked an argument that counted for a great deal in the procedure of the time, by pointing out that he and his fellow suppliants had always been known as people of good name and reputation. Their arrest had been unlawful, for it had been ordered without a preliminary inquiry and without sufficient circumstantial evidence pointing to their guilt. The commissioners had mostly been "well drunk" and had tortured them "inhumanly and unnaturally." Without sufficient old or new indications of their guilt, these tortures had been repeated many times, which was also illegal. The action of the commissioners, in short, had been unlawful from beginning to end. Moreover, they had flouted the orders of the States and the Court to release the prisoners from their cells at Schagen.

All this was reason enough not to put obstacles in the path of the suppliants in their quest for justice. The higher interest of the province of Holland and the entire country also pleaded for this. God, so Jan Jeroenszoon wrote, had favored the common cause for a long time, but if the guilty went unpunished, it was to be feared that that cause would fall under God's wrathful hand, with disastrous consequences. The actions of the commissioners, which went far beyond the murderous brutality of Alba

---

[81] Bor, 638–39.
[82] Apostille of the States of Holland, 5 November 1577, in Bor, 639.
[83] Petition of Jan Jeroenszoon to the States of Holland and Zeeland, with apostille of 15 November 1577, in Bor, 639–40. Bor erroneously dates the apostille 1576.

and his Spanish council, fell within the political responsibility of the States of Holland. They therefore tarnished the honor and reputation of the States and thus of the common cause. The States must consider which course was more likely to promote the general interest: either to overlook the behavior of the commissioners, and thereby forfeit the divine favor hitherto shown to the common cause and the fatherland, as well as their own good name and reputation; or to let the handful of men who had richly deserved it bear all the blame.

There was only one way to achieve the latter result, the way of justice. This was not denied to anyone in all countries of justice, whether they were ruled by kings or emperors, and it should not be denied to the suppliants either. The Pacification of Ghent was irrelevant to their case, since it referred only to hostilities among the various provinces and not to internal disputes among the inhabitants of Holland, who stood under the protection and government of the Prince of Orange and formed members of one province.

Both parties thus invoked the general interest to plead their case. Sonoy, the commissioners, and the towns of the Northern Quarter, on the one hand, had pointed to the political significance of the Pacification of Ghent. Without an amnesty peace was impossible. Jan Jeroenszoon, on the other hand, insisted that the law must be upheld. If the States lost sight of this higher value, the common cause would forfeit both God's favor and its good name among the people. There was much to be said for both arguments, but they were irreconcilable.

The States therefore sought a compromise. On 15 November they resolved that the suppliants' application to purge themselves could not be admitted, "as there was no place for that in the case and matter in question." Although they did not state the reasons for their resolution, they appear to have accepted the argument of Sonoy, the commissioners, and the towns of the Northern Quarter, that the case had been closed by the Pacification of Ghent. At the same time, however, they allowed Jan Jeroenszoon and the other suppliants to bring proceedings before the Court if they felt their rights had been violated by wrongful imprisonment or torture, adding the phrase "either to have their pretended injury, damage or grievance remedied, or for the same to be punished." This meant that the States permitted the suppliants to bring a civil action for compensation, but at the same time they did not rule out criminal proceedings. The States ordered the prosecutor-general to investigate the suppliants' complaints, "to preserve the rights of the King as Count of Holland."[84]

The States' decision was a victory for Jan Jeroenszoon and his followers. Although the States had dismissed their demand for a purge, they had

---

[84] Bor, 640.

allowed them to go to law against Sonoy and the commissioners. That was precisely what the suppliants wanted. The peculiarity of the States' decision, however, was that it had been overtaken by events.

Nine days earlier, on 6 November, the case had again come before the Court.[85] At the hearing the prosecutor informed the defendants that the sheriff of Hoorn, Master Joost Heukesloot, had died in the meantime. After again applying for a postponement the defendants raised the expected objection: the plaintiffs might claim they had suffered wrong in connection with the troubles, but Article I of the Pacification of Ghent stipulated that this must be disregarded. In legal terms, the defendants invoked the *exceptio litis finitae vel rei transactae*. This recourse claimed that the case had already been decided and could not be reopened.[86]

Counsel for Jan Jeroenszoon repeated the by now familiar argument that the terms of the Pacification of Ghent did not apply to this case, for it referred exclusively to those who had been enemies and not to persons who had been on the same side. He demanded the dismissal of the objection and a judgment in default against the defendants who had not appeared, and asked the judge to order the defendants to reply.

In an interlocutory judgment the Court ruled in favor of the plaintiffs. It granted a default against the defendants, who had failed to appear, and declared the plaintiffs "pure, clear and guiltless of the alleged treason."[87] Jan Jeroenszoon and his friends had achieved their first goal: to be cleared of involvement in the treason. Their second objective, to punish the men who had wronged them, was now within reach.

The considerations that led the Court to arrive at its judgment are not clear. It is not impossible that it granted the purge on purely formal grounds, that is, because of the default of the defendants who had not appeared. The records preserved do not identify these men. But it is also possible that the Court simply considered the plaintiffs' involvement in the alleged treason unproven. Presumably the defendants offered no proof of that involvement at the hearing. Their foiled bid to produce a suborned witness cannot have done their case any good either. The important point is that, unlike the States, the Court did not accept the defendants' objection that the case had been closed by the Pacification of Ghent.

Bor says that Jan Jeroenszoon and his fellow plaintiffs let the case drop at this point.[88] In fact it continued to appear on the rolls of the Court of Holland with some regularity for another year and a half, though it was

---

[85] Roll of the prosecutor-general, NA, Hof, inv. no. 5801, 6 November 1577. The parties' arguments are in Bor, 638.

[86] Van Rhee, *Litigation*, 113.

[87] Bor, 638.

[88] Ibid., 640.

never made clear exactly what was still at issue. The plaintiffs were still referred to in the rolls as "impetrants in case of purge," although that purge had long since been granted in full. We must assume that besides their principal claim, the suppliants had made subsidiary claims, on which the judge still had to pronounce judgment after the purge had been granted. It is highly likely that these were claims for compensation. This may have taken the form of financial compensation or of a humiliating public penance, or a combination of the two.[89] Jan Jeroenszoon and his fellow suppliants may also have demanded a criminal penalty. For this, the prosecutor-general would have had to join them as a party in their case, but the surviving documents do not show that he did so.

In any case the matter dragged on at a snail's pace, like all proceedings before the Court of Holland. After the interlocutory judgment of 6 November 1577, granting purge, a long time passed without further events. It was not until 3 and 23 July 1578 that the defendants had to answer the claim. Counsel for the plaintiffs made his rejoinder on 28 October 1578. He demanded the dismissal of the objection raised by the defendants, that the defendants be ordered to answer on two points, and that costs be awarded against them. The Court decided by "dispositive appointment" that the rest of the case would be dealt with by written memorials. This formula indicates that the parties no longer disputed one another's facts, but differed only on the interpretation of the law,[90] presumably still on the application of the Pacification of Ghent. The documents submitted by the parties were considered on 5 December 1578 and 16 February, 1 March, and 24 March 1579.[91]

After this last hearing the case definitively disappeared from the roll, without a final judgment being passed. This was another respect in which the procedure of the Court differed from modern practice. Whereas a modern judge is obliged to pronounce judgment on all matters that come before his court, many cases that appeared before the Court of Holland in the sixteenth century ended without a final judgment. This might be because the parties settled out of court, or because one of them had no funds to continue the proceedings.

This was probably the reason why Jan Jeroenszoon and his followers did not pursue their case. Bor says their advocates advised them not to go on. Because the commissioners themselves had sought to smother the matter under the Pacification of Ghent, they could consider themselves

---

[89] Monballyu, "Onderscheid," 124.
[90] Verhas, *Beginjaren*, 91; Wedekind, *Bijdrage*, 94.
[91] Roll of the prosecutor-general, NA, Hof, inv. no. 5801, 3 July, 23 July, 28 October and 5 December 1578; 16 February, 16 March and 24 March 1579.

sufficiently vindicated; their name and reputation had been adequately defended. To be sure, they had good grounds to present an act of injury (a claim for compensation), and to have the wrong done to them remedied or punished. But because the States of the Northern Quarter had joined Sonoy and the commissioners, it seemed more sensible to renounce further proceedings.

The decision must also have been influenced by the changed political situation. In the spring of 1579 it had long become clear that the ramshackle edifice of the Pacification had collapsed. The king and his governor in the Netherlands had refused to acknowledge the agreement. In the two and a half years since the Pacification had been proclaimed the conflicts between moderates and radicals, Catholics and Protestants, had only grown more intractable. In January 1579 some of the Walloon provinces concluded an agreement among themselves, the Union of Arras, which would later lead to a reconciliation with the king. Then at about the same time the northern provinces joined in the Union of Utrecht, to continue the struggle. A final attempt to resolve the misunderstandings through negotiations, begun in Cologne in May 1579, was a failure. It was now obvious to everyone that the Netherlands were about to be plunged into war again, a war whose outcome was far from certain. No one could have predicted that this time the war would not be fought on the soil of Holland.

For the numerous Catholics in the rebel provinces the resumption of hostilities was nothing short of disastrous. Once again they feared they would be stigmatized as a potential fifth column. In the circumstances it was understandable that Jan Jeroenszoon, Piet El, and Pieter Nanningszoon chose to end their long-drawn-out proceedings against Sonoy and the commissioners. Their good name and reputation had been secured and justice had triumphed, even if they had not won everything they wanted.

The partial victory of Jan Jeroenszoon and his associates over Sonoy and the commissioners calls for an explanation. A sober, perhaps even cynical, view of history tells us that it was very rare under the ancien régime for mere subjects to get their way against the will of their rulers. The powerlessness of simple folk—fugitive clergy, peasants, vagabonds—to influence the course of events during the Revolt has been the main theme of this book.

A great part of the explanation for Jan Jeroenszoon's success may be found in the political and legal culture of sixteenth-century Netherlands in general and specifically of Holland. The Netherlanders regarded their provinces as states in which the rule of law prevailed. This meant that it was widely believed among the population that all government authority was or ought to be subject to the law, even in time of war. The idea of the Netherlands as a group of states under the rule of law was most explicitly expressed in the oath the ruler swore when he was formally invested with his powers. On that occasion he promised his subjects, assembled in their various "estates," that he would "well and faithfully uphold and cause to be upheld" the privileges and freedoms granted by his predecessors, and "furthermore the customs, traditions, usages and rights that they now generally and in particular have and use."[92] Ultimately all authority was derived from that of the prince or ruler; his investiture oath therefore bound all those who served him in positions of authority.

It is well known that this idea came into conflict with the newer view, based on Roman law, that the prince was above the law (*rex legibus solutus*) and as such even created law at his pleasure (*quod principi placuit legis habet vigorem*). In 1572 it was not the question of religion but the traditional view of the place to be assigned to the law that had legitimated the Revolt. Philip's deputy Alba had flouted the laws of the Netherlands and the privileges granted by past rulers. His subjects therefore considered themselves released from the allegiance they owed him.[93]

In his detailed and eloquent petition to the States of Holland and Zeeland Jan Jeroenszoon had claimed that in all countries of justice, no one ought to be denied access to a judge. The confidence the people of sixteenth-century Holland placed in the law is evident from the frequency with which they brought disputes before the highest judicial bodies in the Netherlands, the Great Council of Mechelen, and (to a lesser degree) the Privy Council. Around the middle of the sixteenth century these two bodies together pronounced an average of 170 judgments a year. About 35 percent of these cases originated in Holland and Zeeland.[94] This total may be compared with the roughly 240 cases a year brought before the comparable body in the much larger Holy Roman Empire, the *Reichskammergericht* at Speyer, which furthermore resulted in a much smaller number of final judgments. Certainly in comparison to the total population in the period the Netherlanders were significantly more apt to take their disputes to the highest courts. The Hollanders and Zeelanders (who shared a single sovereign court) were ahead of the other provinces in this trend.

How to explain this preference for resolving conflicts through judicial channels is another question. It is natural to assume that the numerous merchants of Holland and Zeeland would have been especially keen to

---

[92] Cited in De Monté Ver Loren, *Hoofdlijnen*, 208.
[93] Van Gelderen, *Political Thought*, 126–33.
[94] De Schepper, *Belgium*, 16. Holland accounted for 28 percent of the rulings, Zeeland 7 percent.

resolve their disputes by going to law instead of resorting to force. But this would not account for the large proportion of nobles among those who took their cases to the highest courts.

A consequence of the idea of a state ruled by law was that a subject who felt he had been wronged by an illegal act of the authorities could put his case to a judge. Of course this did not mean that he could cite the sovereign before the court, but he could bring proceedings against the sovereign's officers and demand compensation or even punishment of their unlawful deeds.[95] It was assumed that government officials were personally liable for the transgressions or abuses they committed in the exercise of their offices.

The archives of the Court of Holland and Zeeland, the Great Council of Mechelen, and (after 1582) of the High Court of Holland and Zeeland contain many examples of citizens who had been wronged and who turned to these courts for redress, always assisted by their friends and relations. In most cases it was the sheriff or bailiff of their hometown or village whom they accused of corruption, abuse of power, misapplying arrangements for the resolution of disputes, using force, intimidating witnesses, applying torture without good reason or in the wrong way, fraud, illegal confiscation of possessions, arresting a suspect outside his place of residence, and other such misdeeds.[96]

A case very similar to that of Jan Jeroenszoon had occurred seventy years earlier. A locksmith from Alkmaar, Clays Janszoon, had been arrested on a charge of theft by the bailiff of Nijenburg and sheriff of Alkmaar Jan Gerytszoon, roughly handled and imprisoned in the castle of Nijenburg. Clays denied the theft and maintained that as a citizen of Alkmaar he ought to be tried in that town and released on bail. The sheriff refused this, but put Clays on the rack, without the justices being present. Using "piss, vinegar, mustard and rods" among other things, he wrung a confession from him and only released Clays after his father had paid a "composition" of forty-two Flemish pounds. Clays Janszoon was now given leave to bring a civil suit before the Court of Holland against the bailiff for purge, "relief" (annulment) of the composition payment and compensation. The bailiff appealed against an interlocutory judgment of the Court to the Great Council of Mechelen, which took over the further hearing of the case.[97]

---

[95] Hartog, *Onrechtmatige overheidsdaden*, 2; Rijpperda Wierdsma, *Politie*, 173.

[96] Egmond, "Strafzaken"; Blockmans, "Privaat en openbaar domein."

[97] Dossier on the appeal of Jan Gerytz against Clays Janszoon, ARAB, Grote Raad van Mechelen, Dossiers beroepen [appeals], inv. no. 683. I am grateful to Florike Egmond for this reference.

The first point the locksmith made to the Great Council was that he "came from good, honorable people, citizens and inhabitants of Alkmaar," and that he enjoyed an excellent reputation in the town. As a citizen he ought to have been prosecuted in Alkmaar, and not outside the town's jurisdiction. The use of torture had also been unlawful. Clays demanded "honorable betterment" (*amende honorable*) against the bailiff, as well as "profitable betterment" of a thousand gold crowns. In addition he demanded that the bailiff be beheaded; or subsidiarily (alternatively) fined four thousand Carolus guilders and banned from holding office for the rest of his life. The prosecutor-general joined Clays in this criminal demand. In the end the Great Council pronounced its judgment in 1512, five years after the events. On the criminal claim the bailiff was sentenced to pay a fine of four hundred gold Carolus guilders, payable to the Great Council, and on the civil claim to pay Clays compensation of two hundred pounds Flemish. He was also ordered to bear the costs of the proceedings.

The authorities in Holland might have been warned by this precedent. Sonoy also had to answer to the Court of Holland for other matters besides the case of Jan Jeroenszoon. In 1574 he had ordered the arrest of one Pieter Slacht at Purmerend.[98] Slacht had repeatedly allowed his wife, who "was from one of the most tyrannical families in Amsterdam,"[99] to travel to and from the city without a passport, in spite of explicit warnings from Sonoy. The Court allowed Slacht, in his prison in Purmerend, to bring a criminal action against Sonoy, the castellan of Purmerend Jan van den Bouchorst, and others; the process server served writs of summons on Sonoy and the others, and released Slacht from his imprisonment. Because Sonoy did not appear before it, the Court gave Slacht the benefit of three defaults, and there was nothing to stop it pronouncing sentence against the defendants as demanded.

Sonoy was very unhappy about this affair. As in the case of Jan Jeroenszoon he did everything he could to have the case struck off the court roll. On 7 October and 4 November 1576 he wrote to the Prince of Orange asking him to cause the case to be stopped, or at least held over until he

---

[98] Sonoy to the Prince of Orange, 7 October 1576 and 4 November 1576, KHA, inv. no. A 11, XIV C, inv. nos. 37, 38, 39. See also Presentatieboek, 11 January and 15 March 1575, NA, Hof, inv. no. 3788; Roll of the Prosecutor-General, NA, Hof, inv. no. 5801, 8 October 1575; Presentatieboek, NA, Hof, inv. no. 4245, 21 November 1578. For another case of Pieter Slacht before the Court and the High Court, see Verhas, *Beginjaren*, item no. 139; Furneerrol, NA, Hof, inv. no. 4167, 1 June 1579 and 1 August 1579. Pieter Pieterszoon Slacht was buried in Amsterdam on 2 July 1585 (burial register of the New Church, SAA, DTB, inv. no. 1052, fol. 5).

[99] Sonoy to the Prince of Orange, 7 October 1576, KHA, inv. no. A 11, XIV C, inv. no. 37.

could defend himself in person. It was not as a private individual, but as a servant of the authorities, that he had ordered Slacht's arrest. Now he was being constantly harassed by the Court, but he could not appear in person because he had his hands full defending the country, "which in these times was very necessary to prevent all treason."[100] Sonoy also had a similar remonstrance to the prince drawn up by the States of the Northern Quarter. In this matter too the prince refused to interfere in the course of justice. The case remained on the roll for a long time, but the Court never pronounced a final judgment.

Pieter Slacht had thus invoked his right to defend himself against what he saw as the unlawful conduct of servants of the government, with the same success as Jan Jeroenszoon. But although Holland was a country ruled by law, this did not mean that all its inhabitants enjoyed equal protection. Like any other society in ancien régime Europe, society in the Netherlands was divided into estates. The most characteristic feature of such a social order was that its members were in principle unequal before the law. That inequality applied between the three familiar estates of clergy (at least until 1572), nobles, and citizens, but it also took the form of numerous differences of status within each estate. The rights of the citizens of Hoorn were not the same as those of the citizens of Enkhuizen, which in turn differed from those of the burghers of Medemblik or Alkmaar. Furthermore, in this society the better off, the middle and upper classes, who were known as the "people of quality," enjoyed a much stronger position in law than the lower classes of the population.[101] Not for nothing had Jan Jeroenszoon stressed time and again that he and his fellow prisoners were "people of honor, good name and reputation," and that they had clean criminal records.[102]

Not all the victims of Sonoy's investigating commission could say the same. We have seen how unemployed vagrants who roamed from place to place could be tortured simply because of their way of life, and no one sprang to their defense when they were arrested. If they chose to withdraw themselves from the social control of their fellow townsfolk or villagers, then in the eyes of the authorities they must, as it were, pay for that choice by enjoying less legal protection.

Nor were the peasants highly regarded, even if they were freehold landowners. The insignificant village of Benningbroek had city rights, which allowed Pieter Nanningszoon to boast of being a citizen, but in the eyes of the town magistrates and the townspeople this counted for very little. The arrested peasants protested in vain that they were honorable villagers,

[100] Ibid.
[101] Egmond, "Strafzaken."
[102] Bor, 639.

who had always lived respectably.[103] And the only benefit that Nanning Coppenszoon enjoyed as an inhabitant of Wognum, which fell under the jurisdiction of Hoorn, was that the justices of the town should confirm the judgment pronounced by Sonoy and execute it in Hoorn.

Compared with the vagrants and peasants, the townsfolk—at any rate the wealthier citizens—had considerable rights. They could not be arrested until a preliminary inquiry had been held. If they were fortunate they were tried on a criminal charge in the ordinary way, which meant that they were regarded as a party in their own trial. They had the right to inspect the documents in the case, to have the assistance of an advocate, not to be tortured, and to appeal against the verdict. But the cases of Jan Jeroenszoon and others suggest that even the citizens of towns could never take this protection for granted. The magistrates of Hoorn did not lift a finger when Piet El, of whom they had no high opinion, was arrested by the commissioners away from his home. Nor do we have the impression that the magistrates of Medemblik were very concerned about their citizen Sybout Janszoon. On the contrary, in the States of the Northern Quarter the little town sided with the other towns for Sonoy and the commissioners and against Hoorn and the prisoners. And the magistrates of Hoorn only leaped into the breach for Jan Jeroenszoon after his friends had put them under heavy pressure and had won the support of a great part of the citizenry.

Three things worked in Jan Jeroenszoon's favor. In the first place, he was a notable, a graduate in law, well off, the son of a former burgomaster of Edam. Secondly, he was supported by an extensive network of friends and relations. The case would have turned out very differently if they had not exerted themselves to the utmost for Jan Jeroenszoon.[104] And finally the Stadholder intervened at crucial points. The Prince of Orange was politician enough to prefer the release of the prisoners under the terms of the Pacification of Ghent, but when this proved impossible he thought it more important in the long term to uphold the rule of law (the privileges) than to back Sonoy and his colleagues. Jan Jeroenszoon's Catholicism was of no importance in the whole question, either for the magistrates of Hoorn or for the Court of Holland. Had he not sworn a new oath of loyalty to the king, the Stadholder William of Orange, and the burgomasters after his return from Amsterdam?

[103] See above, p. 158.

[104] Bor, 640, says that some friends of Jan Jeroenszoon who wished to act for him were themselves imprisoned. I have not found any further details of this. On the importance of friends and friendship in early modern society see Kooijmans, *Vriendschap*.

Yet the outcome of the case cannot be explained only in terms of the social and political relationships in the province. The missing variable in the equation was Jan Jeroenszoon himself. Perhaps the most surprising element in the story is the Hoorn advocate's zeal for justice, his ingenuity and indomitable tenacity. His fate after 1579, and that of his fellow prisoners and his adversaries, is the subject of the following chapter.

CHAPTER ELEVEN

## Jan Jeroenszoon Again

ON 22 JULY 1610 the Court of Holland wrote to the sheriff of Hoorn to express its disquiet. Reports had reached it that in Wognum, in Hoorn's jurisdiction, "very large gatherings and conventicles were being held by those who practice the papist superstition."[1] That was a dangerous violation of the law and ought not to be tolerated. The sheriff, Nicolaes Boelenszoon, did not reply until 19 September, when he wrote that the "papistical gatherings" were taking place not only in Wognum but also in all the towns and villages of the Northern Quarter.

> In the Northern Quarter the principal instigator and introducer of this is one Jan Jeroenszoon, a native of Middelie, in the jurisdiction of Edam, but resident in Hoorn. This man, being without conscience, a half-hearted jurisconsult and a pleader in inheritance cases, makes bold to believe that by bringing proceedings from the common purse he can wear out the sheriff of Hoorn and other officers, and make them so weary the papists will be freed from harm in this, just as he has already brought proceedings against me.[2]

There can be no doubt that this "half-hearted jurisconsult" and "pleader" was the same man who had made life difficult for Sonoy and the commissioners thirty-five years earlier.[3] Jan Jeroenszoon was now sixty-five, an old man by the standards of his time, but still as active and combative as ever. He had long outlived his former adversaries and was still ready to go to law if it was necessary to defend his rights and those of his co-religionists.

Once the proceedings disappeared from the roll of the Court of Holland, the case of the treason affair in the Northern Quarter was definitively concluded. The suppliants had been cleared of all blame and suspicion, while their opponents had barely escaped the dishonor of a humiliating sentence. Both parties now had to get on with their lives and

---

[1] "Bouwstoffen," 150.

[2] "Papisticque vergaderingen," 316. I have found no trace of the proceedings referred to.

[3] This was already mentioned by Fruin, Dusseldorpius, *Uittreksel*, cix. Although sheriff Claes Boelenszoon himself referred to the question of 1575 in his letter, Van Lommel believes this was a "clever confusion of persons." "Papisticque vergaderingen," 317.

careers, and in the case of the former prisoners, to cope with the traumatic memories of the events of 1575. Apart from Jan Jeroenszoon virtually nothing is known about the later lives of the victims of Sonoy and his Blood Council. Sybout Janszoon, the man from Medemblik who had accepted release under the terms of the Pacification of Ghent, disappeared into the mists of history, from which he had briefly emerged. Piet El can still be followed for a while in the notarial archives of Hoorn, though they do not shed much light on his actions.[4] Pieter Nanningszoon died from the injuries he had received on the rack not long after his release from the Gevangenpoort in The Hague. Presumably he did not live to hear how his case dropped off the rolls in 1579.[5]

We know more about their adversaries, whose lives in the service of the Prince of Orange, the Revolt, and the fledgling Republic all followed a similar pattern. The Revolt had raised them to positions of influence, but in the eyes of most of the inhabitants of Holland they always remained foreigners, outsiders with no sense of proportion or feeling for local conditions. Their unfamiliarity with the way in which the local population was accustomed to conduct its affairs embroiled them in continual conflicts with the local authorities, which not infrequently had to be resolved by the highest judicial body in the province.

Joost Heukesloot, as we saw, had died some time before the Court sat on 6 November 1577.[6] His last years were embittered by fierce quarrels with the magistrates of Hoorn, who in the treason affair had sided with their imprisoned citizens against their own sheriff. The magistrates complained that as a result of his intensive involvement in the work of the commission, Heukesloot had exercised "a bad and lax supervision of justice" in Hoorn, to the irritation of the inhabitants and "all people."[7] It was true that on 27 October 1575, three days after he had given the commissioners leave to subject Jan Jeroenszoon to torture, Sonoy had instructed the town to appoint four sheriff's assistants, but that had not removed the dissatisfaction in the town.[8] In the early spring of 1576

---

[4] Financial arrangement and reconciliation between Pieter Pieterszoon El and his niece Brecht Franssen, 29 February 1596, WFA, Not.A Hoorn, inv. no. 2039, fol. 167. This Pieter Pieterszoon El may also have been a son of Piet El.

[5] Opmeer, *Martelaarsboek*, 270.

[6] See above, p. 213.

[7] Resolution of burgomasters and *vroedschap*, 13 December 1576, WFA, OA Hoorn, inv. no. 91, fol. 83v.

[8] Sonoy to "those of Hoorn," 27 October 1575, WFA, OA Hoorn, inv. no. 4119. They were to be paid a wage of eighty pounds of forty groats Flemish, payable from the estates of ecclesiastics, fugitives, and persons in hiding, "provided that they do not keep disreputable inns or dishonorable or loose women."

the burgomasters complained to the prince that their sheriff was not only "employed with some other commissioners in the affairs of the common cause of the Northland," but had also fallen seriously ill.[9] He paid his sheriff's servants so badly that they left. When he managed, exceptionally, to keep one or two of them, they had to make a living by "brothel keeping," to the scandal of the town and the Christian religion. The burgomasters, who apparently foresaw that Heukesloot was not long for this world, asked the Stadholder not to appoint a new sheriff after Heukesloot's death until he had taken the advice of the magistrates. According to their privileges the new sheriff, unlike Heukesloot, must be a citizen of three years' standing.

The burgomasters' intervention did nothing to improve matters. On 13 December 1576 the sheriff was not yet dead, but the burgomasters had had enough. They and the *vroedschap* begged the prince to replace Heukesloot, "so that the law and justice may be better upheld there." The choice of the new sheriff must be left to the town.[10] In essence it was the same issue as the dispute between Edam and Bailiff Calff a few years earlier. In this case the difficulties were removed by Heukesloot's death. On 23 August 1577 the *vroedschap* authorized Gijsbrecht Duijck to apply for a commission for the office of sheriff, "since it is understood that he is a citizen."[11]

Thanks to the protection of Sonoy and the prince, a great career lay in store for Heukesloot's friend Willem Maertszoon Calff. His quarrelsome character, however, meant that it too was to be punctuated by bitter disputes. In February and March 1576 Sonoy and Baerdesen supported him in his bid for the vacant post of steward, or collector of revenues, of the Vroonlanden near Alkmaar.[12] In September 1576 Sonoy advised the prince to nominate Calff as sheriff of Amsterdam, although the city was still loyal to the king and would not join the prince's cause until May 1578, in the political revolution known as the Alteration. Following this event Calff was in fact appointed to the post, but here, too, he soon made himself impossible.[13] After three years the burgomasters refused to extend his appointment, because an inquiry into his alleged arbitrary conduct had been opened in the meantime. Calff's attempt to persuade the Prince of Orange to force through his reappointment failed because

---

[9] Request of the burgomasters and *vroedschap* to the Prince of Orange, with apostille, 6 April 1576, WFA, OA Hoorn, inv. no. 2496.

[10] Resolution of the burgomasters and *vroedschap*, 13 December 1576, WFA, OA Hoorn, inv. no. 91, fol. 83v.

[11] Resolution of the *vroedschap*, 23 August 1577, WFA, OA Hoorn, inv. no. 91, fol. 86.

[12] Baerdesen to Calff, 31 March 1576, and Sonoy to the Prince of Orange, 26 February 1576, KHA, inv. nos. A 11, XIV C, B 4 and S 31.

[13] Wagenaar, *Amsterdam*, I, 370, 390. See also Verhas, *Beginjaren*, item no. 600.

the Stadholder was unwilling to violate the city's privileges by intervening on his behalf.

The ghosts from Calff's Edam past now seemed to be rearing their heads in Amsterdam, but even this affair was not the end of his official career. After his debacle in Amsterdam Calff was again promoted, this time to be prosecutor-general at the Court of Holland. New posts led to new quarrels, now with the advocate-general Master Ruysch Nicolai. The Court considered the matter and in November 1585 it ruled against Calff, who was found to have behaved in a manner not in accordance with his instructions.[14] A year later Calff, an embittered fifty-three-year-old, died in The Hague.[15]

Willem van Sonnenberg remained Bailiff of Bergen and Brederode at first, but was later appointed Bailiff of Voshol, Monster, and Wateringen in South Holland.[16] In those capacities he became involved in several lawsuits, which he fought out up to the High Council of Holland and Zeeland.[17] The Roman Catholic priest-historian Franciscus Dusseldorpius complained that instead of punishing Sonnenberg severely, as he deserved, the States of Holland had promoted him to be bailiff of the whole Westland, the rural area south of The Hague. In that function Dusseldorpius mentioned Sonnenberg in 1591, when he was living in "the new low-lying district" of The Hague, "so that the reader may understand what kind of people the States are and what sort of servants they look for."[18]

Guillaume Mostaert, as we saw, had been named receiver of ecclesiastical property in the Northern Quarter in July 1576, and had therefore been obliged to resign from the commission.[19] It was not long before he too came into conflict with the local authorities. In the summer of 1577 the magistrates of Schagen, Niedorper Kogge, Sint Maarten, Valkoog, and Eenigenburg successfully applied to the States of Holland to be relieved of the duty to pass on their revenues from the former church lands to the "born Brabanter" Mostaert.[20] Mostaert's birth in Brabant ruled out a further career in Holland. In 1579 the States of Holland rejected his petition "in view of his faithful service and great misfortune [the wound in his leg], to be held and considered as a born Hollander, and as such to be

---

[14] Ruling in the case of *Ruysch Nicolai v. Calff*, 11 November 1585, NA, Hof, inv. no. 5198.

[15] Elias, *Vroedschap*, I, 135.

[16] NA, Grafelijkheidsrekenkamer, Registers, inv. no. 5109 ("First white register of leases of offices"), 18 August 1583, fol. 42r–v. Verhas, *Beginjaren*, items nos. 688 and 941.

[17] Verhas, *Beginjaren*, items nos. 105, 215, 254, 556, 643, 688, 941, 963, 1003.

[18] Dusseldorpius, *Uittreksel*, 154.

[19] See above, p. 197.

[20] RH, 1 July 1577, 16 July 1577, 21 August 1577.

declared fit and capable of holding all offices in Holland."[21] In the same year, however, he acquired citizenship of Alkmaar, and six years later was admitted as a notary in the town.[22]

During the rule of the Earl of Leicester (1585–88) Mostaert again received a commission as receiver of ecclesiastical property in the Northern Quarter and on the islands of Texel, Wieringen, and Vlieland. But in spite of his citizenship Alkmaar still refused to accept a native of Brabant in a post reserved for a Hollander. The town asked the States to ensure that "the country folk are no longer molested by the same Mostaert," and the States responded by canceling his appointment.[23] Mostaert remained a lifelong loyal member of the Reformed Church, to which he had been an early convert, and in June 1596 he represented the classis of Alkmaar as an elder at the synod in Hoorn. He died at Alkmaar in the same year.[24]

Diederik Sonoy remained in his post as governor of the Northern Quarter after 1576, even though the departure of the Spanish army meant there was really no further need for a separate administration there.[25] In 1583, on the orders of the prince and the States of Holland, Sonoy carried out a fierce persecution of Catholics in North Holland, who were holding clandestine services on a large scale in Wognum, Spanbroek, and other villages. These persecutions did not claim the lives of any victims, but they terrified the peasants so effectively that there were no further secret Catholic services for some time.[26]

As an inflexible Calvinist Sonoy supported Leicester against Maurice of Nassau and Oldenbarnevelt.[27] Appealing to a commission he had received from Leicester, he refused to swear an oath of loyalty to Maurice as the new Stadholder, but ensconced himself in Medemblik with his troops, and even withstood a siege. When his patron Leicester left the Netherlands his position became untenable. In 1587 he fled to England and died four years later at the country house of Dijksterhuis near Pieterburen in Groningen.

Finally, even Jacob Michielszoon, the executioner with a conscience, did well in the Dutch Republic, finding employment as public hangman in the city of Utrecht. In July 1584 he briefly reappeared in the limelight

---

[21] Ibid., 8 May 1579.

[22] *NNBW*, II, 946–47; RAA, Inventaris oud-notarieel archief, 113. His name does not appear in the registers of notaries admitted by the Court of Holland. NA, Hof, inv. no. 5929.

[23] Koopmans, "Vreemdelingen," 42.

[24] *Acta*, I, 211; *NNBW*, II, 946.

[25] In 1578 his title was changed to colonel and his salary was reduced at the same time; Ten Raa and Bas, *Staatsche Leger*, I, 254. Later he was called "commander and superintendent of the Northern Quarter and Waterland." Bor, II, 385.

[26] Bor, II, 365.

[27] Den Tex, *Oldenbarnevelt*, I, 409–18.

when, following the murder of the Prince of Orange in Delft, the authorities were in need of an experienced hand to assist in the interrogation and perform the execution of the assassin Balthasar Gérard.[28]

Jan Jeroenszoon resumed his work as a lawyer in Hoorn. As an avowed Catholic he could never hope to sit on the bench of justices, but they nevertheless called on his services as a member of a college of "neutral men" or "good men" to resolve disputes between inhabitants of the town.[29] In 1582 he represented his native village of Middelie and the neighboring villages of Warder and Kwadijk in a quarrel about taxation with the receiver Hendrick Andrieszoon. On this occasion the receiver aroused Jan Jeroenszoon's indignation by claiming his intervention "smacked of stirring up the same villages to unrest and sedition."[30]

Most of Jan Jeroenszoon's clients were his fellow Catholics. In 1583 he appeared as a witness to the joint will of the remaining twelve nuns of the St. Cecilia convent, who instituted one another and the nuns who no longer lived in the convent as their heirs.[31] Two years later he witnessed a statement made by two sisters of the same convent about an annuity certificate they had concealed in the house of a woman of Hoorn during the "time of troubles," to avoid its confiscation, but which they had never seen again.[32] In another case he acted jointly with Jacob Pieterzsoon Pillis and Jacob Simonszoon Potgen, both wealthy and respected Catholics, who, like Jan, had fled the town during the war.[33]

But it was as a merchant and ship owner, not as a legal adviser, that Jan Jeroenszoon made his fortune. Hoorn shared to the full in the spectacular expansion of Holland's economy in the last two decades of the sixteenth century.[34] After 1578 Amsterdam regained its position as the commercial

---

[28] *RH*, 16 July 1574: "paid sixty pounds to Master Jacob Michielszoon, executioner in Utrecht and Master Willem Willemszoon, executioner [in Delft], for the torture and execution performed by them on the murderer." See also *De moord*, 126.

[29] Various notarial protocols: WFA, Not.A Hoorn, inv. no. 2036, fol. 266 (18 June 1591); inv. no. 2036, fol. 288v (7 August 1591), inv. no. 2040, fol. 272v (19 February 1598), inv. no. 2045, fol. 266v (18 January 1605).

[30] Deed of notary Evert Melissen at the request of the peacemakers of Middelie, 2 September 1582, WFA, Not.A Hoorn, inv. no. 2048, fol. 1. See also a deed for the benefit of the burgomasters of Oosthuizen and the peacemakers of Middelie, 25 February 1584, ibid., fol. 141.

[31] After the death of the last survivor the estate was to go to the poor of Hoorn who lived in their own houses; these were more likely to be Catholics, for the inmates of the poorhouse were required to attend Reformed preaching; will of the sisters of the convent of St. Cecilia, 22 April 1583, WFA, Not.A Hoorn, inv. no. 2048, fol. 69.

[32] Statement of Tryn Nanningsdochter of Hensbroek and Hillegont Dirksdochter, 17 May 1585, WFA, Not.A Hoorn, inv. no. 2048, fol. 3v.

[33] Deposition of Jan Jeroenszoon and Jacob Pieterzsoon Pillis, 13 May 1583, WFA, Not.A Hoorn, inv. no. 2048, fol. 79.

[34] Lesger, *Hoorn*, 27–121.

metropolis at the expense of the North Holland ports on the Zuiderzee, but they were still able to profit handsomely from Amsterdam's need for shipping. Hoorn became an important center of freight shipping, and ships fitted out in the town sailed largely under charter to Amsterdam merchants. Timber from Norway was imported through the port of Hoorn, while salt came from France, Portugal, and later also the Caribbean. To accommodate the growth of its merchant fleet, Hoorn's harbor had to be enlarged several times.

The details of Jan Jeroenszoon's business activities are fragmentary, but enough to show that he invested his money in those sectors of the economy that were vital to the commerce of Hoorn and of Holland as a whole, namely salt and the "Straits," or Mediterranean, trade. In 1586 he appears to have taken a share in a ship that sailed in ballast to the "Island of Salt" (the Cape Verde Islands), to return laden with salt. In 1607 he was named as the owner of three ships that carried cargoes of salt, the *Bonte Raven*, the *Jonge Raven*, and the *Waterdrincker*.[35] In 1601 he chartered a ship called the *Swarte Ruyter*, which sailed to Italy for some Amsterdam merchants. This may have been the same ship, financed by a consortium of Amsterdam merchants, that made the legendary voyage to Italy in 1589 and opened up the Mediterranean Sea to the Dutch.[36] His ship the *Swarte Raven* was lost in about 1601 and replaced by the *Jonghe Swarte Raven*.[37] The *Bonte Raven* was seized as enemy property in a Spanish port and redeemed with the aid of a merchant of Delft. The parties disagreed about the repayment, which led to long-drawn-out litigation in the Court of Holland and the High Council of Holland and Zeeland, not definitively resolved until two rulings of 1618 and 1623. Both courts found against Jan Jeroenszoon and his partners.[38]

In 1592 Jan Jeroenszoon made a deposition about his by now deceased "factor, who had been commissioned and delegated to sail to Spain to sell goods carried there on behalf of the deponent [Jan Jeroenszoon]."[39]

---

[35] Deed of indemnity, 28 May 1586, WFA, Not.A Hoorn, inv. no. 2050, fol. 179. For this ship and a judgment of the justices against Jan Jeroenszoon and others (10 October 1588), see WFA, Not.A Hoorn, inv. no. 2051, fol. 7; power of attorney, SAA, Not.A Hoorn, inv. no. 107, fol. 205 (2 October 1607).

[36] Kernkamp and Klaassen-Meijer, "Rekening."

[37] Protest of Jan Jeroenszoon, 22 December 1601, WFA, Not.A Hoorn, inv. no. 2043, fol. 21v; insinuation of Jan Jeroenszoon, 13 June 1602, ibid., fol. 154; deposition of Jan Jeroenszoon, 26 September 1602, ibid., fol. 242v; power of Jan Jeroenszoon, 27 August 1604, WFA, Not.A Hoorn, inv. no. 2045, fol. 166v.

[38] Ruling of the High Council in the case of *Pieter and Jan de Bye et al. v. Jan Jeroenszoon et al.*, NA, Hoge Raad, inv. no. 887, 23 March 1618; ruling in the same case, NA, Hoge Raad, inv. no. 888, 29 November 1623.

[39] Deposition of Jan Jeroenszoon, 31 October 1592, WFA, Not.A Hoorn, inv. no. 2037, fol. 157.

Apparently Jan also took part on his own account in the Mediterranean trade, which had got under way after harvest failures and famine in Italy in the second half of the 1580s created a market for grain. In July 1601 he was one of the four founders, in Amsterdam, of "the company of Barent Sas," to which he contributed 27,000 guilders out of a total of 96,200. The company traded with Spain, from where it also imported goods that originated in Asia and the New World, including ginger and sugar.[40] One of the "chambers" of the United East India Company was based in Hoorn from 1602, but it is not certain that Jan Jeroenszoon invested in the profitable trade to the East Indies.[41]

His shipping and trading ventures made Jan Jeroenszoon a large fortune. As his wealth grew, so did his social standing, reason enough to adopt the quasi-patrician surname Van der Laen, at least from 1582.[42]

Jan Jeroenszoon van der Laen traveled repeatedly to The Hague to plead his case before the Court of Holland and the High Council, and to promote his private affairs.[43] A lengthy case fought out before the bench of justices of Edam, the Court of Holland, and the High Council concerned the estate of the grandson of his brother Gerbrant, which threatened to be lost to the family. The question was complicated, but it throws an unexpected light on the character of Jan Jeroenszoon.[44]

Jan's brother Gerbrant Jeroenszoon had a daughter, Griet, who married one Jan IJsbrantszoon in Edam.[45] The couple had a son, Maerten Janszoon, who was thus Jan Jeroenszoon's great-nephew. Gerbrant Jeroenszoon, Griet Gerbrantsdochter, and Jan IJsbrantszoon had all died. Not long afterward the orphan Maerten Janszoon also died young, without

[40] Partnership agreement, SAA, Not.A Hoorn, inv. no. 34, fol. 27v (July 1601); power of attorney, inv. no. 36, fol. 157v (24 July 1606).

[41] In 1609 a Roman Catholic clerical opponent called him "a slavish follower of... those who favor the trade to the Indies"; Lonius to Eggius, 23 December 1609, UA, OBC, inv. no. 354, fol. 1v. The term *navigationes Indicas* can also include the West Indies trade.

[42] Declaration of Jan Jeroenszoon van der Laen, WFA, Not.A Hoorn, inv. no. 2048, fol. 1 and numerous other places thereafter. The origin of the name Van der Laen is not clear. There is no provable link with the Haarlem patrician family of that name. In Hoorn there was a parcel of land called the Laen. WFA, OA Hoorn, inventaris Gonnet, item no. 1008. Cornelis Albertszoon Verlaen (or Van der Laen) was one of those who left Hoorn during the troubles. On 15 November 1573 he was expelled from the *vroedschap*. *Vroedschap* resolution, 15 November 1573, WFA, OA Hoorn, inv. no. 91, fol. 67v, and Velius, 393. Was Cornelis Albertszoon Verlaen a relative of Griet Frederiksdochter?

[43] Besides the case before the High Council referred to above, see also the ruling of the High Council in the case of *Jacob Claeszoon et al. v. Jan Jeroenszoon et al.*, NA, Hoge Raad, inv. no. 932, 16 March 1608.

[44] Sentence of the High Council in the case of *Jan Jeroenszoon et al. v. Remmet Frederickszoon et al.*, NA, Hoge Raad, inv. no. 689, 26 November 1596.

[45] This Jan IJsbrantszoon was presumably the same man who copied the depositions before notary Van Triere, now preserved in the NHA, for Jan Jeroenszoon's benefit.

230 • Chapter Eleven

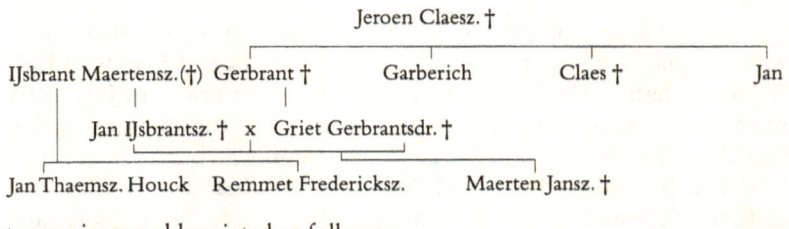

Patronymics are abbreviated as follows:
—z. = —zoon (son);  —dr. = —dochter (daughter)

leaving a will. The question now was: who could claim his inheritance? There were two kinds of law of succession in Holland, each of which gave a different answer to this question. Holland south of the River IJssel observed the originally Zeeland law of *schependom*, which ruled that property ought to revert to the side from which it had come. In the case of the estate of Maerten Janszoon, this would imply that the property Maerten had inherited from his mother Griet Gerbrantsdochter would fall to her relatives, that is, Maerten's great-uncle Jan Jeroenszoon and his great-aunt Garberich Jeroensdochter.

In Holland north of the River IJssel, and therefore in the Northern Quarter, the originally Friesian custom of *aasdomsrecht* had long been recognized. This ruled that in the absence of a descending line, the directly ascending line took precedence over the collateral lines. In the case of Maerten Janszoon this meant that his still living paternal grandfather IJsbrant Maertenszoon would inherit the whole estate, including Maerten's inheritance from his mother. Property that had originally belonged to the estate of old Jeroen Claeszoon would thus fall to an Edam family with which he had had no relationship whatever. After the death of Maerten Janszoon, his grandfather IJsbrant Maertenszoon also died, leaving his heirs Remmet Frederickszoon and Jan Thaemszoon Houck with a claim on Maerten's estate for themselves and their co-heirs.

Because the existence of two laws of succession led to many disputes, the States of Holland had attempted to regulate it in the so-called Political Ordinance of 1 April 1580.[46] In the main this followed the southern *schependomsrecht*, which was regarded as the fairer of the two customs. The regions that had long been used to *aasdomsrecht* successfully opposed this measure, and only a few months later, on 30 July 1580, they obtained from the States of Holland a Moderation, which met their objections.

The suit brought by Jan Jeroenszoon and his sister Garberich (who was represented by her husband Jan Pieterszoon Knechtgens) against Remmet Frederickszoon and Jan Thaemszoon Houck (who acted on behalf of the

---

[46] *Groot Placaet-boeck*, I, 335, art. 19–29; De Groot, *Inleidinge*, II, 190.

other heirs of IJsbrant Maertenszoon), turned on the question of which law of succession applied to the estate of Maerten Janszoon. Jan Jeroenszoon and his brother-in-law Knechtgens invoked the Political Ordinance and claimed half the inheritance; the defendants Remmet Frederickszoon and Jan Thaemszoon Houck relied on the Moderation and demanded the whole. The justices of Edam, the Court of Holland, and finally the High Council all found against Jan Jeroenszoon and his sister and brother-in-law. In all three rulings costs were awarded against the plaintiffs.

It is natural to wonder why such an intelligent and experienced lawyer as Jan Jeroenszoon was persuaded to go to law three times, incurring substantial costs, in a hopeless case. Since the Moderation had been proclaimed, Edam had restored the old rule that the direct ascending line took precedence over the collateral lines. Presumably Jan Jeroenszoon allowed himself to be guided by his sense of justice, rather than by the law in force. He must have considered it unreasonable that property in his family should pass to relations by marriage who had no reasonable claim to it. The same sense of justice that had earlier led him to proceed against Sonoy and the commissioners now played him false.

On another occasion, however, Jan Jeroenszoon's energy and tenacity showed him in a more positive light. One day in late 1601 he was at an inn in Den Oever on the island of Wieringen to discuss business matters concerning the loss of his ship the *Swarte Raven*. In the night a severe storm blew up, which breached the dikes. The village was inundated and the peasants had to evacuate it for higher ground, "with their beasts, wives and children." A few of them tried to stop a great breach in the dike with osier branches, but grew disheartened, "wishing to abandon the work and let the water take its course." But Jan Jeroenszoon, "seeing the great desolation and misery through the water," encouraged them to stand firm and joined in the struggle to hold back the sea. Taking heart from his example, the peasants managed to stop up the hole in the dike, "to the great solace of many sorrowful people."[47]

The suffering and torture that Jan Jeroenszoon had endured as a prisoner of the rebel regime, his years of struggle in the courts against Sonoy and the commissioners, combined with his prominent position as a legally trained counsel and wealthy merchant, inevitably cast him in the almost natural role of leader of the Catholics in Hoorn. Since the resumption of the war their position had not grown any easier. Public services by the Roman rite had been forbidden since 1573, but Catholics were allowed to worship in private houses. In December 1581, however, a new edict declared all meetings of Catholics punishable as criminal offenses. In a

---

[47] Deposition of Jan Jeroenszoon, 26 September 1602, WFA, Not.A Hoorn, inv. no. 2043, fol. 242v.

series of subsequent edicts the States of Holland imposed ever-stricter penalties on clandestine gatherings. Anyone who went on a pilgrimage, had his marriage blessed by a priest, had a child baptized by the Catholic rite, or studied at a Catholic university abroad ran the risk of criminal prosecution. Advocates such as Jan Jeroenszoon who had studied at Leuven were required to revoke the oath they had sworn on graduation and swear a new oath of loyalty.[48]

The States of Holland and the individual towns imposed these restrictions on Catholics' freedom of religion because they still regarded them as potential traitors. A committee of the States of Holland, charged with formulating a new religious policy in 1575, considered that "the public exercise of the papist religion ought to be tolerated, were it not that the papist [priests] and monks, our sworn enemies, had tried to misuse it to stir up trouble."[49] The treason of Count Rennenberg, the Stadholder of the northeastern provinces who reverted to the royalist camp in 1580, the attempts to assassinate William of Orange in 1582 and 1584, and some foiled conspiracies in the 1590s in which the Jesuits were thought to be involved left much ill feeling. The first edict against the Catholics in December 1581 explicitly declared that the States did not wish to burden anyone's conscience or faith, but that gatherings of Catholics could "easily give rise to unrest and disturbances, and bring about guileful plots." Later edicts continued to invoke the safety of the state to justify the prohibition.[50]

In these circumstances it was very difficult to restore Catholic life in the Northern Quarter. The greatest problem was the shortage of priests. Most of the parish clergy had fled, died, left their posts, or turned Protestant and served the new Church. Yet the majority of the population of the Quarter, especially in the countryside, remained faithful to the old Church. In spite of the anti-Catholic legislation they held heavily attended meetings, for example in Grootebroek, Westwoud, Abbekerk, Schoorl, Wognum, and Berkhout.[51] Just as the governments of Charles V and Philip II had failed to enforce the laws against Protestant heresy, so now the States failed to enforce their laws against Catholic worship after the Revolt. As in the time of the Habsburg rulers, this failure was chiefly due to a lack of cooperation from the magistrates in the towns and villages. Only a few of them had joined the new Reformed Church as full members. In the villages above all there were still many Catholics among the magistrates. And just as the Anabaptists had found a safe refuge in the watery landscape decades earlier, so the Catholics turned it to their

[48] Knuttel, *Toestand*, 2–7.
[49] *Oude kerkordeningen*, 117, 129.
[50] Knuttel, *Toestand*, 14.
[51] Ibid., 9.

advantage. In 1610 the sheriff of Grootebroek, where two-thirds of the people were Catholics, complained that it was troublesome and even dangerous to take action because of the narrow roads and abundance of water in the village.[52]

Often the persecuted Catholics successfully resorted to the law for protection. The sheriff of Enkhuizen wanted to persecute a group of Catholics who had held a meeting in the Streek, the rural area between Hoorn and Enkhuizen, at Whitsun 1594. The offenders claimed that they could not be punished because the edicts referred only to the administration of the sacraments. In this case, a simple peasant had merely read out an exposition of a passage from the Gospels. A committee of twelve advocates gave its opinion that this was not forbidden by the letter of the law, but the Court of Holland took the opposite view. Confronted with so many conflicting opinions, the justices of Enkhuizen applied to the States for advice on this thorny question.[53]

In Hoorn, too, the situation was made more difficult by the lack of priests. It was not until the beginning of the seventeenth century that two regular priests settled in the town, a Franciscan and a Jesuit, Gerard Florenszoon, who also served a mission station in Alkmaar. The Jesuit remained in Hoorn only a year, but founded the station Het Klooster (The Monastery), assisted by a wealthy inhabitant, Anna Keijzer. In 1623 a second Jesuit came to Hoorn and set up a second station in the household chapel of another wealthy resident, Thecla Nicolai, called De Kapel (later Het Lam, The Lamb).[54] In 1628 the two stations in Hoorn attracted about five thousand worshipers, more than a third of the total population of the town.[55]

The success of the Catholic mission in Hoorn was to a great extent the work of the Jesuits. This inevitably drew the Catholic faithful into the conflict between the Society of Jesus and the Vicar-Apostolic Sasbout Vosmeer.[56] Now that the old ecclesiastical institutions in the rebellious provinces of the Netherlands had been dismantled, and the region had been declared a mission territory, the Vicar had taken the place of the Archbishop of Utrecht. Vosmeer insisted that all pastoral activities should come under his control, but his claims to authority were not admitted by the Jesuits, who answered directly to their general in Rome and the Pope. The secular and regular clergy glared at one another across what we would now call a cultural divide. The seculars accused the Jesuits of imposing less stringent requirements in order to attract believers, and re-

---

[52] "Bouwstoffen," 151–53: "and that by the length and narrowness of the streets, and the convenience of the water, which comes behind the houses."
[53] *RH*, 26 December 1594; Knuttel, *Toestand*, 11.
[54] Van Hoeck, *Schets*, 47–49.
[55] "Summiere Staat," 187. In 1622 Hoorn had 14,139 inhabitants.
[56] Knuttel, *Toestand*, 46–58; Rogier, *Geschiedenis*, 527–34.

proached them with being legacy-hunters, too keen on money, and therefore of preferring to work with the wealthy.

Relations between the two branches of the clergy reached a nadir in December 1609, when Vosmeer, on his own authority, issued a decree that forbade members of religious orders to administer the sacraments and to preach in places where he had already appointed a pastor. The Catholic faithful who supported a priest not nominated by the vicar, or who allowed him to administer the sacraments, were threatened with excommunication. These crass measures were followed by negotiations with the Provincial of the Jesuits, Florentius de Montmorency, which produced a compromise in the form of the *Articuli* of March 1610. In future the Jesuits would only be allowed to administer the *pastoralia* (baptism, marriage, extreme unction), in places where there was already a pastor, after obtaining his permission; and they would have to give him the names of those to whom they had administered these sacraments. Only where there was no pastor were the Jesuits free to perform these rites, provided that they had been admitted by the Vicar-Apostolic.

Vosmeer's measures were resented in Hoorn, where the Catholic faithful were deeply attached to Gerard Florenszoon's successor, Father Bartholomeus Pleunius S.J. Some leading Catholics, among them Jan Jeroenszoon, wrote a petition pleading the case of the Jesuit fathers. Through Jan Jeroenszoon's mediation this petition was presented to the Bishop of Antwerp, who forwarded it to the Holy See.[57]

The Vicar-Apostolic and other high secular clergy were not amused with Jan Jeroenszoon's intervention. Vosmeer described his letters as "pestilential" and their author as "Societati adictissimus" (highly devoted to the Society of Jesus).[58] The priest of Hoorn, Nicolaus Lonius (Claes Loen), wrote in December to the Haarlem canon Adelbertus Eggius that Jan Jeroenszoon was his chief adversary. This "Joannes Hieronimi" was a slavish follower (*assecla*) of Arboreus (Adriaen Boom S.J., the head of the mission) and of "those who favor the sea trade with the Indies."[59] The last charge was all the more likely to stick, because it was the United East India Company's lobbying that had long delayed the conclusion of a truce with Spain, to which Catholics looked in hopes of gaining freedom to practice their religion. Franciscus Dusseldorpius called Jan Jeroenszoon "one who had formerly suffered much for the faith, but who has strayed from the true path and is eager to make money."[60]

---

[57] "Jezuïeten-staties," 104; the text of the petition on 120–22.
[58] Broedersen, *Tractatus*, 200, 204.
[59] Lonius to Eggius, 23 December 1609, UA, OBC, inv. no. 354, fol. 1v. See also Eggius to Nomius, NHA, Archieven van het Bisdom Haarlem van de Oud-katholieke Kerk, inv. no. 356, 20 March 1610 and 4 May 1610.
[60] Dusseldorpius, *Uittreksel*, 423.

The Catholics in Hoorn brushed aside this criticism from the *missio Hollandica*. Jan Jeroenszoon was their great hero. As the sheriff Claes Boelenszoon had already remarked to his discredit, he had taken the lead in organizing their clandestine meetings.[61] In April 1609 the sheriff broke up a gathering of a hundred Catholics. He began to take the names of those present, but desisted when Jan Jeroenszoon, who was among the surprised congregation, offered to stand surety for them. When the criminal case came to court Jan Jeroenszoon repudiated his surety and thus left the sheriff empty-handed. On another occasion, 15 August 1609, the day of the Assumption of Mary, the sheriff broke into a fortified house outside the town on the Noordermeer, where two hundred Catholics had gathered. He summonsed the owner to appear before the town justices and demanded a fine of two hundred pounds, as the edicts required. The bench of justices acquitted the man.[62]

If the secular clergy needed proof of their charge that the Jesuits were too eager to get their hands on the money of wealthy Catholics, they could point to Hoorn, which was called the *Statio Aurea* (Golden Station). In 1615 three "pious matrons," Anna Keijzer and two daughters of Jan Jeroenszoon, Anna and Hester, gave the colossal sum of forty thousand guilders to endow a new house, which the Society wished to found at Lier near Antwerp.[63] Jan Jeroenszoon was still alive in that year, and it must therefore have been his wealth that his daughters so generously donated to the Society. It is an eloquent proof of both his success in business and his zeal for the cause of the persecuted Catholics in the Netherlands, especially for the Jesuits' contribution.

Jan Jeroenszoon led a quiet and presumably happy family life in Hoorn. He and his wife Griet Frederiksdochter had three daughters, Anna, Hester, and Agatha. Anna was baptized on 1 August 1574, while her parents were living in exile in Amsterdam. Hester was born in Hoorn in 1579 or 1580.[64] Anna and Hester remained unmarried and, as "spiritual virgins," or *klopjes*, may have assisted the clergy who administered the sacraments in secret to the Catholic faithful in Hoorn.

Agatha married Master Reijnier Jacobszoon Cool, a Catholic jurist from Gouda, in 1615.[65] The couple settled in Hoorn and took the surname

---

[61] "Papisticque vergaderingen," 317.

[62] For this raid see Jacobus Odulphi to Eggius, NHA, Bisdom Haarlem van de Oud-katholieke Kerk, inv. no. 354, 23 September 1609.

[63] Van Hoeck, *Schets*, 200; Andriessen, *Jezuïeten*, 286–87.

[64] Baptismal register of the Old Church, SAA, DTB, inv. no. 7714, I, 112. This Anna may have been the child who was buried in the Old Church on 18 October 1574: burial register of the Old Church, SAA, DTB, inv. no. 1041, 100; in that case a later child was again christened Anna. Hester stated in her will of 3 May 1657 that she was seventy-seven years old. Looijesteijn, "Geslacht," 33.

[65] WFA, DTB Hoorn, inv. no. 70, fol. 32, 3 July 1605. For the descendants of Jan Jeroenszoon see Looijesteijn, "Geslacht," 33.

Cools. Reijnier Cools was admitted as an advocate before the Court of Holland in 1604, and like his father-in-law he combined the legal profession with business.[66] Reijnier and Agatha had six sons, of whom the second, Willem, entered the Jesuit order, and the fifth, Lodewijk, became priest of Ilpendam. Their eldest son Hieronymus (Jeroen) married and continued the family line.

We learn something of Jan Jeroenszoon's family life in his last years from a letter written by his eldest grandson Hieronymus from the Catholic town of 's-Hertogenbosch, where he was sent to school. The letter is undated but must have been written in the early 1620s, when the youngest Cools was old enough to go away to school. Hieronymus invited his "beloved grandfather Jan Jeroensen at Hoorn" to spend the summer with him. That would be better than visiting Hieronymus's brothers, who were at school in Mechelen. Hieronymus sent his greetings to "Peethester" (Aunt Hester), but did not mention his grandmother Griet Frederiksdochter, who apparently was already dead.

> Honored grandfather, greetings to you and Aunt Hester. I let you know that I am still well and healthy, God be praised, as I hope that you are. Beloved grandfather, I have understood that you wish to go and lodge in Mechelen this summer. I ask you rather to come here, and then I shall come and visit you and keep you company instead of my brothers. You would be too alone at Mechelen; and also my father and mother will be more easily able to visit you here, and write how things are going in Hoorn. You will easily be able to see how my studies are going, and how I am behaving. Herewith I end, dear grandfather, and commend you to Almighty God, and shall pray for you that you may come over. 's-Hertogenbosch, your grandson obedient in all things, Hieronymus Cools.[67]

Jan Jeroenszoon died in 1623, at the age of seventy-eight, though the precise date is not known. On 13 March 1623 several graves in the choir of the Great Church at Hoorn were registered in the name of the children and grandchildren of Jan Jeroenszoon van der Laen.[68] It may be assumed that he had died shortly before.[69]

---

[66] *Album advocatorum*, 98. In 1617 Reijnier Cools was collaborating with a business partner of Jan Jeroenszoon, Willem Gerritszoon Floor, as a charterer of the *Swarte Raven*. *Bronnen Oostzeehandel*, VI, 82, no. 2144. For his activities as a witness and arbitrator see WFA, Not.A Hoorn, inv. no. 2090 (9 July 1640, 30 April 1643).

[67] Hieronymus Cools to Jan Jeroenszoon (undated), NHA, Aanwinsten, inv. no. 1186.

[68] Conveyance of graves in the church choir, WFA, OA Hoorn, DTB, inv. no. 20 C, nos. 21, 67, 141.

[69] On 12 July 1623 the leading Catholics in Hoorn drew up a document in support of the Jesuits, in which they criticized the secular clergy. The signatories included one Joannes

Jan Jeroenszoon's descendants held his memory in high honor. A transcript of the depositions made before notary Van Triere, produced at Jan Jeroenszoon's request in 1581, was cherished as a relic and handed down in the family from generation to generation. To it were added the letters of Pieter Classzoon Flors and Jan Jeroenszoon from Delft, and the letter from Hieronymus Cools to his grandfather cited above.[70] Jan Jeroenszoon's letter in his own hand from Delft came into the possession of his daughters in the year of his death. One of them, presumably Hester, wrote on the reverse:

> Our father sent this letter from the prison at Delft to the burgomaster Master Jan Corneliszoon Spranger, the father of Jacob Janszoon Spranger, the grandfather of Pieter Trijn and Jan Jacobszoon Spranger. I took it into my keeping, from other letters, from Pieter Trijn in the year 1623.

This modest family archive passed from Jan's daughter Hester to her great-nephew Cornelis Cools, a grandson of her sister Agatha. Cornelis in his turn left the documents to his niece Maria Cornelia Clomp, the daughter of his sister Geertruijt.[71] Maria Clomp, Jan Jeroenszoon's great-great-granddaughter, added a note in her own hand to the collection, which reveals that the descendants of Jan Jeroenszoon owned more than his papers. In good Catholic fashion they also preserved a relic that kept the memory of their ancestor's sufferings green, namely the object the executioner Master Jacob Michielszoon had used to torture Jan Jeroenszoon, and which Hendrik Goltzius had depicted at the request of Pieter Bor (plate 6).

> This is the instrument with which my great-great-grandfather Jan Jeroenszoon, advocate at Hoorn, was tortured, although guiltless, at the castle of Schagen in the year 1575, in the time of the tyrant Sonoy, as P. C. Hooft describes in his *Netherlands Histories* and Velius in his *Chronicle of Hoorn*. And the same has often been told me by the whole

---

van der Laen. "Jezuïeten-staties," 107–8. Had Jan Jeroenszoon's children already bought the grave before their father died, or had Jan Jeroenszoon signed the document before it was closed and dated? Probably the signatory was not Jan Jeroenszoon but his great-nephew Master Jan Claeszoon van der Laen, who also bought a grave on 2 December 1623. WFA, OA Hoorn, DTB, inv. no. 20 C, no. 102. In any case Jan Jeroenszoon was dead by 17 August 1624, when his daughters Anna and Hester, with Johanna Keijzer, had a deed drawn up about the repayment of two loans that Jan Jeroenszoon had given (Deed of Anna and Hester Jansdochter, WFA, Not.A Hoorn, inv. no. 2072, fols. 65v–6).

[70] All these documents are in NHA, Aanwinsten, inv. nos. 1185 and 1186.

[71] Maria Clomp was also active in the semiclandestine Catholic movement. When Father Borsaeus was accused of Jansenism and forbidden to celebrate mass in "The Lamb," his followers met in her house. Van Hoeck, *Schets*, 48.

family of my mama of blessed memory in praise of my great-great-grandfather, assuring me that two rats were placed in this wooden box and it was bound to his bare body, breast and belly, and then coals of fire were put in the copper plate that was nailed on top of the box, so that in their desperation the rats gnawed his body and bit it full of holes. I received this instrument from the estate of my uncle Cornelis Cools, who inherited it from the estate of Hester Jans, my great-grandmother, a daughter of the aforenamed Jan Jeroenszoon, and it has always been highly prized and carefully preserved by our whole family. [signed] Maria C. Clomp.

Maria Clomp died in 1747, unmarried, the last descendant of Jan Jeroenszoon and Griet Frederiksdochter. Her family papers surfaced a century later in the library of the Dutch Historical Society in Utrecht. This venerable institution later presented them to the library of the University of Utrecht, which in 1931 transferred them to the Rijksarchief in North Holland, now the Noord-Hollands Archief, where they can still be consulted.

The humble copper-bound box had lost all recognizable significance without the documentation provided by Maria Clomp. After her death it must have been thrown out as rubbish with the other valueless items in her estate.

CHAPTER TWELVE

# Historiography and Propaganda

THE NORTH HOLLAND treason affair has not gone unnoticed in historiography. Historians have followed two clearly distinct interpretations, a nationalist or pro-States line and a Catholic one. The authors of the first school on the one hand considered themselves the heirs of the Revolt. They took a positive view of its results, but were embarrassed by the excesses committed by the rebels. Catholic historians, on the other hand, regarded themselves and their co-religionists as victims of the Revolt. For them the suspicion of treason was beside the point; the charge had been a mere pretext for the rebels to oppress the Catholics. Sonoy's Blood Council persecuted its victims simply because of their faith. Catholic authors were able to weave this interpretation seamlessly into a long literary tradition of hagiographies and martyrologies.

The first printed account of Hierges's campaign and the abortive plot was not a work of history in the strict sense but a Beggar song, which was sung publicly and lustily throughout the towns and villages of North Holland in the very same summer of 1575.[1] The song has been preserved in the oldest surviving printed collection of Beggar songs, of 1581, in which it bears the title "Of the murderous fire-raising assault in North Holland, plotted by the Monk, in the year 1575." It has been included in every subsequent edition. For about half a century, until the appearance of the works of Velius and Bor in 1617 and 1621, it was the only printed source from which the inhabitants of the young Republic could learn anything of the treason of the Northern Quarter. Their demand for such information is apparent from the frequency with which the Beggar songbook went into new editions, at least nine before 1620.[2]

The song relates in detail how the enemy force of six thousand infantry and seven hundred horsemen tried to force its way into North Holland, and how the danger came not only from outside the sconces but also from inside, because the peasants were ready to admit the enemy:

> They came on the prowl for treason
> That they had stoked from within.
> About five hundred peasants
> Were ready to their hand.

[1] *Geuzenliedboek*, I, 246–49 (no. 107).
[2] Ibid., II, 351–54.

The leader of the plot, "a peasant born in Wognum," in whom readers of this book will recognize Coppen Corneliszoon, had recruited four hundred followers, "not Men alone but Women too," who were to assist the enemy by setting fire to the villages of the Northland. The traitors were to make themselves known to the invaders by wearing "red silk ribbons" on their clothing. The song goes on to praise Sonoy's decisive action to protect the country and the support he found among the majority of the peasants, who remained loyal. When the "papists" appeared before the sconces and gave the agreed signal by burning down the mill at Schoorl, nothing happened.

> The traitors within stand still:
> The plot was already broken,
> They did not get their way:
> Their Captain was a prisoner
> With almost all his followers.

All's well that ends well? First, of course, the fate of the conspirators had to be told. They did not escape their rightful punishment. After the "Devil had broken his neck" the body of the "Captain" was quartered. The would-be fire raisers met a fiery death at the stake. Only the brain behind the conspiracy, one "Colonel" Pieter van Hoef, escaped, but "he will pay for it in the end, who in all his days ever saw such a scoundrel?" The song ends with a prayer to God to protect the country against the enemy, to cause His Church to grow in the Northern Quarter and to bestow wisdom on the Prince of Orange.

This Beggar song has all the qualities of a thriller. The poet, and therefore the singer, unmistakably identifies with the "right" side, which is threatened by a malevolent enemy. Every fellow-townsman or villager, every neighbor, friend, or even family member may be unmasked as a traitor. But thanks to the vigilance of Sonoy and the other followers of the Prince of Orange, the episode had a happy ending. The song closes by placing the affair in a wider moral and political context. The poet praises the heroism of the rebels, exults in the discomfiture of their enemies, and ascribes the fortunate outcome to God's "strong power." It is a true epos with heroes and villains, in which the former barely escape from imminent danger, and the latter come to a bad end. We recognize its picture of the Revolt.

Yet keeping up the morale of the rebel party was not the only object of this song. The Beggar songs served two purposes: propaganda and information. In the absence of daily newspapers they were the quickest and perhaps also the most reliable form of news dissemination. The Beggar songs, "our national trench poetry," were written immediately after the events they described, printed on broadsheets, and sold by itinerant ballad singers for a few coppers.³ The printed format and the ease with which they could be memorized, thanks to their rhymes, meter, and melodies, to some extent counterbalanced the unreliable and unmanageable stream of rumors, the only other source of information available to the people. Through them the latest news could reach even the illiterate majority, who listened as they were sung. The texts drew the moral of events by placing them in their patriotic and biblical contexts. The poetry of the Beggar songs combined the provision of news, the formation of public opinion, history, and propaganda in an inseparable whole.

The song betrays its journalistic function in the fourth line of the first verse by giving the precise date of the invasion ("the twenty-seventh of this May"). The poet mentions a variety of facts, including the size of the invasion force ("about six thousand infantry and seven hundred horsemen"), the identity of the chief plotter ("a peasant born in Wognum"), the red silk ribbons of the conspirators and the name of the elusive "Colonel" Pieter van Hoef. The last two details point to a third function of the song: has anyone recently seen a suspect-looking type wearing red ribbons on his clothing? And who knows where Pieter van Hoef is hiding at the moment?

The precision of the factual information given allows the song to be dated fairly accurately. According to Bor, Coppen Corneliszoon died on 2 June, according to Opmeer, on 14 June.⁴ The song must have been written soon after this event. The text makes no mention of Pieter Nanningszoon of Benningbroek, who was not arrested until mid-July, or of Coppen's son Nanning, who confessed on 6 September and was put to death on 1 October. We may therefore assume that it was written in June 1575, or at the very latest in early July.

As usual in this genre, the author is anonymous. Even so, there are a few clues to his identity. A man who wrote "Let your Church grow here in this Northern Quarter" must have been a supporter and most probably a confessing member of the young Reformed Church. Probably, like most of the Beggar poets, he belonged to one of the chambers of rhetoric. The opening of the last verse, "Prince God, preserve us," is in their typical style. The poet may very well have come from Alkmaar or its neighborhood, where all the facts mentioned in his song occurred.

There is a further sign that our poet was particularly well informed. "The Devil first broke his neck," he wrote of the death of Coppen Corneliszoon on the rack. These were literally the words of the commissioners: "See, he will not tell us the truth, the Devil breaks the rogue's neck."⁵

---

³ For the Beggar songs as a genre see the introduction, ibid., I, vii–xxv.
⁴ For Coppen's death see above, p. 150.
⁵ Deposition of Jacob Michielszoon, NHA, Aanwinsten, inv. no. 1185, fol. 9v; Bor, 626.

Well informed, perhaps a native of Alkmaar or its surroundings, a rhetorician and a Calvinist; we might leave the identification there, if there were not a candidate who fits the profile so well that his name at least must be mentioned. During the siege of Alkmaar an anonymous poet wrote his personal device at the end of a song on that event: "The common cause lives through one."[6] In that motto he betrayed his identity as Dirck Adriaenszoon Valcoogh, whose books, the *Dutch Schoolmasters' Rule* of 1591 and the *Chronicle of Leeuwenhorn of 1595*, both bore the same motto on the title page. It is not impossible that Valcoogh may have been the author of several songs about the events in the Northern Quarter of Holland. The song that described Hierges's invasion and the treason plot may have been one of them.[7]

As was to be expected, Catholic authors gave a totally different picture of the same events. The first work from the Catholic side to refer to the question was a martyrology, a Counter-Reformation polemic. In 1587, the year of the execution of the Catholic pretender to the English throne Mary Stuart, Adriaen Huberti in Antwerp published a curious little book that placed this dramatic event in its international and historical context. Antwerp, 1587: place and date were no coincidence. Two years earlier Alexander Farnese, Prince of Parma, had reconquered the city from the rebels, after which it became a bulwark of the Catholic Reformation.[8] From Antwerp, long a world center of the art of printing, heretics and rebels were attacked in words and images, as well as by arms. The title of the book was *Theatrum crudelitatum haereticorum nostri temporis* ("Theater of the cruelties of the heretics of our time").[9]

The formula of the book is simple: "every picture tells a story." Each odd-numbered page bears an engraving, which depicts how the wicked Protestants have humiliated, tortured, and murdered innocent Catholics. The facing even-numbered page explains the incident illustrated in more detail. Beneath each print are several lines of verse, which supply the necessary classical context in learned humanistic Latin. The outrages of Calvin and his followers, we read, surpass the worst barbarities of classical Antiquity.

In a foreword addressed to "Catholic princes and peoples," the author sets out his intention. He wishes to write a Catholic martyrology that will expose the corruption of Calvin and Beza, Henry VIII and Elizabeth, the Huguenots, and William of Orange. He hopes that Protestant readers will

[6] *Geuzenliedboek*, I, 147–49 (no. 64).
[7] De Planque, *Valcoogh's regel*; Daan, "D. A. Valcoogh." During the hedge preaching outside Alkmaar in 1566 one Cornelis Valcoog, a tailor, collected alms. Was he a relative of Dirck Adriaenszoon? Van Gelder, *Alkmaarse opstellen*, 58.
[8] Thijs, *Van geuzenstad*.
[9] Verstegan, *Theatrum*. See also Buitendijk, *Calvinisme*, 158–61.

be moved to convert when they see what cruelties their co-religionists have perpetrated. Although the sixteenth-century martyrology forms a Protestant genre, the Roman Catholic martyrs certainly cannot be mentioned in the same breath as the Protestants.

> The [Protestant] martyrs were never condemned for their religion, but for their lack of faith; not for their guilt, but for their crimes; not for sound doctrine, but for error; not for steadfastness, but for obstinacy; and that on the grounds of laws that were proclaimed long ago by the emperors. It is a popular adage that it is not the punishment that makes a martyr, but the cause for which he stands.[10]

The author saw the recent event in England in a European perspective. He realized that the struggle between Catholics and Protestants was being fought on several fronts at once. The frontiers between states were less important than the deep gulf that divided Christendom. The religious wars of the sixteenth century, viewed in that light, were the first "world war." The execution of the Queen of Scots was no more than the most recent example of the crimes that heretics all over Europe had committed against the adherents of the old faith.

The book contains four series of prints.[11] The first series of four engravings refers to the outrages inflicted on English Catholics during the reign of Henry VIII. A second series of twelve engravings depicts the cruel deeds of the French Huguenots. A third series of five prints refers to the Netherlands, and illustrates the misdeeds of the Beggars and William of Orange. The final series of eight engravings reverts to England and deals with the persecutions in the reign of Elizabeth, which culminated in the execution of Mary Stuart.

The author of the pamphlet was one Richard Verstegan (ca. 1550–1640), born in London to a family that originated in Gelderland.[12] As a principled Catholic he had had to leave the University of Oxford without taking a degree, and in about 1580 he fled to the continent, where he was to live an adventurous life. In 1583 he was in Paris, where the English ambassador had him arrested for an attempt to print a work that denounced the persecution of Catholics in his native country. He moved to Rome, where his pamphlet eventually appeared in 1582. In 1587 he surfaced in Antwerp, where his *Theatrum* was printed. For the rest of his long and laborious life he devoted himself to active polemics in the service

---

[10] Verstegan, *Theatre* (1st impression, 1587), 15.

[11] Mauquoy-Hendrickx, *Estampes*, III, 378, 593, rejects the previous assumption that the prints were by Johan Wierix.

[12] Rombauts, *Richard Verstegan*; Buitendijk, *Calvinisme*, 155–228; Arblaster, *Antwerp and the World*.

244 • Chapter Twelve

of the Catholic Counter-Reformation. He was so active, in fact, that the English Jesuits gave him a dispensation to read banned heretical books, to enable him to combat heresy even more effectively.

Verstegan's *Theatrum* became a bestseller. The first impression of 1587 was followed by a second in 1588, a third in 1592, and a fourth revised edition in 1604. A French translation followed the Latin original almost at once in 1587, and was reprinted in 1607. A second and freer French translation appeared in 1588. To go into seven editions in twenty years was an achievement not matched even by the Beggar songbook. The use of Latin and French, and the international context in which it placed the clash of faiths, gave the work a much wider market than the Netherlands. In a preface to the French edition of 1588 the printer and publisher wrote that the Latin text published in 1587 had been eagerly bought and read not only in "Flanders" (i.e., the Netherlands), but also in France, Italy, and Spain. A French translation had therefore appeared immediately, but it was full of errors; this had induced "a merchant of France" to produce a better version.

The prints and texts that deal with the "cruel kinds of tyranny practiced by the Beggars in the Netherlands" chiefly portray Catholic clergy who were executed in the early years of the Revolt, including the famous martyrs of Gorcum, Alkmaar, and Roermond. We are concerned with the fifth print (plate 13).[13] It shows a soberly furnished room, in which an unclothed man is bound to a rack. A fire is burning on top of an upturned vessel placed on his belly. Five armed men stand around him. The foxes' brushes they wear in their hats instead of feathers identify them as adherents of the Beggar movement.[14] The facing text explains what is going on here: "Magister Ioannes Hieronymus" of Edam has been arrested with several other Catholics from Hoorn by the Beggars and brought to a place in North Holland called Schagen; there they have been subjected eight times to gruesome tortures, from which some of them have died. The others were then bound fast to the rack on their backs, and upturned vessels were placed on their bellies, in which live rats were put. Fires were lit on top of the vessels, so that the rats were driven to gnaw holes in the men's bellies in their frenzy to escape. Martyred by these tortures, these blessed innocents devoted their souls to God.

How many readers of Verstegan's pamphlet recognized the "martyr" Magister Ioannes Hieronymus of Edam or Hoorn as Master Jan Jeroenszoon? One at least we have already met: the sheriff of Hoorn, Claes Boelenszoon, whose letter to the Court of Holland written in 1610, and referred to above, derisively added:

---

[13] Verstegan, *Theatre*, 66–67.
[14] Van Nierop, "Beggars Banquet," 433–34, and Oosterhuis, "Lumey," 28.

This Jan Jeroenszoon appears as a Saint in a certain book of martyrs, which was printed at Antwerp in the year 1588 with the privilege of the late King of Spain, with figures; wherein it is claimed that he died under torture at the hands of the Beggars and offered his soul to the Lord God.[15]

Conspicuously absent from this passage in the *Theatrum* is any reference to the occasion of the tortures depicted and described, that is, the alleged plot to betray the Northern Quarter. Jan Jeroenszoon was a martyr for the faith and not a suspect on a charge of *crimen laesae majestatis*. It cannot have been easy for the readers of the *Theatrum* to imagine the historical setting of the cruel deeds it illustrated. The only available printed source that gave any account of the treason affair was the Beggar songbook, but that did not name Jan Jeroenszoon, because the song concerned had been composed some months before his arrest. In any case, one can hardly imagine that many readers would have kept the Beggar songbook and Verstegan's *Theatrum* next to each other on their bookshelves.

No one would turn in the first place to Verstegan's pamphlet for accurate information, for it was never his intention to supply it. Facts were not his object, but a means by which he sought to interpret the titanic struggle between the adherents of the ancient Catholic faith and the heretics, between God and the Devil. The text swarms with inaccuracies. The most piquant is the last line of the passage devoted to Jan Jeroenszoon, which says that he died a martyr's death. Evidently the fact that Jan Jeroenszoon was still very much alive must have penetrated to the Antwerp printer at a certain time, for the line was deleted in the revised Latin edition of 1604.

Accurate or not, Verstegan's book has been used as a source by numerous other authors, so that his version of the events has gained a firm place in Catholic devotional literature and historiography. An unprinted Antwerp satirical poem of 1617, by one Gaspard de Coninck, borrows directly from the *Theatrum*. De Coninck wrote of Jan Jeroenszoon:

> At Schagen in Holland the heretics shamelessly
> Seized one named Master Jan Jeroenszoon
> With more Catholics from Hoorn
> Whom they laid [on the rack] with bare bellies upwards.
> They put rats and mice on the naked belly
> Under a copper vessel, on which they lit a fire.
> The rats, feeling the fire take hold,
> Bit the bellies and crept into them.

---

[15] "Papisticque vergaderingen," 317.

> In this cruelty the Beggars gloried
> Because it passed the tyranny of the Huguenots.
> But the martyrs glorified God
> So that he gave them victory and they triumphed.[16]

Even learned authors in the Netherlands and elsewhere relied on Verstegan's work. The Italian Oratorian Tomaso Bozio (Thomas Bosius, 1548–1610), for example, cited the alleged martyrdom of Jan Jeroenszoon in his work *De signis ecclesiae Dei* ("On the Signs of God's Church," Rome 1591–92; Cologne, 1592), to prove his argument that true *patientia*, or endurance under suffering, could only be found in the Catholic Church.[17] Michael ab Isselt, a priest who came from Amersfoort but later settled in Cologne (1550/53–1597), incorporated the account in his *Sui temporis Historia* ("History of His Own Times," Cologne, 1602).[18] He copied the text from the first Latin edition of the *Theatrum*, but misplaced the events in the siege of Alkmaar in 1573. According to Ab Isselt the people of Alkmaar had caught a Spaniard, who offered to betray the plans of the Spanish army to them as the price of his life; after hearing him out the rebels hanged him anyway.[19] Clearly Ab Isselt had heard a garbled version of the treason of the Northern Quarter, for he believed that this Spaniard was the same as the martyr described by Verstegan, Jan Jeroenszoon.

Verstegan's version exerted a curious influence on the Catholic presentation of the event in the supplement added by Arnold de Raisse to the 1626 edition of Johannes Molanus's book on the name days of the Netherlands saints.[20] De Raisse states that the martyrdom of Jan Jeroenszoon was commemorated on 25 June; the description of his martyrdom is derived from Ab Isselt and therefore indirectly from Verstegan. Coppen Corneliszoon and his son Nanning also found a place in this work, with more justification. The martyrdom of the former was remembered on 2 June, that of the latter on 1 October.

De Raisse's account of the martyr's death of the two peasants from Wognum in his calendar of saints cannot have been taken from Verstegan, who did not mention them in his *Theatrum*. De Raisse's chief source was the well-known Dutch martyrology of Petrus Opmeer, *Historia martyrum batavicorum*, which appeared posthumously at Cologne in 1625.[21] Petrus

---

[16] Begheyn, "Antwerps hekeldicht," 214.

[17] Bosius, *De Signis*, I, 839, lib. XI, cap. I, num. VI. On Bosius see *Dictionnaire de théologie*, II, s.v., and *Lexikon für Theologie*, II, s.v.

[18] Ab Isselt, *Sui temporis historia*, 345, 354. On Ab Isselt see Vermaseren, *Katholieke Nederlandse geschiedschrijving*, 50–69.

[19] Cf. Bor, 453.

[20] De Raisse, *Ad natales*, 87, 108, 201. See also Molanus, *Natales*.

[21] Opmeer, *Historia*, and the Dutch translation of 1700, Opmeer, *Martelaarsboek*. For Opmeer see Vermaseren, *Katholieke Nederlandse geschiedschrijving*, 192–96. De Raisse

Opmeer was born at Amsterdam in 1526, but his surname indicates that his family originated in the part of North Holland known as West Friesland. He enjoyed a humanistic education, studied with the learned Petrus Nannius of Alkmaar at the *Collegium Trilingue* in Leuven, and was wealthy enough to devote himself to a life of study. When the Revolt broke out in 1572 he was living in Delft, but he too fled to Amsterdam. After Catholic worship was forbidden in the city following the Alteration of 1578, he returned to Delft, where he died in 1595. His martyrology was published thirty years later by his son.

Opmeer's lengthy account of the affair is of the greatest importance as a source, because he had spoken in person to the victims of Sonoy's investigating commission, so that he obtained his facts at first hand. "I knew Pieter Nanningszoon," he wrote, "whose belly was burned by glowing coals and his breast gnawed through by rats." Even more interesting is his statement that he visited Jan Jeroenszoon, "a very honorable and well to do man, very well known to me for a long time," in his prison cell. That visit must have taken place between February and July 1577, when Jan Jeroenszoon and the others were being held by the Court of Holland as prisoners at Delft and later in The Hague.

Opmeer's description follows the classic pattern of the martyrology. Whereas Verstegan had emphasized the godless corruption of the persecutors, Opmeer stressed the piety of the martyrs, whose lives were sanctified by their deaths.[22] Opmeer presented Coppen Corneliszoon as a "very honorable, gentle and mild-mannered man, modest in his way of life and other virtues. He loved hospitality, and took care to shelter the poor and the exiles in his house, to feed the hungry and to share his means with the poor, as far as was in his power."[23] Opmeer's decision to focus on charity, out of all the Christian virtues he could have chosen, is easily explicable. We know, after all, that the arrested vagrants had agreed with one another to denounce one person for inciting them to commit the alleged treason. It is obvious that they would think of someone who had recently given them shelter or alms.[24] Opmeer's emphasis on Coppen's piety fits the familiar genre of Catholic hagiography. Its evidence, therefore, has little objective value.

Unlike Verstegan, Opmeer does make the connection between the martyrdom of Coppen and Nanning and the abortive invasion of the Northern Quarter. The peasants arrested were not only Catholic, but "rather

---

must have taken 2 June as the day of Coppen's death from Bor, since Opmeer puts it on 14 June.

[22] Vermaseren, *Katholieke Nederlandse geschiedschrijving*, 194.
[23] Taken from the Dutch translation, Opmeer, *Martelaarsboek*, 248.
[24] Bor, 625.

richer than was usually found in that district . . . for Sonoy and the other bloodthirsty commanders, there was no worse crime than to be Catholic and rich, and to own too much land." We have seen that in fact there is nothing to suggest that the arrested peasants were unusually well to do. But since Opmeer's martyrology they have gone down, unchangeably, in historiography as wealthy and Catholic.

What sources did these Catholic authors use? In the case of Verstegan's summary account, the answer can no longer be given, but the most plausible assumption is that he relied on oral tradition. Opmeer says that he spoke to Jan Jeroenszoon in prison, and was shown "authentic documents."[25] We learn what these documents were from the notes of Franciscus Dusseldorpius (1567–1639). His *Annales*, a polemical history of the Revolt from the Catholic point of view, remained in manuscript until 1893, when Robert Fruin edited extracts from them.[26] Dusseldorpius, who misplaced the whole affair in the year 1577, gave a detailed description of the tortures to which the prisoners were subjected. He added that he had seen the depositions made before the notary Willem van Triere at Alkmaar.[27] Residents of the Republic who wanted to find out about the events were not dependent on printed sources alone. Manuscript texts circulated among Catholics and played an important role as long as the printing of seditious Catholic works was forbidden in the Republic.

While Catholic authors paid a great deal of attention to the wrongs inflicted on their fellow believers, there was for a long time a noticeable silence on the States side. After the Beggar song of summer 1575, which described the treason plot somewhat prematurely as a fait accompli, it was nearly forty-two years before the events found a place in a history written from the Protestant side, in the year 1617. The first author who broke the silence was the Hoorn physician Dirck Volckertszoon Seylmaker, better known as Theodoricus Velius (1572–1630), who discussed the history of the countryside of North Holland in detail in the second edition of his *Chronicle of Hoorn* (plate 14).[28] He drew his sources from documents in Hoorn's town archives and from conversations with older fellow townsfolk. Velius evidently also knew the Beggar song of 1575, for he refers to the red silk ribbons the traitors were supposed to have worn and names their leader Pieter van Hoef, who is not identified in any other extant source.

---

[25] Opmeer, *Martelaarsboek*, 255.

[26] Dusseldorpius, *Annales*. For Dusseldorpius see Fruin's introduction to his edition, and Vermaseren, *Katholieke Nederlandse geschiedschrijving*, 69–91.

[27] Dusseldorpius, *Uittreksel*, 153–54. The second and later depositions were made in 1577, which explains Dusseldorpius's mistake in dating.

[28] Velius, 246–49. I have used the third impression of 1648. For Velius see Heeres, "Iets over Velius."

The special significance of Velius's account is not just that he was the first author from the States or Protestant side to lift the veil on the episode, but that he took a remarkably skeptical view of the whole affair. Of Pieter van Hoef, for example, Velius remarked that he was suspected of being in contact with the enemy, but that no one had ever known the whole truth. The plot was a very widespread and persistent rumor, and was accepted as true. Many claimed it was merely a pretext, but most believed that the reports had some basis of fact; only the wrong persons had been arrested. Nanning Coppenszoon had only been brought to accuse others after torture.[29]

Velius's critical detachment is all the more striking because in the first edition of his chronicle of 1604, he had said not a word about the affair, either the invasion of the North or the plot and its aftermath.[30] Why did he ignore the episode in 1604, only to deal with it fully in 1617? In the first place the leaders of the Revolt in the Northern Quarter had put themselves firmly in the wrong; and as long as they were still alive, it was both tactless and dangerous to stir up old memories. Sonoy died in 1597, but the magistrates of the six other towns of North Holland had sided firmly with him against Hoorn and must have felt that the painful topic was best swept under the carpet.

There was, however, another explanation. As long as the war continued, it was imprudent to take up the Catholic cause, certainly while they were suspected of treason. Most of the inhabitants of the Republic favored freedom of conscience for Catholics, while simultaneously distrusting them as a potential fifth column. The suspicion of political unreliability stood in the way of granting religious freedom to Catholics. This situation did not change until 1609, when a twelve years' truce was concluded with Spain. Now that the threat of war was removed for the time being, it was not unrealistic to hope that the truce could be converted into a permanent peace. Since most of those involved in the treason affair had now died, the taboo surrounding it could be broken.

It was no accident that Velius was the man who took the first steps to do so. As a Mennonite he was himself a religious dissenter and therefore a supporter of Johan van Oldenbarnevelt and his party in the religious disputes that divided the Republic during the years of truce. Before Maurice of Nassau's coup and the Synod of Dordrecht changed the face of politics, the Remonstrants had the upper hand in traditionally tolerant Hoorn. Remonstrant preachers preached in the town church, while the

---

[29] Velius, 246–47.
[30] Velius, *Kronijck*, 1st ed., 1604, 197. All he says of the year 1575 is that the peace conference at Breda took place that year; after which Requesens withdrew to Zierikzee, "so that our quarter recovered a little."

Contra-Remonstrants had moved out to worship in a private house. The magistrates of Hoorn, where Velius sat on the *vroedschap*, supported the Remonstrants, the Synod of North Holland the Contra-Remonstrants. It is by no means implausible that Velius deliberately raked up the affair in 1617 indirectly to show the orthodox party in an unflattering light. Sonoy, who was politically responsible for the affair, had been an orthodox Calvinist. In the 1580s he had supported Leicester and his party against Oldenbarnevelt, who now backed the Remonstrants. The Reformed preachers had also played a rather unsavory role in the treason affair. Among them Velius named the Hoorn preacher Jurriaen Ypeszoon, who had attended Nanning Coppenszoon in his last hours. It therefore appears likely that Velius wanted to revive interest in the affair in 1617 as a weapon in the partisan strife that was dividing the Republic at the time. Even such an objective historian as Velius could relate the past with an eye directly on the present. But he did not enjoy this opportunity for long: Maurice's coup in 1618, which brought the Contra-Remonstrants to power, cost Velius his seat in the Hoorn *vroedschap*.

Although Velius has the honor of being the first on the States side to break the silence, the real breakthrough came four years later. In 1621 Pieter Christiaenszoon Bor (1559–1635) published the first two volumes of his magisterial "Origin, Beginning and Continuation of the Wars of the Netherlands," in which he took the narrative of the Revolt as far as 1584 (plate 15).[31] Bor's undertaking compels respect and admiration for its scale and depth, his critical use of sources and the boldness with which he placed the responsibility where it belonged, with the men who held power in North Holland. Bor took fifteen closely printed folios (twenty two-column pages in folio format in the edition of 1679), to uncover the full story of the invasion and the alleged betrayal of the Northern Quarter. That is about twenty-seven thousand words, or sixty pages in the format of the present book. Bor's interest in the Northern Quarter is all the more noteworthy because in the rest of his history his emphasis is chiefly on diplomatic, military, and to a lesser degree ecclesiastical events, and he pays little attention to the role of "ordinary" people in the war. The experiences of the North Holland vagrants, peasants, and citizens stand out clearly.

Bor used exclusively original sources, which he largely reproduced or paraphrased in his text. Because many of these sources have since been lost, his work remains indispensable. These included the correspondence

---

[31] Under the title *Nederlantsche oorloghen, beroerten en borgerlijcke oneenicheyden* ("The Wars, Troubles and Civil Discords of the Netherlands"), 6 vols., 1621–34. Books I to III had appeared earlier (Utrecht, 1595) as had books IV to VI (Utrecht, 1601); they described the Revolt until 1573. A revised reprint of these six books came out as early as 1603.

of Sonoy and the extremely important archive of the commission itself. Bor's access to these archives is proven by the numerous facts that he could have found nowhere else, such as the instruction of the commissioners and the hearings of the imprisoned vagrants.[32]

Bor was in a good position to consult these documents, which were then in the keeping of the Court of Holland. By his marriage in 1613 to Martina Boot, the widow of Willem Sas, a solicitor at the Court of Holland, he became the brother-in-law of François Kriep, the clerk of the Court, through whose influence he "gained much access to the Country's papers, Registers and Resolutions."[33] The States of Holland also supported his work with financial assistance and other facilities. Something of the monumental scope of his work can be read between the lines of a letter in a seventeenth-century hand preserved by chance in an ordinance of Sonoy. This document, the letter says, was used by Pieter Bor and later taken to the Prinsenhof in Haarlem, where all the documents formed a stack more than six and a half feet square.[34]

Bor's work has been described as "dull and dry as dust," and indeed the Utrecht apothecary's son was wary of fine writing. "The principal thing that is required of the Historian is truth and impartiality," as he summarized his scholarly creed.[35] Zeal for the truth, impartiality, and thorough research in the sources are criteria by which one could judge a modern historian, but it would be historically unsound to apply them to a seventeenth-century writer. The aim of renaissance historiography was not, in the first place, to bring to light new facts, but to retell the familiar tale in the most elegant style possible.[36] The historical truth took second place to the pedagogical and edifying purpose: to inspire the present generation to live up to the great deeds of their forefathers.

It is fortunate for posterity that Bor did not regard himself as a historian in this sense. Pieter Christianszoon Bor was trained as a notary. And since the chief task of a notary was and still is to establish, by passing authentic deeds, that a given legal transaction or other fact took place in this way and no other, Bor saw it as his allotted historical task to relate the truth plainly and without partisanship.[37] He did not consider himself learned enough to write "true" history in the sense that the humanists would have attached to the word: "The matter is too heavy for my small understanding."[38]

---

[32] Bor, 624. For Sonoy's correspondence see Fruin, "Prins Willem I," 116.
[33] Janssen, "Pieter Bor," 25.
[34] NHA, Aanwinsten, inv. no. 82.
[35] Janssen, "Pieter Bor," 21–22.
[36] Haitsma Mulier, "Geschiedschrijving."
[37] Janssen, "Pieter Bor," 23.
[38] Ibid., 22.

It must have struck Bor that his detailed treatment of the affair of North Holland formed a rather foreign body in his historical work. At the end of his account he apologizes for spending longer on it than he had planned. The reason for this, he writes, was that its notoriety had spread far beyond the Northern Quarter throughout the Netherlands, and that "it was diversely written and spoken of." A booklet had been printed in Antwerp, which gave a brief account of the whole affair. And Bor would not have been Bor if he had not then incorporated a Dutch version of the full text of the relevant passage from Verstegan's *Theatrum*. Moreover, he continued, other books had appeared in Brabant and elsewhere—unfortunately he did not identify them—that had raised the question without a knowledge of the facts. "Wherefore I wished to narrate the matter as it truly happened, from the authentic documents, deeds, certificates and reports thereof."[39]

This is one of the very few places in which Bor does not confine himself to stating the bare facts, but adds his own opinion. The prisoners, he concludes, owed their lives to the town magistrates of Hoorn, who did so much to defend their privileges. Without their intervention even more people would have lost their lives, since no one dared to stand up for the accused, for fear of falling into the hands of the "cruel" commissioners. Bor laid the chief blame for the outrages committed on the commissioners Calff, Sonnenberg, and Heukesloot, who he believed had misled Sonoy about the true state of the case.[40]

Since Pieter Bor no one has added anything original about the affair. This does not mean that it has not been written about; far from it. In the first place, Bor's detailed account and the shorter versions in Opmeer and Velius formed the sources for all the later authors. Bor's most important successor was the historian and man of letters Pieter Corneliszoon Hooft (1581–1647), who achieved precisely the goal of which Bor had considered himself incapable. In 1642, in finely chiseled prose modeled on the compact style of Tacitus's *Annals*, Hooft presented the citizens of the Republic with a national history that matched their tastes and cultural ambitions.[41] The Amsterdam patrician hardly needed to do any research in the sources, for the spadework had largely been done already by Bor and others. Hooft's elegant classical prose was more easily digestible than the barely paraphrased succession of edicts, ordinances, resolutions, and missives that Bor had served up to his readers.

---

[39] Bor, 640.
[40] Ibid.
[41] Hooft, *Nederlandsche historiën*, 422–29. On Hooft see Groenveld, *Hooft als historieschrijver*.

Even though Hooft has hardly any importance as an independent historical researcher, his version of the events in the Northern Quarter is important, for it was the form in which most inhabitants of the Republic came to know them. Furthermore, his work gives us a good impression of what the educated citizenry thought about them. Because, in Hooft's words, "neither moderation nor manner" was observed in the judicial handling of the affair, the case grew to become "the most odious stain" on the history of the States party up to that time.[42] Hooft also took the opportunity to praise the wise policy of William of Orange, who repressed Sonoy's bitterness and made his Blood Council a scandal.[43] He also added a notable element, which had been absent from Bor, and which was to grow into a cliché in all later versions: the fact that Sonoy was a foreigner, born at Kalkar in the Dutchy of Cleves.

> The eyes grow dim, the fingers numb, with distaste for such grisly and ever-redoubled inhumanities, committed at the instigation (it is true) of one who was no Hollander; but with the connivance nevertheless of some of our fellow countrymen.[44]

The impression one retains from reading Hooft is that the Hollanders had won immortal glory by their heroic struggle for liberation, but that there was bound to be a dark side. The affair of the treason plot was one such black page in the nation's history. Perhaps such a page was unavoidable, when power was wielded by an ex-Beggar who was not even a Hollander, and not in the hands of the moderate regents from patrician families, of whom Hooft was a representative par excellence.

Once put in canonical form by Hooft, the story was available to anyone who wanted to use it for his own purposes. The pamphlet of the Rotterdam physician Daniel Ionktys, "The Rack Refuted and Overcome,"[45] printed about 1650, was based entirely on Hooft and thus indirectly on Bor. This former justice of Rotterdam made grateful use of the detailed descriptions of the tortures inflicted on vagrants and peasants, to support his argument that torture was not only inhumane but also undesirable, because it was not an effective means of discovering the truth.

Catholics, too, could turn the works of Bor and Hooft to their own advantage, even though both men were Protestants. In the Dutch translation of Opmeer's martyrology, published in Cologne in 1700, the original Latin text was substantially augmented "from the writings of those who favor the new ideas."[46] Opmeer's eighteenth chapter, which had related

---

[42] Hooft, *Nederlandsche historiën*, 422.
[43] Ibid., 428.
[44] Ibid., 425.
[45] Ionktys, *Pijnbank*, ca. 1650, and many reprints.
[46] Opmeer, *Martelaarsboek*, chapter xix.

the martyrdom of Coppen Corneliszoon and his son Nanning, was followed by a new chapter nineteen, in which the same material is retold, but this time as a paraphrase of Bor and Hooft.

There is little point in examining in detail the treatment of the question by the States' historians, for none of them added anything new, and none of them matched Hooft's classical form.[47] But as time passed his stylish classicism came to seem rather old-fashioned to the enlightened reading public of the eighteenth century. The Amsterdam historian Jan Wagenaar (1709–1773) met the demand for a modern and enlightened work on the whole of the Dutch past, in his "History of the Fatherland," which appeared in twenty-one volumes from 1749.[48] Wagenaar gave a full account of the treason of the Northern Quarter, but added nothing to the versions of Bor and Hooft, on whom he relied. Even so, his history deserves a mention here, because until well into the nineteenth century it remained the standard work from which the Dutch people drew their knowledge of their country's past. Wagenaar shared the view that the episode had been a stain on the good name of Holland, "although Sonoy, the chief instigator of it, was not a Hollander." Wagenaar's explanation of the events is interesting; he believed the persecutions were launched "to take away from the Romanists once and for all the will to stand up for a change of government." That is, justice was deliberately perverted in the interests of the safety of the state. Wagenaar considered this unacceptable.

In the seventeenth and eighteenth centuries, since the days of Velius and Bor, it had been the pro-States, Protestant authors above all who paid attention to the affair. The Catholics had defended themselves doughtily, especially in the years of the Revolt, when the outcome of the struggle was still uncertain, but once they saw that Protestant rule in the rebel provinces was there to stay, they realized they could expect to gain more from accommodation with it than from confrontation. They therefore kept quiet. Catholic books were mostly printed across the frontier in Antwerp or Cologne. The printing of Catholic literature that could be considered seditious was forbidden in the Republic.[49] Moreover, most of their works were in Latin and read only by a small, cultivated

---

[47] Among others Twisck, *Chronijck*, 1317–18, which was based on Velius before Bor; Ampzing, *Beschryvinge*, 275–76, and Pers, *Ontstelde leeuw*, 295–98, based on Velius and Bor. Brandt, *Geschiedenis der Reformatie*, I, 562–63, based on Velius, Bor, and Hooft, calls the question "a bloody stain on our History." Boomkamp, *Alkmaer*, 367–71 is based on Velius and Bor.

[48] Wagenaar, *Vaderlandsche historie*, VII (1752), 54–61. On Wagenaar, see Wessels, "Jan Wagenaar," and Wessels, "Bron."

[49] Groenveld, "The Mecca of Authors," 67, and the edicts of 1581, 1584, 1587, 1589, and 1594 cited there. Van Gelder, *Getemperde vrijheid*, chapters iii and iv.

public, not least the Catholic clergy, who made use of them in their sermons and pastoral care.

In the nineteenth century the situation was reversed. Nationalist Protestant historiography kept silent about the affair, while Catholics used it to beat the drum loudly for their cause, the emancipation of their religious community.

The liberal, enlightened Protestant historiography that developed in the nineteenth century interpreted the Revolt as a struggle in which a Dutch nation had freed itself from foreign rule. From this perspective it was hard to take a positive view of an affair in which "traitors" had been unjustly treated, and the champions of national freedom had been the villains of the piece. It was difficult to see it as more than a regrettable misfortune, such as otherwise just wars were bound to produce. Protestant historiography therefore kept quiet about the whole question; one must remember that Wagenaar's history was still in print and still read. Only in distant Boston, Massachusetts, did John Lothrop Motley write an epic history of the Revolt for the Anglo-American public, in which he gave a detailed narrative of the alleged plot, following the trusted recipe of transcribing Bor, Hooft, and Wagenaar.[50]

Robert Fruin (1823–1899), the greatest Dutch historian of the nineteenth century, revealed that he was thoroughly familiar with the facts—indeed there was no historical question of importance that he did not know thoroughly—but he dealt with it only in passing. In a long article on the martyrs of Gorcum he pointed out that there had been victims on both sides in the conflict. The persecution of Catholics by the Beggars was as deplorable as the persecution of Protestants by the Inquisition. The Catholic victims of the Revolt, according to Fruin, were hardly known in the Netherlands, where Protestantism was dominant. He therefore considered it his duty, as long as no Catholic historian had emerged who was capable of acquitting himself of the task properly, to relate the history of the excesses of the Revolt impartially.[51] In a footnote he dealt briefly with Sonoy's Blood Council. The gruesome events must certainly not be confused with the persecution of Catholic priests by Sonoy and Lumey during the first months of the Revolt. The peasants arrested were persecuted as "pro-Spanish, not as pro-Roman."[52] In his edition of Dusseldorpius's *Annales* Fruin reexamined the question, but again merely in a footnote.[53] Here he claimed that it was not the commissioners who were to blame

[50] Motley, *Rise of the Dutch Republic*, III, 30–34.
[51] Fruin, "Gorcumsche martelaren," 277–79.
[52] Ibid., 318: "The outrages committed by Sonoy in 1575, although they bear witness to his cruelty, are of another character; Kees Koppens [sic] and his fellow sufferers were tortured because they were pro-Spanish and not pro-Roman."
[53] Dusseldorpius, *Annales*, 493–94.

for the excesses, but torture, which was generally accepted at the time. "The whole conduct of the commissioners, in my opinion, vouches for the good faith of their conviction that the accused were guilty."

Fruin was the first—and the last—author to come to the defense of the commissioners. He may have been provoked to do so by partisan popular Catholic historical works that exploited the question for their own purposes. When Catholic historians reemerged in the nineteenth century, they revived the tradition of Verstegan and Opmeer by depicting the victims of Sonoy's regime as martyrs who had made the ultimate sacrifice for their faith.

Joachim George LeSage ten Broek (1775–1847), the son of a Calvinist minister, and a convert to Catholicism, founded a periodical, *De Godsdienstvriend* ("The Friend of Religion"), of which he also wrote the whole contents. In it he frankly used the treason affair as a weapon in the struggle for Catholic emancipation.[54] The Dutch press had been horrified by the persecution of Protestants in Southern France in 1814. LeSage claimed that these incidents had persuaded Protestants and even some Catholics that Catholicism and religious tolerance were irreconcilable. To prove that Protestants could also be persecutors, he did not choose to rake up the tale of the martyrs of Gorcum and other victims of Lumey, of whom he had given a full account in an earlier issue, but to expose the cruelties of Sonoy in the Northern Quarter, "less extensive but more flagrant because of their added refinements of more cold-blooded, long-drawn-out cruelty."[55] He transcribed his version of the story from the "National Biographical Dictionary" of Jacobus Kok, which in turn went back to Hooft.[56] At the end of his article LeSage felt that he had demonstrated that Protestantism was certainly not tolerant. "You, Protestant, cease your ludicrous vaunting of the spirit of mildness, which you say characterizes Protestantism!"

The North Holland physician W. J. F. Nuyens wrote an eight-volume "History of the Troubles of the Netherlands in the Sixteenth Century," in which he tried to boost the battered self-image of Dutch Catholics by showing that one could very well be both a Catholic and a patriot. His procedure was the same as that of LeSage: the literal copying of someone else's text, in this case the version of Wagenaar. Nuyens used the episode as proof of his argument that Sonoy's reign of terror in North Holland "was just as horrific as, and far more lawless than that of Alba."[57]

[54] For LeSage see Goerris, *Le Sage ten Broek*.
[55] LeSage ten Broek, "Schrikkelijke handel," 121.
[56] Kok, *Vaderlandsch woordenboek*, XXVII, 238–45 (art. "Sonoy").
[57] Nuyens, *Geschiedenis der Nederlandsche beroerten*, I, 213.

The most elaborate version in which the treason of the Northern Quarter was retold to exalt the Dutch Catholics was to be found in the religious monthly "The People's Missionary," a periodical published "under the protection of the Immaculate Mother of God and the Doctor of the Church Alphonsus Maria by several Redemptorist Fathers." The article appeared under the heading "From the days of oppression" and the motto "Praised be Jesus Christ!"[58] Based on Opmeer, Velius, Bor, Hooft, Wagenaar, and others, it was the fullest account to be found in historical literature, but obviously added nothing new, except what sprang from the imagination of the Redemptorist Fathers themselves. They gave free rein to their fantasy, putting speeches into the mouths of the characters in the style of a nineteenth-century children's book: "But the martyr, deploring his former weakness, did not hesitate stoutly to defy the vile, cruel [interrogator]." The Fathers also claimed insight into the victims' innermost thoughts:

> [Nanning Coppenszoon] ardently besought God to forgive him his former weakness [namely, denouncing the innocent], and offered his imminent death to redeem his guilt. The merciful and loving Father certainly consoled and strengthened him and gladly forgave his weakness, if it could be laid to his charge.[59]

The Fathers believed the background to the persecutions lay in the religious intolerance of the new regime. The peasants of Wognum had not been arrested because they were loyal to the king, "as a Protestant writer asserts," but as Catholics. This Protestant writer can of course be none other than Robert Fruin.[60]

The emancipated Catholics of the second half of the nineteenth century continued to reissue the sixteenth- and seventeenth-century martyrologies. In 1879, for instance, a revised edition of Opmeer's book of martyrs, adapted for a modern reading public, was brought out.[61] A Belgian edition of Verstegan's *Theatrum* in French appeared a few years later.[62] In their introduction to the latter the editors admitted frankly that the cruelties of the heretics had occurred long ago, but they had lost none of their relevance, as the frightful experience of the Paris Commune of 1871 had shown. Three hundred years after its first publication the *Theatrum* could still do good service as an unabashed antiliberal polemic.

At the dawn of the twentieth century the treason of the Northern Quarter faded from view. The great surveys of Dutch history and the Revolt

---

[58] "Sonoys bloedraad."
[59] Ibid., 262.
[60] Ibid., 107.
[61] Opmeer, *Katholiek-Nederlandsch martelaarboek*.
[62] Verstegan, *Théatre* (ed. 1883). See the *avertissement des éditeurs*, i–iii.

written in the first half of the century by Blok, Gosses and Japikse, Geyl, Presser, and Enno van Gelder, dismissed it in a line or two.[63] Even L. J. Rogier, in his monumental history of Catholicism in the Northern Netherlands, the last and greatest achievement of the Catholic historiographical tradition, devoted no more than a single extremely soberly phrased paragraph to it.[64] H. A. Enno van Gelder, in his contribution to the *General History of the Netherlands* (1952) was the last author to discuss the affair.

The harvest of four centuries of historiography is not encouraging. When comparing everything that has been written on the affair of the Northern Quarter one can draw two conclusions. The first is that no one has added anything to what Bor published as long ago as 1621. Secondly, it seems that most authors were less interested in the question itself than in the moral argument for which they used it as ammunition. Catholic and Protestant authors reacted to one another. Just as Bor's work had formed a response to Verstegan's *Theatrum*, the Redemptorist Fathers reacted to two footnotes of Fruin. Since the summer of 1575, when the Beggar song about the "murderous fire-raisers" was sung in the towns and villages of the Northern Quarter, historiography and propaganda have been inextricably entwined. The historiography of the Revolt was a continuation of the war by other means.

[63] Petrus Johannes Blok, *History of the People of the Netherlands*, II, 106–7; Gosses and Japikse, *Handboek*, 358; Geyl, *Revolt of the Netherlands*, 141; Presser, *Tachtigjarige oorlog*, 58; Van Gelder, *Revolutionnaire reformatie*, 21–22; Van Gelder, "Strijd," 50 ("a most repellent 'trial' before a popular court").

[64] Rogier, *Geschiedenis van het katholicisme*, 384–85.

CHAPTER THIRTEEN

# Conclusion

For the inhabitants of the Northern Quarter the Revolt in the years 1572–76 was indeed a war, even if it did not last eighty years. Of course, most of the rest of the population did not have to endure anything like the infernal experiences of Jan Jeroenszoon and the other victims of Sonoy's Blood Council, but it is clear that everyone suffered from the misery the struggle brought with it. The war was a civil war of the same type as the conflicts that were tearing France apart at the same time.[1] These *guerras civiles*, as even Spanish contemporaries called them, divided the population of the Netherlands in a way that was without precedent. In 1572 there had been differences of opinion over admitting the Sea Beggars and joining the Prince of Orange's revolt, but the general revulsion from Alba's regime had convinced many that the Beggar bands were the lesser of two evils.

A year later the situation had fundamentally changed. On the one hand the Beggar troops looted churches, assaulted the clergy, and seized property in the areas ruled by the prince and the rebels. On the other hand, the sack of Naarden and the conquest of Haarlem had shown that the government would not yield to pressure and was not prepared to make concessions. The people of the Northern Quarter were in a trap. What was the wise thing to do in the circumstances?

Some of them were ready to defend themselves to the utmost against the king's army. They included, in the first place, the returned exiles and the Calvinists, but also many more who had not yet broken with the Catholic Church and did not intend to do so. With the frightful examples of Mechelen, Zutphen, and Naarden before their eyes, they still preferred the regime of the prince and Sonoy to the lawful government of Alba and Requesens. The plan for the total devastation of the Northern Quarter and its inhabitants, which Hierges tried in vain to put into effect in May 1575, can only have confirmed them in their conviction. But they could not have expected that their struggle for life and liberty would ultimately lead to the independence of the seven northern provinces of the Netherlands. At the time it seemed much more realistic to assume that if they continued the struggle long enough, some sort of compromise with the king would be possible, in which at least some of their grievances would

[1] Benedict, *Reformation*.

be remedied. That was how each of the civil wars in France had ended, in an agreement that granted the rebels certain rights, including a narrowly defined freedom of religion. During the peace negotiations at Breda in 1575, and above all between 1576 and 1579, it appeared that the rebels in Holland and Zeeland would be vindicated in this strategy.

Many others, however, left their homes and "sneaked" away to Amsterdam and elsewhere. Those who chose to stay put regarded them as traitors, but was their decision so irrational? There were many good reasons to await the outcome of events in the relative safety of Amsterdam. The reconquest of the Northern Quarter by the Spanish army appeared to be only a matter of time, and it was clear that even Catholics could expect no mercy. They were attached to the old Church, which had been closed down by the rebels, and moreover the government of Alba and Requesens, however unpopular it might be, was still the lawful authority.

The sources give the impression—which may be misleading—that the "sneakers" were found mainly among the better-off citizenry. Most inhabitants of the Northern Quarter could not have afforded to leave their homes and trades. They hoped to survive the war by accepting the inevitable and not drawing attention to themselves.

The Pacification of Ghent ended the division in the population. The former fugitives now returned to their homes and were readmitted to civic society after swearing a new oath of loyalty to the town and to the Prince of Orange as Stadholder of Holland, apparently without too much difficulty. It appears surprising that the discords and bitterness of 1572–76 did not lead to more problems after the Pacification. Holland's spectacular economic growth, which set in around 1590, must have helped to heal the wounds.

The successful restoration of civic harmony is evidence of social cohesion in the towns of Holland, and indicates that the citizens felt they shared a common fate. Unlike the experience of France, in Holland the sense of civic unity prevailed over religious partisanship. In Paris and most of the other French cities and towns the Catholic majority of the population regarded the Huguenots as a foreign body that tarnished and threatened the sacral unity of the town. In the towns of Holland, in contrast, most citizens felt the greater threat to their ideal of civic unity came from the lawful government, which persecuted Catholic dissidents, Anabaptists, and Calvinists, introduced new taxes, and had relied since 1567 on a "Spanish" army. How the political elite managed, after the war of 1572–76, to attach the citizens in the first place to their towns, in spite of their bewildering confessional diversity, is another story.[2]

---

[2] On this question, Spaans, *Haarlem*. On anti-Calvinist violence in France, Diefendorf, *Beneath the Cross*, and Crouzet, *Guerriers*; there is a comparison between France and the Netherlands in Woltjer, "Violence."

A recurrent theme of this book is the distinction between settled inhabitants and outsiders. The Revolt broke out in 1572 because the towns were unwilling to admit foreign troops, either government forces or the Beggars, and wanted to be responsible for their own defense. When the threat of war increased, the towns reacted in the same way. They confronted all noncitizens with the choice of swearing a citizen's oath or leaving the town. Citizens were by definition people who were known and trusted; by the same definition strangers were suspect. For this reason Amsterdam took an extremely ambivalent attitude to the asylum seekers who flocked to the city during the war years. At the slightest hint of treason the strangers were the first to fall under suspicion.

The vagrants Sonoy rounded up in May 1575 were outsiders par excellence. Their marginal status was even more marked because they came from "the land of the enemy." But their persecutors, the commissioners, Sonoy himself, and the majority of the rebel leadership, were also "foreigners." Heukesloot, who refused to swear the oath of citizenship, was distrusted and hated in Hoorn; Calff fared no better in Edam, and Mostaert's career in Holland was hindered by his birth in Brabant.

In the midst of all the changes and everything that was strange and threatening—Alba, Requesens and the Spanish army, marauders, beggars and vagrants, homeless refugees, the Sea Beggars, bands of mercenaries, and new men in power—the towns and the legal protection they offered their citizens formed an element of stability. There is no need to be sentimental about the spirit of community and social solidarity that is supposed to have characterized the early modern town. But in this "anxious, oppressed, wild time" the importance of social cohesion and concrete assistance can hardly be overstated. To survive one had to feel sheltered somewhere, in a group of family members and relatives ("friends"), a craft guild or fraternity, or in a town. The town formed a sworn community, a quasi-kindred, which was expected to intervene on behalf of its citizens. Only as a citizen could one have access to the law, in which the Hollanders of the sixteenth century placed such remarkable trust. While the vagrants and peasants were led like cattle to the slaughter, citizens could invoke the law even in time of war. Pieter Bor was right to judge that Jan Jeroenszoon and his fellow prisoners owed their lives in the first place to the protection the magistrates of Hoorn offered them.[3]

Karl Marx remarked that history repeats itself, occurring first as tragedy and the second time as farce.[4] That was also the case of the treason of the Northern Quarter. Maria Clomp, the last surviving descendant of Jan Jeroenszoon, had a nephew, Hieronymus (another Jeroen) van Ysselt,

[3] Bor, 640.
[4] Marx, "Achtzehnte Brumaire," 226.

who was thus a great-great-grandson of Jan Jeroenszoon.⁵ Hieronymus van Ysselt was born at Isselt, a country house near Amersfoort, in 1666. He went to the Jesuit school at Emmerich, "as being of the Romish religion," and chose a military career. He served for a year as a cadet and then six years as a volunteer. In 1697 the Peace of Ryswick put an end to the Nine Years' War against France and thus also to Hieronymus's career as a professional soldier.

A year before the peace Hieronymus had appalled his relatives by marrying Elizabeth Clara Bladtwail, who though well off was a Protestant. That was reason enough for his older brother Johan to disinherit Hieronymus and his posterity almost entirely and to name his aunt, Maria Clomp, as his universal heir.⁶ Because Hieronymus was out of work, the newlyweds had to survive on the income from their property. The imminent war of the Spanish Succession seemed to offer a new chance of military glory and a respectable income. Hieronymus therefore applied to his uncle, Cornelis Cools, an advocate in Hoorn, for a recommendation to a commission in a cavalry company. This failed to produce any tangible result, either because his uncle would not recommend him or because the command of the States' army had no use for his services.

Hieronymus resorted to a desperate plan. Armed with letters of recommendation from the ambassadors of France and Spain, he went to the Spanish Netherlands, where he approached the high command of the French army and offered his services to the King of Spain. He would be glad to obtain the rank and salary of a captain of cavalry. Moreover, a ship was to be fitted out on the Zuiderzee, "with which I could put the whole quarter of North Holland under water."

Hieronymus was familiar with the Northern Quarter, where he had spent a large part of his youth. He had chosen three suitable places where the Zuiderzee dike could be cut without too much difficulty. This would inundate the country for at least two years and make it impossible to collect taxes for six to eight years. North Holland was responsible for bearing the costs of eighteen regiments and fourteen warships; the advantage to the Franco-Spanish war effort was obvious. Apart from the command of a cavalry regiment, Hieronymus also demanded an indemnity for his property, because he knew very well that it would be confiscated after such an audacious exploit.

⁵ He was a son of Agatha Cools (d. 1691/95) and Cornelis van Ysselt (1609–1666). His mother, Agatha Cools, was a daughter of Hieronymus Cools (1606–1656) and Maria Maurits (d. 1671). His grandfather Hieronymus Cools was a son of Agatha, the daughter of Jan Jeroenszoon (d. before 1626) and Reinier Cools (d. 1654). Looijesteijn, "Geslacht," passim. For what follows see Beelaerts van Blockland, "Hieronymus van Ysselt."

⁶ Looijesteijn, "Geslacht," 85, 88.

The plan did not remain secret for long. Hieronymus was arrested at his house near Gouda and taken to the Gevangenpoort prison in The Hague on 8 May 1702. The first hearing was on 17 May, and the verdict was pronounced on 21 December. The Court of Holland found him guilty of the crime of lese majesty and sentenced him to be "taken to the place where criminal justice is accustomed to be done, and to be struck with the sword until death follows." His estates were declared forfeit. The sentence was executed the same day.

This time the betrayal of the Northern Quarter was certainly not a fantasy of the nervous authorities. The plan was real. It was concrete and almost palpable in extremely incriminating letters in Hieronymus's own hand, which the prosecutor-general laid before the Court. Hieronymus had made a full confession "without pain or bonds." He had not been able to produce any substantial defense. He claimed that he had not wished to put the plan into effect until he had obtained a commission in a cavalry regiment, a ship had been put at his disposal, and war had broken out; but he had not believed that the war would ever become a reality. Moreover, it was no more than a plan, which had never been put into action. These were lame excuses, and the Court had little patience with them. The counselors acted as might be expected when the country was in peril: with an efficient and orderly trial and a severe but justified sentence.

# Abbreviations

| | |
|---|---|
| ARAB | Algemeen Rijksarchief, Brussels |
| Aud. | Audiëntie [Audience] |
| BBH | *Bijdragen tot de geschiedenis van het bisdom Haarlem* |
| BMGN | *Bijdragen en mededelingen betreffende de geschiedenis der Nederlanden* |
| BMHG | *Bijdragen en mededelingen van het Historisch Genootschap* |
| Bor | Pieter Christiaenszoon. Bor, *Oorsprongk, begin en vervolgh der Nederlandscher oorlogen*, 4th edition, Amsterdam, 1679, vol. I |
| CCG | *Correspondance du Cardinal de Granvelle (1565–1586)*, eds. E. Poullet and Ch. Piot, 12 vols., Brussels, 1877–96 |
| CD | *Corpus documentorum inquisitionis haereticae pravitatis Neerlandicae*, ed. Paul Fredericq, 5 vols., Ghent and The Hague, 1889–1906 |
| CP | *Correspondance de Philippe II sur les affaires des Pays-Bas*, ed. L. P. Gachard, 6 vols., Brussels, 1848–1936 |
| DTB | Doop-, trouw- en begraafboeken [Registers of baptisms, marriages and burials] |
| DWJ | Wouter Jacobsz., *Dagboek van Broeder Wouter Jacobsz (Gualtherus Jacobi Masius) Prior van Stein. Amsterdam 1572–1578 en Montfoort 1578–1579*, ed. I. H. van Eeghen, 2 vols., Groningen, 1959–60 |
| GA | Gemeentearchief [Municipal archives] |
| GNK | Archief van de Gecommitteerde Raden van Westfriesland en het Noorderkwartier [Archives of the Committee of Councelors of West Friesland and the Northern Quarters] |
| Hof | Archief van het Hof van Holland en Zeeland [Archives of the Court of Holland and Zeeland] |
| Hoge Raad | Archief van de Hoge Raad van Holland en Zeeland [Archives of the High Court of Holland and Zeeland] |
| KHA | Koninklijk Huisarchief [Royal House Archives] |
| NA | Nationaal Archief [National Archives], The Hague |
| NHA | Noord-Hollands Archief, Haarlem |
| Not.A | Notarieel archief [Notarial archives] |

| | |
|---|---|
| NNBW | *Nieuw Nederlands Biografisch Woordenboek*, ed. P. C. Molhuysen and P. J. Blok, 10 vols., Leiden, 1911–37 |
| OA | Oud-archief [Town archives before 1811] |
| OBC | Archief van de Oud-bisschoppelijke Cleresij [Archives of the Old Catholic Church] |
| ORA | Oud-rechterlijke archieven [Judicial archives before 1811] |
| RAA | Regionaal Archief Alkmaar |
| RH | *Resolutiën van de Heeren Staaten van Holland en Westvriesland*, 276 vols., The Hague, ca. 1750–98 |
| SAA | Stadsarchief Amsterdam [City archives] |
| SvH | Archief van de Staten van Holland [Archives of the States of Holland] |
| TvG | *Tijdschrift voor Geschiedenis* |
| UA | Utrechts Archief, Purmerend |
| Velius | D. Velius, *Chroniick van Hoorn*, 3rd ed., Hoorn, 1648 |
| WA | Waterlands Archief, Purmerend |
| WFA | Westfries Archief, Hoorn |
| WFON | *West-Frieslands Oud en Nieuw* |

# Bibliography

MANUSCRIPT SOURCES

*Nationaal Archief, The Hague:*

Hof van Holland en Zeeland [Court of Holland and Zeeland]
Hoge Raad van Holland en Zeeland [High Court of Holland and Zeeland]
Grafelijkheidsrekenkamer, rekeningen [Chamber of Accounts, accounts]
Grafelijkheidsrekenkamer, registers [Chamber of Accounts, registers]
Staten van Holland vóór 1572 [States of Holland before 1572]

*Noord-Hollands Archief, Haarlem:*

Gecommitteerde Raden van Westfriesland en het Noorderkwartier [Committee of Counselors of West Friesland and the Northern Quarter]
Nicolaes Ruychaver
Bisdom Haarlem van de Oud-katholieke kerk [Haarlem diocese of the Old Catholic Church]
Collectie losse aanwinsten [Accessions]
Collectie copieën [Copies]

*Utrechts Archief:*

Oud-bisschoppelijke Clerezij [Old Catholic Church]

*Westfries Archief, Hoorn:*

Oud-archief Hoorn
Oud-rechterlijk archief Hoorn
Notarieel archief Hoorn
Oud-archief Enkhuizen
Notarieel archief Enkhuizen
Oud-archief Medemblik
Oud-rechterlijk archief Medemblik
Notarieel archief Medemblik
Gemeentearchief Wognum
Oud-archief Stede Schellinkhout
Oud-archief Stede Westwoud
Oud-archief Stede Grootebroek
Oud-rechterlijk archief Stede Grootebroek
Oud-rechterlijk archief Spanbroek
Oud-rechterlijk archief Niedorp

Oud-rechterlijk archief Sijbekarspel
Huisarchief Weldam [Archives of the house of Weldam]

*Waterlands Archief, Purmerend:*

Oud-archief Edam
Oud-archief Monnickendam
Oud-archief Purmerend

*Regionaal archief, Alkmaar:*

Stadsarchief Alkmaar
Oud-rechterlijk archief Alkmaar
Notarieel archief Alkmaar
Archief van de kerkeraad van de Nederlands-Hervormde Gemeente Alkmaar [Archives of the consistory of the Reformed Church, Alkmaar]

*Stadsarchief Amsterdam:*

Archief Burgemeesters
Archief Vroedschap
Oud-rechterlijk archief
Notarieel archief
Doop-, trouw- en begraafboeken [Registers of baptisms, marriages and burials]

*Koninklijk Huisarchief, The Hague:*

Archief Prins Willem I [Archives of Prince William I]

*Algemeen Rijksarchief [General State Archives], Brussels:*

Raad van State en Audiëntie, fonds zendbrieven [Council of State, missives]
Raad van Beroerten [Council of Troubles]
Grote Raad van Mechelen [Great Council of Mechelen]

*Instituto de Valencia de Don Juan, Madrid*

*Biblioteca Francisco de Zabálburu, Madrid*

PUBLISHED PRIMARY SOURCES

*Acta der provinciale en particuliere synoden, gehouden in de Noordelijke Nederlanden gedurende de jaren 1572–1620*, ed. J. Reitsma and S. D. van Veen, 8 vols., Groningen, 1892–99.
*Album advocatorum. De advocaten van het Hof van Holland 1560–1811*, ed. R. Huijbrecht, S. Scheffers, and S. Scheffers-Hofman, The Hague, 1996.
Ampzing, Samuel, *Beschryvinge ende lof der stad Haerlem in Holland*, Haarlem, 1628.
*Archives ou correspondance inédite de la Maison d'Orange-Nassau*, ed. G. Groen van Prinsterer, 1$^e$ série, 8 vols., Leiden, 1835–47.

Boehncke, Heiner, and Rolf Johannsmeier, *Das Buch der Vaganten. Spieler, Huren, Leutbetrüger*, Cologne, 1987.

Boomkamp, G., *Alkmaer en deszelfs geschiedenissen uit de nagelaten papieren van Simon Eikelenberg, en veel andere echte stukken en bescheiden*, Rotterdam, 1747.

Bor, Pieter Christiaenszoon, *Oorsprongk, begin en vervolgh der Nederlandscher oorlogen*, 4th ed., 4 vols., Amsterdam, 1679–84 (1st ed., 1595 and 1601; 2nd rev. ed., 1603; 3rd rev. and enlarged ed., 1621–34).

Bosius, Thomas, *De signis Eccesiae Dei libri XXIIII*, 3 vols., Cologne, 1592.

"Bouwstoffen voor de kerkelijke geschiedenis van verschillende parochiën thans behoorende tot het bisdom van Haarlem," ed. A. van Lommel, *BBH*, 6 (1878), 146–208.

Brandt, Geeraert, *Historie der reformatie, en andere kerkelyke geschiedenissen, in en omtrent de Nederlanden*, 4 vols., Amsterdam, 1671–74.

———, *Historie der vermaerde zee- en koop-stad Enkhuisen*, Enkhuizen, 1666.

Brant, Sebastian, *Narrenschiff*, ed. F. Zarncke, Leipzig, 1854.

*Brieven en andere bescheiden rakende het beleg van Alkmaar in 1573 naar de oorspronkelijke stukken*, ed. J. J. de Gelder, Alkmaar, 1865.

Broedersen, Nicolaus, *Tractatus historicus II de rebus ecclesiae ultrajectinae, etc.*, Utrecht, 1736.

*Bronnen voor de geschiedenis van de kerkelijke rechtspraak in het bisdom Utrecht in de middeleeuwen*, ed. J. G. C. Joosting and S. Muller, 7 vols., The Hague, 1906–24.

*Bronnen voor de geschiedenis van de Nederlandse Oostzeehandel in de zeventiende eeuw*, ed. P. H. Winkelman, VI, The Hague, 1983.

Buchell, Arent van, *Diarium van Arend van Buchell*, ed. G. Brom and L. A. van Langeraad, Amsterdam, 1907.

*Calendar of State Papers, Foreign Series, of the Reign of Elizabeth, 1558–1589*, ed. Joseph Stephenson et al., 23 vols., London, 1863–1950.

*Corpus documentorum inquisitionis haereticae pravitatis Neerlandicae*, ed. Paul Fredericq, 5 vols., Ghent and The Hague, 1889–1906.

*Correspondance du Cardinal de Granvelle (1565–1586)*, ed. E. Poullet and Ch. Piot, 12 vols., Brussels, 1877–96.

*Correspondance française de Marguerite d'Autriche, duchesse de Parme, avec Philippe II*, ed. H. A. Enno van Gelder, 3 vols., Utrecht, 1925–42.

*Correspondance de Philippe II sur les affaires des Pays-Bas*, ed. L. P. Gachard, 6 vols., Brussels, 1848–1936.

*Dagboek van Broeder Wouter Jacobsz (Gualtherus Jacobi Masius) Prior van Stein. Amsterdam 1572–1578 en Montfoort 1578–1579*. ed. I. H. van Eeghen, 2 vols., Groningen, 1959–60.

Damhouder, Joos de, *Practycke ende handbouck in criminele zaken, etc.*, Leuven, 1555.

*Deuxième livre des procurateurs de la nation germanique de l'ancienne université d'Orléans 1546–1567. Première partie: Texte des rapports des procureurs, I: Texte des rapports 1546–1560*, ed. Cornelia M. Ridderikhoff, Leiden etc., 1988.

*Documenta Anabaptistica Neerlandica. V: Amsterdam, 1531–1536*, ed. A. F. Mellink, Leiden, 1985.
"Dokumenten betreffende de godsdiensttroebelen in het Westkwartier," ed. Marcel Backhouse, *Handelingen van de koninklijke commissie voor geschiedenis*, 138 (1972), 79–381.
Dusseldorpius, Franciscus, *Uittreksel uit Francisci Dusseldorpii Annales 1566–1616*, ed. R. Fruin, The Hague, 1893.
Eppens, Abel, *De kroniek van Abel Eppens tho Equart*, ed. J. A. Feith and H. Brugmans, 2 vols., Amsterdam, 1911.
Erasmus, Desiderius, *The Colloquies of Erasmus*, ed. Craig R. Thompson, Chicago and London, 1965.
Foreest, Nanning van, *Een cort verhael van de strenghe belegeringhe ende aftreck der Spanggiaerden van de stadt Alcmaer gheleghen in Hollandt*, Delft, 1573.
*Het geuzenliedboek. Naar de oude drukken. Uit de nalatenschap van Dr. E. T. Kuiper*, ed. P. Leendertz Jr., 2 vols., Zutphen, 1924–25.
*Groot Placaet-boeck vervattende de placaten . . . van de Staten Generaal der Vereenigde Nederlanden ende van de . . . Staten van Hollandt en West-Vrieslandt mitsgaders van de . . . Staten van Zeelandt*, ed. C. Cau, 9 vols., The Hague, 1658–1796.
Guicciardini, Lodovico, *Descrittione di tutti i Paesi Bassi. Edizione critica*, ed. Bernardina Aristodemo, Amsterdam, 1994.
———, *Beschryvinghe van alle de Nederlanden, anderssins ghenoemt Neder-Duytslandt*, Amsterdam, 1612.
Hooft, P. C., *Nederlandsche Historiën*, 3rd ed., Amsterdam, 1677 (1st ed., 1642).
*Informacie up den staet, faculteit ende gelegentheyt van de steden ende dorpen van Hollant ende Vrieslant, etc.*, ed. R. Fruin, Leiden, 1866.
Ionktys, Daniel, *De pyn-bank wedersproken, en bemagtigt*, Amsterdam, n.d. [ca. 1650].
Isselt, Michael ab, *Sui temporis historia, in qua res toto terrarum gestae, etc.*, Cologne, 1602.
"De jezuieten-staties te Hoorn," ed. F. van Hoeck, *BBH*, 59 (1941), 102–28.
Kernkamp, J. H., and A. J. Klaassen-Meijer, "De rekeningen betreffende de exploratietocht van Den Swerten Ruyter naar het Middellandse zeegebied in 1589/90," *BMHG*, 73 (1959), 3–54.
*Die Kirchenratsprotokollen der reformierten Gemeinde Emden 1557–1620*, ed. Heinz Schilling and Klaus-Dieter Schreiber, 2 vols., Cologne etc., 1992–98.
Kok, Jacobus, *Vaderlandsch woordenboek*, 35 vols. and 3 supplements, Amsterdam, 1785–99.
Kossmann, E. H., and Mellink, A. F., eds., *Texts concerning the Revolt of the Netherlands*, Cambridge, 1974.
"Een kroniek van Medemblik," ed. J. Belonje and R. Kaptein, *BMHG*, 64 (1943), 45–107.
"Lijst van Nederlanders studenten te Orléans (1441–1602)," ed. J. van Kuyk, *BMHG*, 34 (1913), 293–349.
Linden, Joannes van der, *Verhandeling over de judicieele practijcq, of form van procedeeren, voor de hoven van Justitie in Holland gebruikelijk*, 2 vols., Leiden, 1794.

*Matricule de l' Université de Louvain, IV: Févr. 1528–févr. 1569*, ed. A. Schillings, 2 vols., Brussels, 1961–66.
Mendoça, Bernardino de, *Commentaires mémorables de Don Bernardin de Mendoce ( . . .) des guerres de Flandres & Pays Bas depuis l'an 1567 jusques à l'an mil cinq cens soixante et dix-sept*, Paris, 1591.
Meteren, Emanuel van, *Historiën der Nederlanden en haar naburen oorlogen, tot het jaar 1612*, Amsterdam, 1652.
Molanus, Ioannis, *Natales sanctorum Belgii, & eorundem chronica recapitulatio*, Leuven, 1595.
*De moord van 1584: Oorspronkelijke verhalen en gelijktijdige berichten van den moord gepleegd op Prins Willem van Oranje*, ed. J. G. Frederiks, The Hague, 1884.
"Onuitgegeven brieven van Gillis van Berlaimont, heer van Hierges, enz. uit de maanden mei 1576 tot january 1577," ed. J. van Vloten, in *Codex diplomaticus Neerlandicus*, 2nd series, 4th vol., 2nd fasc. (Utrecht, 1860), 264–319.
Opmeer, Petrus, *Historia martyrum batavicorum, sive defectionis a fide maiorum Hollandiae, in duas decades distributa*, Cologne, 1625.
———, *Katholiek-Nederlandsch martelaarboek, of, geschiedenis der Nederlandsche martelaren: De martelaren uit het tijdperk van 't heidendom: Met bijvoeging van levensschetsen der voornaamste Hollandsche heiligen*, ed. W. H. van Hechem, Rijsenburg, 1879.
———, *Martelaarsboek ofte Historie der Hollandse martelaren . . . enz.*, 2 vols., Antwerp, 1700.
*Oude kerkordeningen der Nederlandsche Hervormde Gemeenten (1563–1638) en het concept-reglement op de organisatie van het Hervormd Kerkgenootschap in het Koninkrijk Holland*, ed. C. Hooijer, Zaltbommel, 1865.
"'Papisticque vergaderingen' in het Noorderquartier," ed. A. van Lommel, *BBH*, 1 (1873), 316–20.
Parival, Jean-Nicolas de, *Les délices de la Hollande*, Amsterdam, 1678.
Pers, Dirck Pietersz., *D'ontstelde leeuw of springh-ader der Nederlandscher beroerten*, Amsterdam, 1641.
Pontanus, Johannes Isacius, *Beschrijvinghe der seer wijt beroemde coop-stadt Amsterdam*, Amsterdam, 1614.
Posthumus, N. W., *Nederlandse Prijsgeschiedenis*, 2 vols., Leiden, 1943–64.
Raisse, Arnoldus de, *Ad natales sanctorum Belgii Iohannis Molani auctarium*, Douai, 1626.
*Register van het burgerweeshuis te Edam 1558–1634*, ed. D. Brinkkemper et al., n.p., 1991.
"Rekening van Maerten Ruychaver, thesaurier in het Noorderkwartier, 1572/1573," ed. N. J. M. Dresch, *BMHG*, 49 (1928), 45–127.
*Resolutiën van de Heeren Staaten van Holland en Westvriesland*, 276 vols., The Hague, ca. 1750–98.
"De rooftocht van Dirk Maertensz. van Schagen en zijn bende in 1568 in Noord-Holland," ed. N. J. M. Dresch, *BMHG*, 46 (1925), 312–74.
Rowen, H. H., *The Low Countries in Early Modern Times: A Documentary History*, New York, 1972.

*Sententiën en indagingen van den hertog van Alba, uitgesproken en geslagen in zynen bloedraad . . . 1567 tot 1572*, ed. Jacob Marcus, Amsterdam, 1735.
Schoorel, Dirk burger van, *Chronyk van de stad Medemblik*, Hoorn, 1736.
Soeteboom, Hendrik Jacobsz., *De Nederlandsche beroerten en oorlogen omtrent het Ye en aen de Zaen*, Amsterdam, 1695.
"Summiere staat van de in 1622 in de provincie Holland gehouden volkstelling," ed. J. G. van Dillen, *Economisch Historisch Jaarboek*, 21 (1940), 167–89.
*Troubles réligieux du xvi$^e$ siècle dans la Flandre Maritime 1560–1570. Documents originaux*, ed. E. de Coussemaker, 4 vols., Bruges, 1876.
Twisck, Pieter Jansz., *Chronijck van den onderganc der tijrannen ofte jaerlycksche geschiedenissen in werltlycke ende kercklijke saecken, van Christi geboorte af tot deser tyt toe* . . . , 2 vols., Hoorn, 1619–20.
*Uit de practijk van het Hof van Holland in de tweede helft van de zestiende eeuw*, ed. L. J. van Apeldoorn, Utrecht, 1938.
Velius, D. *Chroniick van Hoorn*, 3rd ed., Hoorn 1648 (1st ed., 1604; 2nd rev. and enlarged ed., 1617).
Verheyden, A. L. E., *Le Conseil des Troubles. Liste des condamnés (1567–1573)*, Brussels, 1961.
"Verslag over den godsdienstigen toestand in Holland en Friesland," ed. J. Kleijntjens, *BBH*, 59 (1941), 52–101.
[Verstegan, Richard], *Theatre de cruautez des heretiques de nostre temps*, Antwerp, 1587, 2nd rev. ed., 1588; 3rd ed., 1607.
———, *Théatre des cruautés hérétiques au 16$^e$ siècle contenant les cruautés . . .* etc., Lille and Brugge, n.d., [1883].
———, *Theatrum crudelitatum haereticorum nostri temporis*, Antwerp, 1587; 2nd ed., 1588; 3rd ed., 1592; 4th rev. ed., 1604.
Verwer, Willem Janszoon, *Memoriaelbouck. Dagboek van gebeurtenissen te Haarlem van 1572–1581*, ed. J. J. Temminck, Haarlem, 1973.
Vloten, J. van, *Nederlands Opstand tegen Spanje in zijne eerste wording, ontwikkeling en verderen voortgang*, 2 vols., Haarlem, 1858–69.
———, "Noordholland in 't geuzenjaar. (Naar de verhoren in 't Belgische Rijksarchief)," *Studiën en Bijdragen op 't gebied der Historische Theologie*, ed. W. Moll and J. G. de Hoop Scheffer (Amsterdam 1870), I, 143–52, 303–42.
Vos, K. "De dooplijst van Leenaert Bouwens," *BMHG*, 36 (1915), 39–70.
Wagenaar, Jan, *Amsterdam in zyne opkomst, aanwas, geschiedenissen, etc.*, 3 vols., Amsterdam, 1760–67.
———, *Tegenwoordige staat der Vereenigde Nederlanden, IV–VIII, behelzende de beschryving van Holland*, 5 vols., Amsterdam, 1742–50.
———, *Vaderlandsche historie, etc.*, 21 vols., Amsterdam, 1749–59.
Walvis, I., *Beschryving der stad Gouda, etc.*, 2 vols., Gouda and Leiden, 1713.
Water, J. W. te, *Historie van het verbond en de smeekschriften der Nederlandsche edelen*, 4 vols., Middelburg, 1776–96.
*Westfriesche stadsrechten.*, ed. M. S. Pols, 2 vols., Utrecht, 1885–88.
Woude, C. van der, *Kronyk van Alckmaar met zyn dorpen . . . tot den jaren 1658, etc.*, The Hague, 1746.

"Zeeland en Holland in 1569. Een rapport voor de hertog van Alva," ed. S. Groenveld and J. Vermaere, *Nederlandse Historische Bronnen uitgegeven door het Nederlands Historisch Genootschap*, II (The Hague, 1980), 103–74.

SECONDARY SOURCES

Aa, A. J. van der, *Aardrijkskundig woordenboek der Nederlanden*, 13 vols. and supplement, Gorinchem, 1839–51.
Abel, Wilhelm, *Massenarmut und Hungerkrisen im vorindustriellen Deutschland*, Göttingen, 1972.
Andriessen, J., *De Jezuïeten en het saamhorigheidsbesef der Nederlanden, 1585–1648*, Antwerp, 1957.
Arblaster, Paul, *Antwerp and the World: Richard Verstegan and the International Culture of Catholic Reformation*, Leuven, 2004.
Aten, Diederik, *"Als het gewelt comt . . ." Politiek en economie in Holland benoorden het IJ, 1500–1800*, Hilversum, 1995.
Augustijn, C., "Anabaptisme in de Nederlanden," *Doopsgezinde Bijdragen*, n.s., 12–13 (1987), 13–28.
Baart de la Faille, R. D., "De beurs van Antwerpen, de bedijking van de Zijpe in 1552 en de schilder Jan van Scorel," in *Handelingen van het elfde Nederlandsche philologen-congres gehouden te Groningen*, Groningen, 1925, 43–44.
Backhouse, Marcel, "Beeldenstorm en bosgeuzen in het Westkwartier," *Handelingen van de Koninklijke geschied- en oudheidkundige kring van Kortrijk*, 38 (1971).
Baelde, M., and P. Van Peteghem, "De Pacificatie van Gent (1576)," in *Opstand en Pacificatie*, 1–62.
Bakhuizen van den Brink, R. C., "Eerste vergadering der Staten van Holland, 19 juli 1572," in *Cartons voor de geschiedenis van den Nederlandschen vrijheidsoorlog*, 2 vols., The Hague, 1891–98, II, 161–211.
Beelaerts van Blockland, W. A., "Hieronymus van Ysselt, onthoofd te Den Haag 21 december 1702," *De Nederlandsche leeuw*, 41 (1923), 145–52.
Begheyn, P. J., "Een Antwerps hekeldicht over Nederlandse martelaren (1617)," *Archief voor de geschiedenis van de katholieke kerk in Nederland*, 26 (1984), 209–17.
Belonje, J., *Het hoogheemraadschap van de uitwaterende sluizen in Kennemerland en West-Friesland 1544–1944*, Wormerveer, 1945.
——, "De polderregering van de Zijpe," *De Navorscher*, 82 (1933), 48–68.
Benedict, Ph., et al., eds., *Reformation, Revolt and Civil War in France and the Netherlands, 1555–1585*, Amsterdam, 1998.
Bergsma, Wiebe, *De wereld volgens Abel Eppens. Een Ommelander boer uit de zestiende eeuw*, Groningen, 1988.
Beuningen, P. Th. van, *Wilhelmus Lindanus als inquisiteur en bisschop. Bijdrage tot zijn biografie (1525–1576)*, Assen, 1976.
Bijleveld, W. J. J. C., "Gegevens omtrent de familie van Mr. Rombout Hoogerbeets, vermaard pensionaris van Leiden," *De Nederlandsche Leeuw*, 42 (1924), 294–97.

Blaas, P. B. M., "Nederlandse geschiedschrijving na 1945," in W. W. Mijnhardt, ed., *Kantelend geschiedbeeld. Nederlandse historiografie sinds 1945*, Utrecht and Antwerp, 1983, 9–47.

Blaupot ten Cate, S., *Geschiedenis der Doopsgezinden in Holland, Zeeland, Utrecht en Gelderland*, 2 vols., Amsterdam, 1847.

Blockmans, Wim, "Privaat en openbaar domein. Hollandse ambtenaren voor de rechter onder de Bourgondiërs," in Jean-Marie Duvosquel and Erik Thoen, eds., *Peasants & Townsmen in Medieval Europe. Studia in honorem Adriaan Verhulst*, Ghent, 1995, 707–19.

Blok, Anton, "Infame beroepen," *Symposion*, 3 (1981), 104–28.

———, "Over de infamie van de scherprechter," *Volkskundig bulletin*, 9 (1983), 179–86.

Blok, P. J., *Geschiedenis eener Hollandsche stad*, 4 vols., The Hague, 1910–18.

———, *History of the People of the Netherlands*, trans. Oscar A. Bierstadt and Ruth Putnam, 5 vols., New York, 1898–1912.

Bodel Nyenhuis, J. T., "Iets over Guillaume of Willem Mostaert, van Alkmaar," *Zuid en Noordhollandsche volks-almanak voor 1845*, I, Gorinchem, 1845, 167–71.

Boeree, Th. A., "Het verraad van hopman Maarten Schets. Een mislukte aanslag op Gouda in 1572," *TvG*, 39 (1924), 195–219.

Bonenfant, P., "Les origines et la caractère de la réforme de la bienfaisance publique aux Pays-Bas sous le règne de Charles Quint," *Revue Belge de philologie et d'histoire*, 5 (1926), 887–904.

Bonnevie-Noël, G., "Liste critique des signataires du Compromis des Nobles," *Vereniging voor de geschiedenis van het Belgisch Protestantisme*, 5th series, 3 (1968), 80–110.

Boogman, J. C., "De overgang van Gouda, Dordrecht, Leiden en Delft in de zomer van het jaar 1572," *TvG*, 57 (1942), 81–112.

Boomgaard, J. E. A., *Misdaad en straf in Amsterdam. Een onderzoek naar de strafrechtspleging van de Amsterdamse schepenbank 1490–1552*, Zwolle and Amsterdam, 1992.

Boon, P. N. M., "Boussu's gevangenschap te Hoorn (1573–1576)," *WFON*, 35 (1969), 78–94.

Bossaers, K. W. J. M., "*Van kintsbeen aan ten staatkunde opgewassen.*" *Bestuur en bestuurders van het Noorderkwartier in de achttiende eeuw*, The Hague, 1996.

Brouwer, D., "West-Friezen van naam: Dr. François Maelson," *WFON*, 15 (1940), 68–84.

Brouwer, J., *Kronieken van Spaansche soldaten uit het begin van den tachtigjarigen oorlog*, Zutphen, 1933.

Buitendijk, W. J. C., *Het Calvinisme in de spiegel van de Zuidnederlandse literatuur der Contra-Reformatie*, Groningen and Batavia, 1942.

Burke, Peter, "Perceiving a Counter-Culture," in *The Historical Anthropology of Early Modern Italy*, Cambridge, 1987, 63–75.

Chartier, Roger, "Les elites et les gueux: Quelques réprésentations," *Revue d'histoire moderne et contemporaine*, 21 (1974), 376–88.

Cordfunke, E. H. P., ed., *Alkmaar ontzet 1573–1579*, Alkmaar, 1973.

Crouzet, Denis, *Les guerriers de Dieu. La violence au temps des troubles de réligion*, 2 vols., Paris, 1990.
Daan, Jo, "Dirck Adriaensz Valcooch," *WFON*, 35 (1968), 71–77.
Darby, Graham, ed., *The Origins and Development of the Dutch Revolt*, London and New York, 2001.
Decavele, Johan, et al., *Keizer tussen stropdragers. Karel V 1500–1558*, Leuven, n.d. [1990].
Deursen, A. Th. van, *Een dorp in de polder. Graft in de zeventiende eeuw*, Amsterdam, 1994.
———, *Mensen van klein vermogen. Het kopergeld van de Gouden eeuw*, Amsterdam, 1991.
*Dictionnaire de théologie catholique*, 15 vols., Paris, 1915–50.
Diefendorf, Barbara, *Beneath the Cross: Catholics and Huguenots in Sixteenth-Century Paris*, New York and Oxford, 1991.
Dillen, J. G. van, *Van rijkdom en regenten. Handboek tot de economische en sociale geschiedenis van Nederland tijdens de Republiek*, The Hague, 1970.
Driessen, A., "Waterland VII; Edam voor de hervorming," *BBH*, 31 (1908), 127–90.
Duke, Alastair, "Dr. Arnold Rosenberger te Alkmaar, 1562–1567: Een raadselachtige figuur uit de tijd der beroerten," *Alkmaars Jaarboekje*, 4 (1968), 70–71.
———, "Nieuwe Niedorp in hervormingstijd," *Nederlands archief voor kerkgeschiedenis*, n.s., 48 (1976), 60–71.
———, "Een onbekende en mislukte aanslag op Heer Balthazar Platander, pastoor van de St. Gommaruskerk, Enkhuizen anno 1557," *Steevast 1993. Jaaruitgave van de Vereniging Oud Enkhuizen te Enkhuizen*, Enkhuizen, 1993, 65–67.
———, *Reformation and Revolt in the Low Countries*, London and Ronceverte, 1990.
Egmond, Florike, "Fragmentatie, rechtsverscheidenheid en rechtsongelijkheid in de Noordelijke Nederlanden tijdens de 17e en 18e eeuw," in Sjoerd Faber, ed., *Nieuw licht op oude justitie: Misdaad en straf ten tijde van de Republiek*, Muiderberg, 1989, 9–22.
———, "Strafzaken in hoogste instantie. Rechtsbescherming, corruptie en ongelijkheid in de vroegmoderne Nederlanden," in Rob Huijbrecht, ed., *Handelingen van het tweede Hof van Holland Symposium, gehouden op 14 november 1997 in de Eerste kamer der Staten-Generaal*, The Hague, 1998, 63–75.
———, *Underworlds: Organized Crime in the Netherlands, 1650–1800*, Cambridge, 1993.
Elias, Johan E., *De vroedschap van Amsterdam*, 2 vols., Haarlem, 1903–05.
Fasel, W. A., "De ontzetviering in Alkmaar in de loop der eeuwen," in *Alkmaars ontzet 1573–1973*, Alkmaar, 1973, 85–196.
Foreest, H. A. van, *Het oude geslacht van Foreest 1250–1570*, Assen, 1950.
Fruin, Robert, "Alva's bril," in *Verspreide geschriften*, VIII, 373–79.
———, *Geschiedenis der staatsinstellingen in Nederland tot den val der Republiek*, ed. H. T. Colenbrander, The Hague, 1922.
———, "De Gorcumsche Martelaren," in *Verspreide geschriften*, II, 277–79.

Fruin, Robert, "Prins Willem in onderhandeling met den vijand over vrede. 1572–1576," in *Verspreide geschriften*, II, 336–84.

———, "Prins Willem I in het jaar 1570," in *Verspreide geschriften*, II, 111–210.

———, *Verspreide geschriften*, 10 vols. and index, The Hague, 1900–1905.

Gelder, H. A. Enno van, *Getemperde vrijheid. Een verhandeling over de verhouding van Kerk en Staat in de Republiek der Verenigde Nederlanden en de vrijheid van meningsuiting in zake godsdienst, drukpers en onderwijs, gedurende de 17e eeuw*, Groningen, 1972.

———, "Een historiese vergelijking. De Nederlandse Opstand en de Franse godsdienstoorlogen," *Verslag van de algemeene vergadering der leden van het Historisch Genootschap*, Utrecht, 1930, 21–42.

———, "De Nederlandse adel en de opstand tegen Spanje, 1565–1572," in *Van beeldenstorm tot pacificatie. Acht opstellen over de Nederlandse revolutie der zestiende eeuw*, Amsterdam and Brussels, 1964, 138–69; previously published in *TvG*, 43 (1928), 1–20, 138–59.

———, *Revolutionnaire reformatie. De vestiging van de Gereformeerde Kerk in de Nederlandse gewesten, gedurende de eerste jaren van de Opstand tegen Filips II, 1575–1585*, Amsterdam, 1943.

———, "De strijd in Holland en Zeeland," in J. A. van Houtte, J. F. Niermeyer, J. Presser et al., eds., *Algemene geschiedenis der Nederlanden*, 12 vols., Utrecht, 1949–58, V, 30–74.

———, *Alkmaarse opstellen*, Alkmaar, 1960.

———, *Geschiedenis der Latijnsche school te Alkmaar. Eerste gedeelte: De Groote School tot 1572*, Alkmaar, 1905.

Gelderen, Martin van, *The Political Thought of the Dutch Revolt, 1555–1590*, Cambridge, 1992.

Gent, M. J. van, *"Pertijelike saken." Hoeken en Kabeljauwen in het Bourgondisch-Oostenrijkse tijdperk*, The Hague, 1994.

Geremek, Bronislaw, *Les fils de Caïn: L'image des pauvres et des vagabonds dans la littérature Européenne du xv$^e$ au xvii$^e$ siècle*, Paris, 1991.

Geus, J. P., "De bewoners van Oudorp, Sint Pancras, Koedijk en Huiswaard in 1575, 'verjaecht, berooft en opgegeten,'" *Alkmaars Jaarboekje*, 8 (1972), 101–9.

———, "De schansen te Schoorldam en Krabbendam, als onderdeel van de verdediging van Westfrieslands westzijde, in 1573 en daarna," *WFON*, 40 (1973), 124–35.

Geyl, P., *The Revolt of the Netherlands (1555–1609)*, London, 1932.

Ginzburg, Carlo, *The Cheese and the Worms: The Cosmos of a Sixteenth-Century Miller*, London, 1980.

Goede, A. de, *Swannotsrecht. Westfriesche rechtsgeschiedenis*, Utrecht, 1940.

———, *Waterland. Westfriesche rechtsgeschiedenis*, 2 vols., Enkhuizen, 1943.

———, "Een Westfriesche grondwet," *Verslagen en mededelingen van de Vereeniging tot uitgaaf der bronnen van het oud-vaderlandsche recht*, 9, fasc. 6 (1944), 614–55.

Goerris, G. C. W., *J. G. Le Sage ten Broek en de eerste faze der katholieken*, 2 vols., Amsterdam, 1947–48.

Goosens, Aline, *Les Inquisitions modernes dans les Pays-Bas meridionaux, 1520–1633*, Brussels, 1997.
Gosses, I. H. and N. Japikse, *Handboek tot de staatkundige geschiedenis van Nederland*, 2nd rev. ed., The Hague, 1927 (1st ed., 1916–20).
Gottschalk, M. K. Elizabeth, *Stormvloeden en rivieroverstromingen in Nederland. II: De periode 1400–1600*, Assen, 1975.
Gouw, J. ter, *Geschiedenis van Amsterdam*, 8 vols., Amsterdam, 1879–93.
Gouw, J. L. van der, "Schieland als koloniaal gebied van Rotterdam," *Rotterdams Jaarboekje* (1977), 235–55.
Graaf, Ronald P. de, *Oorlog om Holland, 1000–1375*, Hilversum, 1996.
Grapperhaus, Ferdinand H. M., *Alva en de tiende penning*, Zutphen, 1982.
Grayson, J. C., "The Civic Militia in the County of Holland, 1560–81: Politics and Public Order in the Dutch Revolt," *BMGN*, 95 (1980), 35–63.
Groenveld, S., "Beeldvorming en realiteit. Geschiedschrijving en achtergronden van de Nederlandse Opstand tegen Filips II," in P. A. M. Geurts and A. E. M. Janssen, eds., *Geschiedschrijving in Nederland, II: Geschiedbeoefening*, The Hague, 1981, 55–84.
———, *Hooft als historieschrijver. Twee studies*, Weesp, 1981.
———, "The Mecca of Authors? States Assemblies and Censorship in the Seventeenth-Century Dutch Republic," in A. C. Duke and C. A. Tamse, eds., *Too Mighty to Be Free: Censorship and the Press in Britain and the Netherlands*, Zutphen, 1988, 63–86.
Groot, Hugo de, *Inleidinge tot de Hollandsche rechtsgeleerdheid*, ed. S. J. Fockema Andreae, 4th ed., 2 vols., Gouda, 1939.
Gutmann, Myron P., *War and Rural Life in the Early Modern Low Countries*, Assen, 1980.
Gutton, J.-P., *La Société et les pauvres en Europe (xvi$^e$–xviii$^e$ siècles)*, Paris, 1974.
Haitsma Mulier, E. O. G., "Geschiedschrijving in het vroeg-moderne Nederland (16$^e$–18$^e$ eeuw): Enige lijnen en patronen," *Holland*, 17 (1985), 185–99.
Hartog, R. H., *Onrechtmatige overheidsdaden in de Republiek der Verenigde Nederlanden. Een onderzoek naar de toenmalige rechtspraktijk*, Deventer, 1971.
Hasselt, Lucas van, "Hoorn's stadsbestuur in vroeger eeuwen," *WFON*, 44 (1977), 78–95.
Heeres, W. G., "Iets over Velius en zijn bronnen," *WFON*, 26 (1959), 119–34.
Heijnsbergen, P. van, *De pijnbank in de Nederlanden*, Groningen, 1925.
Hibben, C. C., *Gouda in Revolt: Particularism and Pacifism in the Revolt of the Netherlands*, Utrecht, 1983.
Hoeck, F. van, *Schets van de geschiedenis der Jezuieten in Nederland*, Nijmegen, 1940.
Hoop Scheffer, J. G. de, *Geschiedenis der kerkhervorming in Nederland van haar ontstaan tot 1531*, Amsterdam, 1873.
Hugenholtz, F. W. N., "Het Kaas- en Broodvolk," *BMHG*, 81 (1967), 14–33.
Jansen, H. P. H., *Hoekse en kabeljauwse twisten*, Bussum, 1966.
Jansen, H. P. H. and P. C. M. Hoppenbrouwers, "Heervaart in Holland," *BMGN*, 94 (1979), 1–26.

Janssen, A. E. M., "Pieter Bor," in P. A. M. Geurts and A. E. M. Janssen, eds., *Geschiedschrijving in Nederland, I: Geschiedschrijvers,* The Hague, 1981, 21–38.

Janssens, Gustaaf, *Brabant in het verweer. Loyale oppositie tegen Spanje's bewind in de Nederlanden van Alva tot Farnese, 1567–1578,* Kortrijk-Heule, 1989.

Jonckheer, L., "Dirk Sonoy, de eerste watergeus (1529–97)," unpublished thesis, Catholic University of Leuven, 1943.

Kaplan, Benjamin J., *Calvinists and Libertines: Confession and Community in Utrecht, 1578–1620,* Oxford, 1995.

———, "Cornelis Cooltuyn," in Hans Hillerbrand, ed., *The Oxford Encyclopedia of the Reformation,* 4 vols., New York and Oxford, 1996, I, 424–25.

Kernkamp, J. H., *De handel op den vijand, 1572–1609,* Utrecht, 1931.

Knappert, L., *Het ontstaan en de vestiging van het protestantisme in de Nederlanden,* Utrecht, 1924.

Knevel, Paul, *Burgers in het geweer. De schutterijen in Holland, 1550–1700,* Hilversum, 1994.

Knuttel, W. P. C., *De toestand der Nederlandsche katholieken ten tijde der Republiek,* The Hague, 1892.

Kok, J. A. de, *Nederland op de breuklijn Rome-Reformatie. Numerieke aspecten van de protestantisering en katholieke herleving in de Noordelijke Nederlanden, 1580–1880,* Assen, 1964.

Kölker, A. J., ed., *De kaart van Noord-Holland door Joost Jansz.—1575— opnieuw uitgegeven,* Purmerend, n.d. [1971].

Kooijmans, Luuc, *Onder regenten. De elite in een Hollandse stad. Hoorn 1700– 1780,* Amsterdam and Dieren, 1985.

———, *Vriendschap en de kunst van het overleven in de zeventiende en achttiende eeuw,* Amsterdam, 1997.

Koopmans, J. W., *De Staten van Holland en de Opstand. De ontwikkeling van hun functies en organisatie in de periode 1544–1588,* The Hague, 1990.

———, "Vreemdelingen in Hollandse dienst 1545–1588. Opmerkingen bij het werk van Briels," in A. H. Huussen, W. E. Krul, and E. Ch. L. van der Vliet, eds., *Vreemdelingen, ongewenst en bemind,* Groningen, 1991, 37–43.

Krahn, Cornelius, *Dutch Anabaptism: Origin, Spread, Life, and Thought (1450– 1600),* The Hague, 1968.

Kuyk, J. van, ed., "Lijst van Nederlanders studenten te Orléans (1441–1602)," *BMHG,* 34 (1913), 293–349.

Lambert, Audrey M., *The Making of the Dutch Landscape: An historical Geography of the Netherlands,* London and New York, 1971.

Lamberts, E., and J. Roegiers, *De Universiteit van Leuven, 1425–1985,* Leuven, 1986.

Lambooij, H. *Getekend land. Nieuwe beelden van Hollands Noorderkwartier,* Alkmaar, 1987.

Lange, P. W. de, "De ontwikkeling van een oligarchische regeringsvorm in een Westfriese stad. Medemblik, 1289–1699," *Hollandse Studiën,* 3 (1972), 119–46.

Le Roy Ladurie, Emmanuel, *Montaillou, village Occitan de 1294 à 1324,* Paris, 1975.

[Lesage ten Broek, J. G.], "Schrikkelijke handel van Diederik Sonoi, omtrent eenige catholijke huislieden en anderen," *De Godsdienstvriend*, 14 (1825), 117-34.
Lesger, C. M., *Hoorn als stedelijk knooppunt. Stedensystemen tijdens de late middeleeuwen en vroegmoderne tijd*, Hilversum, 1990.
*Lexikon für Theologie und Kirche*, 2nd rev. ed., 14 vols., Freiburg im Breisgau, 1957-68.
Lievense-Pelser, E., "De Alteratie en de financiële toestand," *Jaarboek Amstelodamum*, 71 (1978), 38-54.
Lis, Catharina, and Hugo Soly, *Poverty and Capitalism in Pre-Industrial Europe*, Brighton, 1982.
Looijesteijn, H. L. J., "'T geslacht der vrome martelaar. Jan Jeroensz. van der Laen en zijn nageslacht, ca. 1530-1747." MA Dissertation, University of Amsterdam, 1997.
Maltby, William S., *Alba: A Biography of Fernando Alvarez de Toledo, Third Duke of Alba, 1507-1582*, Berkeley, 1983.
Marnef, Guido, *Antwerp in the Age of Reformation, 1550-1577*, Baltimore, 1996.
Mauquoy-Hendrickx, Marie, *Les Estampes de Wierix conservées au Cabinet des Estampes de la Bibliothèque Albert I$^{er}$: Catalogue raisonné*, 3 vols., Brussels, 1978-79.
Marx, Karl, "Der achtzehnte Brumaire des Louis Bonaparte," in Karl Marx and Friedrich Engels, *Ausgewählte Schriften*, 2 vols., Berlin, 1970, 222-316.
Meij, J. C. A. de, *De watergeuzen en de Nederlanden, 1568-1572*, Amsterdam and London, 1972.
Mellink, A. F., *De wederdopers in de Noordelijke Nederlanden, 1531-1544*, Leeuwarden, 1981.
Molhuysen, P. C., and P. J. Blok, eds., *Nieuw Nederlands Biografisch Woordenboek*, 10 vols., Leiden, 1911-37.
Monballyu, J., "Het onderscheid tussen de civiele en de criminele en de ordinaire en de extraordinaire strafrechtpleging in het Vlaamse recht van de 16e eeuw," in H. A. Diederiks and H. W. Roodenburg, eds., *Misdaad, zoen en straf. Aspecten van de middeleeuwse strafrechtsgeschiedenis in de Nederlanden*, Hilversum, 1991, 120-32.
Monté Ver Loren, J. Ph. de, *Hoofdlijnen uit de ontwikkeling der rechtelijke organisatie in de Noordelijke Nederlanden tot de Bataafse omwenteling*, ed. J. E. Spruit, 6th ed., Deventer, 1982.
Motley, John Lothrop, *The Rise of the Dutch Republic*, 3 vols., Philadelphia, n.d. [1856].
Mout, M. E. H. N., "Van arm vaderland tot eendrachtige Republiek. De rol van politieke theorieën in de Nederlandse Opstand," *BMGN*, 101 (1986), 345-65.
Naber, J. C., *Een terugblik. Statistische bewerking van de resultaten van de informatie van 1514*, Haarlem, 1970.
Nierop, H. F. K. van, "*Alva's Throne*—Making Sense of the Revolt of the Netherlands," in Graham Darby, ed., *The Origins and Development of the Dutch Revolt*, London and New York, 2001, 29-47.

Nierop, H. F. K. van, *Beeldenstorm en burgerlijk verzet in Amsterdam, 1566–1567*, Nijmegen, 1978.
———, "A Beggars' Banquet: The Compromise of the Nobility and the Politics of Inversion," *European History Quarterly*, 21 (1991), 419–43.
———, *The Nobility of Holland: From Knights to Regents, 1500–1650*, Cambridge 1993.
———, "Om de vrijheid en de godsdienst. Het beeld van de Nederlandse Opstand," in Herman Beliën and Gert-Jan van Setten, eds., *Dossier Geschiedenisdagen, 1994*, Amsterdam, 1995, 76–87.
———, "De troon van Alva. Over de interpretatie van de Nederlandse Opstand," *BMGN*, 110 (1995), 205–23.
———, *Van ridders tot regenten. De Hollandse adel in de zestiende en de eerste helft van de zeventiende eeuw*, Dieren, 1984.
Noordegraaf, Leo, *Hollands welvaren? Levensstandaard in Holland, 1450–1650*, Bergen, 1985.
Noordegraaf, Leo, and Gerrit Valk, *De Gave Gods. De pest in Holland vanaf de late middeleeuwen*, Bergen, 1988.
Noordeloos, P., "Fugitieve personen in Westfriesland, Edam en Monnikendam," *Archief voor de geschiedenis van de katholieke kerk in Nederland*, 2 (1960), 73–92.
Nuyens, W. J. F., *Geschiedenis der Nederlandsche beroerten in de 16ᵉ eeuw*, 8 vols., Amsterdam, 1865–70.
Oosterhuis, Ton, *Lumey, de vossestaart. Admiraal van de Geuzen*, Amsterdam, 1996.
*Opstand en pacificatie in de Lage Landen. Bijdrage tot de studie van de Pacificatie van Gent. Verslagboek van het tweedaags colloquium bij de vierhonderdste verjaring van de Pacificatie van Gent*, Ghent, 1976.
Orwell, George, *Nineteen Eighty-Four*, in *The Penguin Complete Novels of George Orwell*, Harmondsworth, 1983, 741–925.
Parker, Geoffrey, *The Army of Flanders and the Spanish Road: The Logistics of Spanish Victory and Defeat in the Low Countries' Wars*, Cambridge, 1972.
———, *The Dutch Revolt*, London, 1977.
———, *The Grand Strategy of Philip II*, New Haven and London, 1998.
Persman, J. R., "De bestuursorganisatie in West-Friesland en het Noorderkwartier vanaf de eerste vergadering van de Staten van Noord-Holland in 1573 tot en met 1795," *WFON*, 40 (1973), 136–60.
Pettegree, Andrew, *Emden and the Dutch Revolt: Exile and the Development of Reformed Protestantism*, Oxford, 1992.
Planque, Pieter Antonie de, *Valcooch's Regel der Duytsche Schoolmeesters. Bijdrage tot de kennis van het schoolwezen in de zestiende eeuw*, Groningen, 1926.
Pleij, Herman, *Het gilde van de Blauwe Schuit. Literatuur, volksfeest en burgermoraal in de late middeleeuwen*, Amsterdam, 1979.
Post, R. R., *Kerkelijke verhoudingen in Nederland vóór de Reformatie van ± 1500 tot ± 1580*, Utrecht and Antwerp, 1954.
Posthumus, N. W., *De uitvoer van Amsterdam, 1543–1544*, Leiden, 1971.
Presser, J., *De tachtigjarige oorlog*, Amsterdam, 1941 (published under the pseudonym B. W. Schaper).

Raa, F. G. J. ten, and F. de Bas, *Het Staatsche leger, 1568–1795*, 8 vols., Breda and The Hague, 1911–64.
Rhee, Cornelis Hendrik van, *Litigation and Legislation: Civil Procedure at First Instance in the Great Council for the Netherlands in Malines (1522–1559)*, Brussels, 1997.
Rogier, L. J., *Geschiedenis van het katholicisme in Noord-Nederland in de 16de en 17de eeuw*, 3rd ed., Amsterdam and Brussels, 1964 (1st ed., 1946–48).
Rijpperda Wierdsma, J. V., *Politie en justitie. Een studie over Hollandschen staatsbouw tijdens de Republiek*, Zwolle, 1937.
Rombauts, Edward, *Richard Verstegen, een polemist der Contra-Reformatie*, Brussels, 1933.
Rooden, Peter van, "Dissenters en bededagen. Civil religion ten tijde van de Republiek," *BMGN*, 107 (1992), 703–12.
Scheerder, J., *De beeldenstorm*, Bussum, 1974.
———, "De werking van de Inquisitie," in *Opstand en pacificatie*, 153–65.
Schepper, Hugo de, *"Belgium nostrum," 1500–1650. Over integratie en desintegratie van het Nederland*, Antwerp, 1987.
Schepper, Hugo de, and J.-M. Cauchies, "*Justicie, gracie en wetgeving. Juridische instrumenten van de landsheerlijke macht in de Nederlanden, 1200–1600*," in Hugo Soly and René Vermeir, eds., *Beleid en bestuur in de oude Nederlanden. Liber amicorum Prof. Dr. M. Baelde*, Ghent, 1993, 127–81.
Scheurkogel, J., "Het kaas- en broodspel," *BMGN*, 94 (1979), 189–211.
Schoorl, Henk, *'t Oge. Het Waddeneiland Callensoog onder het bewind van de heren van Brederode en hun erfgenamen, de graven van Holstein-Schaumburg, tot de verkoop aan vier Hollandse heren, ca. 1250–1614*, Hillegom, 1979.
Schulten, C. M., "Beleg van Alkmaar," in *Alkmaar ontzet, 1573–1973*, Alkmaar, 1973, 61–85.
Sigmond, J. P., *Nederlandse zeehavens tussen 1500 en 1800*, Amsterdam, 1989.
Smit, J., *Den Haag in den geuzentijd*, The Hague, 1922.
Smit, J. W., "The present Position of Studies Regarding the Revolt of the Netherlands," in *Britain and the Netherlands: Papers Delivered to the Anglo-Dutch Conference*, II, London, 1960, 11–28.
Sol, C. Chr., "Reformatie en magistraatsbeleid in Hoorn, circa 1560–1573," *Holland*, 20 (1988), 129–50.
"Sonoy's bloedraad," *De volks-missionaris*, 22 (1901), 98–111, 200–207, 257–71.
Spaans, Joke, *Haarlem na de Reformatie. Stedelijke cultuur en kerkelijk leven, 1577–1620*, The Hague, 1989.
Swart, K. W., *William of Orange and the Revolt of the Netherlands, 1572–1584*, ed. R. P. Fagel, M. E. H. N. Mout, and H. F. K. van Nierop, trans. J. C. Grayson, Aldershot, 2003.
Swierstra, N. T., "Historische meidagen in Eukhuizen," *Uit het Peperhuis, Mededelingen over het Zuiderzeemuseum*, 2, fase. 2 (1972), 3–32.
Tanis, James, and Daniel Horst, *Images of Discord: A Graphic Interpretation of the Opening Decades of the Eighty Years' War*, Grand Rapids, 1993.
Tex, Jan den, *Oldenbarnevelt*, 5 vols., Haarlem and Groningen, 1960–72.

Thijs, Alfons K. L., *Van geuzenstad tot katholiek bolwerk. Maatschappelijke betekenis van de Kerk in contrareformatorisch Antwerpen*, n.p. [Turnhout], 1990.
Tóth-Ubbens, Magdi, *Verloren beelden van miserabele bedelaars*, Lochem and Ghent, 1987.
Tracy, James D., "Émigré and Ecclesiastical Property as the Sheet-Anchor of Holland Finance, 1572–1584," in P. Benedict et al., eds., *Reformation, Revolt, and Civil War in France and the Netherlands, 1555–1585*, Amsterdam, 1999, 255–66.
———, *Holland under Habsburg Rule, 1506–1566: The Formation of a Body Politic*, Berkeley, 1990.
Uytven, R. van, "De protestanten," in R. van Uytven, ed., *Leuven "De beste stad van Brabant." I: De geschiedenis van het stadsgewest Leuven tot omstreeks 1600 (Arca Lovaniensis. Artes atque historiae reserans documenta)*, 7, Jaarboek 1978, Leuven, 1980, 257–58.
Vandenbroeck, Paul, *Jheronimus Bosch tussen volksleven en stadscultuur*, Berchem, 1987.
———, *Over wilden en narren, boeren en bedelaars. Beeld van de andere, vertoog over het zelf*, Antwerp, 1987.
Vanhemelryck, Fernand, *Misdadigers tussen rechter en beul, 1400–1800*, Antwerp and Amsterdam, 1984.
Veldman, Ilja M., "Enkele aanvullende gegevens omtrent de biografie van Hadrianus Junius," *BMGN*, 89 (1974), 375–84.
Verhas, Christel, *De beginjaren van de Hoge Raad van Holland, Zeeland en West-Friesland*, The Hague, 1997.
Verhoeff, J. M., *De oude Nederlandse maten en gewichten*, Amsterdam, 1983.
Vermaseren, B. A., *De katholieke Nederlandse geschiedschrijving in de 16e en 17e eeuw over de Opstand*, Maastricht, 1941, 2nd ed., Leeuwarden, 1981.
Vermeer, G. T., "De overgang van Edam naar de zijde van de Opstand in 1572," *De Speelwagen*, 3 (1948), 46–51, 74–80.
Vis, G. N. M., *Cornelis Cooltuyn (1526–1567). De vader van de Hollandse reformatie*, Hilversum, 1995.
———, *Jan Arentsz de mandenmaker van Alkmaar, voorman van de Hollandse reformatie*, Hilversum, 1992.
Vis, G. N. M., and J. J. Woltjer, "De predikanten in Holland in 1566." Unpublished article.
Voets, B., "De hervorming in West-Friesland," *Nederlands archief voor kerkgeschiedenis*, n.s., 35 (1946–47), 65–80, 149–65, 219–44; 36 (1948–49), 1–76.
Vries, Jan de, "De boer," in H. M. Beliën, A. Th. van Deursen, and G. J. van Setten, eds., *Gestalten van de Gouden Eeuw. Een Hollands groepsportret*, Amsterdam, 1995, 281–312.
———, *The Dutch Rural Economy in the Golden Age, 1500–1700*, New Haven and London, 1974.
Vries, Jan de, and Ad van der Woude, *The First Modern Economy: Success, Failure, and Perseverance of the Dutch Economy, 1500–1815*, Cambridge, 1997.
Vrugt, M. van de, *De Criminele Ordonnantiën van 1570. Enkele beschouwingen over de eerste strafrechtcodificatie in de Nederlanden*, Zutphen, 1978.
Waardt, Hans de, *Toverij en samenleving. Holland 1500–1800*, The Hague, 1991.

Waxman, Matthew C., "Strategic Terror: Philip II and Sixteenth-Century Warfare," *War in History*, 4 (1997), 339–47.
Wedekind, W. G. P., *Bijdrage tot de kennis van de ontwikkeling van de procesgang in civiele zaken voor het Hof van Holland in de eerste helft van de zestiende eeuw*, Assen, 1971.
Wessels, L. H. M., *Bron, waarheid en de verandering der tijden. Jan Wagenaar (1709–1773), een historiografische studie*, The Hague, n.d. [1996].
———, "Jan Wagenaar (1709–1773). Bijdrage tot een herwaardering," in P. A. M. Geurts and A. E. M. Janssen, eds., *Geschiedschrijving in Nederland, I: Geschiedschrijvers*, The Hague, 1981, 117–40.
Wielant, Philips, *Practijcke Criminele*, ed. Aug. Orts, Ghent, 1872.
Wiele, Johan van de, "De inquisitierechtbank van Pieter Titelmans in de zestiende eeuw in Vlaanderen," *BMGN*, 97 (1982), 19–63.
Wiesflecker, Hermann, *Kaiser Maximilian I. Das Reich, Österreich und Europa an der Wende der Neuzeit*, 5 vols., Munich, 1971–86.
Wijn, J. W., *Het beleg van Haarlem*, 2nd ed., The Hague, 1982 (1st ed., 1943).
———, "Het Noordhollandse regiment in de eerste jaren van de Opstand tegen Spanje," *TvG*, 62 (1949), 235–61.
Willemsen, Renatus Theodorus Henricus, *Enkhuizen tijdens de Republiek. Een economisch-historisch onderzoek naar stad en samenleving van de 16$^e$ tot de 19$^e$ eeuw*, Hilversum, 1988.
Williams, Roger, *The Actions of the Low Countries*, ed. D. W. Davies, Ithaca, 1964.
Woltjer, J. J, "Het beeld vergruisd?" in C. B. Wels et al., eds., *Vaderlands verleden in veelvoud, I: 16$^e$–18$^e$ eeuw*, The Hague, 1982, 89–98.
———, "Het conflict tussen Willem Bardes en Hendrick Dirkszoon," *BMGN*, 86 (1971), 178–99.
———, *Friesland in hervormingstijd*, Leiden, 1962.
———, *Tussen vrijheidsstrijd en burgeroorlog. Over de Nederlandse Opstand, 1555–1580*, Amsterdam, 1994.
———, "Violence during the Wars of Religion in France and the Netherlands: A Comparison," *Nederlands archief voor kerkgeschiedenis*, 76 (1996), 26–45.
Woude, A. M. van der, *Het Noorderkwartier. Een regionaal historisch onderzoek in de demografische en economische geschiedenis van westelijk Nederland van de late middeleeuwen tot het begin van de negentiende eeuw* (A. A. G. Bijdragen, 16), 3 vols., Wageningen, 1972.
Wytzema, H. J., "Alkmaar voor de keuze: 16 juli 1573," *Alkmaars Jaarboekje*, 6 (1970), 96–100.

# Index of Persons

Adriaenszoon, Cornelis 166
Aelbert from Texel (vagrant) 125
Aelst, Peter van 188
Aker, Claes Gijsbrechtszoon 85
Alba, Fernando Alvarez de Toledo, Duke of 12, 22, 46, 52–56, 58–63, 66, 68–70, 78, 89, 99–100, 105, 119, 137, 142, 164, 174–176, 180, 192, 211, 216, 256, 259–261
Alewijnszoon, Jan 125, 207
Allaertszoon, Dirck 30
Allert (brother-in-law of Nanning Coppenszoon) 137, 156
Allert, Cornelis 32
Allertszoon, Wigger 166
Alveringen, Josua Lord of 114–115, 176
Ambrosius, Jan 134
Amersfoort, Frans Gijsbertszoon van 193, 195
Andrieszoon, Hendrick 227
Anna (from Oudewater) 92
Arboreus see Boom, Adriaen
Arentszoon, Jan 43–44, 47, 62, 106, 108, 171–172
Aris, Pieter schipper 173–174, 178
Ariszoon, Pieter (vagrant) 125, 134, 178, 184
Assendelft, Gerrit Lord of 26

Baerdesen, Willem Dirckszoon 93, 102, 108, 114, 197, 224
Bardesius see Baerdesen
Barentsdochter, Anna 154, 204
Bavaria, Jacqueline Duchess of 24
Beeldsnijder, Joost Janszoon 12–14, 72
Beieren van Schagen, Lords of 26
Bergh, Willem Count van den 59, 70, 116
Berlaymont, Gilles Lord of see Hierges
Beza, Theodorus 42, 242
Bilhamer see Beeldsnijder, Joost Janszoon
Billy see Robles, Caspar de, Lord of Billy
Bladtwail, Elizabeth Clara 262
Blois see Treslong, Willem Blois Lord of
Blok, Petrus Johannes 8, 258
Boeckgen 153–154, 158, 204

Boelenszoon, Nicolaes 222, 235, 244
Boisot, Charles de 114
Bollen, Jannetje Jansdochter 102–103
Boom, Adriaen 234
Boom, Cornelis 179
Boot, Martina 251
Bor, Pieter Christiaenszoon 6, 61–62, 92, 98, 137, 155, 165, 202, 213–214, 237, 239, 241, 250–255, 257–258, 261
Borsaeus 237
Bosch, Hieronymus 126
Bosius, Thomas 246
Bosschuijzen, Frans van 60
Bouchorst, Jan van den 218
Boussu, Maximilien de Hennin, Count of 52, 56, 59, 61–70, 78, 86, 101, 186–187, 193, 195
Bouwens, Lijsbeth 148, 209
Bouwenszoon, Lenaert 37–38, 140, 171
Brandt, Sebastian 121
Brederode, Artus van 201, 206
Brederode, Hendrik Lord of 16, 26, 39, 44–45, 47–48, 54, 104–105, 113, 115
Brederode, Lancelot van 47
Broekhuijsen, Hendrik van 13
Bronckhorst, Dirck van 98
Brueghel, Pieter 126
Brunt, Reijnier 36
Buchelius, Arnoldus 16, 18, 155
Buchell, Arent see Buchelius, Arnoldus
Buijskens, Pieter Luijtgeszoon 60–61
Burghley, William Cecil, Lord 161
Burgundy, Philip Duke of 24

Cabeliau, Jacob 114
Calff, Gerrit Hendrikszoon 151, 167, 201
Calff, Willem Maertszoon 102, 108–113, 119, 131, 151, 155, 159–160, 162, 167, 195, 197, 204, 208, 224–225, 252, 261
Calvin, John 42–43, 122, 242
Camerlingh, Claes 98
Cant, Reinier 114
Carinaeus, Nicolaes 43, 171
Castricomius, Andreas see Castricum, Andries Dirckszoon van

## 286 • Index of Persons

Castricum, Andries Dirckszoon van 42, 45, 49
Cat, Anthonis 184
Charles V, Holy Roman Emperor 16, 27, 39, 99, 118, 232
Claes, Cornelis Grote (justice of Hoorn) 207
Claes Jeroensdochter, Anna 170, 183
Claesdochter, Aecht 170
Claesdochter, Anna 170
Claesdochter, Wendelmoet 34–35, 105
Claeszoon, Fop 148, 166
Claeszoon, Jeroen 169–171, 173–174, 183, 230
Claeszoon, Laurens 47–48
Clant, George 172
Clein, Jan 46
Clerck, Matheus Matheuszoon de 195
Clomp, Maria Cornelia 131, 237–238, 261–262
Clouk, Jan 126, 133, 165
Coek, Jan 125, 128, 133
Coman Vrerick see Kannegieter, Frederick Gerritszoon
Coninck, Gaspard de 245
Cool, Reijnier Jacobszoon see Cools, Reijnier Jacobszoon
Cools, Agatha (Hieronymusdochter) 262
Cools, Cornelis (Hieronymuszoon) 237–238, 262
Cools, Geertruijt (Hieronymusdochter) 237
Cools, Hieronymus (Reijnierszoon) 236–237, 262
Cools, Jeroen see Cools, Hieronymus
Cools, Lodewijk (Reijnierszoon) 236
Cools, Reijnier Jacobszoon 235–236, 262
Cools, Willem (Reijnierszoon) 236
Cooltuyn, Cornelis 29, 41–43, 48, 103, 171
Coornhert, Dirck Volkertszoon 42
Coppensdochter, Hillegont 136–137
Coppenszoon, Nanning 6, 99, 131, 134, 136–137, 149–156, 162–165, 167, 168, 174, 190–191, 193, 207, 210, 220, 241, 246–247, 249–250, 254, 257
Corneliszoon, Coppen 131, 133–134, 136–139, 149–152, 155, 166, 240–241, 246–247, 254
Corneliszoon, Dammas 125, 133
Corneliszoon, Dirck 41

Corneliszoon, Jacob see Corneliszoon, Coppen
Corneliszoon, Jacob (burgomaster of Hoorn) 207
Corneliszoon, Jacob (merchant of Hoorn) 193
Corneliszoon, Jacob (of Spierdijk) 138
Corneliszoon, Pieter 47
Corvinus, Antonius 40
Cremnitz, Hans von 145
Crock, Michiel 118
Cuyper, Thonis 184

Damhouder, Joos de 100, 130, 153, 158
Diemen, Maria van 188
Diemen, Willem van 188
Dijckgraeff, Claes 94, 173–174, 187
Dijkgraaf see Wigger Allertszoon
Dirckszoon, Pieter 47–48
Dirkszoon, Quirijn 125, 129, 133
Dirricxzoon, Jan 184
Doedeszoon, Gerrit 197
Does, Jan 147
Driemunt, Jan 108, 125–126, 131–134, 137, 159, 190, 206
Drunken Pieter 125
Duijck, Gijsbrecht 224
Dusseldorpius, Franciscus 225, 234, 248, 255
Duvenvoirde, lords of 26

Edzard, Count of East Friesland 57
Eggius, Adelbertus 234
Egmond, Jan Count of 25
Egmond, Lamorael Count of 16, 26, 54
Egmond van Kenenburg, lords of 26
Egmond van Kenenburg, Otto van 26
El, Piet 165–167, 169, 179, 184, 187, 190, 192, 195, 200, 202, 205, 207–208, 215, 220, 223
El, Pieter Pieterszoon 223
Elizabeth I, Queen of England 242–243
Emme 139
Enkhuizen, Meinert van 171
Eppens, Abel 152
Erasmus, Desiderius 122
Ewoutszoon, Joost 39

Farnese see Parma, Alexander Farnese, Prince (later Duke) of
Floor, Willem Gerritszoon 236
Florenszoon, Gerard 233–234

Floris V, Count of Holland 23
Flors, Pieter Classzoon 201, 237
Foreest, Dirck van 103
Foreest, Geertruijt van 103
Foreest, Jan van 102–104, 105, 108, 112, 119, 155, 189, 195, 208
Foreest, Jorden van 102
Foreest, Nanning van 103
Franssen, Brecht 223
Frederickszoon, Remmet 231
Frederiksdochter, Griet 173–174, 183, 190, 197, 201, 203–204, 229, 235–236, 238
Friesland, Jet from 125
Fruin, Robert 8, 51, 67, 248, 255–258

Garbrantszoon, Willem Jan 166
Geelcous, Harman 125
Geerloff (vagrant) 125
Gelder, H.A. Enno van 52, 67, 258
Gérard, Balthasar 227
Gerardus (preacher of Graft and De Rijp) 142
Gerbrant Jeroensdochter, Griet 170, 229, 230
Gerritszoon, Roelken alias Nooschert 126, 133–134
Gerytszoon, Jan 217
Geyl, Pieter 52, 67, 258
Glaesmaker, Simon Gerbrantszoon de 32
Goltzius, Hendrik 165, 237
Gons, Jacob Claeszoon 147
Gosses, I. H. 258
Graet or Van Collen, Arent 171
Granvelle, Antoine Perrenot, Cardinal 11, 28, 125
Grave, Willem de 115
Gruwel, Jan 46
Guicciardini, Lodovico 17–18

Haen, Jan de 170
Heemskerck, Maerten van 21
Heilichdach, Pieter Pieterszoon 131
Hendrickszoon, Nicolaes 40
Hendricxzoon, Claes 33
Hennebert, Jacques 175
Henricxzoon, Claes 33
Henry VIII, King of England 242–243
Hermansdochter, Baertgen 134, 136, 153, 155–156, 204
Hermanszoon, Aris 166
Hermanszoon, Claes 193

Index of Persons • 287

Hermanszoon, Pieter 207
Hetersen, Jan 31
Heugelcke, Michiel 104, 134, 155
Heukesloot, Joost 94, 102, 105–109, 119, 126, 131, 136, 155, 157, 159, 163–164, 167–168, 175, 191, 195, 203, 208–209, 213, 223–224, 252, 261
Heukesloot, Maria 105
Hierges, Gilles de Berlaymont, Lord of 3–5, 9, 12–13, 72, 79–82, 86–92, 94, 102, 108, 128, 146–147, 151, 160, 162, 167, 184, 210, 239, 242, 259
Hoef, Pieter van 93, 240–241, 248–249
Hoefnagel, Joris 188
Hogerbeets, Dirck Hendrickszoon 105, 107
Hooft, Pieter Corneliszoon 6, 237, 252–257
Hoogstraten, Antoine de Lalaing, Count of 107
Hornes, Philippe de Montmorency, Count of 54
Houck, Jan Thaemszoon 231
Houtkoper, Pilgrom Janszoon 205
Huberti, Adriaen 242
Hunaeus, Augustinus 171

IJsbrantszoon, Jan 229–230
Ionktys, Daniel 253
Isselt, Michael ab 246

Jacob alias Blaurok 126, 133
Jacobszoon, Gerrit 148, 209
Jacobszoon, Pauwels 207
Jacobszoon, Reylof 32
Jacobszoon, Tonis 207
Jacobszoon, Wouter 1–5, 9, 13, 74–75, 87, 93–94, 101, 140–141, 143, 177, 178, 181–182, 183, 186
Jan Jeroensdochter, Agatha (Aecht) 235–237, 262
Jan Jeroensdochter, Anna 183, 235
Jan Jeroensdochter, Hester 235–238
Jansdochter, Neel 169–170
Jansdochter, Stijn 153–154, 157, 190, 204
Janszoon, Clays 217–218
Janszoon, Cornelis 134, 136, 150, 155, 204
Janszoon, Jacob 126, 134
Janszoon, Jan 125, 128, 134
Janszoon, Lambrecht 111–112
Janszoon, Maerten 229–231

288 • Index of Persons

Janszoon, Pieter (of Buiksloot) 125–126, 128, 134, 165
Janszoon, Pieter alias Geelcous (of Koudum) 126, 128, 134, 207
Janszoon, Sybout 165, 187, 202–203, 205, 220, 223
Janszoon, Ysebrant 126, 133
Janszoon alias Jeroenszoon, Claes 170, 173
Japikse, N. 258
Jeroensdochter, Garberich 170, 183, 230
Jeroenszoon, Claes 230
Jeroenszoon, Gerbrant 170, 183, 229–230
Jeroenszoon, Jan 5–7, 131, 165–176, 178–179, 183–197, 199–208, 210–223, 227–231, 234–238, 244–248, 259, 261–262
Jezus, Dirck 166, 184
Joncx, Pietge Pieterszoon 87, 165–166, 210
Joosten, Gerrit 125, 129, 133
Joosten, Jan 125, 129, 133
Joosten, Michiel 125, 129, 133
Joosten, Teunis 156
Jordaenszoon, Jan 46–48
Junius, Hadrianus 21

Kannegieter, Frederick Gerritszoon 173, 207
Keeszoon, Jan 125, 129, 134
Keijzer, Anna 233, 235, 237
Kistenmaker, Jacob Jacobszoon 206
Knechtgens, Jan Pieterszoon 230–231
Kok, Jacobus 256
Kriep, François 251

Laen, Jan Claeszoon van der 237
Laen, Jan Jeroenszoon van der see Jeroenszoon, Jan
Lalaing, Antoine de, see Hoogstraten
*Landwijff*, the Waterland see Maertenszoon, Willem
Lanoy, Matheus de 188
Laurenszoon, Anthonis 139
Leicester, Robert Dudley, Earl of 118, 226, 250
Leonardus (parish priest of Sijbekarspel) 40
LeSage ten Broek, Joachim George 256
Lieuwe (chaplain of the West Church of Enkhuizen) 42
Loeff, Jan Corneliszoon 162

Lonius, Nicolaus (Claes Loen) 234
Loon, Pelgrom van 201, 206
Loosen, Sebastiaen 194–195, 203
Lumey, Willem van der Mark, Lord of 52, 66, 69, 73, 98, 119, 255–256
Luther, Martin 30, 32–33, 122

Maekschoon see Maelson
Maelson, François 197
Maelson, Jacob Pieterszoon 196–197, 203
Maertenszoon, Clement 41, 45–46
Maertenszoon, IJsbrant 230–231
Maertenszoon, Willem 124–125
Maertes, Arian (wife of Pilgrom Janszoon) 205
Magdaleen (daughter of Wigger Allertszoon Dijkgraaf) 166
Malsen, Maria van 113
Margaret of Parma (Margaret of Austria, Duchess of Parma) 39–40, 43, 54
Maritgen (wife of Wigger Allertszoon Dijkgraaf) 166
Mary of Hungary (Mary of Austria, Queen of Hungary) 35
Maurits, Maria 262
Maximilian I, Holy Roman Emperor 13, 24–25
Melissen, Lammert 173
Meliszoon, Evert 148
Meliszoon, Jan 170
Melles, Neel Jan van 32
Mendoça, Bernardino de 87
Menéndez, Pedro 78
Michiels, Jacquemina 205–206
Michielszoon, Jacob 104, 131, 135, 153–154, 156–157, 159, 163–164, 167, 187, 190, 204–206, 226, 237
Michielszoon, Jan 142, 196
Midwoud, Claes van 32
Minne (vagrant) 125
Molanus, Johannes 246
Mondragon, Christoforo de 161
Monnik (vagrant) 125
Montmorency, Florentius de 234
More, Thomas 122
Morillon, Maximilien 11, 28, 55–56, 61, 125
Mostaert, Guillaume 46, 115, 188–189, 195, 197, 205, 208, 225–226, 261
Motley, John Lothrop 51, 67, 98, 255
Murmellius, Johannes 21

Nanningszoon, Claes 204–205
Nanningszoon, Pieter 6, 131–132, 134, 136–138, 149, 151–152, 155–157, 160, 162–163, 165–167, 169, 178, 187, 190, 192, 195, 199–200, 202, 204–205, 207–208, 210, 215, 219, 223, 241, 247
Nannius, Petrus 21, 247
Nassau, Henry of 172
Nassau, John Count of 140
Nassau, Louis of 44, 59, 69, 128
Nassau, Maurice Count of 118, 226, 249–250
Nicolai, Ruysch, 225
Nicolai, Thecla 233
Noircarmes, Philippe de Sainte-Aldegonde, Lord of 101
Nuyens, Willem Jan Frans 256

Oldenbarnevelt, Johan van 118, 197–198, 226, 249–250
Oostland, Claes Corneliszoon van 111
Opmeer, Petrus 17, 21, 137, 139, 241, 246–248, 252–253, 256–257
Orange, William Prince of 3–5, 44, 51, 53–54, 59–62, 66, 69, 73, 77, 85–87, 94–95, 96, 98–99, 101, 107, 110–116, 118–119, 127–128, 140–141, 143, 146, 148–149, 152, 159, 161, 172, 176, 178–180, 184, 187, 188, 194–196, 198, 200, 206, 212, 218–220, 223–225, 227, 232, 240, 242–243, 253, 259–260
Otszoon, Jan 144
Ottenszoon, Willem 31

Parival, Jean-Nicholas de 16
Parma, Alexander Farnese, Prince (later Duke) of 242
Pecklap, Hendrick Gerritszoon 108
Peelt, Gerard 31
Pelser, Louris de 125
Petri, Jan *see* Pieterszoon, Jan (parish priest of Castricum)
Philip II, King of Spain, 51, 54, 75, 78–81, 86, 87, 89–90, 97, 99, 113, 118, 216, 232
Pierszoon, Jan (justice of Hoorn) 207
Pieter, Hansgen alias Deelbecker 125
Pieterszoon, Adriaen 166
Pieterszoon, Ben 166
Pieterszoon, Cornelis (parish priest of Krommeniedijk) 30

Pieterszoon, Cornelis (vagrant) 125, 129, 133
Pieterszoon, Gerrit 125, 128–129, 133
Pieterszoon, Jan (from Opperdoes) 40
Pieterszoon, Jan (justice of Hoorn) 207
Pieterszoon, Jan (parish priest of Castricum) 46
Pieterszoon, Laurens 40
Pieterszoon, Maerten (vicar in Hoorn) 41
Pieterszoon, Marten (justice of Benningsbroek) 166
Pilgromsdochter, Maritgen 204–205
Pillis, Jacob Pieterszoon 166, 178, 227
Platander, Balthazar 41
Pleunius, Bartholomeus 234
Potgen, Jacob Symonszoon 184, 227
Presser, J. 258
Puthaeck, Dirck 94

Raisse, Arnold de 246
Ravesteijn, Cornelis van 142
Rennenberg, George de Lalaing, Count of 232
Requesens y Zúñiga, Luis de 3, 4, 75, 79–82, 86, 87, 88–90, 91, 198, 249, 259–261
Reyer (priest of Schoorl and Camp) 47–48
Reyerszoon, Claes 197
Rhoon, Catharyne van 188
Rhoon, Pieter van 188, 195, 208
Rhoon, Pieter van, jr. 188
Rijswijk, Cornelis van 63, 68
Ripperda, Wigbolt 144
Robles, Caspar de, Lord of Billy 57, 90
Roeloffszoon, Claes 126, 133–134
Roest, Barent 166
Rogier, L. J. 258
Rol, Jan Simonszoon 73
Rootgen (vagrant) 125
Ruychaver, Maerten 115
Ruychaver, Nicolaes 117, 144–146

Samplon, Michiel 91
Sas, Barent 229
Sas, Willem 251
Saxony, Albert Duke of 25
Schaft, Jan Taemszoon 144
Schagen, Dirck Maertszoon van 107, 143, 192
Scheeltkens, Claes 47–48
Scheltius, Nicolaes *see* Scheeltkens, Claes
Schets, Maerten 101

## Index of Persons

Schijtgelt, Willem Pieterszoon 166, 184
Schilder, Vrerick Gerritszoon 207
Schipper from Flushing (vagrant) 125
Schoenmackers, Jannytge 32
Schoorstienveeger, Heynrick 94
Scorel, Jan van 21
Seylmaker, Dirck Volckertszoon *see* Velius, Theodoricus
Simonszoon, Menno 37
Slacht, Pieter 218–219
Smit, Jan Pieterszoon 111
Sonnenberg, Willem van 44, 47, 102, 104–105, 108, 131, 159, 162, 189, 194–195, 201, 204, 208, 225, 252
Sonoy, Diederik 5, 13, 15, 61–67, 71, 73, 76–77, 81–88, 90, 93–96, 98–100, 102–104, 105, 108, 112, 113–120, 125–127, 129, 132, 136, 141–142, 144–147, 149, 151, 154–156, 158, 160–165, 167–169, 174, 176, 178, 179, 186, 188–197, 199–200, 203–206, 208–210, 212–213, 215, 218–220, 222–224, 226, 230, 237, 239–240, 247–256, 259, 261
Sonoy, Joost 113
Spaarndam, Guerte van (Old Guerte) 186
Spranger, Jacob Janszoon 237
Spranger, Jan Corneliszoon 201, 237
Spranger, Jan Jacobszoon 237
Steenwijk, Koenraad van 144
Steynemolen, Maria van 105
Steynemolen, Rombout van 105
Stoffelaer, Thijs 163
Stralen, Antoon van 188
Stralen, Jan van 188
Stuart, Mary, Queen of Scots 242–243
Sweerszoon, Jacob 166
Swieten, Adriaen van 98
Symons, Reynken 126, 133, 165
Symons, Roomken *see* Symons, Reynken
Symonszoon, Wouter 165

Tambergen, Lord of (lieutenant of Hierges) 91
Tapper, Ruard 41
Tassis, Juan Baptista de 77
Texel, Adriaen Corneliszoon 131, 206
Thaemszoon, Jaep 144
Thijszoon, Cornelis 144
Thomas (vagrant) 125
Thomaszoon, Pieter 110
Thoorenburg, Jacob van 197, 203
Toledo, Don Fadrique de 70–72
Treslong, Willem Blois van 52
Triere, Anna van 205
Triere, Barbara van 205
Triere, Captain Van 144
Triere, Jan Baptista van 205
Triere, Joseph van 205
Triere the elder, Guillaume van 205
Triere the younger, Guillaume van 46, 131, 134, 136, 149, 153, 156, 187, 203–206, 229, 237, 248
Trijn, Pieter 237

Ulricus (preacher in Winkel) 142

Valck, Cornelis in the 156
Valcoog, Cornelis 242
Valcoogh, Dirck Adriaenszoon 242
Valdéz, don Francisco de 89, 101
Veen, Jan Claeszoon 173
Velius, Theodoricus 9, 32, 128, 147, 164, 176, 237, 239, 248–250, 252, 254, 257
Verduyn, Gerbrant 166, 184
Verlaen, Cornelis Albertszoon 229
Vermertlen, Michiel *see* Heugelcke, Michiel
Verstegan, Richard 243–248, 252, 256–258
Visscher, Jan Maertenszoon 196–197, 201, 207
Vives, Juan Luis 122–123
Vosmeer, Sasbout 233–234
Vrerickszoon, Pieter Vrerickszoon 144
Vrientszoon, or Vincentszoon, Jelys 34
Vries, Pieter Jacobszoon de 126, 129

Wagenaar, Jan 6, 254–257
Warendel, Jacob van 66
Wely, Bernard van 201
Westwoud, Pieter Claeszoon 184
Wielant, Filips 100, 130, 158
Wierix, Johan 243
Wigger (pastor of Petten) 46
Willem II, Count of Holland, King of the Romans 22
Willemszoon, Pieter 207
Willemszoon, Willem 210, 227
William, Holy Roman Emperor *see* Willem II, Count of Holland, King of the Romans
William II, Count of Holland 23

Winter, Jan Corneliszoon 31–32
Witcop, Harman (alias Harman van Emden, alias Jacob Folkertszoon van Leeuwarden) 125
Woerden van Vliet, Jan van 114, 194–195, 203
Wolff, Cornelis van der 98
Woltjer, J. J. 52
Wormer, Jan van 125
Woude, A. M. van der 10

Ypeszoon, Jurriaen 164, 250
Ysselt, Cornelis van 262
Ysselt, Hieronymus van (Corneliszoon) 261–263
Ysselt, Johan van (Corneliszoon) 262

Zas, Laurens Jacobszoon 29, 41
Zevender, Frederik van 114
Zwinglius, Huldrych 47, 122
Zythopeus, Gijsbertus 142

# Index of Places

Aalst 198
Aartswoud 140
Abbekerk 232
Alkmaar 4–5, 8–10, 13, 16, 19, 21–22, 24–25, 29, 38, 40–41, 43–48, 53, 56, 65–67, 71–72, 77–78, 82–84, 86–87, 89, 93–95, 99, 101–103, 105, 107–108, 112, 114–115, 117–118, 124, 130, 132–134, 136, 146, 150, 153, 155, 165, 168, 172, 178, 180, 188–189, 197, 201, 204–207, 217–219, 224, 226, 233, 241–242, 244, 246–248
Amersfoort 193, 246, 262
Amstelland 109
Amstelveen 89–90
Amsterdam 1–5, 9, 13, 18, 20–21, 28, 30–31, 36, 38–39, 42–45, 47, 55, 57, 60, 66, 68–69, 71–76, 78–80, 81, 86, 89, 93, 101, 108–109, 110, 114–115, 118, 123–127, 140–141, 143, 154, 161, 165–167, 171, 176–178, 180–183, 197, 218, 220, 224–225, 227–229, 247, 252, 260–261
Anjum 126
Antwerp 17–18, 42, 44, 61, 81, 86, 89, 188–189, 205, 242–243, 245, 252, 254
Asperen 44
Assendelft 18, 26, 46
Avenhorn 144
Axwijk 171

Bakkum 26, 125
Baltic Sea 20, 31, 55–56, 73, 75, 81
Barndegat 77, 81, 86, 116
Barsingerhorn 26, 37–38, 46, 57, 82, 140, 142
Beemster 14, 19, 83
Beets 38, 106, 144–145
Benningbroek 129–130, 136–142, 146–149, 165–166, 207, 209, 219, 241
Bergen 26, 44, 46, 57, 95, 102, 104, 143, 225
Bergermeer 16
Berkhout 44, 129, 143–144, 232
Betuwe 4

Beverwijk 2, 4, 25, 72–73, 87–92, 94, 98, 125–126, 128–129, 133, 147, 151, 160, 184
Binnenwijzend 129, 147
Blokker *see* Oosterblokker; Westerblokker
Boston Massachusetts 255
Bovenkarspel 140, 142
Brabant 3, 18, 43, 69–70, 198, 225–226, 252, 261
Breda 3, 77, 79, 102, 160, 249, 260
Brederode 95, 102, 104, 225
Brill 28, 44, 52, 54, 59–62, 67–68, 109
Broek in Waterland 9, 83
Broek op Langendijk 143
Broekerhaven 90
Bruges 122
Brussels 1, 26, 41, 43, 100, 123, 173
Buiksloot 126, 128
Buren 4, 92, 160–161
Burghorn 26

Callantsoog 13, 26, 44, 49, 56–57, 104
Camp 26, 46–47, 57
Cape Verde Islands 228
Caribbean 228
Castricum 26, 46
Cleves, Duchy of 113, 118, 253
Cologne 125, 215, 246, 254

Delfland 26
Delfshaven 31
Delft 30, 44, 101, 105, 140, 173, 201–202, 205, 207, 227–228, 237, 247
Denmark 55, 114
Diemerdijk 76, 116, 144
Diemermeer 2, 76
Diemerzeedijk 116
Dokkum 126, 133, 165
Dordrecht 18, 66, 68–69, 101, 115, 161, 177
Duiveland 161
Durgerdam 38, 140

East Friesland 20, 28, 37, 48–49
East Indies 229, 234
Eastland *see* Baltic Sea

294 • Index of Places

Echte 126
Edam 20, 24, 36, 38, 40, 43–44, 48, 53, 56–57, 64, 66–67, 84, 90, 93, 102, 109–112, 115, 160, 169–173, 180–181, 183, 220, 222, 224–225, 229, 231, 244, 261
Eenigenburg 37, 46–48, 225
Egmond 26, 40, 67, 72, 105
Egmondermeer 16
Emden 28, 31, 42–43, 49, 60–62, 75, 103, 109, 171
Emmerich 262
Ems 74, 75
Enghien (Hainault) 126
Enghien-les-Bains 126
England 18, 20, 161, 226, 243
Enkhuizen 13, 19, 24–25, 38, 41–42, 45–46, 48–49, 51, 53–54, 56, 59–69, 73–74, 81, 84–85, 87, 89–90, 94, 114, 133–134, 142–144, 166, 175, 180, 196, 203, 219, 233

Fijnaart 161
Flanders 18, 24, 26, 43, 44, 81, 142, 198, 244
Flushing 52–54, 60, 68, 110
France 20, 59, 113, 228, 244, 259–260, 262
Friesland 42, 57, 63, 73, 75, 126, 162

Galgendijk 56, 83, 87
Gdansk 28, 55
Geestmerambacht 24, 56, 87, 146
Gelderland 118, 243
Geneva 42
Germany 18, 20–21, 55, 59, 73, 105
Ghent 99
Gorinchem 68, 244, 255–256
Gouda 1, 4, 68, 98, 100–101, 123–124, 161, 235, 263
Gouwzee 117
Graft 82, 142, 143
Groet 57, 91
Groningen 57, 63, 126, 129, 152, 226
Grootebroek 24, 38, 93, 129, 133, 140, 142, 196, 233
Grosthuizen 143–145

Haarlem 1–3, 8, 17, 21, 24–25, 36–37, 56, 70, 71–73, 75–78, 80–81, 102, 104, 114, 116, 125–126, 128–129, 133–134, 140, 165, 178, 181, 189, 251, 259
Haarlemmermeer 77

Hague, The 25–26, 29, 31, 34, 38, 41, 44, 97, 106–107, 113, 202, 206, 223, 225, 229, 247
Hamburg 28
Hanseatic cities 57
Harenkarspel 26
Haringhuizen 57, 82
Harlingen 73, 86
Hasselt 36
Hauwert 129, 133, 144–146, 165
Heemskerk 25–26, 46
Heiloo 124–125
Hem 24
Hensbroek 26, 142
's-Hertogenbosch 236
Hobreede 145
Holland 5, 8–11, 17–18, 21–23, 25–26, 28, 37, 42–44, 49, 52–60, 68–70, 72, 77, 78–80, 86–88, 91, 95–96, 99–100, 104–107, 113, 115, 118–119, 122, 125, 139, 143, 146, 160–161, 168, 172, 177, 198, 211–212, 215–216, 218–219, 223, 225–227, 230, 242, 245, 254, 260–261
Holy Roman Empire 99, 105, 216
Hondsbosse Zeewering 14, 83
Hoogkarspel 24, 38, 140
Hoogwoud 129–130, 133, 136
Hoorn 5, 10, 18–19, 21, 23–24, 29–35, 38–42, 44–46, 48, 51, 53–54, 56, 63–67, 73, 74–76, 81, 84–85, 87, 89, 91, 93, 95, 99, 101–102, 105–109, 114–116, 122, 125–126, 131, 136, 142–149, 157, 162–169, 171, 173–180, 183–188, 190–197, 200–202, 205, 207, 209–211, 213, 218–223, 226, 228–229, 231, 233–237, 244–245, 248–250, 252, 261–262
Huigendijk 14–15, 56, 65, 77, 83
Huisduinen 13, 26, 57, 78, 140, 167
Huiswaard 87

IJ, River 1, 3, 10–13, 16, 19, 21–22, 37, 43, 68, 72–77, 84, 87, 110, 115–116
IJssel, River 230
Ilp, Den 44
Ilpendam 26, 49, 83, 84, 145, 236
Italy 20–21, 228–229, 244

Jisp 9, 36

Kalf, Het 83–84, 87
Kalkar 113, 253
Katwoude 112

Keins 57
Kennemerland 10–11, 14, 22–25, 36, 46, 49, 72, 82, 104, 144, 146
Klundert 161
Knollendam 36
Kolhorn 13, 37–38, 57, 140
Korsloot 14
Koudum 126, 134, 207
Krabbendam 67, 83–84, 87–88, 147, 160, 166
Krimpen 160
Krommenie 9, 14, 18, 84, 125–126, 128–129, 133
Krommeniedijk 18, 30, 84
Kwadijk 24, 112, 227

La Goletta 79
Lambertschaag 147
Landsmeer 9, 38, 140
Langedijk 83, 118, 140, 142
Leiden 8–9, 12–13, 25, 30, 44, 76, 79, 86, 123, 160, 164, 183, 188
Leuven 21, 29, 41, 48, 102, 113, 171–172, 188, 232, 247
Lier 235
London 21, 243
Lübeck 28
Lutjebroek 24
Luxemburg 153

Maas, River 52, 59, 73
Madrid 79
Marsdiep 73–74
Mechelen 69–70, 78, 102, 205, 236, 259
Medemblik 13, 19, 20, 24, 29, 31, 38–40, 43–44, 48, 53, 56, 62–63, 66–68, 84, 89, 90, 106, 114, 116, 144, 166, 176, 182, 187, 203, 219–220, 223, 226
Mediterranean Sea 79, 90, 228
Middelburg 53, 69, 200
Middelie 24, 38, 112, 140, 169–172, 222, 227
Midwolda 126, 134
Midwolde 126, 134
Midwoud 32, 126, 129, 134
Monnickendam 20, 28, 30–32, 34–36, 38, 43–44, 48, 53, 57–58, 64, 66, 82, 84, 90, 93, 102, 109, 111, 126, 139, 171–172, 180
Mons (in Hainault) 59, 69
Monster 225
Mook Heath (Mookerheide) 9, 128, 172

Muiden 1, 4, 77, 116, 125
Münster 36–37

Naarden 1, 70, 78, 102, 126, 128, 140, 177–178, 259
Nek 26
Nibbixwoud 87, 133, 144–146, 165, 166, 210
Niedorper Kogge 225
Nieuwe Niedorp 37, 46–47, 57, 77, 129, 133, 140–142, 162, 188
Nieuwendam 73
Nijenburg 217
Noorderdijk 162
Noordermeer 235
North Holland *passim*
North Sea 10, 13, 73
Northern Quarter *passim*
Northland *passim*
Norway 19, 21, 228

Obdam 26, 139
Oever, Den 231
Oge, 't *see* Callantsoog
Oldambt 126
Ommelanden (of Groningen) 126
Oosterblokker 129, 147
Oosterland 40
Oosthuizen 145
Oostwoud 129, 148
Oostzaan 18, 46
Opmeer 129, 140
Opperdoes 40
Orléans 105, 188
Oude Niedorp 25, 57, 77, 129
Oudendijk 145
Oudewater 9, 87, 92, 160–161
Oudkarspel 15, 48
Overijssel 36
Oxford 243

Papendrecht 160
Paris 21, 126, 243, 260
Petten 13, 26, 46–47, 57, 67, 82–84, 90, 129, 140, 205
Pieterburen 226
Poland 55
Portugal 19–21, 55, 228
Purmer 14, 76, 82–83
Purmer Ee 14
Purmerdijk 169

296 • Index of Places

Purmerend 14, 26, 36, 43, 48, 76, 83–85, 115, 117, 128, 140–141, 145, 147, 218
Purmerland 26, 84
Putten 188

Ransdorp 18, 38, 140
Regensburg 99
Rekerdijk 83–84, 87
Rekere, River 82, 87–88, 91, 94
Rijp, De 142–143
Roermond 244
Rome 41, 243, 246
Rotterdam 31, 253
Ruigenhil 161
Rustenburg 83

Santander 79
Schagen 43, 46, 57, 67, 77, 82, 136, 142, 143, 151, 156, 162, 167, 169, 174, 185–187, 189–190, 192, 198–202, 203, 204, 207, 211, 225, 244–245
Schardam 140, 145
Schellingwoude 57
Schellinkhout 24
Schermer 14–15, 19, 22, 77, 82, 140
Schermer island 14–15, 19, 82
Schoonhoven 87, 91, 160–161
Schoorl 26, 46–49, 57, 67, 87, 91, 94, 102, 232, 240
Schoorldam 83–84, 88, 91, 160
Schouwen 161
Sijbekarspel 40, 46, 129, 134, 140, 147–148, 166, 207
Sint Maarten 46–47, 83, 140, 225
Sint Maartensrecht 26
Sint Pancras 46
Sound 20, 55
South Holland 1, 4, 8, 10, 26, 39, 68–69, 72–73, 76–77, 85, 87–88, 97, 113, 119, 126, 146, 183, 194, 200, 206, 225, 228
Southern Quarter *see* South Holland
Spaarndam 13
Spain 18, 20, 55, 78, 90, 229, 244, 249, 262
Spanbroek 129, 133, 226
Speyer 206
Spijkerboor 147
Stavoren 63, 68, 73
Streek district 46, 48, 66, 144, 233
Sweden 55, 114

Terschelling 38
Texel 19, 25, 29, 38–39, 78, 142, 226
Tunis 79
Twisk 40, 46, 129, 147

Uitgeest 125
Utrecht 3, 4, 12–13, 16, 21, 31–32, 39, 59, 63, 65, 75–76, 81, 89, 92, 95, 98, 113, 116, 118, 123, 132, 140, 206, 226, 227, 238, 251

Valkoog 83, 225
Veenhoop 24
Velsen 10–11, 26
Vianen 26, 44, 104
Vlie 74
Vlieland 19, 29, 38, 226
Voshol 225
Vroonlanden 77, 114, 146, 224

Waard 14–15
Waarder mere 77
Wadden Islands 37–38, 57
Wadway 147, 207
Warder 24, 112, 227
Warmenhuizen 26, 46–47, 67, 141
Watergang 38, 140
Wateringen 225
Waterland 10–11, 14, 17–18, 20, 22–23, 26, 28, 35–38, 44, 46, 66–67, 72, 76–77, 79–80, 81, 82, 87, 95, 102, 109–112, 124, 127, 141–142, 144, 146, 171
Werverhoof 43, 129, 133
West Friesland 10–11, 14, 19, 22–24, 32, 35, 37, 42, 46, 78, 106–107, 126, 127, 130, 142, 162, 180, 247
Westerblokker 44, 129, 147, 177
Westland 225
Westphalia 36
Westwoud 18, 24, 147, 232
Westzaan 18, 84
Wieringen 19, 25, 38, 40, 226, 231
Wijk aan Zee 89
Winkel 57, 140, 142
Woerden 160
Wognum 24, 99, 129–131, 133, 136–147, 149, 151, 162, 164, 166, 220, 222, 226, 232, 240–241, 246, 257
Wormer (mere) 14, 76, 82–83
Wormer (village) 9, 13, 36, 76, 82, 84, 128
Wormerveer 9

Zaan, River 14, 66–67, 76, 82–83
Zaan district 14, 19, 30, 35, 82, 144
Zaandam 38, 67, 140
Zandvoort 104
Zeeland 1, 5, 8–9, 39, 52–53, 59, 68–70, 73, 78–79, 85, 88, 95, 100, 115, 126, 161, 198, 200, 216, 260, 263
Zeevang 14, 23, 46, 85, 95, 102, 109–112, 146, 171
Zierikzee 9, 161, 198, 249
Zijpe (channel in Zeeland) 161
Zijpe (North Holland) 14, 22, 48, 56, 71, 77, 82, 87, 117, 166, 189
Zuiderwoude 9
Zuiderzee 13, 19, 21, 61, 63, 67, 73–74, 76–77, 81–83, 90, 101, 147, 162, 177, 186, 228, 262
Zunderdorp 9
Zutphen 59, 70, 78, 102, 116, 259
Zwaag 23, 32, 129, 139–140, 162, 204

GPSR Authorized Representative: Easy Access System Europe - Mustamäe tee
50, 10621 Tallinn, Estonia, gpsr.requests@easproject.com

www.ingramcontent.com/pod-product-compliance
Lightning Source LLC
Chambersburg PA
CBHW021648230426
43668CB00008B/551